Towards Uniformity

Towards Uniformity

The 2nd Annual MAA Schlechtriem CISG Conference

13 March 2010, Hong Kong

Conference in Honour of Peter Schlechtriem 1933-2007

Ingeborg Schwenzer and Lisa Spagnolo (eds.)

eleven international publishing

Published, sold and distributed by Eleven International Publishing
P.O. Box 85576
2508 CG The Hague
The Netherlands
Tel.: +31 70 33 070 33
Fax: +31 70 33 070 30
Website: www.elevenpub.com

Sold and distributed in USA and Canada
International Specialized Book Services
920 NE 58th Avenue, Suite 300
Portland, OR 97213-3786, USA
Tel: 1-800-944-6190 (toll-free)
Fax: +1 503 280-8832
orders@isbs.com
www.isbs.com

Eleven International Publishing is an imprint of Boom uitgevers Den Haag.

Photograph by Prof. I. Schwenzer, reproduced with kind permission of Ms. V. Schlechtriem & prof. I. Schwenzer

ISBN 978-94-90947-10-1

Printed in The Netherlands

Table of Contents

Preface

This book presents the papers of the 2nd Annual MAA Peter Schlechtriem CISG Conference, held on 13 March 2010 in Hong Kong. The conference takes place on an annual basis, alternating between Hong Kong and Vienna, with the first conference held in Vienna on 2 April 2009.[1]

The annual conference is named in honour of Peter Schlechtriem, who sadly passed away in 2007. Professor Schlechtriem was a leading scholar in the field of international commercial law, and an inspiration to many. We hope that the conference will act as a permanent reminder of his scholarship. In presenting papers at the conference, we honour his great contribution to our field.

The theme of the 2010 conference was 'Towards Uniformity'. The day was notable for the flow of good food and lively discussion of issues relating to the extent to which uniformity has been achieved, and ways in which it might be enhanced. The event was graciously hosted by the Law School of the City University Hong Kong, and its location naturally lent itself to a closer look at harmonization of sales law in the Asian region, a vital topic for international trade.

This book contains valuable contributions which provide new empirical research relating to the CISG. Ingeborg Schwenzer and Christopher Kee demonstrate the current state of acceptance of the CISG globally in their chapter which provides the results of an important large-scale empirical study under the auspices of the Global Sales Law Project. John Gotanda's contribution compares the results of awards in CISG arbitrations in CIETAC on the one hand, and international investment awards on the other. Anna Rogowska presents her survey of UK professors in this volume. As the UK remains one of the few leading trade jurisdictions not to have acceded to the CISG, this is a valuable insight into UK legal education on the CISG.

Uniformity in relation to specific issues is also explored. In a very thoughtful piece on the extremely pertinent issue of inclusion of standard terms by various means of email, websites and hyperlinks, Sonja Kruisinga examines the issue from the perspective of what is required by the CISG, from the specific perspective of current developments in the Netherlands.

1 Papers from the first conference, 'Conference in Honour of Peter Schlechtriem (1933-2007): Issues on the CISG Horizon' were collected and published in a special edition of the *Vindobona Journal of International Commercial Law & Arbitration* (2009) Vol. 13(1).

The chapter by Lisa Spagnolo reconsiders the role of *iura novit curia* and waiver in the common situation where litigants fail to present arguments on the CISG but instead cite inapplicable domestic sales law. The role of the CISG within Asia is the topic of a number of chapters in this book. Many nation states within Asia are predominantly Muslim, and Gary Bell takes a look at the much neglected topic of whether the CISG is compatible with Islamic law, and with legal values within Asia. In one of the very first insights into the CISG in South Korea, the honourable Judge Chang-ho Chung provides a very complete picture comparing the CISG with the Korean Civil Code, detailing the establishment of special chambers of expertise within the courts, and a history of CISG cases in South Korea to date. The chapters by Fan Yang and Weidi Long each also examine a subject upon which little has been written thus far: whether the CISG applies in the Special Administrative Region of Hong Kong, and when it might apply to Hong Kong counterparties. In his chapter on the CISG in Japan, Hiroo Sono explores the effect of the CISG on Japanese reform of the Civil Code, while Yasutomo Sugiura considers whether Japan should now accede to the Limitations Convention following its accession to the CISG. Increasingly the world has watched as the economic influence of the Asian region within global trade has grown. Bruno Zeller examines the relationship between the CISG and ASEAN, including the extent and effect of the proliferation of agreements between ASEAN nations. Websites referenced in the footnotes to each chapter were last accessed on 16 December 2010.

Thanks must go to the MAA for once again organizing this event, and to the sponsors, host and supporters: UNCITRAL, City University of Hong Kong, Mannheimer Swartling & Hong Kong Corporate Counsel. The event would not be possible without the support of Professor Dean Wang of the School of Law, City University of Hong Kong, and Assistant Professor Fan Yang who, before she had even relocated to Hong Kong, was instrumental in bringing the conference to it. In particular, the conference was a success largely due to the organizational skills of Mr. Arno Eisen. We also thank Ms. Rebecca Lanctot, and the MAA chairpersons Felix Lautenschlager, Elisabeth Opie, Romesh Weeramantry and Arno Eisen.

Naturally, we extend our thanks to all who contributed to this volume. Finally, and most importantly, our warmest gratitude for the wonderful and patient editing work performed by Alain Hosang, who brought this book to life.

Ingeborg Schwenzer & Lisa Spagnolo
Basel & Melbourne
Editors

16 December 2010

Foreword

Opening Address of the Conference

The United Nations Convention on Contracts for the International Sale of Goods, 1980 (CISG) has become a fundamental text of international trade law in several ways. Indeed, it has gone beyond the original purpose of enhancing the predictability of the law applicable to international contracts for the sale of goods and modernizing the substantive rules, and is increasingly used as the blueprint for domestic law reform, not limited to the contract for sale of goods. It has therefore become a prominent legal model, circulating thanks to its prestige and attracting in turn the attention of the broader comparative law community.

If we look back at its path towards success, we see that the CISG has travelled a long way to obtain wide application: the suggestion, first born in Central Europe, soon won the support of Socialist countries (at the same time promoters of the new-born UNCITRAL), consolidated its influence on the two sides of the Atlantic ocean, and attracted some fans in Africa and the Middle East, regions where further expansion is possible. The CISG has been adopted by 76 States, but by 28 of the 30 countries most active in international trade. There is therefore a clear correlation between engagement in commercial activity and adoption of this text. At the same time, the need to insist on the dissemination of information and promotion of this text in developing countries, where the benefits arising from its adoption may actually be even greater, becomes equally clear.

The most promising approach to further expand the reach of the Convention seems now based on its possible contribution to regional economic integration. Indeed, universal texts may provide at no cost a modern legislative framework operating both at the regional and at the global level. This may be the case of the Association of South-East Asian Nations (ASEAN). While ASEAN countries have so far adopted the CISG only to a limited extent, their most important commercial partners have already done so. This is especially true at the regional level, where all ASEAN partners in the 'ASEAN plus three' economic space (*i.e.*, China, Japan and the Republic of Korea) have now adopted the Convention, as did other important commercial partners such as Australia and New Zealand. The UNCITRAL secretariat regularly receives news on the progress made in various ASEAN States towards the adoption of the CISG. The fact that this Conference will discuss this approach is therefore particularly timely and welcome, as is the decision to include in the analysis the Convention on the Limitation Period in Contracts for the International Sale of Goods, a text that complements the CISG and may provide an important additional contribution to uniformity in this field, but that has been unfortunately sometimes neglected for reasons unrelated to its actual content.

As we know, one of the staunchest supporters of the CISG is the People's Republic of China. China was an original signatory of the CISG, and its deposit of the instrument of ratification, on the same day as the USA and Italy, triggered the entry into force of the Convention. These formal signs of support reflect well the importance that China attaches to the CISG. Indeed, adoption of this treaty is considered as a landmark in the legislative work associated with the 'opening up and reform' policy, which paved the way to remarkable economic development. Lately, we have learned that the favour of Chinese parties for the application of the Convention to contracts for the sale of goods is inducing a change in the other countries who are parties to the Convention, leading to rethink of the practice of 'opting out' of the CISG terms.

This success story could inspire other countries looking at sources for international and domestic trade law reform. It also provides important evidence of the flexibility of the provisions of the CISG, which proved to be adequate both for the Chinese economy of thirty years ago and for that of today, thus offering a fair and neutral legislative ground to cross-border traders. Despite the great achievements made, some important details in the application of the CISG in China are still open for discussion, namely, the possibility to extend the territorial application of the CISG to the Special Administrative Regions of Hong Kong and Macao, and the possibility to withdraw the declarations lodged by China upon ratification. Such steps would further increase the level of uniformity and predictability in the application of the CISG inside and outside China. This conference may provide an important contribution to better understanding these issues.

The adoption of the CISG may mark a fundamental point in trade law reform, but it is only a starting point. At the time of entry into force in a legal system, the CISG is like a new-born baby: healthy, energetic, full of promises, but not yet self-sufficient. Initiatives like this conference and the moot arbitral courts are welcome as they provide the necessary tools to better understand the Convention and, in particular, the uniform and transnational spirit that inspired its drafting and should lead its interpretation and application. In this spirit, we gladly welcome this event and wish a fruitful and enriching experience to its participants.

Renaud Sorieul
The Secretary, UNCITRAL

New Challenges for the Uniformisation of Laws: How the CISG is Challenged by 'Asian Values' and Islamic Law

Gary F. Bell[*]

1 Introduction

The efforts at the uniformisation[1] of laws by the United Nations Commission on International Trade Law (UNCITRAL) and the many other European uniformisation initiatives are often presented simply as efforts at bridging the gaps between civil law and common law traditions.[2] The commercial rules of these two legal traditions are of European and therefore, dare I say, of Christian origin. Because of colonisation and 'modernisation', the rules of either the civil or common law were and are still often assumed to be applicable to trade almost everywhere in the world and a uniform law that would take into account these two traditions was and is still often assumed to have universal appeal.

In this chapter, I will challenge this assumption that only Western law (civil and common law) and only state law need be taken into account when trying to create uniform laws for international trade. I will argue that Asian traditions should be taken into account, but more importantly, I will argue that Islamic law poses great challenges to the movement to create uniform laws for international commerce, and that comparative legal scholarship should take Islamic law into account and look beyond civil and common law approaches

* Associate Professor, Faculty of Law, National University of Singapore; Director of the Asian Law Institute (ASLI).

1 A *unification* of laws would replace a plurality of national laws with one unique law – it would leave no place for national laws. The CISG is therefore rather an effort at *uniformisation* of law – each nation adopts a uniform law but the national laws remain in their plurality as options which the parties may chose, and arguably, the CISG is part of the national law in those nations where it is adopted. *Harmonisation* of law does not require a common legal text – it is a kind of coordination of different national laws so that they reach similar results, but without necessarily adopting a common legislative text. For a comparison of unification, uniformisation and harmonisation, see S. Nadaud, *Codifier le droit civil européen*, 52 (2008). The term 'uniformisation' (sometimes with a 'z') is rarely used in English but has been used and I find it useful.

2 Socialist law was also a concern, but is increasingly less so.

and rules. As an example of why uniformisation and comparative scholarship should take into account Asian traditions and Islamic law, I will look at the CISG[3] and show, first, that Asian approaches to law should be taken into account in the interpretation of the CISG and second, and more importantly, that the CISG, as it stands, is incompatible with many aspects of Islamic commercial law and particularly with the requirements of the law of Islamic finance, and that therefore the CISG is likely to be rejected by those who wish to finance their international sales and other transactions in accordance with Islamic law.

Relatively few Asian countries have adopted the CISG. Although the largest Asian country, China, has adopted the CISG, the next three largest Asian countries India, Indonesia and Pakistan, have not.[4] In a previous article I had argued that Asian countries should adopt the CISG rather than seek their own regional harmonisation.[5] Most of them in any event have most of their commercial law of sale governed by the leftover laws of their former colonial masters or a Western law they have adopted in order to 'modernise' – they almost all mainly use the civil law or the common law for their commercial sales, rather than Asian laws. Since the CISG is a good compromise between these two Western legal traditions, at first sight there seems to be no reason why this compromise could not work well for the uniformisation of these Western laws in Asia.

There are, however, two concerns raised against the CISG in Asia, both of which were mentioned but not fully addressed in this author's previous article. In this chapter, I will first very briefly address the concern that many Asian countries may have values that are different from the Western values embodied in both the civil and the common law, values which in practice modify how the civil law and the common law are applied and work in Asia. There is of course not one set of 'Asian values' all across Asia but some have argued that, particularly in East and Southeast Asia, contracts are more relational than transactional – that what is valued is the long-term relationship between trusted partners rather than the specifics of a particular contract. Therefore, the specific text of a contract should not be insisted upon, and the parties should be flexible enough to adapt the contract to new circumstances in order to maintain the relationship and the trust rather than the specific contract. One would look at contractual relationships as expressions of a partnership rather

3 United Nations Convention on Contracts for the International Sale of Goods (CISG), Vienna, 11 April 1980, available at <http://www.uncitral.org/uncitral/en/uncitral_texts/sale_goods/1980CISG.html>.

4 The population of these three countries together is greater than that of China, see *CIA, The World Factbook, Field Listing: Population*, available at <https://www.cia.gov/library/publications/the-world-factbook/fields/2119.html>. However, China's external trade is many times greater than the external trade of these three countries combined, see *CIA, The World Factbook, Country Comparison: Export*, available at <https://www.cia.gov/library/publications/the-world-factbook/rankorder/2078rank.html>.

5 G. Bell, 'Harmonisation of Contract Law in Asia – Harmonising Regionally or Adopting Global Harmonisations – The Example of the CISG', 2005 *Singapore Journal of Legal Studies* 362.

than as separate individual deals creating absolute rights. It is argued that these so-called 'Asian values' shape contract law in parts of Asia, even though the black letter law enacted in Asia is similar to what it is in the West. The CISG might be ill-adapted for such relational approaches to contract law, lacking a clear obligation to act in good faith, an obligation to renegotiate in cases of changed circumstances and arguably, a requirement that the long-term relationship between the parties be fully taken into account in the interpretation of the contract.

The second concern that I will address in greater length is that the CISG is incompatible with Islamic law. There is the oft-cited Article 78 CISG that provides for interest, something Islamic law prohibits, but if this were the only problem it could be dealt with through an exclusion of that article by the parties.[6] The problem is more fundamental. In the 1970s, when the CISG was being negotiated, socialist law was taken into account but not Islamic law. At the time it seemed that socialist law had a future, and that Islamic law did not. We now know that the contrary was true. Islamic law has seen a great resurgence and Islamic financing is today a hot topic and a very significant industry.

How does Islamic financing relate to the international sale of goods? Because interest is prohibited, Islamic financing often takes the form of a *murabaha*, a kind of contract of sale. In order to finance an acquisition by its client, the Islamic bank actually buys the goods for a price and resells them to its client for a higher price payable through fixed (non-aleatory) instalments with no interest (a kind of *vente à tempérament* or instalment sale). This kind of financing is liberally allowed in some schools of Islamic law (*Madhaheb*, singular: *Madh'hab*), in particular in the Shafi'i school which is dominant in all of Southeast Asia (including Malaysia, Singapore and Indonesia). This is not without controversy within Islamic legal scholarship (the main criticism being that the use of *murabaha* for financing is just a disguise for what is in reality interest or *riba*) but it remains that today the *murabaha* is the most commonly used method of Islamic financing and is a thriving and fast developing business.[7]

Many *murabaha* contracts are international contracts. Is the *murabaha* contract compatible with the CISG? It seems that it is not as the CISG does not take into account the many requirements of the *murabaha* and of Islamic contract law in general. This does not bode well for the adoption of the CISG by Islamic countries, and, even if it is adopted, it is likely

6 Art. 6 CISG.

7 See A. Saeed, *Islamic Banking and Interest – A Study of the Prohibition of Riba and its Contemporary Interpretation* 77 (1996).

that it will be excluded by the parties to Islamic transactions as the CISG seems incompatible with the *murabaha* contract.

Before looking at whether the so-called 'Asian values' and the *murabaha* contract of sale are compatible with the CISG, let us first look at the status of the ratification of the CISG in Asia and in Muslim-majority countries, as a kind of sombre reality check.

2 The Status of the CISG in Asia and in Muslim Countries

As we know the CISG has been a very successful convention if we measure that success by the total number of countries that are parties to the Convention and the amount of international trade between these parties.[8] When, however, we look at the geographical distribution of the parties to the CISG, it becomes clear that the coverage in Asia[9] and Africa remains patchy. The CISG is popular in East Asia: China, South Korea and, since recently, Japan are parties to the CISG.[10] However, in the Association of Southeast Asian Nations (ASEAN) only one country out of ten (Singapore) is a party to the CISG. In South Asia, no country is a party – not India, not Pakistan, not Bangladesh, nor Sri Lanka. A few countries of Central Asia have joined,[11] but fewer countries have adopted the CISG in West Asia: only Georgia, Iraq, Lebanon, Syria and Israel. The fact that the adoption of the CISG is not widespread in Asia does not necessarily mean that there are reasons specific to Asia for not adopting the CISG – it might have nothing to do with a potential conflict with so called 'Asian values' – but nonetheless, it is an interesting phenomenon to note.

The CISG is even less present in Muslim-majority countries. There are 193 countries in the world (UN members)[12] of which 47 are Muslim-majority countries.[13] This means that

8 See I. Schwenzer & P. Hachem, 'The CISG – Successes and Pitfalls', 57 *Am. J. Comp. L.* 457 (2009), available at <http://www.cisg.law.pace.edu/cisg/biblio/schwenzer-hachem.html>.

9 J. Mowbray, 'The Application of the United Nations Convention on Contracts for the International Sale of Goods to E-Commerce Transactions: The Implications for Asia', 7 *Vindobona Journal of International Commercial Law & Arbitration* 121 (2003), stating that '[t]here are also regions where participation in the CISG is noticeably lacking. One of these regions is Asia'.

10 A detailed list of the currently 78 countries that have ratified the CISG and 76 Contracting States (two countries will become Contracting States within a year) can be found at <http://www.uncitral.org/uncitral/en/uncitral_texts/sale_goods/1980CISG_status.html>.

11 Namely Kyrgyzstan, Uzbekistan, and Mongolia, if it is considered as Central Asia, as opposed to East Asia.

12 A detailed list can be found at <http://www.un.org/en/aboutun/index.shtml>.

13 The Pew Forum estimates that there are 50 Muslim-majority countries and territories out of 232 countries and territories in the world, see Pew Forum on Religion & Public Life, Mapping the Global Muslim Population: A Report on the Size and Distribution of the World's Muslim Population, October 2009, available at <http://pewforum.org/uploadedfiles/Topics/Demographics/Muslimpopulation.pdf>. However, since we are concerned with the ratification of the CISG, it is the number of sovereign countries, rather than territories,

78 out of 193 or 40.4% of all countries have ratified the CISG.[14] However, only 9 out of 47, or 19% of Muslim-majority countries have done so: Albania, Egypt, Iraq, Kyrgyzstan, Lebanon, Mauritania, Syria, Turkey and Uzbekistan. This is in sharp contrast with 66 out of 146 or 45% of non Muslim-majority countries that have ratified the convention.[15]

Again, we should not rush to the conclusion that the reason why these countries have not ratified the CISG is the fact that they are Muslim-majority – in the vast majority of these countries most international commercial sales are governed by a Western law – civil law or common law. The different rates of ratification may have more to do with the fact that most of them are developing countries – 29 out of 30 OECD countries (developed countries), including Turkey, have ratified the convention, but the rate of ratification is much lower in the developing world. Nonetheless, with the greater importance of Islamic financing, and the increasing number of Muslims who hope that Islamic commercial law can be restored to its former glory, the ratification of the CISG in these countries may become more problematic as the years pass.

3 'Asian Values' and the CISG

Asian countries increasingly see the need for uniform or harmonised law at least in commercial matters, but the adoption of international uniform laws has nonetheless often been slow in many parts of Asia. Should there be an Asian uniformisation, or should Asian nations simply adopt internationally negotiated uniform law? Do the internationally negotiated laws sufficiently take into account the legal traditions of Asia, or are they simply compromises between the main Western legal traditions (civil and common law)?

Let us be frank here: the CISG did not take into account non-Western legal traditions; not at all. This is not surprising as most Asian jurisdictions had been forced to abandon their Asian legal traditions and rely mainly on Western legal traditions imposed in most instances through colonisation (or the threat of it that led to a so-called 'modernisation', *i.e.* Westernisation of the law in the case of Japan, China, Thailand etc.). Islam had a very long and

---

that is important to note. I have therefore decided to rely on the list of UN members for the total number of countries (193). In the 50 countries and territories named as majority Muslim in the Pew Forum report, three are not countries at this point: Palestine, West Sahara and Mayotte. There are therefore 47 Muslim-majority countries which is confirmed by a compilation of mainly CIA statistics, available at <http://en.wikipedia.org/wiki/List_of_Muslim_majority_countries>.

14 See *supra* note 10.

15 These numbers are arrived at by subtracting the number of Muslim-majority countries from the total number of countries, and the number of Muslim-majority countries that have adopted the CISG from the total number of countries that have adopted it.

very successful tradition of commercial law. In fact, the Prophet Muhammad himself was a merchant. Yet, it was not taken into account simply because the CISG was negotiated by States and therefore state law, and that meant Western colonial laws in Asia and the Islamic world were taken into account, since colonialists had rejected any role for Islamic and Asian laws in commercial sales, and the law of the decolonised or modernised Asian and majority-Muslim states reflected this.

Islamic law is not state law and can never truly be state law,[16] and this may also explain why when negotiations took place between states it was not taken into account. The same is true for some other Asian legal traditions.

Are there 'Asian values' that are not reflected in the CISG that make its adoption inappropriate for Asia? I put 'Asian values' in inverted commas. There has been years of debate as to whether Asians in general have common 'Asian values'. Some of the proponents of Asian values have in fact promoted the concept as a way of resisting the promotion of so called 'universal human rights' by arguing that human rights were Western values, and that Asians had their own values. I am not here using 'Asian values' in that generalising sense. How could it be that the Jews, Christians, Muslims, Hindus, Buddhists and others living from the Suez Canal all the way to Japan, share one set of values? People of different cultures and religions do have, to some extent, different values. Many of the values are the same, but some are indeed very different. It is just as dangerous to make generalisations about Asian values as it is dangerous to make generalisations about human rights. Nonetheless, there is among many Asians an increasing consciousness that their legal traditions or their cultures are somewhat different. There are studies about why people in some Asian countries may be less litigious[17] – cultural explanations of why legal transplants from the West do not lead to the same results in Asia.[18]

Under the leadership of Professor Naoki Kanayama of Japan, some scholars from Asia have just begun work on the *Principles of Asian Contract Law*, and the presumption is that they would be quite different from the *Principles of European Contract Law*.[19] There is therefore a sense that Western legal transplants in Asia are transformed and become dif-

16 The sources of Islamic law are not found in the State, but in the *Quran*, the *Sunna* etc.

17 See, *e.g.*, E.A. Feldman, 'Law, Culture, and Conflict: Dispute Resolution in Postwar Japan', in D.H. Foote (Ed.), *Law in Japan – A Turning Point*, 50 (2008).

18 B. Tabalujan, 'Why Indonesian Corporate Governance Failed – Conjectures Concerning Legal Culture', 15 *Colum. J. Asian L.* 141 (2001). For an analysis of why U.S. efforts to transplant U.S. law often do not work in Asia, see J. deLisle, 'Lex Americana?: United States Legal Assistance, American Legal Models, and Legal Change in the Post-Communist World and Beyond', 20 *U. Pa. J. Int'l Econ. L.* 179 (1999).

19 The work on the *Principles of Asian Contract Law* is in its preliminary stages and the Principles have not yet been published.

ferent in some respects. I cannot speak for every Asian country (or for any for that matter) but I do specialise in Indonesian law and I can assure you that the attitudes of Indonesians toward contracts are often quite different from the attitudes of most Westerners. One could say that many Indonesians have a relational approach to contracts rather than a transactional approach.[20] I think this might also be true in some other East Asian/Southeast Asian countries. The specific transaction and therefore the letter of the contract is not what is most important, but the ongoing relationship between the parties is what matters most. This affects how binding the text of the contract is, at least in the minds of the parties and culturally. Let me take two examples.

3.1 Merger Clauses

There often is in Indonesia a real incomprehension of some Westerners' attitude of insisting on the letter of the contract whatever the circumstances, and therefore merger clauses are seen as very foreign. The idea that, through a merger clause, a contract could be reduced to a writing and that nothing of the relationship, context and discussions between the parties could be used in interpreting the contract seems almost insane. In Indonesian culture, context is everything and the relationship requires that you do not take the wording of the contract out of context.

In the first draft of the Principles of Asian Contract Law (PACL), it was proposed that the following text be adopted on merger clauses:

> Art. 4. A clause stating that the writing embodies all the terms of the contract (merger clause) is void, unless its rationality is demonstrated.[21]

It therefore seems that the Indonesian approach to merger clauses is shared by many Asian countries.

---

20 Of course, relational theories of contract are not exclusively Asian. See, *e.g.*, I.R. Macneil, 'Contracts: Adjustment of Long-Term Economic Relations under Classical, Neoclassical, and Relational Contract Law', 72 *Nw. U. L. Rev.* 854 (1977-1978); and I.R. Macneil, 'Reflections on Relational Contract Theory After a Neoclassical Seminar', in H. Collins, *et al.* (Eds.), *The Implicit Dimensions of Contract*, at 207 (2003). The argument here is that on a spectrum in many Asian countries a relational approach to contract law would be stronger.

21 Early draft of the *Principles of Asian Contract Law*. Copy on file with the author.

There is nothing in the CISG on merger clauses but the *CISG Advisory Council Opinion No. 3*[22] states that such merger clauses are permitted although 'in determining the effect of such a Merger Clause, the parties' statements and negotiations, as well as all other relevant circumstances shall be taken into account'.[23] This seems to reflect a more 'Western' approach.

In fact, such a Western approach can be found in the Indonesian Civil Code, which is based on the old Dutch Code.[24] The Indonesian Civil Code has a 'plain meaning rule' which lends some support to merger clauses:

> Art. 1342. If the wording of an agreement is clear, one shall not deviate from it by way of interpretation.
>
> Art. 1343. If the wording of an agreement is open to several interpretations, one shall ascertain the intent of the parties involved rather than be bound by the literal sense of the words.

Yet, the general attitude in Indonesia seems to be to go to Article 1343 directly, thus ignoring the Dutch limitation on recourse to interpretation and context. There is an allergy to the merger clauses that are typically imposed by foreign parties, and it seems that this attitude is shared in some other Asian countries.

3.2 Good Faith

Another issue is the need to behave in good faith. Good faith is of course a general duty in Western civil law traditions. But this duty is much more extensive in Islamic law and in the indigenous *adat* laws of Indonesia.[25] In Islamic law the very fairness of every transaction is often a condition of its validity. Aleatory obligations are not allowed as they can lead to unfairness. In *adat* laws there is also a communal aspect that must be taken into account and therefore rights cannot be insisted upon as absolute, but are subject to com-

22 CISG-AC Opinion No. 3, Parol Evidence Rule, Plain Meaning Rule, Contractual Merger Clause and the CISG, 23 October 2004, Rapporteur: Professor Richard Hyland, Rutgers Law School, Camden, NJ, USA, available at <http://www.cisgac.com/UserFiles/File/CISg%20AC%20Opinion%203%20English.pdf>.

23 CISG-AC Opinion No. 3, *supra* note 22, para. 3.

24 The Indonesian Civil code was adopted in Dutch for Indonesia as the *Burgerlijk Wetboek voor Indonesie*, promulgated on 30 April 1847, by Ordinance (in Dutch, *Staatsblad*, in Indonesian, *Ordonansi*) No. S 1847-23. The Code is known in Indonesian unofficial translations as the *Kitab Undang-Undang Hukum Perdata*.

25 *Adat* laws are the local customary laws found in Indonesia. They are very diverse, each ethnic group having its own *adat*. For example, the Minangkabau are Muslims but follow matrilineal inheritance rules from their indigenous *adat*. However, the various *adat* laws generally share some common features.

munity needs and approval (a radical form of abuse of rights doctrine or social function of rights).[26]

When interpreting the civil law concept of good faith found in the Indonesian civil code, the Indonesian courts seem to have gone further much faster than their European Dutch and French counterparts in creating more extensive obligations, maybe influenced by Islamic and *adat* legal cultures. They have held that contracts had to be re-negotiated when currency fluctuations made them unfair (not following closely the then Dutch and French precedents on this issue). For example, after World War II, Indonesian courts have, when faced with radical depreciation and inflation, intervened by refusing to enforce an unjust contract price and based this intervention on the need to act in good faith.[27] This was at a time when their French and Dutch counterparts would not have done so as radically. Later cases were even more liberal in enforcing good faith, which led the leading Indonesian contract law academic to conclude: 'It appears that several decisions in Indonesia indicate that the judge, based on equity (*kepatutan*) can change the basic rights and obligations of the contract without having to mention many reasons and that all that is necessary is the opinion of the court that the content of the contract is not fair.'[28]

However, when these Indonesian precedents were invoked in the midst of the late 1990s Asian financial crisis, in the majority of cases the matter was decided by foreigners sitting as arbitrators, and they rejected that Indonesian interpretation of the principle of good faith, insisting instead on the letter of the contract.[29]

26 In fact the very use of the concept of an individual 'right' in *adat* law is problematic. 'Rights and duties are not absolute or fixed principles but are relative according to the proper behaviour adat requires from specific individuals. There is no conception of the individual as a fixed point of normative reference which is absolute and independent of circumstance. Obligation varies depending upon circumstance and upon an individual's position (in status, or kinship relationship) within or without the adat universe', M.B. Hooker, *Adat Law in Modern Indonesia*, 54 (1978).

27 See the case of Mahkamah Agung, 28 May 1953, No 62aK/Sip/1952 under the name of 'Jual-Beli Bersyarat' published in H.1953 – 2 & 3, reported in part in J. Satrio, *Hukum Perikatan – Perikatan Yang Lahir Dari Perjanjian – Buku II*, at 170-172 (1995). The Indonesian Courts' approach in that respect may have been closer to the German courts' approach at the time.

28 My translation of Satrio, *supra* note 27, at 230.

29 For example, in the arbitration cases of *Himpurna Cal. Energy Ltd. (Bermuda) v. PT (Persero) Perusahaan Lestrik Negara (Indonesia)*, 14 *Mealey's Int'l Arb.* Rep. A-1 (December 1999) and *Patuha Power Ltd. (Bermuda) v. PT (Persero) Perusahaan Lestrik Negara (Indonesia)*, 14 *Mealey's Int'l Arb.* Rep. B-1 (December 1999), the arbitral tribunal refused to apply the Indonesian good faith precedents even though Indonesian law applied, and rather applied Dutch precedents, yet, later in the award, with respect to the quantum of the damages, the tribunal applied the concept of abuse of rights as understood in international arbitration, which strangely looked more European than Indonesian.

Some Indonesian jurists may look at the CISG with suspicion as it has no clear duty to act in good faith, and they may therefore fear that the interpretation of the CISG may be inconsistent with the Indonesian concept of good faith.

3.3 *Conclusion on 'Asian Values'*

Although I do understand very well the concern of many Asian colleagues, it seems that in relation to the civil law, often the very same provisions of the French, Dutch or German civil codes enacted within Asian countries in Asian languages, are sometimes interpreted differently. This is certainly true – the civil codes transplanted in Asia have taken a life of their own given the socio-cultural environment in which they have been transplanted. But transplanted they have been, for better or for worse, and lawyers from Japan, China and Indonesia for example, are not arguing from outside the civil law tradition, but, within that tradition, from a Japanese, Chinese or Indonesian perspective. In my view, there is therefore no need to fear unification, but simply a need to try to influence it, and more importantly, to influence the interpretation of instruments such as the CISG. If there are Asian approaches to the interpretation of contracts and to the interpretation of the CISG, the best way to assert this is to participate in the uniformisation effort and to influence the interpretation of the CISG. In my view, the cultural arguments only go so far – understandably, there are many interpretations of civil or common law traditions around the world – that is the very starting point of efforts at uniformisation. What I do not hear from colleagues is the radical argument that the CISG is fundamentally incompatible with civil law or common law as applied in Asia. Therefore, although I see this challenge as real – uniformisation efforts should be more sensitive to Asian approaches to law – it is not fundamental in that these jurists do participate in civil and common law traditions and therefore can influence their development. The challenge brought by the resurgence of Islamic law is far more fundamental.

4 Islamic Law, the *Murabaha* and the CISG

4.1 *The Lack of Contact Between the CISG and the Islamic Law Academic Communities*

I should state at the very outset that I am not an expert on Islamic law and I am not a Muslim (not that this would make me an expert on Islamic law). I do not speak Arabic and therefore I have no access to the sources of Islamic law in their original language. I therefore ask for the indulgence of colleagues trained in Islamic law. The reader who seeks a full understanding of Islamic law and Islamic finance, including the *murabaha* contract of sale, would be well advised to consult the writing of Islamic law scholars.[30] This chapter is not an authoritative exposition of the relevant Islamic law of sale – its goal is much more humble.

I am an academic in Singapore writing on the CISG and specialising on Indonesian law. Being in Singapore, I have followed with interest the development of Islamic finance in Singapore and in neighbouring Indonesia and Malaysia. Islamic banking is by all accounts a growing industry with a growing market. Even Western banks are increasingly involved in this expanding market and offer Islamic instruments. Assets managed under Islamic banking laws could reach USD 1.6 trillion by 2012.[31] It is estimated that about 75% of Islamic financing is done through the *murabaha* contract of sale[32] and many of these sales (and this would often be the case in Singapore) are international sales. Since Singapore is a party to the CISG some of these Islamic international sales could be in part governed by the CISG. Would they still be Islamic if they were governed by the CISG, or are the parties to the *murabaha* contract well advised to systematically exclude the application of the CISG? There is almost no research published on this issue.

There seem to be two entirely separate academic worlds that are not in contact with one another. On the one hand, the CISG academic community (of which I am part) does not seem to realise that the development of Islamic financing in this region and around the world means that many contracts for the international sale of goods are and increasingly will be governed by Islamic law. The CISG was conceived to reconcile the different rules of the civil law, common law and socialist law but it is ill-equipped to reconcile the differences between Islamic law and Western laws, and therefore the CISG is likely to be excluded in all Islamic finance sale contracts. Given how much is written on the CISG generally, and given that close to a quarter of the world population is Muslim and that Islamic financing is a growing industry in which most large Western banks are also active, it is astonishing that the issue of the compatibility or incompatibility of the CISG with Islamic law has not been more fully considered by the CISG academic community.

On the other hand, Muslim scholars are busy building up the modern Islamic finance intellectual framework and have not had time to consider the CISG and its potential effect

30 For an introduction to Islamic law generally, see W.B. Hallaq, *An Introduction to Islamic Law* (2009). For an introduction to Islamic financing including the *murabaha* contract of sale, see M. Ayub, *Understanding Islamic Finance* (2007).

31 F. Richter, *Islamic finance assets seen at $1.6 trln by 2012*, Reuters, 8 April 2009, available at <http://www.reuters.com/article/idUSL894329020090408>.

32 Saeed, *supra* note 7, at 77.

on Islamic financing transactions. It does not help of course that the vast majority of Muslim-majority countries are not parties to the CISG – these scholars usually do not have to worry too much about whether the CISG is reconcilable with Islamic law as their countries usually are not parties to the CISG (although some Muslim-majority countries, such as Egypt and Turkey, are parties, and Singapore, where Muslims are in the minority but where Islamic finance is thriving, is also a party). In any event, if the CISG could apply to a *murabaha* contract, the scholars will most certainly recommend that it should be excluded as the CISG has no Islamic credentials. For a transaction to be considered Islamic, banks usually ask a council of Islamic scholars to confirm that their standard transactions conform to Islamic law, and I am unaware of any opinion by such a council of scholars that has considered whether, if the CISG were used, the transaction could still conform to Islamic law.[33] I am no Islamic scholar but from the little knowledge I have, it does not seem that the CISG can be used for Islamic finance without compromising the very Islamic nature of the transaction.

In any event, Islamic law is not state law – its sources are in the *Quran*, the *Sunna* and other sources, many scholarly. It is supra-national rather than international and for international Islamic sales, the parties may share the same Islamic law even if they are in different countries, and there is therefore no real need to have recourse to the CISG – Islamic law can be a transnational 'uniform law' chosen by the parties.[34]

There must be very few academics (if any) who have full credentials in the classical Islamic law of sale, are active in the development of modern Islamic finance and are experts on the CISG. But there is a need to start the dialogue. Some colleagues with an interest in Islamic law and specialising in the CISG have written on the topic, but at the Pace database on the CISG[35] I could find only two full articles on Islam and the CISG out of 1400 full articles available.[36] There is obviously very little research being done on whether the CISG is compatible with Islamic law, and more precisely with the *murabaha*.

---

33 My knowledge is indeed anecdotal and not reliable, but I have tried to find an instance where the issue was considered and have failed.

34 It should be said however that there is in fact great diversity in Islamic law not only between *Sunni* and *Shia* Muslims but even for example within *Sunni* Islam which has four main schools of law (*a Madh'hab*): the *Maliki*, *Hanafi*, *Shafi'i* and *Hanbali* schools. Each school may be significantly different from the other on many points of law, including on some details of the *murabaha* contract, so the parties should choose a school of law. Most Southeast Asian Muslims belong to the *Shafi'i* school.

35 See Pace University CISG Database, available at <http://www.cisg.law.pace.edu/cisg/text/case-annotations.html>.

36 There seem to be only three law review articles at the Pace University website that refer to Islamic law. See, *e.g.*, F. Akaddaf, 'Application of the United Nations Convention on Contracts for the International Sale of Goods (CISG) to Arab Islamic Countries; Is the CISG Compatible With Islamic Law Principles?', 13 *Pace Int'l L. Rev.* 1 (2001), and T. Twibell, 'Implementation of the United Nations Convention on Contracts for

To some extent, this is understandable. There are lots of civil law and common law scholars working on the CISG because, from the time the discussions that led to the CISG started, the goal has been to harmonise civil and common law approaches to contracts to sale. Civil law and common law scholars were heavily involved in the negotiation of the CISG. Muslims scholars were not. We have to remember that these negotiations took place in the 1970s before the full emergence of modern Islamic financing and at a time when most governments in Muslim-majority countries were led by secularists who saw no role for Islamic law in commercial transactions. However, times have changed and there is now a market for Islamic transactions, including the Islamic sale of goods and financing. There is therefore a need for those of us specialising in the CISG to look at Islamic law and vice versa.

I will very briefly describe some aspects of the *murabaha* contract as I understand it (and apologies for any shortcoming on my part in describing the contract) so that my colleagues specialising on the CISG can understand the growing importance of Islamic law as a governing law for many international sales of goods and the incompatibility of the CISG with that law.

4.2 *Islamic Contract Law in General*

The contract of *murabaha*, like all Islamic contracts, is governed by the general rules of Islamic contract law. Islamic contract law could be described as encouraging good faith and honest behaviour between parties. There is a prohibition against the undertaking of uncertain, risky and undetermined obligations that are associated with the concept of deceit or *gharar* – such obligations are invalid. A price, for example, must be certain and determined and may not be aleatory (it cannot be a market price on a future date as this would be speculative).[37] There is also the prohibition of interest (*riba*).[38] As we shall see, many of these general rules of contract law could in fact be inconsistent with the CISG.

---

the International Sale of Goods (CISG) Under Shari'a Law: Will Article 78 of the CISG Be Enforced When the Forum Is an Islamic State?', 9 *International Legal Perspectives* 25 (1997). The third does not directly address the CISG but provides an interesting perspective on the resurgence of the Islamic legal tradition: O. Azziman, *La traditionalisation du droit: Tradition juridique islamique et droit privé marocain*, Saggi, Conferenze e Seminari 11, available at <http://cisgw3.law.pace.edu/cisg/biblio/azziman.html>. There were five more articles mentioned in the bibliography (no full text), but they were general introductions to, or comparisons of aspects of Islamic law.

37 Ayub, *supra* note 30, at 214.

38 N.A. Saleh, *Unlawful Gain and Legitimate Profit in Islamic Law: Riba, Gharar, and Islamic Banking* (1992).

4.3 The Murabaha

In the *murabaha*, an eventual buyer asks an eventual seller to buy a specific good which will be resold in turn to the eventual buyer ('buy this book and I will buy it from you'). The seller in the *murabaha* contract is in some way a middle-man but he is neither a partner, nor an agent or *mandataire* of the eventual buyer – the two sales are independent. The sale to the eventual buyer will be for the original price paid by the eventual seller for the goods, plus his expenses, plus a mark-up (which can be a percentage of the original price for example) all of which must be fully disclosed to the buyer. If there is no truthful and complete disclosure of the price, expenses and mark-up, then the contract is invalid (null, void).[39]

In classical times, this contract was originally used for purely commercial purposes and not as a way of financing a transaction. For example, one could say 'on your next trip to Baghdad, buy me this book up to this price and I will buy it from you for the price you paid plus 10 percent plus your expenses'. This type of transactions was not specifically mentioned in the *Quran* or in any *Hadith*,[40] but both Malik and Shafi'i, the founders of two of the four main schools (*Madhaheb*) of Islamic law, specifically approved the *murabaha* and later some *Hanafi* scholars also approved it.[41]

It must be noted, however, that in classical times the price was usually paid in full in one instalment. It was only later that the *murabaha* started to be used with deferred payment, usually by instalments, and thus became a financing instrument. 'You will buy a carpet for me at this price and I will pay you back that price plus your expenses plus 20% over the next year in twelve equal instalments.' It became an instalment sale (*une vente à tempérament*) which of course may look like a sale with interest being charged for deferred payment, but is technically a sale for a higher price. An Islamic bank for example could buy train carriages for a price and would resell them to a train operator for that price plus expenses (insurance etc.) plus a mark-up, the total price to be paid back by instalments over ten years. In more complex schemes (including double sales) the *murabaha* is used almost as a legal fiction, to support what is, in all other respects, a loan of money.

Some Muslim scholars look unfavourably or critically on this financial use of the *murabaha*. They say it mimics interest charges and is simply an indirect way of offering the same kind

39 Ayub, *supra* note 30, at 218.

40 Saeed, *supra* note 7, at 76.

41 *Id.*, at 77 *et seq.*, for an account of the position taken by classical scholars.

of financing non-Muslim banks offer.[42] However, in defence of this use of the *murabaha*, it is not the case that the bank is simply lending money, as there are many other conditions that must be fulfilled. For example, it must follow the general rules of the contract of sale (some mentioned above) and some rules specific to the *murabaha*:

- The transaction must involve goods against money – it cannot be used for the trading of currencies or precious metals.[43]
- The seller must own and have at least a notional or constructive possession of the goods before they are resold to the buyer (hence there is an assumed risk for the seller).[44]
- The object must be determined and assigned to the buyer at the time of the contract of sale, not later.[45]
- If there is an intrinsic defect in the good, the buyer has a right to rescind the sale as the seller had an obligation to reveal any such defect.[46]
- As mentioned above, the original price, the expenses and the mark-up, *i.e.* profit, must be disclosed precisely to the buyer.
- If the seller lies about original price, all schools agree: the contract is invalid. If the seller mistakenly states the original price, some schools allow the seller to save the contract by reimbursing the difference to the buyer, others do not.[47]
- The payment may be agreed to be deferred but the contract cannot give the option between deferred payment and immediate payment – nothing must be aleatory, therefore, if an option is offered it must be solved by the time of the acceptance of the offer to contract.[48]
- There cannot be any interest for late payment, but according to some councils of scholars formed by the banks, there can be a penalty equal to the profit the bank could have on investment if the debtor has the ability to pay and refuses to pay (there can be no such penalty if the debtor does not have the ability to pay).[49]

Again, this very short summary by a non-expert is not intended to be a reliable source of knowledge on the *murabaha* but is intended to allow a preliminary comparison with the CISG to determine whether the CISG is reconcilable with the *murabaha*.

---

42 'It has been conveniently ignored that accepting the time value of money logically leads to the acceptance of interest. [...] If Islamic law can allow *murabaha* financing as it is practiced under Islamic banking then the question is, "Is there any moral basis for not allowing fixed interest on loans and advances?"': Saeed, *supra* note 7, at 95.

43 Ayub, *supra* note 30, at 217.

44 *Id.*, at 214.

45 *Id.*

46 Saeed, *supra* note 7, at 85.

47 Ayub, *supra* note 30, at 218.

48 *Id.*, at 215.

49 *Id.*, at 231.

4.4 *Is the CISG Compatible With the* Murabaha?

4.4.1 Uncertainty of Price and Other Details

As was mentioned before, the Islamic contract of *murabaha* does not allow for any uncertainty as to the price to be paid. In fact the parties must determine the price (as in French law) – they may not let the price be determined by a third party or a market (unlike French law), or leave it open so that a judge will determine what a reasonable price should be (unlike *e.g.* in most common law jurisdictions). Islamic law requires certainty of obligations and abhors uncertainty, risk and speculation. The same is true with respect to other details such as place and time of delivery.

It therefore seems that this is inconsistent with the CISG. Of course, we know that Article 14(1) CISG states that an offer is 'sufficiently definite if it [...] expressly or impliedly fixes or makes provisions for fixing the price'. This would allow the parties to agree that the price will be determined by a third party or by the market price on a certain market on a certain day in the future.[50] Such provisions would be invalid in Islamic law as the contract would be speculative in nature and the parties' obligations would be uncertain.

Article 55 CISG also provides that

> [w]here a contract has been validly concluded but does not expressly or implicitly fix or make provision for determining the price, the parties are considered, in the absence of any indication to the contrary, to have impliedly made reference to the price generally charged at the time of the conclusion of the contract for such goods sold under comparable circumstances in the trade concerned.

This would also seem to go against the prohibition against uncertainty in contract: the parties may not know and may disagree on the price generally charged – an unacceptable uncertainty in Islamic law. The CISG also provides that, unless the parties agree otherwise, the goods are to be delivered within a reasonable time[51] which is not an entirely certain point in time.

50 I. Schwenzer (Ed.), *Schlechtriem & Schwenzer, Commentary on the UN Convention on the International Sale of Goods* (CISG), 263 (2010).

51 Art. 33 CISG.

4.4.2 Certainty of Goods Sold

In many ways, the goods have to be determined under Islamic law. The goods sold must have been determined and assigned to the contract – one cannot sell a ton of rice which is not separate from ten other tons at the time of the contract. Also there can be no future sale – the seller must be the owner at the time of the contract. This is inconsistent with Articles 31(b) and 32(1) CISG.

4.4.3 Good Faith Contract

Islamic law is a moral and religious law. Its aim is to have people follow the right path, the one pleasing to God. Honesty and good faith are, in this respect, high moral and religious duties. Parties to contracts must enter into them in good faith and perform them in good faith. All Islamic contracts are what the Romans would have called a 'good faith contract' (of which the contract of sale was one).

Unlike other contracts of sale under Islamic law, in the *murabaha*, there is even a further obligation of full transparency (other contracts of sale for example do not require the seller to reveal the price he paid for the goods). There must be perfect transparency as to the price paid by the seller, his expenses and the mark-up. If the seller does not reveal these prices or is dishonest about them, the contract is invalid.

There is obviously no such broad obligation to act in good faith under the CISG. Article 7(1) CISG only provides that in interpreting the convention 'regard is to be had [...] to the need to promote [...] the observance of good faith in international trade'. Even if a general duty to act in good faith could be found to be a general principle of the CISG under Article 7(2) CISG (something which is controversial), such a duty would only be secondary – such a general principle would be relevant only when questions concerning matters governed by the convention are not expressly settled within it. A general principle of good faith under Article 7(2) CISG would have a limited supplementary role. In any event, none of the specific good faith requirements relating to the *murabaha* (revealing the original price for example) are included expressly in the CISG or would be likely to be included in a general principle to act in good faith under the CISG.

One could argue that these specific requirements (disclosure of price paid by the seller etc.) are questions of validity under Islamic law and therefore could be governed by the Islamic law through Article 4(a) CISG: the CISG is not concerned with the validity of the contract. However, it is clear that validity was an issue the CISG intended to leave to national state law, rather than religious law – and there seems to be some uncertainty in Western private international law as to whether an invalidity under Islamic law would be recognised by state courts.[52] Thus Article 4(a) CISG is not entirely reassuring for parties to a *murabaha*.

4.4.4 Non-Conformity of the Goods

Any non-conformity of the goods in a *murabaha* contract means that the contract may be rescinded under Islamic law. The CISG on the other hand, makes the avoidance of the contract for non-conformity conditional on the breach being fundamental.[53]

4.4.5 Interest

It is well known that Islamic law prohibits interest. By contrast, Article 78 CISG gives an entitlement to interest to an aggrieved party.

4.4.6 Conclusion on the CISG and Islamic Law: Some Clear Incompatibilities

There are indeed many ways in which CISG clashes with Islamic law. It is not surprising given that there was no attempt to take Islamic law into account when writing the CISG. Bridging the gap between civil and common law was the easy part – both are (Christian) Western laws that share almost exactly the same values. Islamic law is more religiously and morally grounded than Western laws and therefore is quite different in many ways from Western laws.

It will be interesting to see how Islamic law develops over the next decade. The resurgence of Islamic law is not an easy process and some have even argued that it is not possible to restore Islamic law in its classical form, and that therefore Islamic law will develop in a different shape and form, one compatible with 'modernity'.[54] In Islamic financing however, Islamic law has already re-emerged. There will be debates for years as to whether it has re-emerged in the right form, but the market for Islamic financing is so large that it is likely that Islamic law in that field will become even more important in the years to come.

It seems to me, however, that there is no way to reconcile the CISG with Islamic law, and since it is unlikely that the CISG could be amended, Islamic lawyers would be well advised to exclude the CISG when they want their *murabaha* contract to be valid under Islamic law.

52 See, *e.g.*, *Beximco Pharmaceuticals Ltd v. Shamil Bank of Bahrain E.C.* [2004] EWCA Civ 19, where a governing law clause that explicitly referred to both English law and Sharia, was interpreted as referring to English law. This was not a CISG case, but nonetheless shows the reluctance of national courts to give force to Islamic law as a governing law.

53 Arts. 49(1)(a) and 25 CISG.

54 W. Hallaq, 'Can The Shari'ah be restored?', in Y.Y. Haddad & B.F. Stowasser (Eds.), *Islamic Law and the Challenges of Modernity*, 21 (2004).

5 Conclusion: Reflection on the Future of the Uniformisation of Laws

Clearly, the CISG did not take into account 'Asian values' and attitudes toward laws, nor did it take into account Islamic law. As far as Asian values and attitudes toward Western law are concerned, I have mentioned that in my view the best solution is for Asian countries to become parties to the CISG and to try to influence its interpretation and development.

However, when it comes to Islamic law, there are clear incompatibilities, and therefore, there seems to be no hope that the CISG can bridge the gap between Islamic law and Western law.

The most important issue that this raises is not so much with respect to the CISG but with respect to future efforts at uniformisation and harmonisation. Should UNCITRAL as well as other organisations and the legal scholars interested in the uniformisation of laws and the harmonisation of laws try to take Islamic law into account in the future? To answer this question, more comparative and collaborative research should be undertaken by Western law scholars (be they in the West or elsewhere) and Islamic law scholars. Assuming, however, that in some respects, Islamic law has greatly different values and sources of law (sources that cannot be amended by national legislation), is the UNCITRAL model of intergovernmental negotiations and compromises even compatible with the very nature of Islamic law (a non-state law)? Would academic collaboration, rather than intergovernmental negotiations, be a more appropriate forum to compare Western and Islamic law?

If Muslims feel that the uniformisation of laws would make them lose their identity and their religious law, is uniformisation even worth pursuing? Aren't alternative choices of law a good thing – something that even the CISG recognises when it states that the parties are free to exclude the CISG and choose another law (Art. 6 CISG)? Is diversity not a good thing, at least in some respects?

Islamic law challenges many of our assumptions on the need and the desirability of harmonisation and uniformisation and I personally look forward to the debates and the possibility of greater legal pluralism that the resurgence of Islamic law may bring.

The Application and Use of the CISG in South Korea

Chang-ho Chung[*]

1 Abstract

Along with developments in South Korean politics and the economy, there has also been a significant improvement in the Korean judiciary. The Korean judiciary has consistently striven to be independent and realize legal stability and constitutionalism. Furthermore, the Supreme Court of Korea has made every effort to resolve international disputes more efficiently by expanding the application and use of the United Nations Convention on Contracts for the International Sale of Goods (CISG).[1]

On 17 February 2004, South Korea acceded to the CISG, which then entered into force on 1 March 2005. South Korea made no declarations or reservations at the time of accession.

As differences between the CISG and the Korean Civil Code (KCC)[2] still remain, South Korea is in the process of amending the KCC to fill the gap between national law and the Convention.

There has been a need to establish trial chambers of expertise to address international lawsuits in a prompt and fair manner, and now most of the district courts and high courts in South Korea have trial chambers specializing in international lawsuits.

Several court decisions applying the CISG have been handed down by South Korean judges, and those decisions will be reported to CLOUT (Case Law on UNCITRAL Texts) by the national CLOUT correspondent, who is also a South Korean judge.

---

* Bachelor of Law from Seoul National University in 1989, Master of Law from Seoul National University in 1991 (International Law); Judge, South Korea, Gwangju District Court.

1 United Nations Convention on Contracts for the International Sale of Goods (CISG), Vienna, 11 April 1980, available at <http://www.uncitral.org/uncitral/en/uncitral_texts/ sale_goods/1980CISG.html>.

2 Arts. 467, 530, 534 & 568 Korean Civil Code.

2 CISG Accession and Application

On 17 February 2004, South Korea acceded to the CISG, which entered into force on 1 March 2005.[3] South Korea made no declarations or reservations at the time of accession.

With the entry into force of the CISG in Japan as of August 2009, most of South Korea's largest trading partners – the United States, China, Japan, Singapore, Germany and Mexico – are likewise Contracting States. The application of the CISG to sales transactions among these countries could have significant implications for the promotion of trade, as trade between these countries potentially subject to the Convention is worth a total of some USD 175.5 billion, accounting for approximately half of South Korea's total trade in 2009.[4]

Worldwide, the potential is even greater with experts estimating that 'about seventy to eighty percent of all international sales transactions are potentially governed by the CISG'.[5] Nine out of the ten leading trade nations are party to the CISG and as of September 2010, there are 76 member states. As parties become more familiar with its application and functioning in practice, the CISG is likely to gain greater acceptance among both the legal and business communities and play an increasingly important role in stimulating trade by decreasing the risks and costs of dispute.

Widely regarded as 'one of the success stories in the field of the international unification of private law',[6] the application and use of the CISG in South Korea nevertheless remains largely underappreciated due in part to its relatively recent entry into force and the paucity of English translations of Korean case law in which the CISG was applied.

In order to better acquaint readers with the CISG's application and use in South Korea, Part 3 of this article will outline the civil procedure for lawsuits on international transactions in South Korea to provide the context for the treatment of the CISG cases there. The comparison of the Korean Civil Code and the CISG will then be discussed in Part 4. Six specific issues – formation of contract, obligations of the seller, place of delivery, breach of contract, intention or negligence and foreseeability – will be considered. Since the entry

3 A detailed list of the CISG Contracting States can be found at <http://www.uncitral.org/uncitral/en/uncitral_texts/sale_goods/1980CISG_status.html>.

4 The export trade of South Korea in 2009 was worth a total of approximately USD 355.1 billion, see CIA World Fact Book, available at <https://www.cia.gov/library/publications/the-world-factbook/index.html>.

5 I. Schwenzer & P. Hachem, 'The CISG – Successes and Pitfalls', 57 *Am. J. Comp. L.* 457 (2009), available at <http://www.cisg.law.pace.edu/cisg/biblio/schwenzer>.

6 P. Huber, 'Some Introductory Remarks on the CISG', 2006 *Internationales Handelsrecht* 228, available at <http://www.cisg.law.pace.edu/cisg/biblio/huber.html>.

into force of the CISG in South Korea, several court decisions applying the CISG have been handed down and will be briefly summarized in Part 5. The Supreme Court of Korea has realized the importance not only of the CISG but also of the United Nations Commission on International Trade Law (UNCITRAL) and its other instruments, and has made every effort to expand the understanding and application of the UNCITRAL instruments. Those efforts will be reviewed in Part 6. Finally, some evaluations and suggestions will be given as concluding remarks in Part 7.

3 Civil Procedure for Lawsuits on International Transactions

3.1 *Jurisdiction*

At the beginning of its judicial modernization in the middle of the 20th century, South Korea adopted the European civil law system as the basis for its general legal system. Since then however the Anglo-American legal system has also served as a model for a number of new and amended laws, with the result that the Korean legal system now features a combination of both civil law and common law systems.

The Korean judicial system comprises six types of courts within a three-tier hierarchy: the Supreme Court on the top tier, the High Courts (Appellate Courts) and the Patent Court sharing the second, and the District Courts, the Family Court and the Administrative Court occupying the third.[7]

The determination of which court has proper jurisdiction depends on the financial sum in controversy. Where the amount in controversy does not exceed 100 million Korean Won (approximately USD 100,000), a single judge of the district court is entitled to hear the case. If the amount in controversy exceeds 100 million Korean Won, a three-judge panel of the district court has jurisdiction to hear the case.

On matters of venue, a plaintiff may, in principle, file a lawsuit in the district court where the defendant has residence. The parties may agree on a proper forum for the lawsuit to be brought.

7 Aside from these six courts, South Korea has a Constitutional Court which adjudicates on the constitutionality of laws. Furthermore, the Constitutional Court adjudicates on impeachment proceedings, dissolution of a political party, competence disputes and constitutional complaints. Further information about the South Korean Constitutional Court can be found at <http://english.ccourt.go.kr>.

Regarding international jurisdiction, Article 2 of the Private International Law[8] provides that the court has international jurisdiction in the event the party concerned or the issue of contention has substantial relevance with South Korea. The Supreme Court has stipulated as follows:

> The determination of international jurisdiction should follow the basic idea of aiming to achieve impartiality between the parties, and appropriateness, speediness and economy of adjudication, and should, more concretely, take into account not only private interests such as impartiality between the parties, convenience and predictability, but also interests of the court as well as of the state such as appropriateness, speediness and efficiency of adjudication, and effectiveness of judgment. The issue of which interest among such diverse interests deserves protection should be determined reasonably, applying in each individual case the objective criteria of substantial relationship between the court and the parties, and substantial relationship between the court and the case in dispute.[9]

3.2 *Source of Law*

Written laws are the primary sources of law in South Korea[10] and treaties duly concluded and promulgated under the Constitution and generally recognized rules of international law have the same force as the domestic laws of South Korea.[11]

The CISG is one of those treaties and the provisions of the CISG apply to the relevant subject matter of international lawsuits. If the subject matter of an international lawsuit is not governed by the CISG, then private international law would determine the applicable law. Also, if parties agree to exclude the application of the CISG or derogate from or vary the effect of any of its provisions prior to concluding a sales contract in accordance with Article 6 CISG, relevant domestic laws, as determined by the rules of private international law, will apply.

8 Art. 2 para. 1 Private International Law of South Korea.

9 Supreme Court of South Korea, 2002Da59788, 27 January 2005.

10 Korean legislation in English can be obtained on the Korea Legislation Research Institute's website at <http://elaw.klri.re.kr/eng/main.do>. The Global Legal Information Network (GLIN) also provides a summary of each law in English at <http://www.glin.gov/search.action>.

11 A list of bilateral and multilateral treaties that South Korea has signed and ratified can be obtained on the website of the South Korean Ministry of Foreign Affairs and Trade at <http://www.mofat.go.kr/english/political/treaties/what/index.jsp>.

Court decisions, law reviews, journals and archives are the secondary sources of law in South Korea.[12] There is no principle of *stare decisis* or precedent in the Korean legal system. However, a higher court's decision in the judicial hierarchy prevails over that of a lower court in a specific case. A higher court can uphold, reverse or remand the judgment of the lower court based on either its own fact-finding or legal interpretation, while the Supreme Court can do so only by legal interpretation.

3.3 *Trial Chambers of Expertise*

Unlike general domestic lawsuits, lawsuits on international transactions cause many difficult problems with regard to jurisdiction, applicable law, service, communication and enforcement. Not all judges are familiar with international instruments. Therefore, a need arose to establish trial chambers of expertise to address international lawsuits in a prompt and fair manner.

Most of the district courts and high courts in South Korea have trial chambers specializing in international lawsuits. In principle, those chambers handle the following cases: cases on international transactions such as international sales contracts, letters of credit and financial transactions; cases on international marine transport and international air transport; cases on marine insurance and cases where the defendant is the Korea Export Insurance Corporation; and lawsuits on approval and enforcement of court decisions or arbitration awards reached in a foreign nation.

The Seoul Central District Court has two trial chambers of expertise specializing in international lawsuits, and each chamber handles about 100 cases a year. The judges working in those chambers have organized a Research Association to share their experience and knowledge with other judges and lawyers. In addition, the Supreme Court of Korea has organized a team of research judges in order to let them study the international lawsuits appealed to the Supreme Court and then report the results to the Justices of the Supreme Court.

The establishment of the trial chambers of expertise has enhanced consistency in the processing criteria and promoted efficiency in handling the courts' cases.

12 The Supreme Court of South Korea provides court decisions, laws, journals and other useful legal services free of charge on its website at <http://eng.scourt.go.kr/eng/main/Main.work>.

3.4 *Service and Interpreters*

The service of documents is done in accordance with the Judicial Alliance Treaty or the Convention on the Service Abroad of Judicial and Extrajudicial Documents in Civil or Commercial Matters.[13] In the event the treaty does not apply, the documents may be delivered by transmission to the court in jurisdiction through diplomatic channels.

Translations must be attached to the documentary evidence submitted to the court in a foreign language. The court may designate an interpreter in case interpretation is required in the interrogation of foreign witnesses. Attorneys calling such a witness may provide their own interpreter unless the other party objects.

3.5 *Judicial Mediation and Arbitration*

3.5.1 Judicial Mediation

The parties involved in international lawsuits tend to be more interested in the future impact on their business rather than the recovery of the losses caused by the dispute, and those parties usually resort to international arbitration or international private mediation. However, in South Korea, judicial mediation by the judges is also available in the overall litigation process.

Judicial mediation may be accessed in two ways. The plaintiff may file a case against the court asking for judicial mediation. Alternately, even after the normal litigation process has commenced, a judge may decide either on his own initiative or upon application by a party to change from normal litigation to judicial mediation if it is considered to be necessary owing to exceptional circumstances.

Judicial mediation can be presided over only by judges, sometimes with the assistance of relevant experts. At an appropriate stage of the mediation proceedings, one or more third persons can be joined as a party.[14] If the parties agree on a settlement of the dispute during the judicial mediation, the judges record the settlement in the form of a court decision, which is final and binding on the parties. If the judicial mediation fails, the case returns to the normal litigation process.

---

13 Convention on the Service Abroad of Judicial and Extrajudicial Documents in Civil or Commercial Matters, The Hague, 15 November 1965, available at <http://hcch.e-vision.nl/upload/conventions/txt14en.pdf> South Korea joined the Convention on 13 January 2000, and the Convention took effect as of 1 August 2000.

14 Art. 16 Judicial Mediation Law of South Korea.

3.5.2 Arbitration

The arbitral institution in South Korea is the Korea Commercial Arbitration Board. It has its own International Arbitration Rules[15] and the number of the international arbitration cases it handles has increased rapidly thanks to the fast-growing volume of business with China.

4 COMPARISON OF THE KOREAN CIVIL CODE AND THE CISG

4.1 Formation of the Contract

As regards the revocability of an offer, the CISG provides in Article 16(1) CISG that until a contract is concluded, an offer may be revoked if the revocation reaches the offeree before an acceptance has been dispatched, while Article 527 of the Korean Civil Code (KCC)[16] provides that an offer is irrevocable.

Concerning late acceptance, Article 21 CISG provides that a late acceptance is nevertheless effective as an acceptance if, without delay, the offeror orally so informs the offeree or dispatches a notice to that effect, while Article 530 of the KCC provides that the offeror may regard the late acceptance as a counter-offer.

As regards the modification of an offer, the CISG in Article 19(1) CISG provides that a reply to an offer that purports to be an acceptance but contains additions, limitations or other modifications is a rejection of the offer and constitutes a counter-offer. However, according to Article 19(2) CISG, a reply to an offer that purports to be an acceptance but contains additional or different terms that do not materially alter the terms of the offer constitutes an acceptance, unless the offeror, without undue delay, objects orally to the discrepancy or dispatches a notice to that effect. The KCC in Article 534 KCC provides that an acceptance to an offer containing conditions or modifications is a rejection of the offer and constitutes a counter-offer.

4.2 Obligations of the Seller

Article 30 CISG separates the seller's obligation to deliver the goods and hand over documents from the seller's obligation to transfer the property, providing that the seller must

---

15 The Rules of International Arbitration for the Korean Commercial Arbitration Board as approved by the Supreme Court of Korea on 25 January 2007.

16 Art. 527 Korean Civil Code.

deliver the goods, hand over any documents relating to them and transfer the property in the goods as required by the contract and the Convention. The KCC does not separate those obligations of the seller and states only the seller's obligation to transfer the property in the goods.[17] However, the seller's obligation to transfer the property in the goods is interpreted by the courts to include an obligation to deliver the goods and hand over documents.

4.3 *Place of Delivery*

Article 31(c) CISG provides that if the seller is not bound to deliver the goods at any other particular place, then the seller must place the goods at the buyer's disposal at the place where the seller had his place of business at the time of the conclusion of the contract. Article 467 KCC provides that any delivery of goods should be made at the buyer's place of business.

Article 31(a) CISG provides that if the contract of sale involves carriage of the goods, the seller's obligation to deliver consists in handing the goods over to the first carrier for transmission to the buyer. The KCC is silent on this issue, so a seller in the same situation would in principle make delivery at the buyer's place of business.

4.4 *Breach of Contract*

The CISG does not distinguish between failure to perform obligations and delivery of defective goods and simply uses the unitary concept of breach of contract.[18] In contrast, the KCC does distinguish failure to perform obligations from delivery of defective goods, and it furthermore divides failure to perform obligations into three categories: delayed performance, impossible performance and defective performance.

4.5 *Intention or Negligence*

The CISG does not require the aggrieved party to demonstrate intention or negligence by the party who has failed to perform in order to exercise remedies. In contrast, Article 390 KCC requires this party to prove the breaching party's intent or negligence in order to hold him liable for failure to perform, although delivery of defective goods renders him liable for damages regardless of the presence or absence of intention or negligence.

17 Art. 568 Korean Civil Code.

18 See, *e.g.*, Art. 45(1) CISG.

If the failure by the seller to perform any of his obligations under the contract or this Convention amounts to a fundamental breach of contract,[19] then Article 49(1)(a) CISG allows the aggrieved party to declare the contract avoided, regardless of the presence or absence of intention or negligence. Pursuant to the KCC, however, an aggrieved party may declare the contract avoided only when the other party's breach is intentional or negligent.

4.6 *Foreseeability in Determining the Extent of Damages*

Article 74 CISG provides that liability for damages for breach of contract by one party consists of a sum equal to the loss, including loss of profit, suffered by the other party as a consequence of the breach and limits it by requiring that such damages

> may not exceed the loss which the party in breach foresaw or ought to have foreseen at the time of the conclusion of the contract, in the light of the facts and matters of which he then knew or ought to have known, as a possible consequence of the breach of contract.

Article 393 KCC distinguishes between two categories of damages – ordinary damages and special damages – and provides that damages due to extraordinary circumstances may be recovered only when they were foreseen or ought to have been foreseen.

5 Court Decisions

5.1 *Seoul High Court: 2008-14857*

The CISG was first applied in South Korea by the District Court of Eastern Seoul on 16 November 2007 in a ruling on a supply contract dispute between a Korean company and Chinese company.[20] The decision was appealed to the Seoul High Court and its decision on 23 July 2009 was not appealed.[21]

5.1.1 Facts of the Case

The plaintiff was a Chinese company, the Hangzhou Oran Teakwuryung Limited, located in Hangzhou City, Zhejang Province, while the defendant, the Tai Korea Company, Limited, was a Korean company.

19 The definition of a fundamental breach is laid down in Art. 25 CISG.

20 Seoul Eastern District Court 2006, Ka-hap 6384, 16 November 2007.

21 Seoul High Court 2008, Na 14857, 23 July 2009.

The two parties concluded a contract of sale on 20 June 2005 under which the plaintiff agreed to deliver 93,430 kg of duck feathers to the defendant in multiple shipments in exchange for a total of USD 1,337,189. Delivery was to begin in July 2005 and the defendant was to make payment upon receipt of each shipment.

Between 22 June 2005 and 27 August 2005, the plaintiff delivered 51,156 kg of feathers worth USD 764,349 to a location specified by the defendant, and received USD 401,980 in payment.

However, the plaintiff failed to deliver a shipment of 9,635 kg of duck feathers (USD 13 per kg) due for delivery to the defendant by 25 August 2005. The defendant was forced to buy 6,985 kg of duck feathers (USD 17.8 per kg) in replacement from another company on 6 September 2005 and paid USD 52,387.50 for the delivery.

The defendant gave notice of a declaration of avoidance of the contract to the plaintiff on 20 October 2005.

5.1.2 Application of the CISG

The parties to this contract had places of business in different states, China and South Korea, both of which are CISG Contracting States. The CISG therefore was applicable according to Article 1(1)(a) CISG. However, Article 4 CISG states that 'this Convention governs only the formation of the contract of sale and the rights and obligations of the seller and the buyer arising from such a contract'. Any subject matter which does not fall under the CISG is governed by the law determined by private international law.

5.1.3 Avoidance

Article 73(1) CISG provides that for contracts for delivery by instalments, if

> failure of one party to perform any of his obligations in respect of any instalment constitutes a fundamental breach of contract with respect to that instalment, the other party may declare the contract avoided with respect to that instalment.

Further, according to Article 73(2) CISG, if failure regarding any instalment 'gives the other party good grounds to conclude that a fundamental breach of contract will occur with respect to future instalments [...]' then the contract may be declared avoided in relation to future instalments.

In addition, Article 25 CISG defines the fundamental breach as a breach which 'results in such detriment to the other party as substantially to deprive him of what he is entitled to expect under the contract, [...]' unless such a result was unforeseen and not foreseeable by 'a reasonable person of the same kind in the same circumstances'.

The contract between the plaintiff and the defendant in this case was a contract for delivery of goods by instalments. The plaintiff's failure to deliver the duck feathers due by 25 August 2005 constituted a fundamental breach with regard to that instalment and gave the defendant good grounds to conclude that a fundamental breach of contract would occur with respect to future instalments.

Therefore the contract between the plaintiff and the defendant, except for the 51,156 kg of feather worth USD 764,349 that had been already delivered, was avoided by means of the declaration dated 20 October 2005.

5.1.4 Damages

In addition to Article 74 CISG which provides for damages 'equal to the loss, including loss of profit, suffered by the other party as a consequence of the breach', Article 75 CISG provides for recovery of 'the difference between the contract price and the price in the substitute transaction' where a substitute transaction is entered within a reasonable time after the contract was avoided.

Since the plaintiff failed to deliver the duck feathers that were supposed to be delivered to the defendant by 25 August 2005, the defendant had to buy duck feathers in replacement from another company and pay for the delivery. Therefore, the plaintiff was obliged to pay the defendant the difference between the contract price and the price in the substitute transaction, which amounted to USD 33,528 [(USD 17.8 – USD 13) x 6,985 kg] and further damages, the delivery cost of USD 52,387.

5.1.5 Set-off

The defendant claimed damages for the purpose of set-off. Since the CISG contains no provision with regard to set-off, the Private International Law of Korea determines the governing law. Article 26 of the Korean Private International Law provides that the governing law for set-off is the seller's law, which meant that Chinese law was the governing law.

5.2 *Seoul High Court: 2008-20319*[22]

5.2.1 Facts of the Case

The plaintiff was a Chinese company, while the defendant was a Korean individual. Between 28 September 2005 and 10 May 2006, the plaintiff delivered clothing worth USD 168,047.90 to the defendant and the defendant sold the clothing to other buyers. Because of a delay in delivery and defects of the clothing, the defendant had to pay damages to those buyers.

5.2.2 Application of the CISG

The parties had their places of business in different states, China and South Korea, and both states are CISG contracting states. Therefore, the CISG applied according to Article 1(1)(a) CISG.

5.2.3 Damages

As mentioned above, Article 74 CISG provides that the breaching party is liable for damages for loss suffered, provided the amount does

> not exceed the loss which the party in breach foresaw or ought to have foreseen at the time of the conclusion of the contract, in the light of the facts and matters of which he then knew or ought to have known, as a possible consequence of the breach of contract.

Since the plaintiff failed to deliver as required by the contract, the defendant had to pay damages to the other buyers. Considering the fact that the plaintiff had delivered clothing to the defendant since 2003, the plaintiff could foresee such damages at the time of the conclusion of this contract as a possible consequence of a breach of contract. Therefore, the plaintiff was ordered by the court to pay a sum equal to the loss suffered by the defendant.

5.3 *Seoul Central District Court: 2007-19698*[23]

5.3.1 Facts of the Case

The plaintiff was a Korean company and the defendant was a Spanish company. The two parties entered into a contract on 6 September 2006 under which the defendant agreed to supply the plaintiff with clothing worth USD 227,000.

---

22 Seoul High Court 2008, Na 20319, 12 February 2009.

23 Seoul Central District Court 2007, Ka-hap 19698, 5 December 2008.

The defendant sent a sample of the clothing to the plaintiff but the plaintiff made a declaration of avoidance of the contract to the defendant in January 2007, arguing that the materials used for the clothing did not comply with the quality required by the contract.

The plaintiff bought substitute clothing of the same description from another company and claimed damages from the defendant to recover the difference between the contract price and the price in the replacement transaction.

5.3.2 Application of the CISG

The parties to this contract had places of business in different states, the CISG Contracting States of South Korea and Spain, thus the CISG applied to the case according to Article 1(1)(a) CISG.

5.3.3 Conformity with the Contract

Article 35(1) CISG provides that the 'seller must deliver goods which are of the quantity, quality and description required by the contract', and, according to Article 35(2)(a) CISG, unless

> the parties have agreed otherwise, the goods do not conform with the contract unless they are fit for the purposes for which goods of the same description would ordinarily be used.

The contract between the plaintiff and the defendant specified only the quantity and did not require any special quality. Furthermore, the plaintiff failed to prove that the clothing delivered by the defendant was not fit for the purposes for which clothing of the same description would ordinarily be used.

5.4 *Seoul Central District Court: 2007-97810*[24]

5.4.1 Facts of the Case

The plaintiff was a Singaporean company and the defendant was a Korean company. The two parties concluded a contract of sale on 1 March 2004 under which the plaintiff agreed to supply the defendant with crude oil in exchange for the defendant opening a letter of credit by 24 March 2004.

24 Seoul Central District Court 2007, Ka-hap 97810, 19 December 2008.

The defendant failed to open a letter of credit by 24 March 2004 and the plaintiff made a declaration of avoidance of the contract to the defendant on 15 April 2004. The plaintiff had to resell the crude oil to another buyer.

5.4.2 Application of the CISG

The CISG applied to the case, since the parties had their places of business in different states, Singapore and South Korea, both of which are CISG Contracting States according to Article 1(1)(a) CISG.

5.4.3 Obligation to Pay the Price

Article 53 CISG requires the buyer to pay the price, and Article 54 CISG provides that this obligation 'includes taking such steps and complying with such formalities as may be required under the contract or any laws and regulations to enable payment to be made'. Article 61(1) CISG enables the seller to exercise the rights provided in Articles 62 to 65 CISG if the buyer fails in this obligation, and Article 64(1)(a) CISG provides that the seller 'may declare the contract avoided if the failure by the buyer to perform any of his obligations under the contract or this Convention amounts to a fundamental breach of contract [...]'.

The court held that the defendant's failure to open a letter of credit was a failure to perform his obligation to pay the price complying with formalities required under the contract. Such a failure by the defendant amounted to a fundamental breach of the contract, enabling the plaintiff to declare the contract avoided.

5.4.4 Damages

Article 74 CISG facilitates recovery of losses where they are either foreseen by the breaching party at the time of conclusion of the contract, or ought to have been foreseen at that time 'in the light of the facts and matters of which he then knew or ought to have known'. As mentioned above, Article 75 CISG allows recovery of the 'difference between the contract price and the price in the substitute transaction' where the replacement transaction was entered within a reasonable time of avoidance. The amount recoverable under Article 75 CISG is in addition to 'any further damages recoverable under article 74 [CISG]'.

Since the defendant failed to perform his obligation, the plaintiff had to resell the crude oil to another buyer at a lower price. Considering the provisions of this contract and the usage, the defendant either foresaw or ought to have foreseen at the time of the conclusion of this contract that his failure to perform his obligation would lead the plaintiff to pay extra charges for the storage of the crude oil as a possible consequence of the breach of the contract. Therefore, the court held that the defendant was entitled to recover the difference between the contract price and the price in the substitute transaction and the extra payment for the storage.

5.4.5 Mitigation of the Loss

Article 77 CISG provides that

> [a] party who relies on a breach of contract must take such measures as are reasonable in the circumstances to mitigate the loss, including loss of profit, resulting from the breach. If he fails to take such measures, the party in breach may claim a reduction in the damages in the amount by which the loss should have been mitigated.

The defendant claimed a reduction in the damages in accordance with Article 77 CISG, but was unable to prove that the plaintiff failed to take reasonable measures to mitigate the loss.

6 Other Efforts by the Supreme Court of Korea

6.1 Legal Attaché

The Supreme Court of Korea regularly dispatches a Korean judge with more than 15 years of experience to the Permanent Mission in Vienna as a Legal Attaché to add his or her knowledge and experience to the Korean delegation to UNCITRAL, UNIDROIT and the Hague Conference on Private International Law (HCCH).

Residing in Vienna, the Legal Attaché attends all Working Group meetings of UNCITRAL held in both Vienna and New York including Commission sessions. Every time the Legal Attaché attends meetings, he or she compiles a detailed report including translations of all Working Papers and the relevant Korean legal systems in order to help Korean lawyers, professors, students and lawmakers understand the details of the work carried out by the Commission.

The reports of the Legal Attaché on the meetings and issues of UNCITRAL have helped Korean lawyers to become more familiar with UNCITRAL instruments and to gain a better understanding of the CISG's important role. The Legal Attaché's understanding of issues dealt with by UNCITRAL working groups plays a key role with regard to the adoption of UNCITRAL instruments.

6.2 CLOUT

The Supreme Court of Korea also has appointed a Korean judge as a national CLOUT correspondent since 2009, because the judge is ideally placed to collect court decisions relating to the CISG or other instruments of UNCITRAL.

South Korea has not yet recorded many court decisions relating to the CISG, and not all will emanate from the Supreme Court of Korea. However, the Supreme Court of Korea has established a team to translate major Supreme Court decisions into English. Should a Supreme Court decision relating to the application or interpretation of the CISG arise, the whole decision will be translated in full into English and then sent by the correspondent to CLOUT to be made available globally on the CLOUT website.[25]

6.3 Research team

Not only the Legal Attaché and the CLOUT correspondent but also many other Korean judges are keenly interested in UNCITRAL instruments, and a research team to study them has been established with financial support from the Supreme Court of Korea. Each member of the team chooses a specific issue that he or she is especially interested in and may have the opportunity to attend the relevant working group meeting of UNCITRAL on that issue with the Legal Attaché.

Judges attending such meetings are also expected to file a detailed report including further research relating to the specified area of interest, for subsequent distribution to the entire judiciary. These reports make reference to reports by the Legal Attaché, and help inform deliberation on the position to be taken by the delegation.

6.4 International Judicial Symposium

The Supreme Court of Korea hosted a Judicial Symposium on the theme of 'International Trends in Business Insolvency Procedures' in 2009, and invited many prominent lawyers and professors from all over the world to participate, including the Secretary of UNCITRAL as a keynote speaker.

25 The English version of the CLOUT website is available at <http://www.uncitral.org/uncitral/en/case_law.html>.

The Symposium is hosted by the Supreme Court of Korea every two years under an UNCITRAL related theme, thus enabling lawyers and professors from all over the world to share their views and experiences relating to UNCITRAL instruments.

6.5 *Judicial Exchange and Cooperation Program*

Under the theme of 'Improvement of Judicial Fairness and Effective Judicial Administration', the Supreme Court of Korea has hosted a Judicial Exchange and Cooperation Program for foreign judges with financial support from the Korea International Cooperation Agency since 2002.

From 2002 to 2005, the Supreme Court of Korea invited judges from Vietnam and Mongolia to participate in the program. Since 2006, the Supreme Court has expanded the number of programs and the number of countries receiving invitations. Since 2009, the Supreme Court has been sharing not only information on the Korean judicial system but also experience relating to South Korea's participation in UNCITRAL meetings and adoption of UNCITRAL instruments. UNCITRAL also understands the importance of this program and has pledged its collaboration.

6.6 *Future Work*

Trade and investment between South Korea and North Korea has increased greatly in recent years, and both countries have taken measures to establish a dispute resolution mechanism that could be applied to these transactions. For that purpose, both have developed not only procedural laws but also substantial laws and hope that the UNCITRAL instruments such as the CISG and the Model Law on International Commercial Arbitration[26] could serve as a common reference point.

South Korea is in the process of amending the Korean Civil Code to fill the gap between the KCC and the CISG. Since the KCC has been recognized as a very successful code in South Korea, most South Korean lawyers and professors have hesitated to amend the KCC in accordance with the CISG, and it was suggested that the Amendment Committee should undertake to carefully define the list of provisions which might need to be addressed in a revised version of the KCC. This process is still in its early stages.

---

26 UNCITRAL Model Law on International Commercial Arbitration, Vienna, 21 June 1985, With Amendments as Adopted in 2006, available at <http://www.uncitral.org/pdf/english/texts/arbitration/ml-arb/07-86998_Ebook.pdf>.

7 Conclusion

The development of the Korean judiciary since its modernization began some sixty years ago has helped to lay the foundation for South Korea's remarkable economic growth and political maturation. The Korean judiciary has consistently striven to be independent and realize legal stability and constitutionalism. Without this effort, it would not have been possible to promote the country's economic and social stability.

Given South Korea's economic and political ties with the rest of the world, a key part of the judiciary's development has been the Supreme Court's efforts to resolve international disputes more efficiently by expanding the application and use of the CISG.

The need to establish trial chambers of expertise to address international lawsuits in a prompt and fair manner has been addressed, and now most of the district courts and high courts in South Korea have trial chambers specializing in international lawsuits.

South Korean judges have handed down several court decisions applying the CISG, and the national correspondent, who is also a South Korean judge, will report those decisions to CLOUT.

As differences between the CISG and the KCC still remain, South Korea is in the process of amending the KCC to fill the gap between national law and the Convention. The measures referred to above are expected to assist lawmakers, law practitioners and scholars in the revision process, which will hopefully result in greater consistency in the CISG's interpretation and application, and in broader acceptance of the CISG among the legal and business communities in Contracting States.

Yin & Yang: A Comparison of Monetary Remedies in International Investment and Transnational Commercial Disputes

John Y. Gotanda[*]

1 Introduction

According to conventional wisdom, the global recession should result in a boom for international arbitration as investments and deals go down with the economy. This prediction certainly has proven true for many international arbitral institutions handling commercial disputes.[1] In fact, in 2008, at the height of the global recession, the China International Economic and Trade Arbitration Commission (CIETAC) saw a record 548 new international cases – a 28% increase over 2007.[2] However, the prediction has not proven true for investment arbitrations. In 2008, the International Centre for the Settlement of Investment Disputes (ICSID) reported a 43% decrease from 2007.[3]

To be sure, these two types of arbitration are very different. International disputes filed with CIETAC often involve commercial matters that are governed by the United Nations Convention on the International Sale of Goods (CISG).[4] By contrast, cases before ICSID

---

* J.D., Professor of Law, Villanova University School of Law, U.S.A; Director of the J.D./M.B.A. Program, Associate Dean for Academic Affairs and for Faculty Research.

1 B. Anstey, *Global Recession – Trends in Arbitration*, K&L Gates LLP, Arbitration World, March 2009, available at <http://www.klgates.com/newsstand/Detail.aspx?publication=5391#recession>. According to Anstey, in 2008, the International Chamber of Commerce, the London Court of International Arbitration, the Arbitration Chamber of the Stockholm Chamber of Commerce, and the American Arbitration Association (International) all reported increases in new claims over the prior year, see *id.*

2 *Id.*

3 L. Ahee & R. Walck, 'Investment Arbitration Update, As of December 31, 2008', 6 *Transnational Dispute Management* 1, at 3 (2009), available at <http://www.gfa-llc.com/images/Investment_Arbitration_Update_2008_-_TDM.pdf> (cited as: *Update 2008*).

4 United Nations Convention on Contracts for the International Sale of Goods (CISG), Vienna, 11 April 1980, available at <http://www.uncitral.org/uncitral/en/uncitral_texts/sale_goods/ 1980CISG.html>. See F. Yang, 'The Application of the CISG in the Current PRC Law and CIETAC Arbitration Practice', 2006 *Nordic Journal of Commercial Law*, Issue 2, 1, at 19, available at <http://www.njcl.fi/2_2006/article4.pdf>.

offer a mix of public and private international law, involving claims of expropriation, discriminatory treatment, or unfair or inequitable treatment under an investment treaty, as well as breach of contract.[5]

Yet, we can learn much from comparing the awards in these disputes. Such a comparison might not only shed light on how well each system is functioning, but may also help explain the results. In addition, it may help predict future outcomes and the costs associated with resolving commercial or investment claims, thereby helping create more efficient systems for resolving these disputes.

This paper examines monetary remedies in international commercial and investment arbitrations. It will compare data from publicly available CISG contract disputes resolved between 1989 and 2006 under the auspices of the China International Economic and Trade Arbitration Commission (CIETAC-CISG) with publicly available investment treaty arbitration (ITA) awards decided between 1996 and June 2009. Specifically, it examines: (1) who is winning; (2) what the successful parties are winning in terms of damages; (3) whether tribunals award the cost of the proceedings, including the fees and expenses of the arbitrators (collectively arbitration costs) and the parties' legal costs, including attorneys' fees (collectively parties' costs) and, if so, how the tribunals apportion them; and (4) the length of time these disputes take to resolve. In relation to cases surveyed, the present study concludes: (1) CIETAC-CISG claimants are more successful than ITA claimants; (2) CIETAC-CISG claimants win a larger percentage of their claims than ITA claimants; (3) CIETAC-CISG tribunals are more likely to shift arbitration costs to the losing party; (4) parties' costs are awarded infrequently in both CIETAC-CISG and ITA disputes; and (5) ITA disputes take significantly longer to resolve than CIETAC-CISG disputes.

2 Overview

This study examines two types of cases. The first is commercial disputes governed by the CISG. The second is investment disputes.

In general, the CISG, by its terms, applies to all international sales contracts between parties from signatory countries.[6] To date, over 70 countries have adopted the CISG, including

5 L. Ahee & R. Walck, 'Investment Arbitration Update, As of December 31, 2007', available at <http://www.gfa-llc.com/images/Investment_Arbitration_Update_12-31-07.pdf> (cited as: *Update 2007*).

6 Art. 1(1)(a) CISG. See also *Filanto, S.p.A. v. Chilewich International Corp.*, 789 F.Supp. 1229 (S.D.N.Y 1992), 14 April 1992, CISG-online 45, available at <http://cisgw3.law.pace.edu/cases/920414u1.html>.

nine out of the ten leading trading nations.[7] In fact, commentators noted that 'it can be estimated that about seventy to eighty percent of all international sales transactions are potentially governed by the CISG'.[8]

The three countries reporting the largest number of CISG case loads are Germany, China, and Russia.[9] Interestingly, while the United States was one of the first countries to adopt the CISG, its courts have not generated a large number of cases.[10] One commentator speculates that the unfamiliarity of U.S. courts with the CISG has led many American attorneys to contractually opt out of the CISG.[11] By contrast, Chinese parties have shown a preference for the CISG over Chinese domestic law.[12] As U.S. trade with China increases, so, too, will American parties' exposure to the CISG.[13]

Many disputes between Chinese and foreign parties are resolved under the auspices of CIETAC, China's largest arbitral institution. CIETAC panels have decided hundreds of cases involving the CISG, with about one quarter of those studied involving U.S. parties.[14]

While the CISG involves commercial disputes between mainly private parties, investment disputes are between governments and foreign investors. As noted, investment disputes often involve a mix of public and private international law. Investment disputes can be

---

7 I. Schwenzer & P. Hachem, 'The CISG – Successes and Pitfalls', 57 *Am. J. Comp. L.* 457, 459 (2009), available at <http://www.cisg.law.pace.edu/cisg/biblio/schwenzer-hachem.html>. The ten leading trading nations are Belgium, China, France, Germany, Italy, Japan, The Netherlands, Russia, the United Kingdom, and the United States. Of these, only the United Kingdom has not adopted the CISG. See generally, A. Kritzer, *et al.*, *International Contract Manual* (2009).

8 Schwenzer & Hachem, *supra* note 7, at 475.

9 Kritzer, *et al.*, *supra* note 7, noting reported case loads as 448, 341, and 248 respectively. The study further speculated that the number of CISG cases in China is actually much higher because 85% of CISG cases are CIETAC-CISG cases and CIETAC-CISG waits three years before publicly releasing information on decided cases.

10 See *Taming the Dragons of Uniform Law Case Law: Sharing the reasoning of courts and arbitral tribunals, Chart of 1,791 'tamed and assigned dragons'*, available at <http://www.cisg.law.pace.edu/cisg/text/queen-mary.html>, reporting that the case load of United States is 109 cases, and that the case loads of China, Germany, Russia and Switzerland far exceed those of the United States. China, the United States and Italy adopted the CISG on 11 December 1986. See also F. Yang, 'CISG in China and Beyond', 40 *UCC Law Journal* 373 (2008).

11 Yang, *supra* note 10, at 375.

12 Yang's study found that Chinese parties had a preference for the CISG over domestic law, as they often chose to apply the CISG in domestic disputes and in other contexts where it might otherwise not be applicable. See *id.*, at 376.

13 *Id.*, at 375.

14 See *id.*, at 375 (Yang reports that 268 of the 320 Chinese cases on the PACE CISG Database were CIETAC arbitration awards, 74 of which involved the U.S. as a party).

resolved through a variety of forums, including litigation in national courts, private arbitration, and arbitration pursuant to a treaty or convention.[15]

One of the most popular forums for resolving investment disputes is ICSID, which is an institution of the World Bank. ICSID was established pursuant to the 1966 Convention on the Settlement of Investment Disputes between States and Nationals of Other States (known as the ICSID Convention or Washington Convention) to facilitate the settlement of disputes between governments and private foreign investors.[16] In general, ICSID is applicable to disputes that: (1) are legal in nature, (2) arise directly out of an investment, (3) involve an investor that is a national of another Contracting State, and (4) are submitted with the written consent of both parties allowing ICSID to hear the dispute.[17] Governments often give written consent through signing a treaty, a contract or through local law.[18] Investors give consent by filing a claim with ICSID, typically invoking jurisdiction pursuant to a bilateral investment treaty (BIT) or a multilateral treaty such as the North American Free Trade Agreement (NAFTA).[19] To date, over 150 countries have signed the ICSID Convention and over 300 cases have been filed with ICSID.[20]

3 The Data

This study collects data from CIETAC-CISG cases, and ICSID cases. It also considers the results of previous studies examining CIETAC-CISG cases and ITA disputes.

---

15 M. Dimsey, *The Resolution of International Investment Disputes*, 8 *et seq.* (2008).

16 Convention on the Settlement of Investment Disputes between States and Nationals of Other States, Washington, 18 March 1965, available at <http://icsid.worldbank.org/ICSID/ICSID/RulesMain.jsp>.

17 O. Garcia-Bolivar, Special Report on ICSID Jurisdiction, BG Consulting, at 1 (2008), available at <http://www.bg-consulting.com/docs/report_icsid_jurisdiction.pdf>.

18 *Id.*, at 3.

19 North America Free Trade Agreement, San Antonio, 17 December 1992, available at <http://www.nafta-sec-alena.org/en/view.aspx?conID=590>. See also Garcia-Bolivar, *supra* note 17, at 3.

20 It should be noted that investment disputes could arise in other forms, including ad hoc arbitration, see R. Herrera, *Global Trends in Investment Treaties and Investor-State Arbitration*, at 2 (2008), available at <http://www.fiesp.com.br/derex/negociacoes_interncionais/pdf/raul%20r.%20herrera%20-%20global%20trends%2 0in%20investment% 20treaties%20and%20investor-state%20arbitration.pdf>.

3.1 *CIETAC-CISG Data*

In 2008, the Institute of International Commercial Law commissioned the translation of several hundred CIETAC-CISG awards that involved the CISG.[21] These awards range in date from August 1988 to December 2007.[22] Dr. Allan Shwedel, on behalf of the Institute of International Commercial Law, analyzed 265 of these cases to determine *inter alia* who was winning, the amounts parties claimed, and what successful parties were awarded.[23] Using the 265 cases translated by the Institute, the present study also examines the same 265 CIETAC-CISG cases to see if arbitration costs and parties' costs were awarded and, if so, in what amounts, and how such costs were divided amongst parties. It also looks at the length of time taken to resolve the disputes.

3.2 *Investment Awards Data*

To date, there have been several studies of investment awards. Perhaps the most well-known is a study conducted by Professor Susan Franck which examined 52 publicly available investment awards decided before June 2006.[24] Professor Franck's study analyzed who was more successful: investors or governments, what investors claimed in damages and what the successful claimants were awarded.[25] She later conducted a second study looking for the presence of bias based on the income level of respondent governments and presiding arbitrators.[26] In both studies, Professor Franck focused on investment disputes decided by institutions and by ad hoc tribunals.

---

21 For a detailed list of the awards, see the webpage of the PACE University Institute of International Commercial Law, CIETAC Arbitration Awards, First 321 Case Translations, available at <http://cisgw3.law.pace.edu/cisg/text/CIETAC-CISG-awards.html>.

22 *Id.* The cases only went up until 2007 because CIETAC-CISG waits three years before releasing awards publicly.

23 A. Shwedel, *The Institute of International Commercial Law of the Pace University School of Law: Analysis and Translation of CIETAC-CISG Awards* (2 March 2009) (on file with the author) [cited as: *IICL study 3/2/2009*]. The Institute's study originally consisted of 288 cases that were translated. One case was excluded because it involved a claim for equitable relief. Also excluded were cases in which: (1) both parties were from the PRC, Hong Kong, or Macau, (2) the countries of the parties involved were unknown, (3) both parties were from the USA, or (4) neither party was from the PRC. The exclusion of these cases lowered the study to a total of 265 cases.

24 S. Franck, 'Empirically Evaluating Claims about Investment Treaty Arbitration', 86 *N.C. L. Rev.* 1, at 25 (2008).

25 *Id.*, at 6.

26 S. Franck, 'International Investment Arbitration: Winning, Losing and Why', *Columbia FDI Perspectives*, No. 7, 15 June 2009.

Two other well-known studies of investment awards were conducted by Global Financial Analytics.[27] One study examined publicly available ICSID awards rendered in 2007 and the other examined awards rendered in 2008.[28] These studies analyzed the claims raised, what successful parties were awarded, why cases were dismissed, and how long disputes took to resolve.[29] A current study also examined publicly available ICSID awards decided between 1996 and June 2009 to determine whether tribunals awarded arbitration costs and parties' costs and, if so, how such costs were allocated amongst parties.[30] It also examined the length of time it took to resolve the disputes.

3.3 *Results*

This section reports on whether claimants or respondents as a whole are winning, the amounts that claimants are being awarded, whether tribunals are awarding arbitration costs and parties' costs, and the length of time it takes to resolve CIETAC-CISG and ITA disputes.

3.3.1 Who Is Winning?

The Institute of International Commercial Law's study of 265 CIETAC-CISG arbitration awards found that claimants prevailed and were awarded damages in 87% of those cases.[31] By contrast, Professor Franck's study of 52 ITA awards decided before 1 June 2006 found that investors won and received damages awards in 38.5% of those cases.[32] In other words, governments won more often in the ITA cases studied.

---

27 Global Financial Analytics offers companies financial consulting, analysis, and expert witness testimony in arbitration and litigation. It is based in Washington, D.C., and works with companies worldwide. See <http://www.gfa-llc.com>.

28 Ahee & Walck, *Update 2008, supra* note 3; Ahee & Walck, *Update 2007, supra* note 5.

29 Ahee & Walck, *Update 2008, supra* note 3, at 2.

30 For a list of cases used, see <http://ita.law.uvic.ca/chronological_list.htm>. Cases with no English translation were excluded from the results. Cases decided under NAFTA but using ICSID Additional Facility Rules were included because those rules are similar to the ICSID Rules with regard to the awarding of attorneys' fees and costs.

31 *IICL Study 3/2/2009, supra* note 23, at 1.

32 Franck, *supra* note 24, at 49. Susan Franck studied ICSID disputes as well as UNCITRAL disputes.

Chart 1. Claimant Success Rate in CIETAC-CISG and Investment Disputes[33]

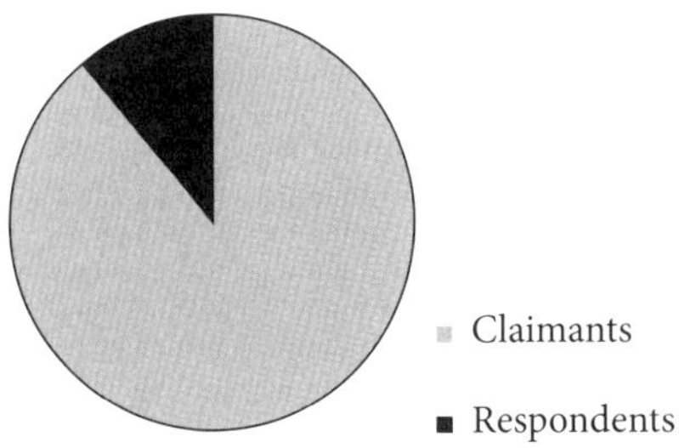

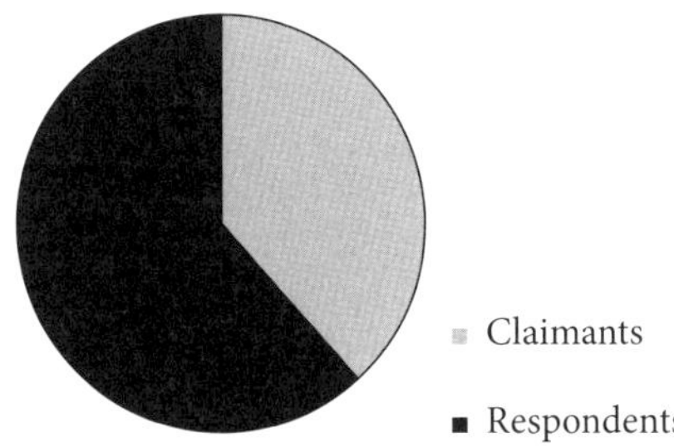

A study by Global Financial Analytics of 29 investment arbitration awards rendered in 2007 seems to support this conclusion. The Global Financial Analytics study determined that: (1) expropriation was found in only 10% of the cases in which it was claimed; (2) discriminatory treatment was found in 13% of the cases in which it was claimed; and (3) unfair or inequitable treatment was found in 26% of the cases in which it was pled.[34] Similarly, in its 2008 study, Global Financial Analytics determined that claimants 'were successful in obtaining *something* in exactly half of the matters'. (emphasis added)[35] Although all of these studies are limited, they indicate that CISG claimants tended to win more often than in investment arbitrations studied by Professor Franck.

3.3.2 What Are Successful Parties Winning?

To measure claimants' success in CIETAC-CISG and ITA disputes, the present study examined the amount of the initial claims and the amount that claimants ultimately recovered. CIETAC-CISG claimants made smaller claims than their ITA counterparts, but on average recovered a larger percentage.

In CIETAC-CISG cases studied, the median claim was USD 175,090 and the median recovery was USD 87,636.[36] Additionally, the mean claim was USD 373,130 and the mean recovery was USD 181,838.[37]

33 Based on the results of the studies by Franck, *supra* note 24, and *IICL Study 3/2/2009, supra* note 23, at 1.

34 Ahee & Walck, *Update 2007, supra* note 5, at 7. Global Financial Analytics only looked at ICSID arbitration cases.

35 Ahee & Walck, *Update 2008, supra* note 3, at 7.

36 A. Shwedel, *The Institute of International Commercial Law of the Pace University School of Law: Analysis and Translation of CIETAC-CISG Awards* (6 August 2010) (on file with author) (cited as: *IICL study 8/6/2010*), at 8. Dr. Shwedel adjusted the claims and awards for inflation to 2008 U.S. dollars. He also adjusted the dataset to eliminate outlier claims, resulting in a dataset of 254 cases.

37 *Id.*

By contrast, in ITA disputes, claimants asserted much larger claims and were correspondingly less successful. Professor Franck's study found that the median amount claimed was approximately USD 59 million, but the median award was zero.[38] This shows that most ITA claimants did not recover. Professor Franck also found that the mean claim was approximately USD 340 million, but the mean award was USD 10.4 million.[39]

Chart 2. What Parties are Winning: A Comparison of Median Claims and Awards[40]

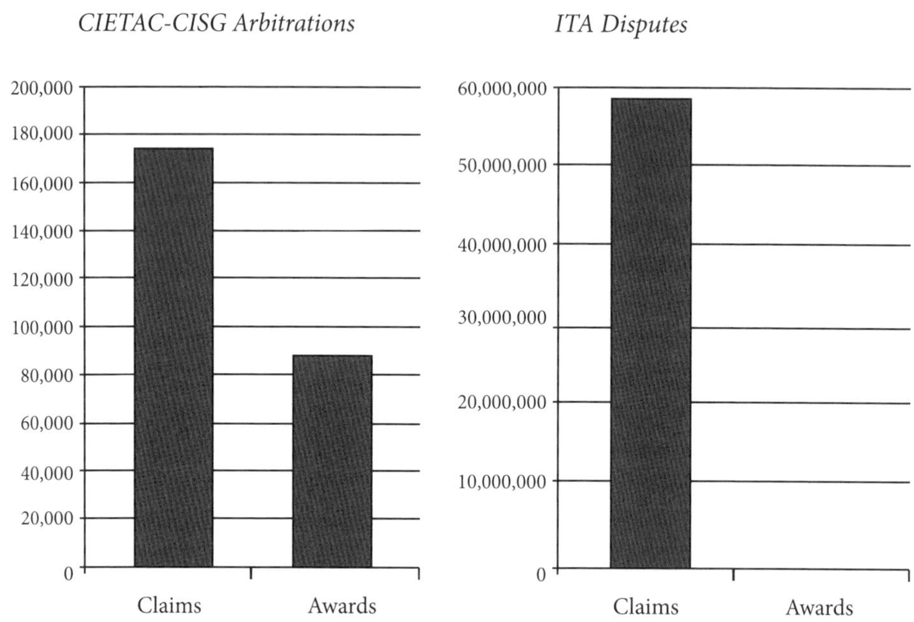

38 Frank, *supra* note 24, at 58, note 254 and 258.

39 *Id.*, at 58.

40 Based on the results of the studies by Franck, *supra* note 24, at 49 *et seq.*, and *IICL Study 8/6/2010, supra* note 36, at 8.

Chart 3. What Parties are Winning: A Comparison of Mean Claims and Awards[41]

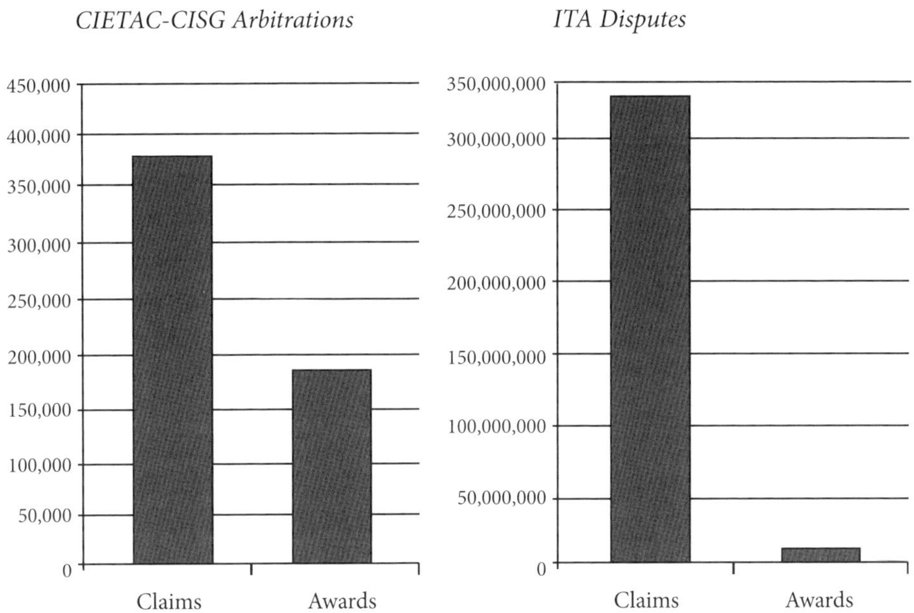

The Global Financial Analytics' study of 2007 ICSID awards found that successful claimants sought a total of USD 3.14 billion in compensation, and received USD 932 million. In addition, Global Financial Analytics reported that for awards in 2007, 'the average recovery was about one-third of the amount claimed'.[42] For awards in 2008, Global Financial Analytics found that claimant recovery dropped to 18.6% of the amount claimed.[43] These two studies posted different results from the Franck study because Global Financial Analytics looked at the average recovery of successful claimants, whereas Professor Franck looked at the recovery of all claimants.[44] Thus, Professor Franck's average recovery figure includes cases in which the claimants were unsuccessful (including cases dismissed for lack of jurisdiction), whereas Global Financial Analytics' recovery figure does not. The International Institute of Commercial Law's study also looked at only those CIETAC-CISG awards in which the claimants were successful. It found that the median claim in those cases was

41 Id.
42 Ahee & Walck, *Update 2007, supra* note 5, at 7-12.
43 Ahee & Walck, *Update 2008, supra* note 3, at 7.
44 It is also possible that Susan Franck's inclusion of UNCITRAL and other non-ICSID disputes while Global Financial Analytics use of only ICSID disputes, could account for some differences in their findings.

USD 171,331 and the median recovery was USD 119,019.[45] Additionally, the mean claim was USD 413,246 and the mean recovery was USD 233,652.[46] In addition, the average recovery was 60% of the amount claimed.[47]

Chart 4. Average Recovery of Amounts Claimed by Successful Claimants[48]

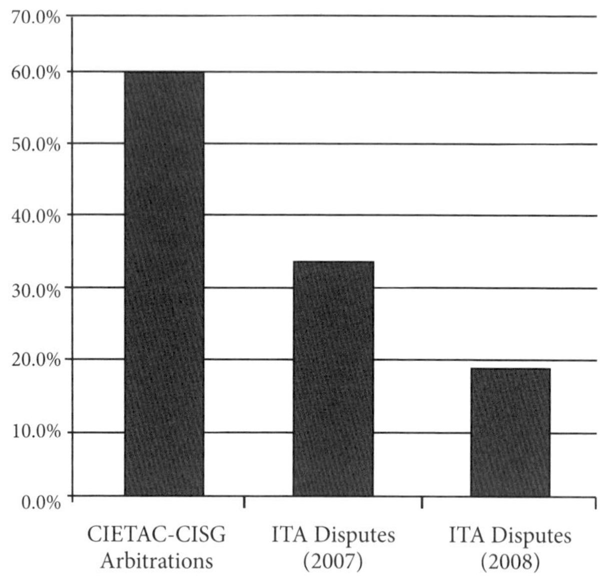

In short, these studies show that CISG claimants are both more likely to prevail and, when they do so, are more likely to receive awards that more closely approximate the size of their claims.

3.3.3 Expenses: Amounts and Allocation

In CIETAC-CISG and ITA cases, whether a tribunal may award arbitration costs and parties' costs often depends on applicable laws and rules.[49] The rules of CIETAC provide that,

45 A. Shwedel, *The Institute of International Commercial Law of the Pace University School of Law: Analysis and Translation of CIETAC-CISG Awards* (24 July 2010) (on file with the author), at 19. The number of cases in this dataset was 239 cases.

46 *Id.*

47 *Id.*, at 27. The median was 77%.

48 Based on results of studies by Ahee & Walck, *Update 2007, supra* note 5, at 7-12, and Ahee & Walck, *Update 2008, supra* note 3, at 7, and *IICL Study 8/6/2010, supra* note 36, at 8.

49 The practice in almost all countries, excluding the United States, is for a successful party to recover the costs of the proceedings and attorneys' fees. This practice is known as the costs follow the event principle. In the

> [t]he arbitral tribunal has the power to decide in the award, according to the specific circumstances of the case, that the losing party shall compensate the winning party for the expenses reasonably incurred by it in pursuing its case.[50]

Thus, the awarding of both arbitration costs and parties' costs under the CIETAC rules is discretionary.

In ITA disputes, the rules of the most widely used institution, ICSID, allow arbitration tribunals to

> assess the expenses incurred by the parties in connection with the proceedings, and [to] decide how and by whom those expenses, the fees and expenses of the members of the Tribunal and the charges for the use of the facilities of the Centre shall be paid.[51]

Thus, as is the case under the CIETAC rules, ICSID tribunals are given broad discretion in shifting the costs.[52]

United States, the practice is for each party to bear its own expenses. This practice is known as the American Rule, see J. Gotanda, *Supplemental Damages in Private International Law (*1998).

50 Art. 46(2) CIETAC Arbitration Rules provides that '[i]n deciding whether the winning party's expenses incurred in pursuing the case are reasonable, the arbitral tribunal shall consider such factors as the outcome and complexity of the case, the workload of the winning party and/or its representative(s), and the amount in dispute, etc.'. The China International Economic and Trade Arbitration Commission (CIETAC), Arbitration Rules, effective as of 1 May 2005, available at <http://cn.cietac.org/Rules/rules.pdf>. See also China International Economic and Trade Arbitration Commission (CIETAC), Arbitration Fee Schedule, effective as of 1 May 2005, available at <http://www.cietac.org.cn/english/fee/fee.htm>. In addition, CIETAC-CISG tribunals have interpreted the CISG to allow for the award of costs and fees as damages.

51 Art. 61 ICSID Convention, *supra* note 16. The majority of awards did not provide the numerical amounts of arbitration costs awarded. Instead, they simply ordered each party to pay a percentage of the costs. Therefore, the median claim was chosen to be plugged into the CIETAC fee structure to approximate the median cost of CIETAC arbitration. Determined from author's own study of the CIETAC-CISG Cases. For a detailed list of the awards, *see* the webpage of the PACE University Institute of International Commercial Law, CIETAC Arbitration Awards, First 321 Case Translations, available at <http://cisgw3.law.pace.edu/cisg/text/CIETAC-CISG-awards.html>.

52 The ICSID additional facility rules also provide for arbitrator discretion, see the ICSID Additional Facility Rules, Washington, 10 April 2006, available at <http://icsid.worldbank.org/ICSID/StaticFiles/facility/AFR_English-final.pdf>. Art. 58(1) ICSID Additional Facility Rules states that '[u]nless the parties otherwise agree, the Tribunal shall decide how and by whom the fees and expenses of the members of the Tribunal, the expenses and charges of the Secretariat and the expenses incurred by the parties in connection with the proceeding shall be borne. The Tribunal may, to that end, call on the Secretariat and the parties to provide it with the information it needs in order to formulate the division of the cost of the proceeding between the parties'.

CIETAC-CISG arbitration tribunals almost always award arbitration costs and base them on a fee structure that calculates them as a percentage of the amount of money claimed.[53] To illustrate, under CIETAC's fee schedule, it would cost USD 12,252 to arbitrate the average claim of USD 373,130, not including parties' costs.[54] It would cost USD 7,301 to arbitrate the median claim of USD 175,090, exclusive of parties' costs.[55] When determining who should pay these costs, arbitrators most frequently shifted arbitration costs completely to the losing party.[56]

Unlike CIETAC-CISG disputes, the cost of ICSID arbitration is based on the actual cost to the tribunal that is hearing a case.[57] In this circumstance, the cost of the arbitration consists of the fees of the arbitrators, often determined on an hourly basis, the expenses of the tribunal, any fees of any experts or administrators employed by the tribunal and any institutional fees. Many ICSID tribunals allocate the arbitration costs without providing the total amount of actual costs. Thus, it is difficult to determine the average cost of ICSID arbitration. However, it is certain that the cost is significantly higher than in a CIETAC-CISG arbitration. Professor Franck determined that the average cost of ITA arbitration was USD 581,332.[58] In approximately 80% of the ICSID cases studied, arbitrators split the costs of arbitration equally among parties.[59] Therefore, ICSID tribunals often did not shift arbitration costs.

---

53 Determined from author's own study of the CIETAC-CISG Cases. For a detailed list of the awards, see the webpage of the PACE University Institute of International Commercial Law, CIETAC Arbitration Awards, First 321 Case Translations, available at <http://cisgw3.law.pace.edu/cisg/text/CIETAC-CISG-awards.html>. See CIETAC Arbitration Fee Schedule, *supra* note 50.

54 Mean Claim = USD 373,130
USD 373,130 x 6.84 (exchange rate) = 2,552,209 CNY
First 1,000,000 CNY costs 35,000 CNY
Remaining 1,552,209 CNY charged at 2.5% rate = 38,805 CNY
35,000 CNY + 38,805 CNY +10,000 CNY processing fee = 83,805 CNY
83,805 CNY / 6.84 = USD 12,252

55 Median Claim = USD 175,090
USD 175,090 x 6.84 (exchange rate) = 1,197,616 CNY
First 1,000,000 CNY costs 35,000 CNY
Remaining 197,616 CNY charged at 2.5% rate = 4,940 CNY
35,000 CNY + 4,940 CNY +10,000 CNY processing fee = 49,940 CNY
49,940 CNY / 6.84 = USD 7,301

56 Costs in CIETAC-CISG arbitration were allocated at a 0/100 ratio in 52% of cases and a 50/50 ratio in 8% of cases. For a detailed list of the awards, see the webpage of the PACE University Institute of International Commercial Law, CIETAC Arbitration Awards, First 321 Case Translations, available at <http://cisgw3.law.pace.edu/cisg/text/CIETAC-CISG-awards.html>.

57 Art. 61 ICSID Convention, *supra* note 16.

58 Franck, *supra* note 24, at 69.

59 Costs were allocated in a 0/100 ratio in 17% of cases. UNCITRAL arbitrators more frequently shifted the costs of arbitration to the losing party (in 71% of disputes the losing party paid more than 50% of the arbitration costs). This difference is attributable to the difference between ICSID and UNCITRAL rules on

Chart 5. Distribution of Arbitration Costs in CIETAC-CISG Disputes and ITA Disputes[60]

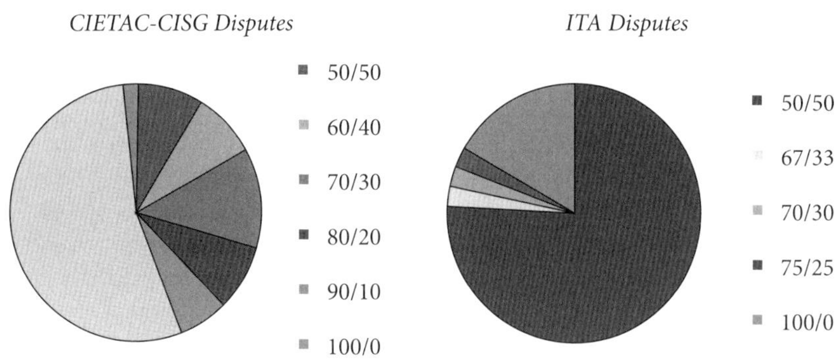

Both CIETAC-CISG and ICSID claimants recovered parties' costs at low frequencies. In CIETAC-CISG disputes, attorneys' fees were awarded in 28% of all cases in the current study.[61] In ICSID disputes, parties' costs were awarded in 16% of all cases.

Chart 6. Percent of Cases Awarding Parties' Costs

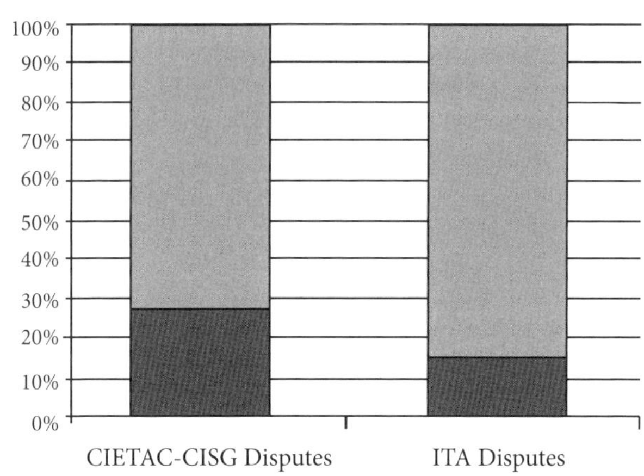

awarding costs and fees. Determined from author's own study of 139 ICSID cases. For cases used, see <http://icsid.worldbank.org/ICSID/FrontServlet?requestType=GenCaseDtlsRH&actionVal=ListConcluded>.

60 Based on the results of the author's own study presented in this chapter.

61 In disputes settled under the UNICTRAL Arbitration Rules, attorneys' fees were awarded in 43% of all cases. This difference may be attributable to the difference between UNCITRAL and ICSID Rules on the awarding of costs and fees.

3.3.4 Length of Disputes

The current study also examines the average time it took to resolve disputes before each institution, measuring the time from the dates that the claims were filed to the dates of the final awards. The average CIETAC-CISG dispute took approximately one year to resolve.[62] By contrast, ITA disputes took an average of approximately four years to resolve.[63]

Chart 7. Length of Disputes

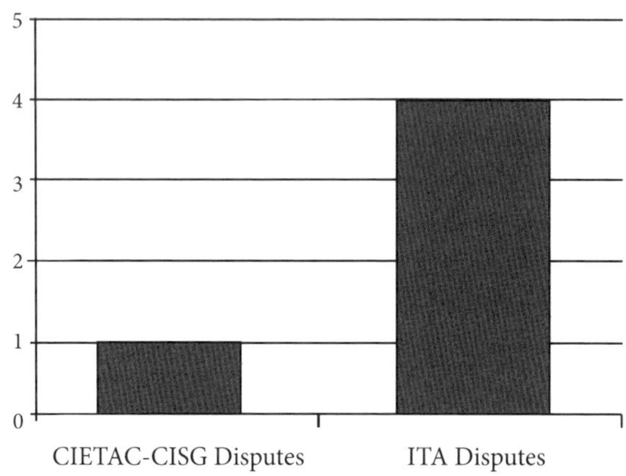

The two studies conducted by Global Financial Analytics examined the length of ICSID awards rendered in 2007 and 2008. They considered both cases dismissed on jurisdictional grounds as well as those decided on the merits. The studies found that the average length of a case in 2007 was five years, while the average length of an ICSID case decided in 2008 was four years.[64] Global Financial Analytics hypothesized that this disparity could indicate a downward trend in the length of investment disputes, but conceded that an increase in awards on jurisdiction in 2008 could also be the cause of this result.

62 Calculated by taking the average of time between a claim being filed and resolved of the cases available at CIETAC Arbitration Awards, First 321 CISG Translations, available at <http://cisgw3.law.pace.edu/cisg/text/CIETAC-CISG-awards.html>.

63 Calculated by taking the average of time between a claim being filed and resolved, starting with those cases resolved between 1996 and June 2009, including those dismissed for lack of jurisdiction, see the ITA Chronological Listing of Newly Released Awards, Decisions and Orders, available at <http://ita.law.uvic.ca/chronological_list.htm>. The average UNCITRAL case took 3.7 years to resolve.

64 Ahee & Walck, *Update 2008, supra* note 3, at 7. Global Financial Analytics found that the disputes took 5 years to resolve in 2007 and 4 years in 2008. The Global Financial Analytics study stated that this indicated a downward trend in the length of investment disputes.

4 Conclusions

4.1 Winners and Losers

Claimants in CIETAC-CISG disputes almost always won, while their counterparts in ITA disputes prevailed in only 40% of cases. These statistics may result from the difference in the nature of these disputes, a difference that ultimately has an impact on the rules concerning liability and damages.

In investment cases, the involvement of a government, often acting in a sovereign capacity, greatly complicates disputes and makes the legal regime more complex. These investment disputes often involve complex claims of expropriation, breach of treaty, discrimination, unfair or inequitable treatment and defences of necessity and abuse of rights – all of which raise difficult legal issues.[65]

By contrast, CISG cases involve the sale of goods, typically between private parties, and a legal regime consisting of a well-developed code.[66] Furthermore, there are over 2,500 reported decisions by courts and arbitral tribunals involving the CISG and a wealth of scholarly commentary on the Convention, all of which aids parties in understanding and applying the CISG and in promising a more uniform interpretation of the Convention by tribunals. Accordingly, it is easier for CISG claimants to determine if they have a meritorious claim and for tribunals to find liability warranting relief.[67]

65 Ahee & Walck, *Update 2007, supra* note 5, at 7 *et seq.*

66 P. Schlechtriem & I. Schwenzer, in I. Schwenzer (Ed.), Schlechtriem & Schwenzer, *Commentary on the UN Convention on the International Sale of Goods (CISG), 'Introduction I'* (2010).

67 There is little evidence of bias in the CIETAC and ICSID disputes that would skew these conclusions. In CIETAC-CISG disputes, bias would most likely present itself in awards in favor of Chinese natives over foreign parties and for sellers over buyers. The Institute of International Commercial Law conducted a study of CIETAC-CISG cases to look for bias towards Chinese parties. The study found that Chinese and non-Chinese claimants succeed at nearly identical rates and recovered close to the same percentages of their claims. Thus, no bias towards Chinese parties was found, see *IICL Study 3/2/2009, supra* note 23, at 1. In investment disputes, the prospect of bias towards governments has worried some commentators. Recently, Susan Franck conducted a study to examine the possibility of this type of bias. Excluding settlements, she found that governments won 58% of the time and that investors won in 39% of cases. Franck's study also looked at arbitrator bias based on the country both arbitrators and governments were from. She found evidence that arbitrators from middle income countries tended to favor high income countries in their awards. Other than this, no other evidence of bias was found. Franck, *supra* note 26, at 2-3.

4.2 Recoveries

In cases studied, CIETAC-CISG claimants won a much larger percentage of their claims than ICSID claimants did. This remains true even when looking only at the recoveries of successful claimants.[68] One may again attribute this result to the difference in the nature and complexity of these disputes. That is, ITA disputes involve complex issues and high claims that are difficult to quantify. For example, in investment arbitrations involving expropriations, claimants may seek to recover the value of their business that was taken. Determining damages in this circumstance is a much more complicated process; no set of uniform rules is consistently followed.

For example, one of the most common methods parties and tribunals use to calculate the value of a business is the Discounted Cash Flow (DCF) method.[69] The DCF method works by projecting the net cash flow for a certain time period into the future and then discounting it back to present value as of the date of the wrongful act taking into account inflation and risk. This process often involves experts making a number of projections, assumptions and subjective determinations.[70]

Thus, calculations of damages each using reasonable approaches may result in very different conclusions concerning the value of a claimant's damages. Indeed, some commentators have called this practice more of an art form than a science.[71]

By contrast, in commercial disputes, the CISG provides detailed provisions for calculating damages derived from well established principles found in many national laws. For example, Articles 74 CISG provides that '[d]amages for breach of contract by one party consist of a sum equal to the loss, including loss of profit, suffered by the other party as a consequence of the breach'.[72] In addition, Articles 75 CISG allows calculation of damages through a straightforward method of taking the difference between the contract price and the price in the substitute transaction when there has been an avoidance of the contract.[73] Articles 76 CISG allows for recovery of the difference between the current price of the goods and the contract price, where there has been no cover transaction.[74] Because this framework provides clear, familiar and relatively easy to apply rules, parties should be able

68 Ahee & Walck, *Update 2008, supra* note 3, at 5-7.
69 J. Gotanda, 'Recovering Lost Profits in International Disputes', 36 *Geo. J. Int'l L.* 61, at 90 (2004).
70 *Id.*, at 90.
71 *Id.*, at 91.
72 Art. 74 CISG.
73 Art. 75 CISG.
74 Art. 76(1) CISG.

to determine with a reasonable degree of certainty the damages that would be recoverable under the Convention in the event of a breach of contract.

Another factor that may help to explain the difference between CIETAC-CISG and ITA recoveries is that in CIETAC arbitration, arbitration costs are based on the amount in dispute.[75] Thus, in theory, it is less likely that claims will be inflated beyond what a party thinks that they can actually recover. In this regard, CIETAC's practice is similar to that of the ICC. The ICC has found that this system

> encourage[s] the efficient handling of cases within a financial framework that is proportionate to the amount at stake in the arbitration. The fact that the scales are based on the sum in dispute also has the virtue of discouraging the submission of frivolous claims.[76]

As noted, in ITA disputes, the arbitration costs are based primarily on actual fees and expenses incurred; therefore, there is no similar mechanism for keeping them low.[77]

4.3 *Arbitration and Parties' Costs*

Winning parties in both CIETAC-CISG and ICSID disputes were generally unsuccessful at recovering parties' costs. This is especially interesting in the CIETAC-CISG context where arbitrators frequently shifted arbitration costs, yet were reluctant to award parties' costs. It should be noted that this finding is similar to an ICC study which concluded that arbitrators frequently shifted arbitration costs but were reluctant to award parties' costs.[78]

It is unclear why CIETAC-CISG arbitrators would not follow the costs follow the event principle. One possibility is that parties in CIETAC-CISG disputes do not regularly seek parties' costs. In my study of these cases, the issue of parties' costs rarely arose. In addition, in the few cases where parties requested their expenses, the arbitrators refused to award parties' costs, because, in their view, the claimant did not prove their claims for costs and

75 CIETAC Arbitration Fee Schedule, *supra* note 50.

76 ICC Webpage, Introduction to Arbitration, available at <http://www.iccwbo.org/court/arbitration/id4089/index.html>.

77 Some commentators note, however, that in cases where the amount in dispute is large, but the legal and factual issues are straight forward, the ICSID fee structure may wind up costing less than the approaches used by the ICC and CIETAC, see W. Craig, *et al.*, *International Commercial Arbitration*, at 31 (2000).

78 A report that tracked ICC awards from 1989-1991 revealed that when the Claimant won, the Respondent was ordered to pay all or most of the arbitration costs 81% of the time. In contrast, the same was true in only 50 % of those cases with respect to the Respondent paying some portion of the Claimant's legal fees.

fees with a sufficient degree of certainty. Thus, it is possible that parties did not request their costs because litigating the issue would have been expensive and unlikely to result in a successful verdict.

Another reason may be that where an arbitrator has broad discretion to award costs and fees, the arbitrator may decline to do so because such practice gives each side a 'partial victory' and, thus, the arbitrator will enhance his or her chances of being appointed in other cases. In other words, this practice is unlikely to lead either claimants or respondents to infer a pattern of favouritism and it will be attractive to risk-averse disputants, ultimately increasing the possibility of future appointments and reducing challenges to serving as an arbitrator in other cases.[79]

In investment disputes, a party almost always requests a ruling requiring the other party to pay its litigation expenses. It is possible that the high cost of ICSID arbitration creates more incentives for parties to seek awards of costs and fees. However, because the awards often involve millions of dollars, tribunals may hesitate to award these large amounts.

In addition, as one arbitrator noted, the rules governing ITA disputes allow arbitrators to use their discretion when choosing to award costs.[80] This discretion may have generated a policy of awarding costs and fees only in the 'case of spurious claims or bad faith litigation tactics'.[81] It is unclear, however, why this arbitral practice has evolved. Perhaps, then, costs and fees were awarded infrequently in ICSID disputes because most disputes did not involve bad faith conduct.

4.4 *Time for Resolving Disputes*

Not surprisingly, the current study found ITA disputes took longer to resolve than CIETAC-CISG disputes – on average four times longer. One factor increasing the length of ITA disputes is that in many ITA disputes, it takes years to determine whether the arbitration tribunal has jurisdiction. For example, in cases studied, the average time it took to litigate the issue of jurisdiction in an ICSID dispute was about 2.7 years. To be sure, some of this time is spent on appointing the tribunal and on other administrative matters, but there is no doubt that it takes a significant amount of time to resolve jurisdictional issues, which

79 R. Posner, 'Judicial Behavior and Performance: An Economic Approach', 32 *Fla. St. U. L. Rev.* 1259, at 1260 *et seq.* (2004).

80 See also *International Thunderbird Gaming Corporation v. Mexico*, UNCITRAL (NAFTA), 26 January 2006, available at <http://www.naftaclaims.com/Disputes/Mexico/Thunderbird/Thunderbird_Award.pdf> (T. Walde, concurring), para. 123.

81 *Id.*

in ITA disputes may be complicated. In contrast, jurisdiction in CIETAC-CISG disputes is based on the contract between the parties. Therefore, jurisdiction is easier to determine and less likely to be a source of litigation.

5 Summary

In general, this study shows that the CISG appears to provide a more predictable legal regime for determining liability and damages than do the legal rules used in ITA disputes. As a result, CIETAC-CISG disputes are relatively quick and inexpensive to resolve. Perhaps, as more ITA cases are decided, more uniform practices will emerge, and ultimately lead to a more predictable and efficient system.[82]

82 *Continental Casualty Company v. Argentine Republic*, ICSID Case No. ARB/03/9, 5 September 2008, available at <http://ita.law.uvic.ca/documents/ContinentalCasualtyAward.pdf> (stating that the practice of awarding compound interest in ICSID awards has evolved through the use of case precedent). See also *International Thunderbird Gaming Corporation v. Mexico*, UNCITRAL (NAFTA), 26 January 2006, available at <http://www.naftaclaims.com/Disputes/Mexico/Thunderbird/Thunderbird_Award.pdf> (T. Walde, concurring) (discussing precedent in ICSID cases). See furthermore T. Cheng, 'Precedent and Control in Investment Treaty Arbitration', 30 *Fordham Int'l L.J.* 1014, at 1015 (2007).

Incorporation of Standard Terms under the CISG and Electronic Communication

*Sonja A. Kruisinga**

1 Introduction

International trade has always played an important role in the Netherlands. The Dutch East India Company (*Vereenigde Oostindische Compagnie*, or *VOC*), which was established in the 17th century, was the first multinational corporation in the world and the first company to issue stocks and shares.[1] For a long time, the East India Company was the largest trading company that did business with Asia, buying tea, porcelain and silk in China. However, the importance of international trade for the Netherlands is not matched by attention to the CISG.[2] In the same year as the CISG entered into force in the Netherlands, 1992, the new Civil Code for the Netherlands (*Burgerlijk Wetboek*) was enacted.[3] The entry into force of the CISG was, unfortunately, overshadowed by the introduction of the new Civil Code.

The increased use of electronic communication worldwide has altered the position of international trade. This has given rise to new legal questions. This paper will focus on one of these new issues and will discuss the incorporation of standard terms in a contract that is governed by the CISG and the use of electronic communication. When discussing the issue of general terms and conditions, one can distinguish between different questions. First of all, it needs to be determined whether any general terms and conditions have become part of the contract. If the general terms and conditions are in a language other than the language in which the contract is drafted, one may wonder whether such general terms and conditions can become part of the contract at all. If the contracting parties both

* Associate Professor of Commercial Law, Molengraaff Institute of Private Law, Utrecht University, the Netherlands.

1 P. van Schilfgaarde & J. Winter, *Van de BV en de NV*, at 31 (2009).

2 United Nations Convention on Contracts for the International Sale of Goods (CISG), Vienna, 11 April 1980, available at <http://www.uncitral.org/uncitral/en/uncitral_texts/sale_goods/1980CISG.html>.

3 Enactment of the Netherlands Civil Code: 'besluit van 17 April 1991, Staatsblad 200'. Since its enactment in 1992, the Netherlands Civil Code has been amended frequently.

use their own, and thus differing, general terms and conditions, a situation arises which is termed the 'battle of the forms' and the pertinent question is which conditions the parties have agreed upon. If contracting parties have a long-term business relationship, one of the parties may have assumed that they had established a general usage between them of applying one set of general terms and conditions. Finally, there are usually special requirements for the treatment of jurisdiction and arbitration clauses, and for choice of law clauses.

This paper will focus on only the first point, that is, the position of the offeror which is concluding an international sales contract for the first time with its counterparty, and which would like to incorporate its own standard terms in the contract. What would such a party need to do in order to ensure that its general terms and conditions become a binding part of the international sales contract that is about to be concluded? This question will be discussed in Part 2 of this article. In particular, this article will address the use of electronic communication in this respect, including attention to the question whether a reference in the offer to the company's website – which contains the general terms and conditions – is sufficient to incorporate these terms in an international sales contract which is governed by the CISG (Part 3). In this respect, a short comparison will be made with Dutch national contract law. An amendment to the Dutch Civil Code recently agreed by the Dutch legislator has given rise to similar questions as those arising under the CISG (Part 4).

2 Standard Terms and the CISG

2.1 *No Special Provisions Concerning Standard Terms*

The CISG does not contain any special rules regarding the inclusion of standard terms and conditions in a contract. At the time when the CISG was drafted, a proposal was made to expressly regulate the incorporation of general terms and conditions in the Convention. This proposal was rejected, however, on the ground that the Convention already contained rules for interpretation of the content of the contract.[4] Thus, even though the CISG does not contain any special rules regarding the inclusion of standard terms in a contract, the CISG is applicable to this issue. This has also been confirmed in case law and literature.[5]

4 U. Schroeter, in I. Schwenzer (Ed.), Schlechtriem & Schwenzer, *Commentary on the UN Convention on the International Sale of Goods (CISG)*, Art. 14 para. 33 (2010), with further references.

5 *Id.*; German Federal Supreme Court, 31 October 2001, CISG-online 617, 2002 *Internationales Handelsrecht* 14, translation available at <http://cisgw3.law.pace.edu/cases/011031g1.html>; French Supreme Court, 16 July 1998, CISG-online 344, translation available at <http://cisgw3.law.pace.edu/cases/980716f1.html>.

The question whether any general terms and conditions have been agreed upon by the parties will therefore have to be determined on the basis of the provisions of the CISG dealing with contract formation and contract interpretation. Articles 14 to 24 CISG concern the formation of contracts. The starting point of these provisions is that an international sales contract comes into being by an offer and acceptance.[6] Regarding the content of an offer, Article 8 CISG is of importance.[7]

When determining whether a party's standard terms are incorporated in a sales contract, it must first of all be ascertained whether the standard terms were part of the offer, which was the basis of the contract and which was accepted by the offeree. According to Article 8(2) CISG, it has to be determined whether, according to the understanding of a reasonable person of the same kind as the offeree, it was clear that the offeror intended to include its general terms and conditions in the contract. An effective inclusion of general terms and conditions first requires that the intention of the offeror to incorporate its general terms and conditions in the contract is apparent to the recipient of the offer. In addition, the question arises whether a reference to standard terms suffices to incorporate these terms in an international sales contract, or whether it is necessary to transmit the text of the standard terms to the offeree.

Whether general terms and conditions are part of the offer can follow from the negotiations between the parties, the existing practices between the parties, or international custom. Very interesting issues may arise in this respect. However, these will not be discussed in this paper which concentrates on the situation in which a seller is negotiating a new international sales contract with a prospective buyer. If a seller is about to conclude an export contract which will be governed by the CISG, the question arises what such a seller needs to do in order to validly insert its standard terms in the contract. Literature and case law show that different approaches exist with regard to this issue.

See also *Château des Charmes Wines Ltd. v. Sabaté USA, Sabaté S.A.*, 328 F.3d 528 (9th Cir. 2003), CISG-online 767, 2003 *Internationales Handelsrecht* 295, available at <http://cisgw3.law.pace.edu/cases/030505u1.html>. The Supreme Court of the Netherlands, 28 January 2005, CISG-online 1002, translation available at <http://cisgw3.law.pace.edu/cases/050128n1.html>, held that if a contract is governed by the CISG, questions concerning matters governed by this Convention, which are not expressly settled therein, are to be settled in conformity with the general provisions on which the Convention is based, on the basis of Art. 7(2) CISG. The court therefore held that the question whether a party has consented to the formation of a contract and the general terms and conditions which are part of that contract, belongs to the matters which are governed by the CISG.

6 Arts. 14 to 24 CISG.

7 P. Mankowski, in F. Ferrari, *et al.* (Eds.), *Internationales Vertragsrecht, EGBGB – CMR – CISG – FactÜ, Kommentar*, Vor Art. 14 CISG para. 21 *et seq.* (2007).

2.2 Divergent Approaches in Case Law

There have been some divergent approaches in case law on the question whether a seller can suffice by inserting a reference to standard terms in the contract. For example, in a case decided by the Belgian *Tribunal Commercial de Nivelles* on 19 September 1995, it was held that a reference to standard terms is sufficient to incorporate these terms in an international sales contract governed by the CISG.[8] A French decision from the same year took a somewhat more stringent approach, holding that the standard terms that were printed on a standard form were not applicable because they were printed on the back of the offer and the offeror failed to point this out to the offeree.[9]

In a case decided by the German Federal Supreme Court, the *Bundesgerichtshof* (BGH), on 31 October 2001, it was held that it must be possible in a reasonable manner for the recipient of a contractual offer to become aware of the standard terms.[10] The BGH explicitly held that, according to the CISG, the offeror intending to rely on standard terms must transmit the text of the conditions to the offeree or make the text of the conditions available in another way. The court, very clearly, explained the rationale of its decision.

First, it placed the burden of making general terms and conditions available on the party using the general terms, since the recipient can often not foresee which clauses he is agreeing to in a specific case as significant differences exist between the standard terms used in different countries due to the different national legal systems and customs. Secondly, the court held that it is readily possible for the party using standard terms to attach these terms to its offer. The court held that imposing an obligation on the other party to inquire about clauses that have not been transmitted and burdening him with the risks and disadvantages of unknown standard terms of the counterparty would contradict the principle of good faith in international trade (Art. 7(1) CISG) as well as the general obligations of cooperation and information provision by the parties.

As will be illustrated in Part 2.4, the literature has both agreed with and rejected this decision. In the case law, however, the decision by the *Bundesgerichtshof* was followed, for

---

8 Nivelles Commercial Court, 19 September 1995, not published, Case No. R.G. 1707/93, available at <www.law.kuleuven.be/ipr/eng/cases/1995-09-19.html>.

9 Paris Court of Appeal, 13 December 1995, CISG-online 312, translation available at <http://cisgw3.law.pace.edu/cases/951213f1.html>. The same was held by the Düsseldorf Court of Appeal, 30 January 2004, CISG-online 821, 2004 *Internationales Handelsrecht* 108, translation available at <http://cisgw3.law.pace.edu/cases/040130g1.html>. But see Amsterdam Court of Appeal, 24 April 1997, *NIPR* 1999 no 169, which held that for the application of standard terms, it is sufficient that the full text of such terms is printed on the back of the order form.

10 German Federal Supreme Court, 31 October 2001, *supra* note 5.

example, by the German Courts of Appeal of Düsseldorf and Munich.[11] The reasoning of the German Federal Supreme Court in its aforementioned decision was also explicitly followed by a number of judicial decisions in the Netherlands.[12] From the perspective of a uniform interpretation of the CISG, it is interesting to note that in some of these decisions, the courts explicitly referred to the German Federal Supreme Court's findings. It was one of the first occasions on which courts in the Netherlands explicitly referred to foreign case law when applying the CISG. A somewhat different approach may have been taken by the Austrian Supreme Court (*Oberster Gerichtshof*) which, in its decision of 17 December 2003, seemed to accept that standard terms may be validly incorporated in a contract even if they are not made part of the offer, provided that there is a clause referring to these terms which is so clear that a reasonable party in the same position as the recipient would have understood it.[13] The court held that the addressee must be referred to the standard terms in such a way that it could not reasonably be unaware of those standard terms. The decision by the court was, however, based on a different issue: the court held that the standard terms were not applicable because they were drafted in another language than that of the contract itself. Whether or not the standard terms were handed over was therefore no longer a crucial issue in this decision.

2.3 *The Influence of the Principles and the DCFR*

In some cases it has been held that in the interpretation of the CISG it is important to take notice of the UNIDROIT Principles of International Commercial Contracts (UNIDROIT Principles)[14] and the Principles of European Contract Law (PECL).[15] These cases all con-

11 Düsseldorf Court of Appeal, 21 April 2004, CISG-online 915, 2005 *Internationales Handelsrecht* 24, translation available at <http://cisgw3.law.pace.edu/cases/ 040421g3.html>; München Court of Appeal, 14 January 2009, CISG-online 2011, 2009 *Internationales Handelsrecht* 201, translation available at <http://cisgw3.law.pace.edu/cases/090114g1.html>.

12 Utrecht District Court, 21 January 2009, CISG-online 1814, translation available at <http://cisgw3.law.pace.edu/cases/090121n1.html>; Rotterdam District Court, 25 February 2009, CISG-online 1812, translation available at <http://cisgw3.law.pace.edu/cases/090225n1.html>; Zutphen District Court, 14 January 2009, *Nederlandse Jurisprudentie Feitenrechtspraak* 2009 No. 244; Amsterdam District Court, 3 June 2009, *Landelijk Jurisprudentie Nummer* BK0976, which all explicitly refer to the decision of the German Federal Supreme Court, 31 October 2001, *supra* note 5. See also Arnhem District Court, 16 December 2009; *Landelijk Jurisprudentie Nummer* BK8904.

13 Austrian Federal Supreme Court, 17 December 2003, CISG-online 828, 2004 *Internationales Handelsrecht* 148, translation available at <http://cisgw3.law.pace.edu/cases/031217a3.html>.

14 UNIDROIT International Institute for the Unification of Private Law, UNIDROIT Principles of International Commercial Contracts (2004), Rome, April 2004, available at <http://www.unidroit.org/english/principles/contracts/principles2004/integralversionprinciples2004-e.pdf>.

15 Principles of European Contract Law, 1999, available at <http://frontpage.cbs.dk/law/commission_on_european_contract_law/PECL%20engelsk/engelsk_partI_og_II.htm>. See also 's-Hertogenbosch District Court, 16 October 2002, CISG-online 816, translation available at <http://cisgw3.law.pace.edu/cases/021016n1.html>;

cerned contracts for the international sale of goods between parties having their places of business in different European states. The courts, and the arbitral institution, held that it is a matter of interpretation of the CISG to determine whether, and to what extent, a party has to be informed about the general conditions of its counterparty. It was considered that the aforementioned UNIDROIT Principles give some guidance in this respect.

The UNIDROIT Principles do not provide whether the text of the standard terms has to be transmitted to the other party. The Official Comments state that standard terms contained in a contract document itself are binding upon the mere signature of the counterparty, unless they appear on the reverse side and not referred to in the contract document itself. There must be express references to standard terms in a separate document.[16] Article 2:104(1) PECL, however, states that standard terms may only be invoked against a party which did not know of them if the party using the conditions 'took reasonable steps to bring them to the other party's attention before or when the contract was concluded'. Terms are not appropriately brought to a party's attention by a mere reference to them in a contract document, according to Article 2:104(2) PECL.

In the aforementioned case law, it was held that according to this provision in the PECL, a mere reference to general conditions does not suffice to incorporate these conditions in an international sales contract which is governed by the CISG.[17] Thus, the general conditions must be attached to the contract, or must be made available to the offeree in another way. In this respect, it is interesting to note that a very similar provision is contained in the Draft Common Frame of Reference (DCFR).[18] These provisions are thus in accord with the position that was taken by the *Bundesgerichtshof* in its aforementioned decision of 2001.

Amsterdam District Court, 3 June 2009, CISG-online 2065, available at <http://cisgw3.law.pace.edu/cases/090603n1.html>; Netherlands Arbitration Institute, 10 February 2005, CISG-online 1621, available at <http://www.globalsaleslaw.org/content/api/cisg/urteile/1621.pdf>.

16 See Official Comments to Art. 2.1.19 UNIDROIT Principles, available at <http://www.unilex.info/dynasite.cfm?dssid=2377&dsmid=13637&x=1>, para. 3.

17 *Supra* note 15.

18 C. von Bar, *et al.* (Eds.), *Principles, Definitions, and Model Rules of European Private Law, Draft Common Frame of Reference (DCFR)* (2009). A full online version of the DCFR is available at <http://ec.europa.eu/justice_home/fsj/civil/docs/dcfr_outline_edition_en.pdf>. Art. II. – 9:103(1) DCFR provides that standard terms may only be invoked against a party who was not aware of these terms if the party supplying the terms took reasonable steps to draw the other party's attention to these terms, before or when the contract was concluded. Art. II. – 9:103(3)(b) states that terms are not sufficiently brought to the other party's attention by a mere reference to them in a contract document.

2.4 Divergent Perspectives in the Literature

Some authors have agreed with the approach taken by the *Bundesgerichtshof*.[19] Other authors, however, disagree while stating that a general duty to transmit the text of standard terms should be rejected.[20] According to these scholars, a mere reference to the standard terms can suffice. What should be decisive, in their view, is whether the other party could reasonably be expected to be aware that its contracting party would like to include its standard terms in the contract. To achieve this, it would be sufficient that the required reference to the standard terms is clear and understandable for a reasonable person within the meaning of Article 8(2) CISG. Moreover, upon inquiry, it must be possible to become aware of the terms in a reasonable manner. Such an inquiry is not in all cases unreasonable for the other party. If the contracting parties have established a long-standing business relationship, it would indeed be useless to require that the text of the standard terms be transmitted for every new contract.

However, if parties are concluding an international sales contract for the first time, I would submit that the offeror is then required to transmit the text of its standard terms if it wishes to include these terms in the contract that is about to be concluded. Thus, I tend to agree with the ruling of the German Federal Supreme Court of 2001, especially because of its rationale, that in international transactions the content of standard terms can vary extensively due to the different legal systems of the countries where the contracting parties have their places of business. More importantly, standard terms usually contain provisions which are in the interest of the party using them and may include a choice of law clause, a dispute settlement clause, a retention of title clause or clauses excluding or limiting liability. As the CISG is a non-mandatory convention, these clauses may be essential for the outcome of a dispute that arises out of an international sales contract. For the party intending to use its standard terms it is easily possible, especially if electronic communication is used, to attach its standard terms to its offer. As the provisions therein generally favour the party using the standard terms, it is, in my view, for that party to carry the burden of transmitting the text of the standard terms to the other party.

---

19 U. Magnus, 'Incorporation of Standard Contract Terms Under the CISG', in C. Andersen & U. Schroeter (Eds.), *Sharing International Commercial Law across National Boundaries, Festschrift for Albert H. Kritzer on the Occasion of his Eightieth Birthday*, 303, at 318 *et seq.* (2008); Schroeter, *supra* note 44, Art. 14 para. 36 *et seq.*; Mankowski, *supra* note 7, Vor Art. 14 CISG para. 28 *et seq.*; B. Piltz, 'AGB in UN-Kaufverträgen', 2004 *Internationales Handelsrecht* 133.

20 K. Berger, 'Die Einbeziehung von AGB in internationale Kaufverträge', in K. Berger, *et al.* (Eds.), *Zivil- und Wirtschaftsrecht im Europäischen und Globalen Kontext, Private and Commercial Law in a European and Global Context, Festschrift für Norbert Horn zum 70. Geburtstag*, 3 (2006); T. van Wechem, *Toepasselijkheid van algemene voorwaarden*, at 111 *et seq.* (2007); M. Schmidt-Kessel & L. Meyer, 'Allgemeine Geschäftsbedingungen und UN-Kaufrecht', 2008 *Internationales Handelsrecht* 177; M. Schmidt-Kessel, in I. Schwenzer (Ed.), *supra* note 4, Art. 8 para. 57.

3 Standard Terms and Electronic Communication in the CISG

The increased use of electronic communication gives rise to some new questions. It is generally acknowledged that international sales contracts can be concluded by electronic means.[21] When discussing the use of electronic communication with respect to standard terms, a distinction needs to be made. Standard terms can be contained in an attachment to an e-mail, or they can be retrieved from a website, either via a link from the website on which the offer is available, or via a link in the e-mail that constitutes the offer. The user of the standard terms may also, in its offer, refer to its website where the standard terms are to be found.

If a seller is doing business for the first time with its counterparty, I would be inclined to follow the stringent requirements that were set by the *Bundesgerichtshof*. This means that the offeror has to make the text of the standard terms available to the offeree. The aim is to ensure that the offeree is not obliged to search for the standard terms of the offeror. If the parties have used electronic communication for the formation of their contract, it would suffice for the offeror to include its standard terms in an attachment to the e-mail or in the e-mail itself.[22] By doing so, the offeror has clearly transmitted the text of the standard terms to the offeree and the offeree will be able, even at a later stage, to consult the text of the standard terms.

In my view, a mere reference to the company's website, where the standard terms are to be found, does not suffice for the incorporation of such standard terms in an international sales contract governed by the CISG.[23] The rationale of the stringent requirement that was set by the German Federal Supreme Court is that the burden of informing the other party rests, as the court explicitly held, on the offeror.

---

21 CISG-AC Opinion No. 1, Electronic Communications under CISG, 15 August 2003, Rapporteur: Professor Christina Ramberg, Gothenburg, Sweden, available at <http://www.cisgac.com/default.php?ipkCat=128&ifkCat=143&sid=143>.

22 Mankowski, *supra* note 7, Vor Art. 14 CISG para. 33 *et seq.*; Schroeter, *supra* note 4, Art. 14 para. 44; I. Schwenzer & F. Mohs, 'Old Habits Die Hard: Traditional Contract Formation in a Modern World', 2006 *Internationales Handelsrecht* 239.

23 P. Huber, 'Standard Terms under the CISG', 13 *Vindobona Journal of International Commercial Law & Arbitration* 123, at 133 (2009), stating that it is doubtful whether it is sufficient for the user of standard terms to simply send a link to a website where its standard terms can be downloaded. See also Piltz, *supra* note 19, at 134 *et seq.*; Magnus, *supra* note 19, 303, at 323; Mankowski, *supra* note 7, Vor Art. 14 CISG para. 33 *et seq.* But see A. Stiegele & R. Halter, 'Nochmals: Einbeziehung von Allgemeinen Geschäftsbedingungen im Rahmen des UN-Kaufrechts – Zugänglichmachung im Internet', 2004 *Internationales Handelsrecht* 169; Berger, *supra* note 20, 3, at 17 *et seq.*

First of all, it is not reasonable for the offeree to have to search for standard terms, to be found somewhere on the company's website, on which there may even be a number of different standard terms for different transactions.

Secondly, if a company changes its standard terms, an offeree could never be sure which general terms and conditions it agreed to by returning to the website at a later stage. Moreover, the risk that the standard terms can be unilaterally modified by the user subsequent to the formation of the contract should not be borne by the offeree, for whom such conditions are usually disadvantageous. The argument that this can be counteracted by printing the standard terms at the time of the conclusion of the contract should fail, as it is not for the offeree to print the standard terms, but for the offeror to make sure that the offeree has free access to the standard terms which are applicable to their contract. Had the offeror included the standard terms in the offer, such confusion could have been prevented.

The same is true, from my perspective, with regard to standard terms which can be retrieved from a website, either via a link from the website where the offer is available, or via a link in the e-mail that constitutes the offer.[24] First of all, the offeree must be able to easily examine the standard terms if a dispute arises about the performance of the contract and, secondly, it has to be clear to which standard terms a party has agreed. A website may be temporarily inaccessible, a risk which should not be borne by the offeree. Finally, the offeror would be able to change its standard terms in the meantime. It is, in any event, advisable for a party that intends to insert its standard terms in an international sales contract to insert the text of the standard terms in an email, as this will allow it – at a later stage – to prove that it sent the text of the terms. The burden of proof in this respect will be addressed in more detail in Part 5 of this article.

The aforementioned reasoning seems to be consistent with Article II. – 9:103(2) DCFR, which provides that if a contract is to be concluded by electronic means, the party supplying standard terms may only invoke these terms against the other party if they are made available to the other party in textual form. This provision seems to imply that the text of the conditions as such, contained in a document, must be transmitted to the other party.[25] This is also in accordance with a recent amendment to the Netherlands Civil Code.

24 But see Schwenzer & Mohs, *supra* note 22, at 241; Schroeter, *supra* note 4, Art. 14 para. 49 *et seq.*
25 See also Huber, *supra* note 23, at 133, note 42.

4 Standard Terms and Electronic Communication in the Netherlands Civil Code

The aforementioned questions have also been considered by the legislator in the Netherlands. For contracts concluded by electronic means, the Netherlands Civil Code already allowed standard terms to be made available to the other party by electronic means, before or at the time of the conclusion of the contract. This has to occur in such a way that the text of the standard terms can be saved, or otherwise stored, by the other party and that they are accessible for later perusal.[26] In 2008, the Dutch Minister of Justice proposed an amendment to the Dutch Civil Code.[27] The suggested amendment makes it possible to make standard terms available by electronic means even if the contract itself has not been concluded by electronic means. If the contract is not concluded by electronic means, explicit consent of the other party will be required.[28] It is not clear, however, what amounts to *explicit* consent.[29]

The Minister of Justice has stated that as to the requirement of making the general terms and conditions available, the complete text of the standard terms could be inserted in an attachment to an e-mail or inserted as a hyper link in an e-mail through which the other party can consult the text of the applicable standard terms with one click.[30] The first option mentioned by the Minister is, in my view, undisputed. The second option, however, fails

26 See Art. 6:233(b) and Art. 6:234(1)(c) Netherlands Civil Code. For a translation, see H. Warendorf, *et al.*, *The Civil Code of the Netherlands* (2009). It has to be noted, however, that some of these provisions have a limited scope of application. These provisions cannot be invoked by a party that has validly inserted the identical (or almost identical) standard terms repeatedly in its contracts, as provided by Art. 6:235(3) Netherlands Civil Code. Moreover, and even more importantly, legal entities (*rechtspersonen*) can generally not rely on Arts. 6:233 and 6:234 Netherlands Civil Code. The same is true, generally, for companies having 50 workers or more at the time of the conclusion of the contract, according to Art. 6:235(1) Netherlands Civil Code.

27 The title of the proposed amendment is: 'Wetsvoorstel Wijziging van enige bepalingen van het Wetboek van Burgerlijke Rechtsvordering en het Burgerlijk Wetboek teneinde naast het in deze bepalingen gestelde vereiste van schriftelijkheid ook ruimte te bieden aan de ontwikkelingen op het gebied van het elektronisch verkeer', proposing amendments to some of the provisions of the Netherlands Civil Code and the Netherlands Code of Civil Procedure in order to provide for the developments in the area of electronic commerce. See *Kamerstukken II* 2007/08 31 358, available at <www.officielebekendmakingen.nl>.

28 Such consent is not required if the contract is concluded by electronic means: in such cases, the other party chose itself to contract by electronic means. See *Kamerstukken II* 2007/08 31 358 no 3 at. 9-10, available at <www.officielebekendmakingen.nl>.

29 D. Beenders, 'Informatieplicht bij algemene voorwaarden; verdeeldheid in de praktijk', 6777 *Weekblad voor Privaatrecht Notariaat en Registratie* 903, at 903-905 (2008), C.B.F.M. Westerhuis, 'Algemene voorwaarden; elektronisch gebruik en toepasselijkheid anno 2008', 21 *Juridisch up to Date* 21, at 21-24 (2008) and T.H.M. van Wechem, 'Wetsvoorstel 31 358: een hamerstuk met losse eindjes', 1 *Contracteren* 4 (2010).

30 *Kamerstukken II* 2007/08 31 358, no 3, at 9-10, available at <www.officielebekendmakingen.nl>.

to ensure that the offeree is allowed access to the text of the standard terms at all times, as was argued in Part 3 above.

The Minister of Justice has explicitly pointed out that a mere reference to the address of a website is insufficient, because the other party would then have to search on that website for the standard terms which are applicable to its contract.[31] If a buyer has to actively search for the text of the standard terms, this is not to be regarded as offering a reasonable opportunity to become aware of the standard terms, as is required.[32] This amendment was agreed upon by the Dutch legislator as at 16 February 2010 and entered into force on 1 July 2010.[33]

It is clear that lawyers are struggling with the aforementioned questions and there is still some legal uncertainty in this respect. For example, the Court of Appeal of 's-Hertogenbosch, in a decision on 13 October 2009 in which the Netherlands Civil Code was applied, held that a mere statement that the standard terms can be viewed on the website of the company was sufficient to incorporate the standard terms into the contract without handing over the standard terms as such.[34] This case concerned a contract that was concluded by electronic means; it did not concern a contract for the sale of goods, but a storage contract. The claim concerned the costs for storage of groundnut kernels. At the bottom of an e-mail, the party using the standard terms stated:

> Storage activities are subject to the Warehouse Conditions Amsterdam-Rotterdam [...]. A copy of these conditions will be sent to you free of charge immediately upon your request or they can be viewed on [website].

The standard terms were posted on the named website and could be downloaded there. According to the court, this had to be regarded as providing the other party with a reasonable opportunity to become aware of the standard terms used. This clearly differs from the approach taken by the Minister of Justice. A number of other cases that were decided by courts of first instance, however, show that a mere reference to the fact that the standard terms can be viewed on a website is not sufficient to warrant the conclusion that the standard terms have been made available to the other party.[35]

---

31 *Id.*

32 *Kamerstukken I* 2008/09 31 358, C at 3-6, available at <www.officielebekendmakingen.nl>.

33 *Staatsblad* 2010, at 222, available at www.officielebekendmakingen.nl.

34 's-Hertogenbosch Court of Appeal, 13 October 2009, *Landelijk Jurisprudentie Nummer* BL1921. A similar line of reasoning was adopted by the Haarlem District Court, 29 August 2007, *Landelijk Jurisprudentie Nummer* BB2576.

35 In some of these cases, the contract was concluded by electronic means, and in some it was not, Maastricht District Court, 20 January 2010, *Landelijk Jurisprudentie Nummer* BL1980; Zwolle District Court, 14 January

Even though the aforementioned provisions in the Dutch Civil Code do not apply to international contracts and do not even apply to all national commercial contracts, the rationale of these provisions can be used as a source of inspiration for international commercial contracts that are governed by the CISG. I would submit that in order to incorporate standard terms in an international sales contract governed by the CISG, it does not suffice only to refer to a website which contains the company's standard terms.

According to the Dutch Civil Code, a party using standard terms which does not take the aforementioned provisions into account, will not be able to rely on these standard terms. The sanction that the Dutch Civil Code uses in this respect is that the offeree may annul the standard terms.[36] These provisions in the Dutch Civil Code thus relate to content control. However, if the CISG is applicable to a particular contract, the Dutch provisions do not play any role. Although control over the validity of standard terms is, in principle, a matter of domestic law, in my view this is not so in relation to the matters of content discussed in this chapter. While it may not yet be fully certain whether, according to the CISG, a party using standard terms is required to transmit the text of these conditions to the other party, it is certain that this question is governed by the CISG.

5 Burden of Proof

It is possible that the aforementioned issues are solved in practice through the division of the burden of proof. It is well established nowadays that the CISG governs the division of the burden of proof. First of all, for the interpretation under Article 8(2) CISG, the general rule applies that the party that stands to benefit bears the burden of proof.[37] Moreover, if a party claims that its declaration has reached the other party, then it bears the burden of proving its claim.[38] Thus, the burden of proving whether any standard terms are incorporated in a contract rests with the party relying on the standard terms.[39]

If this party has included the standard terms in an attachment to an e-mail or in the e-mail itself, it has not only clearly transmitted the text of the standard terms to the other party, but it will generally also be able to prove which standard terms it inserted in the contract at hand. If the offeror has used a hyperlink in its e-mail which contains the offer, or if it

2009, *Landelijk Jurisprudentie Nummer* BI3429; Roermond District Court, 11 August 2009, *Landelijk Jurisprudentie Nummer* BJ5160; Utrecht District Court, 23 July 2008; *Landelijk Jurisprudentie Nummer* BF0016; Zutphen District Court, 19 August 2009, *Landelijk Jurisprudentie Nummer* BJ5577.

36 Art. 6:233 (b) Netherlands Civil Code.

37 Schmidt-Kessel, *supra* note 20, Art. 8 para. 67.

38 Schroeter, *supra* note 1, Art. 24 para. 43.

39 *Id.*, Art. 14 para. 76.

has used such a link on the website where the offer was to be found, the offeror will have to prove that it had made the text of the conditions available. It may, however, be difficult to prove the exact contents of the standard terms if the website had meanwhile been altered.

The question whether or not a hyperlink is sufficient for the incorporation of standard terms will, in my view, have to be answered through the division of the burden of proof.[40] This, again, was also confirmed in the recent amendment to the Dutch Civil Code. Concerning the amendment, the Minister of Justice stated that if a dispute arises concerning the question whether the party using standard terms has provided the other party with a reasonable opportunity to take note of these standard terms, the burden of proof rests with the party using the standard terms. The Minister states that the way in which the offeror does this, is up to him. He further adds that a confirmation of receipt by the other party will surely help, but that there are also other possibilities.[41]

6 Conclusion

Standard terms are often used by companies in international trade. Such terms are drafted in advance and are meant to be incorporated into a contract without negotiating them with the other party. As the CISG is a non-mandatory convention, these clauses may turn out to be essential for the outcome of a dispute that arises out of an international sales contract. There is, however, still some legal uncertainty with respect to the insertion of standard terms by using electronic communication.

First of all, the provisions and case law discussed show that contracting parties which are doing business abroad would be well advised to always add their general terms and conditions to their offers. For contracts that are concluded by the use of electronic communication, it is suggested that the standard terms should always be sent as an attachment to an e-mail message, or the text of the standard terms be placed in full in the e-mail message itself. This will allow the party seeking to rely on the standard terms, later on, to prove which standard terms were transmitted to the offeree. Transmission of the text of the standard terms is, in my view, required under the CISG if a party concludes an international sales contract with a counterparty with which it has not previously done business.

40 See also E.C. Kraan-Beekman, 'Leerstukken – Elektronisch contracteren, maar toch de pen (moeten) hanteren?', 3 *Contracteren* 80, at 81 (2009).

41 *Kamerstukken I* 2009/10 31 358, E at 7. See also T.H.M. van Wechem, 'Twee arresten over bewijslast en algemene voorwaarden (HR 21 september 2007, NJ 2007, 565 en HR 11 juli 2008, LJN: BD1394, C07/012HR)', 3 *Contracteren* 68, at 68-70 (2008).

It is in my view neither sufficient to merely refer to the company's website where the standard terms can be found, nor to place a hyperlink in an e-mail message that gives direct access to the website. First of all, the offeree must be able to easily examine the standard terms if a dispute arises about the performance of the contract and, secondly, it has to be clear to which standard terms a party agreed. A website can be temporarily inaccessible, a risk which should not be borne by the offeree, and the offeror could change its standard terms in the meantime. Moreover, in such cases, it will also be rather complex for the offeror to prove that it made the standard terms available to the other party.

As e-mail and internet are increasingly used for the conclusion of international sales contracts, the questions discussed in this paper will inevitably attract further attention in the next decade. It is to be hoped that this will lead to a uniform approach in this respect.

The Reach of the CISG in China: Declarations and Applicability to Hong Kong and Macao

Weidi Long[*]

1 Introduction

The aim of the United Nations Convention on Contracts for the International Sale of Goods[1] (hereinafter 'CISG' or 'Convention') is to promote worldwide uniformity in dealing with disputes arising from international sales.[2] To date, the CISG has gained worldwide acceptance,[3] and its story has been one of worldwide success.[4] Yet its success is still a fragile one.[5] Indeed, uniformity does not follow automatically from uniform rules.[6] Homeward trends and '*lex forism*' are in the way.[7] Automatic opt outs have led to under utilisation of the CISG in some jurisdictions.[8] Apparently, many of these contributing

---

* PhD Candidate, Wuhan University, P.R. China; PhD Candidate, University of Groningen, The Netherlands; LLB, Sun Yat-sen University; Co-Founder and Editor, CISG-China Database. The author is indebted to Lisa Spagnolo for her invaluable support without which this chapter would not have been completed. The author is also grateful to the late Professor Albert Kritzer, Luca Castellani, Dr. Ulrich Schroeter, Professor Mary Keyes, Professor Yuqing Zhang, and Dr. Qingming Li, for their support in one way or another. An earlier draft of this chapter was presented at the Second Annual Peter Schlechtriem CISG Conference held in Hong Kong on 13 March 2010. This article is also dedicated to the memory of Al Kritzer.

1 United Nations Convention on Contracts for the International Sale of Goods (CISG), Vienna, 11 April 1980, available at <http://www.uncitral.org/uncitral/en/uncitral_texts/sale_goods/ 1980CISG.html>.

2 P. Schlechtriem, 'The Borderland of Tort and Contract: Opening a New Frontier?', 21 *Cornell Int'l L.J.* 467, at 472 (1988).

3 P. Schlechtriem & I. Schwenzer, in: I. Schwenzer (Ed.), Schlechtriem & Schwenzer, *Commentary on the UN Convention on the International Sale of Goods (CISG) Introduction* (3rd ed., 2010) (cited as: *Commentary on the CISG* (3rd ed.)).

4 I. Schwenzer & P. Hachem, 'The CISG - Successes and Pitfalls', (Spring) 57 *Am. J. Comp. L.* 457, at 478 (2009).

5 *Id.*, at 458.

6 B. Zeller, *CISG and the Unification of International Trade Law 4-5* (2007). See also C. Andersen, 'Furthering the Uniform Application of the CISG Sources of Law on the Internet', 10 *Pace Int'l L. Rev.* 403, at 404 (1998).

7 See generally F. Ferrari, 'Homeward Trend and Lex Forism Despite Uniform Sales Law', 13 *Vindobona Journal of International Commercial Law & Arbitration* 15-42 (2009) (cited as: *Homeward Trend).*

8 See L. Spagnolo, 'The Last Outpost: Automatic CISG Opt Outs, Misapplications and the Costs of Ignoring the Vienna Sales Convention for Australian Lawyers', 10 *Melbourne Journal of International Law* 141 (2009) (cited as: *Last Outpost*); L. Spagnolo, 'A Glimpse Through the Kaleidoscope: Choice of Law and the CISG (Kaleidoscope Part I)', 13 *Vindobona Journal of International Commercial Law and Arbitration* 135 (2009)

factors to the fragility of its success are external. Yet there are reasons from within the CISG as well.[9] These include, *inter alia*, the declarations authorized by the Convention,[10] to which this chapter is addressed. To explore this part of the CISG story in a specific context, the chapter takes a 'field trip' to China, a significant territory in the map of the CISG where both the successes and (perhaps minor) pitfalls go hand in hand.

On 11 December 1986, the People's Republic of China (hereinafter 'P.R. China' or 'China') approved the CISG with two declarations under Article 95 and Article 96 CISG. As of 1 January 1988, the CISG came into force in China.[11] Over the past 20 years, the CISG has had phenomenal impact in China, proof of which is twofold.

First, the CISG has greatly influenced the evolution of Chinese domestic contract law. Before the Chinese delegation attended the 1980 Diplomatic Conference in Vienna (hereinafter 'Vienna Conference'), China did not have domestic legislation on the subject of contract law, for the country was under a strictly planned economy until the Reform and Opening-up in 1978. However, to some extent, the rationales learnt by the Chinese delegation at the Vienna Conference triggered the enactment of Chinese domestic contract law and special regulation for international trade. Around the time of China's approval of the CISG, several sets of private law rules were promulgated, *i.e.*, the 1981 Economic Contract Law, the 1985 Foreign-Related Economic Contract Law (hereinafter '1985 FECL'), the 1986 General Principles of Civil Law (hereinafter '1986 GPCL') and the 1987 Technology Contract Law.[12] On 1 October 1999, China took a further step towards the unification of

---

(cited as: *Kaleidoscope Part I*); L. Spagnolo, 'Rats in the Kaleidoscope: Rationality, Irrationality, and the Economics and Psychology of Opting In and Out of the CISG (Kaleidoscope Part II)', 13 *Vindobona Journal of International Commercial Law and Arbitration* 157 (2009) (cited as: *Kaleidoscope Part II*); L. Spagnolo, 'Green Eggs and Ham: The CISG, Path Dependence, and Behavioural Economics of Lawyers' Choices of Law in International Sales Contracts', 6 *Journal of Private International Law* 417 (2010) (cited as: *Green Eggs and Ham*).

9 See generally H.M. Flechtner, 'The Several Texts of the CISG in a Decentralized System: Observations on Translations, Reservations and other Challenges to the Uniformity Principle in Article 7(1)', 17 *Journal of Law and Commerce* 187 (1998) (cited as: Several Texts of the CISG).

10 For discussion on the declarations under the CISG, see generally U.G. Schroeter, 'Backbone or Backyard of the Convention?: The CISG's Final Provisions', in: C. Andersen & U. Schroeter (Eds.), *Sharing International Law across National Boundaries: Festschrift for Albert H. Kritzer on the Occasion of his Eightieth Birthday* (cited as: *Kritzer Festschrift*), 428 (2008) (cited as: *Backbone or Backyard*).

11 See CISG: Participating Countries – China (PRC), <http://cisgw3.law.pace.edu/cisg/countries/cntries-China.html>.

12 Thus, between 1 July 1985 and 30 September 1999, the basic applicable laws for international sales in the Chinese legal system were the 1986 General Principles of Civil Law (cited as: GPCL) and 1985 Foreign-Related Economic Contract Law (cited as: FECL), and from 1 October 1999 to the present, they are the 1986 GPCL and 1999 Contract Law. The 1986 GPCL embodies general rules, while the 1985 FECL and 1999 Contract Law set forth more specific provisions. With respect to a given matter on which both the 1986 GPCL and the 1985 FECL/1999 Contract Law apply, the 1985 FECL/1999 Contract Law shall prevail. The

domestic contract law by enacting the Contract Law of the P.R. China (hereinafter '1999 Contract Law'), which repealed the 1981 Economic Contract Law, the 1985 FECL and the 1987 Technology Contract Law. During the drafting of both the 1985 FECL and the 1999 Contract Law, the CISG was one of the most important sources of reference.[13]

Second, with China's active participation in international trade, a great many Chinese cases have been decided under the CISG. To date, the CISG has been applied in one way or another in around 60 Chinese court decisions, and more than 320 arbitrations organized by the China International Economic and Trade Arbitration Commission (hereinafter 'CIETAC').[14] But this is only the count of cases that have been reported thus far. In view of the absence of a regular case reporting system in China,[15] the striking number of Chinese cases reported still appears to be a fraction of the total.[16] Not surprisingly, the application of the CISG in China has been engaging increasing attention from Chinese courts, arbitral tribunals and commentators.[17]

---

texts of these statutes are available at <http://www.lawyee.net>. For a more detailed account of the Chinese legal framework regarding international trade, see generally F. Yang, 'The Application of the CISG in the Current PRC Law & CIETAC Arbitration Practice', 2006 *Nordic Journal of CommercialLaw* 2, available at <http://www.njcl.fi/2_2006/article4.pdf>. Considering that the cases decided under the 1985 FECL fall within the scope of the present paper, the provisions of the 1985 FECL will be discussed where necessary, although they ceased to be in effect in 1999.

13 See S. Han, 'The CISG and Its Impact on China', in: F. Ferrari (Ed.), *The CISG and Its Impact on National Legal Systems*, 71 (2008). The legislators of the 1999 Contract Law endeavoured to develop a new contract law which would reflect the recent contractual developments and demands taking place in commercial practice. To this end, they cooperated with the academic circle more closely than ever before, and referred extensively to international and foreign experience. They have also conducted detailed comparisons and discussions of many foreign contract laws and international uniform laws, the CISG and the UNIDORIT Principles being the main references. See D. Ding, 'China and CISG', in: M.R. Will (Ed.), *CISG and China: Theory and Practice*, 25, at 33 (1999).

14 This is the count according to the Pace CISG Database, available at <http://cisgw3.law.pace.edu> and CISG-China Database, available at <http://aff.whu.edu.cn/cisgchina/en>.

15 So far, only selected Chinese court decisions have been reported. Han, *supra* note 13, at 73. In terms of arbitral awards, the CIETAC awards released so far are not as current as commentators would like them to be. In fact, CIETAC releases awards on the CISG three years after they were rendered, see P. Mitchard, 'Is CIETAC Leading Arbitration in Asia into a New Era of Transparency?', 2009 *Asia Pacific Arbitration Review*, at note 27 and accompanying text, available at <http://www.GlobalArbitrationReview.com>.

16 Spagnolo, *Kaleidoscope Part I*, *supra* note 8, note 35-37, observing the safe assertion would be that the number of Chinese CISG cases is enormous. It is speculated that CIETAC will soon overtake all other international arbitral institutions in terms of CISG case numbers, see F. Yang, 'CISG, CIETAC Arbitration and the Rule of Law in the PR of China: A Global Jurisconsultorium Perspective', in: *Kritzer Festschrift*, *supra* note 10, 600, at 601.

17 For an interesting discussion on how the increasing involvement of China in the application of the CISG may force CISG exposure on other (reluctant) jurisdictions, see Spagnolo, *Kaleidoscope Part I*, *supra* note 8, at 138 *et seq*; Spagnolo, *Kaleidoscope Part II*, *supra* note 8, at 172 *et seq*; Spagnolo, *Green Eggs and Ham*, *supra* note 8, at 420 *et seq*.

So far, there has been a wealth of literature on China and the CISG,[18] covering a wide range of topics including the impact of CISG on Chinese domestic law,[19] comparisons between CISG and Chinese contract law,[20] and the application of CISG in Chinese courts and CIETAC arbitration.[21] Among them, China's declarations under the CISG have come under the spotlight.[22] The declarations by China under Articles 95 and 96 CISG have long been causing confusion in theory and in practice. More recently, two purported Article 93 CISG declarations by China, respectively regarding Hong Kong and Macao Special Administrative Regions (hereinafter 'SARs'), have led to remarkably divergent decisions on the applicability of the CISG to SARs, further adding to the current uncertainty in practice.

This chapter will examine the diverse approaches to the effect of China's declarations in theory and in practice.[23] In so doing, it seeks to identify the underlying problems, and explore what can be done to improve the *status quo*. Part 2 of this chapter will examine the effect of China's Article 95 CISG declaration, followed by a proposition to eliminate

---

18 See Bibliography of CISG, Materials in Chinese, <http://cisgw3.law.pace.edu/cisg/biblio/biblio-chi.html>.

19 See, *e.g.*, Ding, *supra* note 13, at 25-37; B. Zeller, 'CISG and China', in: M.R. Will (Ed.), *CISG and China: Theory and Practice*, 7 (1999); Han, *supra* note 13.

20 See, *e.g.*, C. Wang, 'A Comparison Between the CISG and the FECL (Part I)', 3 *Chinese Legal Science* 106 (1989); C. Wang, 'A Comparison Between the CISG and the FECL (Part II)', 4 *Chinese Legal Science* 114 (1989); C. Wang, 'A Comparison Between the CISG and the FECL (Part III)', 5 *Chinese Legal Science* 115 (1989); J. Shen, 'Declaring the Contract Avoided: The U.N. Sales Convention in the Chinese Context', 10 *N.Y. Int'l L. Rev.* 7 (1997) (cited as: *Declaring the Contract Avoided*); Y. Yang, 'Suspension Rules under Chinese Contract Law, the UCC, and the CISG: Some Comparative Perspectives', 2008 *China Law & Practice* 23, at 23-27, available at <http://cisgw3.law.pace.edu/cisg/biblio/yang.html>.

21 See, *e.g.*, M.S. Jacobs & Y. Huang, 'An Arbitrator's Power and Duties Under Art. 114 of Chinese Contract Law in Awarding Damages in China in Respect of a Dispute under a Contract Governed by CISG', 20 *Mealey's International Arbitration Report* 39 (2005); D. Wu, 'CIETAC's Practice on the CISG', *Nordic Journal Commercial Law* 1 (2005); F. Mohs & B. Zeller, 'Penalty and Liquidated Damages Clauses in CISG Contracts Revisited', 21 *Mealey's International Arbitration Report* 1 (2006); Yang, *supra* note 12; A.E. Butler, 'Contracts for the International Sale of Goods in China', 21 *International Litigation Quarterly* 3 (2006); M. Koehler & Y. Guo, 'The Acceptance of the Unified Sales Law (CISG) in Different Legal Systems: An International Comparison of Three Surveys on the Exclusion of the CISG's Application Conducted in the United States, Germany and China', (Spring) 20 *Pace Int'l L. Rev.* 45 (2008); Y. Xiao & W. Long, 'Selected Topics on the Application of the CISG in China', 20 *Pace Int' L. Rev.* 61 (2008) (cited as: *Selected Topics).*

22 See, *e.g.*, X. Wang & C.B. Andersen, 'The Chinese Declaration Against Oral Contracts Under the CISG', 8 *Vindobona Journal International Commercial Law & Arbitration* 145 (2004); U.G. Schroeter, 'The Status of Hong Kong and Macao Under the United Nations Convention on Contracts for the International Sale of Goods', 16 *Pace Int'l L. Rev.* 307 (2004) (cited as: *Hong Kong and Macao*); Yang, *supra* note 12.

23 All the arbitration awards reviewed in this chapter are reported by the China International Economic and Trade Arbitration Commission (cited as: CIETAC). The English versions of these awards are available online through the Pace Law School CISG Database at <http://www.cisg.law.pace.edu/cisg/text/casecit.html#china>. In addition, as of 2 December 2007, around 30 further CIETAC cases have been reported since the publication of the two articles concerning arbitral practice on the CISG, *i.e.* Wu, *supra* note 21, and Yang, *supra* note 12.

the confusion. The effect of China's Article 96 CISG declaration will then be dealt with in Part 3, leading up to a similar solution to the problems hitherto encountered. The respective status of Hong Kong and Macao will be treated from a historical perspective in Part 4, based on which possible improvements relative to the current situation will be suggested. Illustrations follow in Part 5, in which the application of the CISG to SARs will be analyzed in typical scenarios. Finally, some evaluations and suggestions will be given as concluding remarks in Part 6.

2 Indirect Application: The Article 95 Declaration

Pursuant to Article 1(1)(b) CISG, the CISG applies 'indirectly' where the parties do not have their places of business in different Contracting States as required by Article 1(1)(a) CISG, but conflicts rules refer to the law of a Contracting State, and the parties have their places of business in different states (though not different Contracting States). China filed a declaration pursuant to Article 95 CISG, which is designed to exclude such 'indirect' application.[24] In general, the effects of Article 95 CISG declarations are controversial.[25] Yet in China, it is even more so than in other jurisdictions.[26] The following discussion is confined to the effect of the declaration on the courts of Mainland China. The extension of this declaration to SARs, as well as its effect on the courts of other Contracting States, will be examined in Part 5.[27]

2.1 *Effect of the Declaration*

At the time of its declaration, China had envisaged separate legislation on international trade (of which the 1985 FECL later formed part), so as to protect the immature domestic market and to buffer the impact of the rapid Reform and Opening-up.[28] China's declaration

---

24 China's declaration pursuant to Art. 95 CISG states: 'The People's Republic of China does not consider itself to be bound by subparagraph (b) of paragraph 1 of article 1 [...]' CISG: Participating Countries – China (PRC), available at <http://cisgw3.law.pace.edu/cisg/countries/cntries-China.html>. Art. 95 CISG provides: 'Any State may declare at the time of the deposit of its instrument of ratification, acceptance, approval or accession that it will not be bound by subparagraph (1)(b) of article 1 of this Convention.'

25 For a synopsis of the pros and cons on the subject, see Spagnolo, *Last Outpost, supra* note 8, at 143-144.

26 So far, the Contracting States that have made Art. 95 CISG declarations are Armenia, China, Canada, the Czech Republic, Singapore, Slovakia, St Vincent and the Grenadines, and the U.S. Canada withdrew its declaration on 31 July 1992. *See* Status of the CISG, available at <http://treaties.un.org/Pages/ViewDetails.aspx?src=TREATY&mtdsg_no=X-10&chapter=10&lang=en#10>. It is believed that despite the general controversy regarding the effects of Art. 95 CISG, the 'core principle [...] is clear'. See I. Schwenzer & P. Hachem, in: *Commentary on the CISG* (3rd ed.), *supra* note 3, Art. 1 para. 37.

27 See *infra* notes 229, 233-243 and accompanying text.

28 It is believed that the Chinese delegation became aware of this idea at the Vienna Conference, see Yang, *supra* note 12, at 7.

may also have been influenced by the fact that the U.S. had made its own Article 95 CISG declaration to protect U.S. traders from being deprived of the use of their familiar domestic law, without the countervailing gain of supplanting the foreign law of trading partners in non-contracting states.[29]

Against this background, some commentators believe that the declaration is intended to prevent the application of the CISG to contracts where one of the parties has its place of business in China and the other in a non-contracting state.[30] Other scholars observe that its purpose is to ensure the application of Chinese domestic law, where selected by conflicts rules, in cases involving a party in China. According to the latter understanding, where parties have their places of business in China and a non-contracting state, respectively, the CISG may still apply under Article 1(1)(b) CISG if conflicts rules point to the law of a Contracting State other than China.[31] True, in that case, it would be perverse to apply the Contracting State's domestic law, especially when that state has not entered an Article 95 CISG declaration.[32] Nevertheless, to interpret Article 95 CISG in a uniform manner, one must stay true to the wording of this provision. Since China has declared under Article 95 CISG that 'it will not be bound by' Article 1(1)(b) CISG, this declaration discharges China from the obligation to apply CISG whether conflicts rules refer to the law of China or any other Contracting State, irrespective of whether Chinese parties are involved. This being said, it should be stressed that the declaration does not by any means prohibit application of the CISG. Nevertheless, the effect of this declaration is indeed undermined by several cases within the scope of Article 1(1)(b) CISG in which the CISG was applied by virtue of Chinese domestic law or as evidence of international usages.[33]

---

29 Other states shared China's concern that domestic traders be protected by a declaration excluding Art. 1(1)(b) CISG. For example, representatives from Czechoslovakia were concerned about the impact of Art. 1(1)(b) CISG in denying their traders the benefit of domestic codes for international trade, *see id.*

30 Z. Chen & J. Wu, 'On the Application of the CISG in China: With Comment on Article 142 of the GPCL', 2004 *Legal Science* 112, at 116.

31 G. Wang, 'The Sphere of Application and Principles of Interpretation of the CISG', in: *Chinese Yearbook of International Law*, 239 at 249 (1989). But see P. Schlechtriem, in: P. Schlechtriem & I. Schwenzer (Eds.), *Commentary on the UN Convention on the International Sale of Goods (CISG)*, Art. 1 para. 41 (2nd ed., 2005) (cited as: *Commentary on the CISG* (2nd ed.)). Schlechtriem seemed to indicate that in the present scenario, the CISG will apply only if the Contracting State whose law is determined by conflict rules has not made a declaration under Art. 95 CISG.

32 M. Bridge, *The International Sale of Goods* 543 (2007) (cited as: *International Sale of Goods*). Similarly J. Honnold & H. Flechtner (Eds.), *Uniform Law for International Sales under the 1980 United Nations Convention* (2009). Bridge correctly pointed out that Honnold's conclusion is based on conflict-of-laws considerations, but not on the forum's treaty obligations under the CISG. Bridge, *id.*, at note 216.

33 For further references in this respect, see Xiao & Long, Selected Topics, *supra* note 21, at 68-72.

China's Article 95 CISG declaration has also been regarded as having influence on parties' rights to opt in to the CISG at the level of conflict of laws.[34] In a sales case submitted to the Shanghai Commission of CIETAC involving differences between a Chinese seller and Korean buyer, decided before South Korea's accession to the CISG, it was held the CISG could not apply under Article 1(1)(a) CISG. The Tribunal ruled that the parties had chosen the CISG by basing their claims and defences on it in the hearings. However, under the belief that the declaration by China against Article 1(1)(b) CISG precluded application of the CISG to contracts between parties from China and non-contracting states, the Tribunal concluded that party autonomy should be restricted in the instant case and the CISG should not apply.[35] The reasoning of this award derives from the above view,[36] *i.e.*, China's Article 95 CISG declaration prohibits the application of the CISG to contracts where the parties are in China and a non-Contracting State respectively. Accordingly, the declaration is considered as creating a mandatory rule which prohibits parties from opting in to the CISG in the present scenario.[37] In the present author's opinion, however, the Article CISG 95 declaration only releases China from the obligation to apply the CISG in cases described under Article 1(1)(b) CISG,[38] but does not prohibit its application. Thus, in Mainland courts and CIETAC arbitrations (seated in the Mainland and applying Mainland conflict rules), opting-in to the CISG at the conflict-of-laws level should be allowed insofar as it is permissible under the Mainland conflict of laws.[39]

2.2 *Potential Withdrawal of the Declaration*

Recently, China's potential withdrawal of the declaration has raised concerns. It is submitted that the declaration should be withdrawn mainly for four reasons. First and foremost, as mentioned, rapid economic development has contributed to the change of China's

34 For the permissibility of opting-in to CISG in Mainland courts and CIETAC arbitrations, see *infra* notes 252-266 and accompanying text.

35 See Chen & Wu, *supra* note 30, at 115. However, a contrary position was taken in another similar case where the parties also intended their choice of the CISG to operate at the level of conflict of laws. In that case, a dispute arose between a Chinese seller and a Japanese buyer who designated 'Chinese law, international conventions and international usages' as the applicable law. Manifestly, the CISG could not apply under Art. 1(1)(a) CISG because Japan was not a Contracting State. Nevertheless, the Xiamen Intermediate People's Court deferred to the parties' choice and applied the CISG. See *Sanming Tsusho (Japan) Corp. v. Fujian Zhangzhou Metals & Minerals Import & Export Co.*, Xiamen Intermediate People's Court, August 1994 (Xiajing Chuzi No. 124).

36 See Chen & Wu, *supra* note 30, at 116.

37 *Id.*

38 Similarly Honnold & Flechtner (Eds.), *supra* note 32, at 44, para. 47.6 (observing that Art. 95 CISG merely frees the declaration state from Art. 1(1)(b) CISG).

39 But see Schlechtriem, in: *Commentary on the CISG* (2nd ed.), *supra* note 31, Art. 95 para. 3 ('As a rule, [...] a reservation state will not apply the CISG in such a situation [...]'). For the permissibility of choosing the CISG in its own right under Mainland conflicts law, see *infra* notes 252-266 and accompanying text.

domestic legislation with one single body of law, *i.e.*, the 1999 Contract Law, replacing the separate pieces of legislation on domestic and international contracts. Legislators of the 1999 Contract Law have made frequent references to the CISG, and the application of the two sets of rules will lead to quite similar, if not identical, results. Thus, one of the initial intended functions of the declaration, that is, to protect traders in China through domestic legislation on international trade that differs from the CISG, has been largely undermined. Further, should the CISG apply under Article 1(1)(b) CISG where conflicts rules lead to Chinese law, the interests of China and Chinese parties would not be prejudiced, since the CISG provides Chinese parties with protections similar to those under the 1999 Contract Law.[40]

Second, where the law of a contracting state other than China is referred to by conflict rules, withdrawal of the declaration will enable the application of the CISG, which would not only relieve Chinese courts from proof of foreign laws, but would also protect Chinese parties from foreign laws with a body of neutral international law. Third, with 76 states having adopted the CISG (and more to be expected),[41] including most of China's major trade partners, the effect of the declaration has been and will continue to be minimal in any event.[42] Last but not least, withdrawal of the declaration will not only eliminate confusion as to the declaration's effects, but will also contribute to uniformity in the outcome of trade disputes by retaining the application of the CISG.[43]

If the Chinese government wishes to withdraw the declaration, it may do so, pursuant to Article 97(4) CISG, at any time by a formal notification in writing addressed to the depositary, *i.e.*, Secretary-General of the UN. This procedure worked well for Canada, the only country so far which has withdrawn its Article 95 CISG declaration.[44] In accordance with Article 97(4) CISG, such withdrawal will take effect on the first day of the month following the expiration of six months after the date of receipt of the notification by the depositary.

---

40 Xiao & Long, *Selected Topics*, *supra* note 21, at 68.

41 So far, the CISG has not entered into force in Ghana and the Bolivarian Republic of Venezuela, see UNCITRAL Status 1980 – United Nations Convention on Contracts for the International Sale of Goods, <http://www.uncitral.org/uncitral/en/uncitral_texts/sale_goods/1980CISG_status.html>.

42 See similarly Bridge, *International Sale of Goods*, *supra* note 32, at 545.

43 Other good reasons have been given for a possible withdrawal of Singapore's Art. 95 CISG declaration. See G.F. Bell, 'Why Singapore Should Withdraw Its [Article 95] Reservation to the United Nations Convention on Contracts for the International Sale of Goods (CISG)', 9 *Singapore Yearbook of International Law* 55, at 61-70 (2005) (cited as: *Singapore*). Some of these reasons hold good for the case of China as well.

44 For more details on the Canadian withdrawal, see *id.*, at 71.

The withdrawal will also have to be effectuated in Chinese domestic law. The Constitution of the P.R. China (hereinafter 'Chinese Constitution') is silent on the approaches to the implementation of treaties in China. Nevertheless, it is generally believed that China adopts a monist approach to the implementation of treaties on civil and commercial matters in internal law.[45] In this respect, attention is drawn to Article 142(2) 1986 GPCL, which provides:

> If any treaty concluded or acceded to by the P.R. China contains provisions differing from those in the civil laws of the P.R. China, the provisions of the former shall apply, unless the P.R. China has announced reservations to these provisions.[46]

This provision enforces the principle of *pacta sunt servanda* in Chinese domestic law. Notwithstanding its misleading wording which is open to criticism,[47] the provision manifestly incorporates treaties on substantive civil and commercial matters into Chinese internal law. Yet under Chinese law, it is unclear whether a certain procedure must be fulfilled for a given treaty to be implemented.[48] In the case of CISG, before and after the Convention entered into force on 1 January 1988, a number of administrative directives,[49] judicial interpretations[50] and other official documents[51] were issued. These instruments either notified the Chinese stakeholders of China's approval of the CISG and its entry into force, or directed Mainland courts to apply the CISG when its basic requirements were

45 See Y. Xiao, *Principles of Private International Law*, 291-300 (2007); W. Zhu & Q. Li, *The Law of Treaties*, 223-224 (2008).

46 This provision concerns treaties on substantive civil and commercial matters. Similarly, Art. 236 1982 Civil Procedure Law of P.R. China (amended 2007) provides: 'If any treaty concluded or acceded to by the P.R. China contains provisions differing from those in this Law, the provisions of the former shall apply, unless the P.R. China has announced reservations to these provisions.' This provision deals with treaties on procedural civil and commercial matters.

47 The wording of this provision has directed Chinese courts to base the application of CISG on the condition that the CISG 'contains provisions differing from those in the civil laws of the P.R. China', rather than on the conditions set forth by Art. 1 CISG. For further references, see Xiao & Long, *Selected Topics*, *supra* note 21, at 70-71.

48 According to the Law of the P.R. China on the Procedure of Conclusion of Treaties, Arts. 15 and 16, treaties to which China is a contracting party should be officially published. Yet it is unclear whether this is the precondition for the effectuation of treaties in China. See Xiao, *supra* note 45, at 292.

49 See, *e.g.*, Notice of the Implementation of CISG, 87 Waijingmao Fazi No. 2, issued by the then Ministry of Foreign Trade and Economic Cooperation on 22 January 1987; Notice on Several Issues Regarding the Implementation of the CISG, issued by the then Ministry of Foreign Trade and Economic Cooperation on 4 December 1987, available at <http://www.lawyee.net>.

50 See, *e.g.*, Notice on Circulation of the Notice of the Implementation of CISG, Fa (Jing) Fa (1987) No. 34, issued by the Supreme People's Court on 10 December 1987.

51 See, *e.g.*, Memorandum of the National Working Meeting on Adjudication of Economic Cases Involving Foreign, Hong Kong and Macao Elements in Coastal Regions, Fa (Jing) Fa (1989) No. 12, issued by the Supreme People's Court on 12 June 1989.

met. Although it is unclear whether these instruments *de iure* effectuated the CISG in China, they indeed *de facto* facilitated its implementation in China. Thus, if China withdraws the Article 95 CISG declaration, it seems advisable, and necessary in practice, that similar directive instruments be issued to realize the effect of the withdrawal.

If directive instruments are needed in the event of withdrawal, they should ensure withdrawal is (*de facto*) effectuated internally on the same day as it takes effect internationally.[52] Moreover, another two issues need to be addressed in the directive instruments: the applicability of the CISG to offers made before the withdrawal, and its applicability to contracts concluded before the withdrawal. In this regard, an agreeable formula has been advanced for the potential withdrawal by Singapore.[53] This formula derives from analogy to Article 100 CISG, which deals with the entry into force of the Convention in a Contracting State.[54] The present author proposes that the same formula be adopted by China in the event of withdrawal. Thus, the directive instrument(s) may contain the following guidelines:

> (1) When, under Article 1(1)(b) CISG, the rules of private international law lead to the application of the law of a Contracting State, the CISG applies to the formation of a contract only when the proposal for concluding the contract is made on or after the date when China's withdrawal is to take effect.
>
> (2) When, under Article 1(1)(b) CISG, the rules of private international law lead to the application of the law of a Contracting State, the CISG applies only to contracts concluded on or after the date when China's withdrawal is to take effect.

---

52 This proposal also draws on the experience of Canada. When Canada withdrew its Art. 95 CISG declaration, it made sure that its internal legislation and the withdrawal came into force on the same day. A similar proposal was also advanced for Singapore. See Bell, *Singapore*, *supra* note 43, at 71-72.

53 The proposed transitional measures for Singapore are as follows: '(1) When, under Article 1(1)(b), the rules of private international law lead to the application of Singapore law, the CISG applies to the formation of a contract only when the proposal for concluding the contract is made on or after the date when Singapore's withdrawal is to take effect. (2) When, under Article 1(1)(b), the rules of private international law lead to the application of Singapore law, the CISG applies only to contracts concluded on or after the date when Singapore's withdrawal is to take effect.' See Bell, *Singapore*, *supra* note 43, at 70-71.

54 Art. 100 CISG provides: '(1) This Convention applies to the formation of a contract only when the proposal for concluding the contract is made on or after the date when the Convention enters into force in respect of the Contracting States referred to in subparagraph (1)(a) or the Contracting State referred to in subparagraph (1)(b) of article 1. (2) This Convention applies only to contracts concluded on or after the date when the Convention enters into force in respect of the Contracting States referred to in subparagraph (1)(a) or the Contracting State referred to in subparagraph (1)(b) of article 1.'

3 FORMAL VALIDITY: THE ARTICLE 96 CISG DECLARATION

3.1 *Wording of the Declaration*

Upon approval of the CISG, China made the following declaration:

> The People's Republic of China does not consider itself to be bound by...article 11 as well as *the provisions in the Convention relating to the content of article 11.*[55]

The wording of this declaration has given rise to doubts as to its qualification as an Article 96 CISG declaration.[56] Indeed, unlike the declarations made by other countries under Article 96 CISG, this declaration is not couched in the precise phraseology called for by Article 96 CISG.[57] It only expressly refers to Article 11 CISG, and does not directly mention Article 29 or Part II of the CISG. Nor does it declare that the cited provisions do not apply where a party's place of business is in China, and hence it is unclear under what circumstances China intends to exclude the application of these provisions. Moreover, it fails to identify the CISG provision pursuant to which the declaration was made. Yet it is premature to conclude that the unclear wording renders the declaration ineffective. Here, it is worth noting that the position of Articles 12 and 96 CISG is 'take it or leave it'. Thus, if any 'non-written form' provision of Article 11, Article 29 CISG or Part II is to be excluded, they are to be excluded altogether. Further, Article 98 CISG stipulates that no reservations are permitted except those expressly authorized in the CISG. Therefore, to determine the effect of China's declaration, it is necessary to examine whether the declaration can be located within the wording of Articles 12 and 96 CISG.

In this respect, regard is to be had to the intention of China. First, at the time of China's declaration, China had already promulgated the 1985 FECL, a regulation specifically relating to international contracts involving Chinese parties. Under the 1985 FECL, written

55 See Status of the CISG, *supra* note 26 (emphasis added).

56 See Schroeter, *Backbone or Backyard, supra* note 10, at 450.

57 Art. 96 CISG provides: 'A Contracting State whose legislation requires contracts of sale to be concluded in or evidenced by writing may at any time make a declaration in accordance with article 12 that any provision of article 11, article 29, or Part II of this Convention, that allows a contract of sale or its modification or termination by agreement or any offer, acceptance, or other indication of intention to be made in any form other than in writing, does not apply where any party has his place of business in that State.' So far, apart from China, Argentina, Armenia, Belarus, Chile, Estonia, Hungary, Latvia, Lithuania, Paraguay, Russian Federation and Ukraine have also made use of Art. 96 CISG. Estonia withdrew its declaration on 9 March 2004. All the declarations, except for the one by China, resemble the wording of Art. 96 CISG. See CISG: Table of Contracting States, available at <http://www.cisg.law.pace.edu/cisg/countries>.

form was required for a contract, its modification, termination by agreement, any offer, acceptance, and other indication of intention.[58] Given this requirement for written form concerning all aspects of a contract, it stands to reason that the declaration's wording 'the provisions in the Convention relating to the content of article 11' refers to Article 29 CISG and the relevant provisions of Part II.[59] Thus, the declaration fits within the pigeonhole of Articles 12 and 96 CISG.

Second, the 1985 FECL made it clear that the written form requirement under the statute was aimed at international contracts involving Chinese parties.[60] China's need for protection of Chinese (state-owned in particular) entities against claims unsupported by a written agreement, and the rationale it learned from the U.S.S.R. at the Vienna Conference,[61] would naturally lead to China's intention to exclude the application of the 'non-written form' provisions of the CISG to contracts involving parties whose places of business were in China. Such an exclusion is expressly authorized by Articles 12 and 96 CISG. Indeed, there is no reason why China's declaration should be treated differently from the Article 96 CISG declarations filed by other countries which share(d) the same concerns and needs.

3.2 *Effect of the Declaration*

The effect of China's Article 96 CISG declaration is a matter of dispute. The following discussion centres upon the effect of the declaration on Mainland courts. The extension of this declaration to SARs, as well as its effect on the courts of other Contracting States, will be examined in Part 5.[62]

---

58 See, *e.g.*, Art. 7 1985 FECL provides: '[A] contract shall be formed as soon as the parties to it have reached a written agreement on the terms and have signed the contract. If an agreement is reached merely by means of letters, telegrams or telex and one party requests a signed letter of confirmation, the contract shall be formed only after the letter of confirmation is signed . . . . '. Written form was also required under Art. 32 1985 FECL, regarding modification and termination by agreement.

59 See Y. Zhang, *Uniform Law for International Sales: Commentary on the United Nations Convention on Contracts for the International Sale of Goods* 103 (2009) (stating that China has declared under Art. 96 CISG against the relevant provisions of Art. 11, Art. 29 and Part II of the CISG). Note that the cited author was former Director, Department of Treaty and Law, Ministry of Commerce of the P.R. China.

60 See Art. 2 1985 FECL.

61 The law of the U.S.S.R. imposed strict formal requirements for the making of foreign trade contracts. In the UNCITRAL proceedings, representatives of the U.S.S.R. indicated that the preservation of these requirements was of great importance to protect established patterns for creation of foreign trade contracts. See Honnold & Flechtner (Eds.), *supra* note 32, at 186, para. 128. The fact that the State was responsible for international trade in the U.S.S.R. may have led to such concerns. A similar situation also existed in China in the 1980s, where state-owned entities were actively taking part in international trade on behalf of the PRC. See Wang & Andersen, *supra* note 22, at 155.

62 See *infra* notes 229-232 and accompanying text.

In the Chinese literature, opinions are divergent as to whether the Article 96 CISG declaration *per se* imposes a requirement of written form in cases involving Chinese parties. Some commentators advocate that, in cases concerning parties from China and another Contracting State, contracts must be concluded in written form.[63] This position has found support not only in numerous CIETAC arbitrations,[64] but also in foreign court decisions.[65] This view is unconvincing in that the Article 96 CISG declaration only relieves China from the obligation to recognize contracts in all forms, but imposes no obligation to enforce only written contracts.[66] Moreover, in view of the *erga omnes* effect of the declaration, this understanding would result in universal applicability of the (then) written form requirement under Chinese law.[67] Further, it may even encourage other states to make an Article 96 CISG declaration in order to extend the influence of its own law, which would undermine the goal of establishing uniform sales law.[68]

Other writers rely upon Article 21 of the Vienna Convention on the Law of Treaties (hereinafter 'Vienna Treaty Convention'),[69] which deals with legal effects of reservations and of objections to reservations, in interpreting the effect of China's Article 96 CISG declaration. According to this view, in cases involving parties from China and another Contracting State, the effect of the declaration depends on whether the other state has made an Article 96 CISG declaration. If it has not, the effect of the declaration depends on whether that other state raised an objection to the declaration.[70] This understanding is flawed in that the Vienna Treaty Convention itself indicates that its application is only residuary,[71] let alone the doubtful applicability of its Article 21 to declarations under the

63 Z. Chen, 'Comments on the Formality of Contracts for International Sale of Goods' (in Chinese), 1997 *Legal Science* 25-26. This is nowadays the minority view in other jurisdictions. For a synopsis of the literature holding this view in other jurisdictions, see P. Schlechtriem & M. Schmidt-Kessel, in: *Commentary on the CISG* (3rd ed.), *supra* note 3, Art. 12 para. 2.

64 See, *e.g.*, CIETAC Arbitration proceeding, China, 6 September 1996, available at <http://cisgw3.law.pace.edu/cases/960906c1.html>; CIETAC Arbitration proceeding, China, 31 December 1997, available at <http://cisgw3.law.pace.edu/cases/971231c1.html>. See similarly CIETAC Arbitration proceeding, China, 17 October 1996, available at <http://cisgw3.law.pace.edu/cases/961017c1.html>.

65 See, *e.g.*, Supreme Court, Austria, 31 August 2005 (7 Ob 175/05v), available at <http://cisgw3.law.pace.edu/cases/050831a3.html>, (cited as: *Tantalum case*). In that case, the court of first instance seemingly considered that China's Art. 96 CISG declaration mandates the application of Chinese law. Interestingly, although at the time China had already adopted the 1999 Contract Law permitting oral contracts, the court of first instance deemed that written form was still required under Chinese law.

66 See P. Si, 'The Nature of Declarations', 1997 *Legal Science* 23.

67 Schroeter, *Backbone or Backyard, supra* note 10, at 442.

68 Honnold & Flechtner (Eds.), *supra* note 32, at 189.

69 United Nations, Treaty Series, Vol. 1155, at 331 (2005).

70 See W. Ding, 'Two Viewpoints on the Formality of Chinese Contracts for International Sale of Goods' (in Chinese), 1997 *Legal Science* 24, at 24-25.

71 Art. 20(a) Vienna Convention on the Law of Treaties, Vienna, 23 May 1969, available at <http://untreaty.un.org/ilc/texts/instruments/english/conventions/1_1_1969.pdf> (cited as: Vienna Treaty

CISG.[72] Since Articles 12 and 96 CISG contain sufficiently clear rules on the effect of the declaration, there is simply no room for the Vienna Treaty Convention to come into play.

When determining the effect of the declaration, regard is to be had to the text of Article 12 CISG, which clearly provides the effect of the declaration is merely that 'any provision of article 11 [and other provisions of the CISG permitting non-written form] does not apply'. No contrary indications concerning the meaning of the wording of Article 12 CISG can be found from the legislative history of the CISG.[73] Accordingly, the declaration only excludes the application of relevant provisions of the CISG, but leaves the matter of formal validity to the applicable law determined by the forum's conflicts rules. Currently, this seems to be the prevailing view across the globe,[74] and has gained worldwide support in practice.[75] Yet even within this school of thought, opinions remain divided on whether, if the forum's conflict rules lead to the law of a non-declaration state, Article 11 CISG or the domestic rules as to form of that state should prevail.[76]

Convention), provides: '[A]cceptance by another contracting State of a reservation constitutes the reserving State a party to the treaty in relation to that other State if or when the treaty is in force for those States'. See also Schroeter, *Backbone or Backyard, supra* note 10, at 4-7.

72 It has been argued that 'the reservations addressed by Article 21 [Vienna Treaty Convention] are selective and not general. Reservations declared under private law conventions are, however, general in nature... They have a general character and therefore are not subject to Article 21': J. Basedow, 'Uniform Private Law Conventions and the Law of Treaties', *U. L. Rev.* 731, at 741 (2006-4).

73 See Honnold & Flechtner (Eds.), *supra* note 32, at 191; J. Rajski, in: C.M. Bianca and M.J. Bonell (Eds.) *Commentary on the International Sales Law: The 1980 Vienna Sales Convention* (cited as: *Bianca & Bonell Commentary*), Art. 96 para. 1.2 (1987).

74 See, *e.g.*, Honnold & Flechtner (Eds.), *supra* note 32 at 188-189; Schlechtriem & Schmidt-Kessel, in: *Commentary on the CISG* (3rd ed.), *supra* note 3, Art. 12 para. 2; Bridge, *International Sale of Goods, supra* note 32, at 559; Rajski, *ibid*, Art. 12 para. 2.3.

75 *Adamfi Video v. Alkotók Studiósa Kisszövetkezet*, Metropolitan Court, Hungary, 24 March 1992 (12.G.41.471/1991/21), available at <http://www.cisg.law.pace.edu/cisg/wais/db/cases2/920324h1.html>; *Vital Berry Marketing NV v. Dira-Frost NV*, Rechtbank van Koophandel Hasselt, Belgium, 2 May 1995 (A.R. 1849/94, 4205/94), available at <http://www.cisg.law.pace.edu/cisg/wais/db/cases2/950502b1.html>; *J.T. Schuermans v. Boomsma Distilleerderij/Wijnkoperij*, Supreme Court, Netherlands, 7 November 1997 (16.436), available at <http://www.cisg.law.pace.edu/cisg/wais/db/cases2/971107n1.html>; Supreme Court, Austria, 22 October 2001 (1 Ob 77/01g), available at <http://www.cisg.law.pace.edu/cisg/wais/db/cases2/011022a3.html>; Presidium of the Supreme Arbitration Court of the Russian Federation, Russia, 20 March 2002 (Resolution No. 6134/01), available at <http://www.cisg.law.pace.edu/cisg/wais/db/cases2/020320r1.html>; *Forestal Guarani S.A. v. Daros International, Inc.*, 613 F.3d 395, (3rd Cir.), United States, 21 July 2010, available at <http://cisgw3.law.pace.edu/cases/100721u1.html>.

76 For positions in favour of the domestic rules as to form of the non-declaration state, see Honnold & Flechtner (Eds.), *supra* note 32, at 189-191; Bridge, *International Sale of Goods, supra* note 32, at 559-560; Flechtner, *Several Texts of the CISG, supra* note 9, at 196-197. For arguments in favour of Art. 11 CISG, see P. Schlechtriem & M. Schmidt-Kessel, in: *Commentary on the CISG* (3rd ed.), *supra* note 3, Art. 12 para. 3; Schroeter, *Backbone or Backyard, supra* note 10, at 443-444.

Nonetheless, at the time when the writing requirement under the 1985 FECL was in force, the intense debate on the above issue would not be of practical significance in Chinese courts and CIETAC arbitrations. Given China's need at the time for protection of Chinese entities against claims unsupported by written agreements, the rule as to written form under the 1985 FECL would be qualified as an expression of overriding mandatory rules or *lois d'application immediate*, which served China's crucial interests that must be preserved.[77] In fact, as evidenced by the Argentine court decision on *Qûilmes Combustibles v. Vigan*,[78] other declaration states – which consider their declarations under Article 96 CISG to be essential – would probably, for reasons of (positive) public policy, also apply their own rules of form.[79] Thus, in cases involving parties from China before Mainland courts, the writing requirement under the 1985 FECL would claim application to the contract regardless of the law which may otherwise apply. In fact, in a number of Chinese cases involving a Chinese party, the 1985 FECL rules on written form were directly applied for reasons which were unclear from the record.[80] These decisions would have been justified had the tribunals expressly applied the rules in the name of overriding mandatory rules. The overriding application of these rules would also be possible in foreign courts, if the forum state's conflict of laws dictated respect for a third country's mandatory rules.[81]

At the present time, however, the divergent approaches to the effect of China's declaration may be of practical relevance in Chinese courts and CIETAC arbitrations. Since the 1999 Contract Law – which repealed the 1985 FECL – recognizes contracts in any form,[82] the

---

77 W. Li, 'Discussion on Several Cases Concerning the Formation of Contracts for International Sale of Goods: A Comparison Between the CISG, UCC and Chinese Contract Law', 3 *Study of Comparative Law* 117, at 121 (2004) (expressly advocating such a qualification).

78 Appellate Court, Argentina, 15 March 1991, available at <http://cisgw3.law.pace.edu/cases/910315a1.html>. Abstract available at <http://www.unilex.info>. The suit was filed by an Argentine buyer against a Belgian seller. The Court observed that the agreement was not contrary to the Argentinian public policy rule which provides that international contracts for the sale of goods must be made in writing. Note that Argentina was and is still an Art. 96 CISG declaration state.

79 See also F. Enderlein & D. Maskow, *International Sales Law* 383 (1992).

80 See, *e.g.*, CIETAC Arbitration proceeding, China, 29 March 1999, available at <http://cisgw3.law.pace.edu/cases/990329c1.html> (*Caffeine case*); CIETAC Arbitration proceeding, China, 29 September 1997, available at <http://cisgw3.law.pace.edu/cases/970929c1.html>; CIETAC Arbitration proceeding, China, 8 October 1997, available at <http://cisgw3.law.pace.edu/cases/971008c1.html>.

81 Similarly Bridge, *International Sale of Goods*, *supra* note 32, at 559 ('A court in a non-declaring State should therefore apply its own choice of law rules on formal validity, taking account of the mandatory rules of another State to whatever extent is consistent with the provisions of the Rome Convention as enacted in the Contracts (Law Applicable) Act 1990').

82 In regard to formal validity, contracts in all forms are permitted, the only exception being that the relevant laws and regulations require, or the parties agree to employ, written form: Art. 10 1999 Contract Law. Art. 36 1999 Contract Law further provides that, notwithstanding the requirement of written form under relevant laws and regulations or as agreed by parties, if one party has fulfilled its major obligations and the other party has accepted performance, the contract has been concluded even though no written form is used.

Chinese rules as to form can no longer be considered as internationally mandatory rules. Thus, the matter of formal validity should be determined by the law applicable pursuant to conflict rules. Interestingly, in the more recent *Carl Hill v. Cixi Old Furniture Trade Co., Ltd.*,[83] where the CISG was considered applicable, the Court, without any choice of law process, held that an oral contract was valid. The scenario was repeated in *Zhuhai Zhongyue New Communication Technology Ltd. v. Theaterlight Electronic Control & Audio System Ltd.*[84] It is unclear from the record whether the effect of China's Article 96 CISG declaration was ever considered by these courts.[85] Nevertheless, given Chinese courts' comfort for direct application of the *lex fori* (which is *pro* freedom as to form in nature), the practical relevance of the above-mentioned approaches might regrettably turn out to be insignificant.

Recently, doubts have been raised as to whether, since current Chinese domestic law no longer requires written form for contracts,[86] China is still entitled to an Article 96 CISG declaration.[87] Here, it is irrelevant whether the legislation of the SAR requires contracts to be concluded in or evidenced by writing. The 'writing' requirement in domestic law is only a precondition for filing an Article 96 CISG declaration.[88] It has no bearing on the effect of the declaration. Therefore, the force of the declaration remains unaffected. The only way to remove the effect of the declaration is to withdraw it in accordance with Article 97(4) CISG.[89] This is not only out of respect for the provisions of the CISG, but is also in the interest of certainty and predictability in international transactions.[90] Having said that, the current inconsistency between China's declaration and Chinese domestic law would easily lead to doubts in practice.[91]

Apparently, the Chinese legislators' attitude towards the formality of contracts has changed to give parties more freedom of choice and meet the ever-changing needs in practice.

83 Cixi People's Court, China, 18 July 2001 ((2001) Cijing Chuzi No. 560), available at <http://cisgw3.law.pace.edu/cases/010718c1.html>.

84 Guangdong High People's Court, China, 11 January 2005 ((2004) Yue Gaofa Minsi Zhongzi No. 274), available at <http://cisgw3.law.pace.edu/cases/050111c1.html>.

85 Interestingly, recent discussion on *Carl Hill v. Cixi Old Furniture Trade Co., Ltd.* poses the question as to whether the Art. 96 CISG declaration should be invoked *sua sponte* by Chinese courts. See J. Huang, 'Direct Application of International Commercial Law in Chinese Courts: Intellectual Property, Trade, and International Transportation', 5 *Manchester Journal of International Economic Law* 105, at 111-113 (3/2008).

86 For the prerequisites to an Art. 96 CISG declaration, see *supra* note 57.

87 See Xiao & Long, *Selected Topics*, *supra* note 21, at 86; Wang & Andersen, *supra* note 22, at 152; Yang, *supra* note 12, at 15.

88 See Flechtner, *Several Texts of the CISG*, *supra* note 9, at 196.

89 Schroeter, *Backbone or Backyard*, *supra* note 10, at 436.

90 Wang & Andersen, *supra* note 22, at 163-164.

91 Similarly Yang, *supra* note 12, at 15.

3.3 *Possible Withdrawal of the Declaration*

Notwithstanding the disagreement in Chinese scholarship and jurisprudence regarding the effect of the declaration, the major concern in China has been the possible withdrawal of the declaration. The dominant view, that the declaration should be withdrawn,[92] is preferable for two main reasons.

First, the rapid socio-economic developments of recent decades have led to a much more open attitude of China towards international trade, which is well manifested by the replacement of the 1985 FECL by the 1999 Contract Law. The conservative position reflected by an Article 96 CISG declaration seems contradictory to this attitude. The inconsistency between the declaration and China's policy favoring international commerce is especially apparent in view of the fact that China has signed the 2005 United Nations Convention on the Use of Electronic Communications in International Contracts,[93] which applies to the use of electronic communications in connection with the formation or performance of a contract between parties whose places of business are in different States. Further, the declaration may also sap the confidence of the foreign parties in Sino-foreign sale of goods.[94] Second, withdrawal of the declaration would eliminate all the confusion in practice concerning the effect of the declaration, and promote certainty and predictability in the international sale of goods.[95]

If China wishes to withdraw the Article 96 CISG declaration, what has been proposed above for the possible withdrawal of China's Article 95 CISG declaration applies *mutatis mutandis* here. In particular, if directive instruments are needed in the event of withdrawal, they should ensure that the withdrawal is effectuated internally on the same day as it takes effect internationally. Moreover, the directive instrument(s) may contain the following guidelines:

> (1) The provisions of Article 11, Article 29, and Part II of this Convention, that allow a contract of sale and its modification and termination by agreement and

92 See Zhang, *supra* note 59, at 572; Y. Xiao, 'On the Application of Rules of Private International Law Treaties in China', in: L. Zeng, *et al.* (Eds.), *Wuhan University Collections of Lectures on International Law*, 80, at 87 (2006); Yang, *supra* note 12, at 13-16; Wang & Andersen, *supra* note 22; Ding, *supra* note 70, at 25. For the contrary minority view, see, *e.g.*, L. Zhu, 'No Conflict Between Chinese Contract Law and the Declaration by the PRC', 1997 *Legal Science* 23, at 24.

93 United Nations Convention on the Use of Electronic Communications in International Contracts, G.A. Res. 60/21, U.N. Doc. A/RES/60/21 (9 December 2005). For discussion on China's experience with the Convention, see, *generally*, Q. He, *The Latest Developments of Uniform Contract Law*, 338-350 (2007).

94 Wang & Andersen, *supra* note 22, at 163.

95 Xiao & Long, *Selected Topics*, *supra* note 21, at 86.

any offer, acceptance, and other indication of intention to be made in any form other than in writing, apply to the formation of a contract only when the proposal for concluding the contract is made on or after the date when China's withdrawal is to take effect.

(2) The provisions of Article 11, Article 29, and Part II of this Convention, that allow a contract of sale and its modification and termination by agreement and any offer, acceptance, and other indication of intention to be made in any form other than in writing, apply only to contracts concluded on or after the date when China's withdrawal is to take effect.

4 The Status of SARs: Article 93 Declarations?

On 1 July 1997, Hong Kong was returned to China. Macao followed suit on 20 December 1999. Ever since, the respective status of the two SARs under the CISG has continuously generated confusion in practice. This undesirable situation has engaged the increasing attention of commentators who are split on the issue.[96] At the outset, two issues should be distinguished; the implementation of the CISG within SARs, and the applicability of the CISG to SARs. The former is cast in an intranational setting, focusing on the implementation of treaties in domestic law. In comparison, the latter is to be addressed from an international perspective, as it centres upon the question whether, according to the CISG, SARs fall within the territorial scope of the Convention. Thus, for example, the opinion that 'the courts in Hong Kong are unlikely to apply the CISG'[97] should not be taken as contrary to the argument that the CISG is applicable to Hong Kong.[98] For present purposes, 'the status of SARs' is concerned with the question whether the CISG is applicable to SARs or, in other words, whether SARs fall within the territorial scope of the CISG.

Under Article 1 CISG, Hong Kong may fall within the sphere of the CISG only if it is (part of) a Contracting State. A region's status as (part of) a Contracting State is important in

96 G.F. Bell, 'Harmonisation of Contract Law in Asia - Harmonising Regionally or Adopting Global Harmonisations - The Example of the CISG', 2005 *Singapore Journal of Legal Studies* 362, at 364, note 10 ('[T]he government of the People's Republic of China has not filed a notification with the Secretary General of the UN and therefore one would assume that the CISG does not apply in Hong Kong'); Chen & Wu, *supra* note 30, note 36. *Contra*: Schroeter, *Hong Kong and Macao*, *supra* note 22.

97 This view was shared by Xiao & Long, *Selected Topics*, *supra* note 21, at 61, note 2.

98 The two issues were appropriately distinguished by L. Wolff, 'Hong Kong's Conflict of Contract Laws: Quo Vadis', 6 *Journal of Private International Law* 465, at 480 (2010). See *Innotex Precision Limited v Horei Image Products, Inc.*, 679 F. Supp. 2d 1356, (N.D. Ga.), United States, 17 December 2009, available at <http://cisgw3.law.pace.edu/cases/091217u1.html>.

determining the applicability of the CISG,[99] not only in the normal cases described under Article 1 CISG, but also in other somewhat special scenarios.[100] Thus, if the status of SARs is unclear, this will lead to divergent decisions on the applicability of the CISG, which will in turn undermine the uniformity of CISG's application. The following discussion will in turn examine the respective status of Hong Kong and Macao under the CISG. Where necessary, the implementation of the Convention in the regions will also be treated briefly.

4.1 *The Case of Hong Kong*

4.1.1 Before the Handover

In 1842, Hong Kong Island was ceded to the United Kingdom under the Treaty of Nanking. Subsequently, the ceded region extended to part of the Kowloon Peninsula and Stonecutter's Island under the Convention of Peking in 1860. In 1898, the Convention for the Extension of Hong Kong Territory granted to the United Kingdom a 99-year lease of Lantau Island and the adjacent northern lands, which became known as the New Territories.[101] Due to their unequal character, these treaties are not recognized by China. Accordingly, it is China's position that sovereignty over the region was never transferred to the U.K.[102] Nevertheless, until the 'handover' of Hong Kong, China was not in possession of the power to conclude international treaties for the region.[103] Consequently, although the CISG was approved by China in 1986 and entered into force in 1988, this had no legal effect for Hong Kong. On the other hand, since the U.K. – which was responsible for the international

99 For an elaboration on the significance of the status as a 'Contracting State', see Schroeter, *Hong Kong and Macao, supra* note 22, at 309-311.

100 See, *e.g.*, a trilateral transaction with the seller in China, the broker in Hong Kong, and the buyer in Germany. This was the scenario in the *Vitamin C case*, CIETAC Arbitration proceeding, China, 18 August 1997, available at <http://cisgw3.law.pace.edu/cases/970818c1.html>. There could also be contracts with multiple parties with one of them from Hong Kong. See, *e.g.*, *Hannaford v. Australian Farmlink Pty Ltd.* Federal Court, Australia, 24 October 2008 (SAD 251 of 2005), available at <http://cisgw3.law.pace.edu/cases/081024a2.html>. For comments on this case, see Spagnolo, *Last Outpost, supra* note 8, at 203-204.

101 X. Zhang (Ed.), *Hong Kong Law in a Nutshell*, 1 (2006).

102 For this reason, it is China's contention that no 'transfer' of sovereignty took place upon the handover on 1 July 1997, since China merely 'resumed the exercise of sovereignty over Hong Kong'. The quoted wording was employed in section 1 of the Sino-British Joint Declaration, full text available at <http://www.hkbu.edu.hk/~pchksar/JD/jd-full2.htm>. Similar position was shared by O. Dörr, 'Cession', in: R. Wolfrum (Ed.), *The Max Planck Encyclopedia of Public International Law*, para. 4 (online ed., 2008), available at <http://www.mpepil.com>. According to Dörr, the so-called New Territories 'always remained under Chinese territorial sovereignty, while their administration was granted to the British for 99 years'.

103 According to Section 4 of the Sino-British Joint Declaration, during the period from 27 May 1985 to 1 July 1997, the U.K. was responsible for the administration of Hong Kong.

relations of Hong Kong at the time – was not a party to the CISG,[104] the Convention was not applicable to Hong Kong.[105]

This status of Hong Kong under the CISG at the time was noted in the Italian decision on *Italdecor s.a.s. v. Yiu's Industries (H.K.) Ltd*,[106] where the performance of a contract between a Hong Kong seller and an Italian buyer was disputed, and the conflict rules led to the application of the law of Italy as a Contracting State.[107] The Milan Court of Appeals correctly based its application of the CISG on Article 1(1)(b) CISG, rather than on Article 1(1)(a) CISG which requires that parties have their places of business in two different Contracting States.[108] Indeed, although the CISG was not in force in Hong Kong, it would still apply if a court of a Contracting State[109] was seized of the case and the requirements under Article 1(1)(b) CISG were satisfied.

In addition to Article 1(1)(b) CISG, there were other grounds on which the CISG was applied to contracts involving parties from Hong Kong. In the Chinese decision on *Xiamen Trade Co. v. Lian Zhong (Hong Kong) Co.*,[110] concerning a contract between parties from Mainland and Hong Kong, the CISG was applied based on agreement by the parties during

104 To date, the U.K. remains a non-contracting state to the CISG. See Status of the CISG, *supra* note 26.

105 Accordingly, the Hong Kong courts would not be bound to apply the CISG, see D.J. Lewis, 'The UN Convention for the International Sale of Goods: Implications for Hong Kong and China', in: 1988 *Law Lectures for Practitioners* 243, at 248.

106 *Italdecor v. Yiu's Industries*, Appellate Court Milan, Italy, 20 March 1998, available at <http://cisgw3.law.pace.edu/cases/980320i3.html>.

107 Initially, the law of Hong Kong was applicable pursuant to conflict rules. However, Hong Kong law could not be ascertained in that case. Consequently, the Court ruled that the Italian law applied.

108 See similarly *Chinese goods case*, Hamburg Arbitration proceeding, Germany, 21 March 1996, available at <http://cisgw3.law.pace.edu/cases/960321g1.html>. Probably also *Kahn Lucas Lancaster, Inc. v. Lark International Ltd.*, U.S. District Court, (S.D.N.Y.), 1997 WL 458785, 6 August 1997, available at <http://cisgw3.law.pace.edu/cases/970806u1.html>. But see *Zheng Hong Li Ltd. (Hong Kong) v. Jill Bert (Switzerland) Ltd.*, Supreme People's Court, China, 20 July 1999 ((1998) Jing Zhongzi No. 208), available at <http://cisgw3.law.pace.edu/cases/990720c1.html>. In that case, the CISG was somehow applied at first instance to a contract concluded in 1996 by parties from Hong Kong and Switzerland respectively. On appeal, the Supreme People's Court ruled that the CISG should not apply, because the parties had chosen to apply Chinese law. The Court did not touch upon the issue as to whether the requirements under Art. 1(1)(a) CISG had been satisfied.

109 Since the CISG was not applicable to Hong Kong, the Hong Kong courts would not be bound to apply the CISG. Rather, the courts would employ their own conflict rules to determine the applicable law of the contract. Nevertheless, if the conflict rules led to the application of the law of a Contracting State, the CISG would apply (as foreign law). See Lewis, *supra* note 105, at 248.

110 Xiamen Intermediate People's Court, China, 5 September 1994, available at <http://cisgw3.law.pace.edu/cases/940905c1.html>. See also *Lianzhong Enterprise Resources (Hong Kong) Ltd. v. Xiamen International Trade & Trust Co.*, Xiamen Intermediate People's Court, China, 20 April 1993, available at <http://cisgw3.law.pace.edu/cases/930420c1.html>.

the hearings.[111] Similarly, in a number of CIETAC arbitrations involving parties from Mainland and Hong Kong, the CISG was applied via the parties' designation during the arbitral proceedings.[112] Moreover, the CISG was somehow referenced in the *Cement case*[113] and *White cardboard scrap paper case*,[114] where Chinese law was the *lex causae*. In these cases, it was unclear whether the CISG merely had persuasive value in the application of Chinese law, or the Convention *per se* was considered as the (jointly) applicable law. Finally, in some other cases, the CISG was applied to contracts involving Hong Kong parties, but the reasons for such application were missing in the decisions.[115] Although these approaches are diverse and sometimes inappropriate, they usually had no bearing on the judges' or arbitrators' opinion on the status of Hong Kong under the CISG. Indeed, the status of Hong Kong seldom gave rise to confusion prior to the handover.

4.1.2 After the Handover

After Hong Kong as a whole was returned to China on 1 July 1997 in accordance with the Joint Declaration of the Government of the United Kingdom of Great Britain and Northern Ireland and the Government of the People's Republic of China on the Question of Hong

111 The approaches taken by these cases may invite criticism for two reasons. First, according to the Chinese conflict rules, the parties have the freedom to choose Chinese law, Hong Kong law, Macao law or foreign law. It may well be argued that choice of international rules such as the CISG in their own right was not permitted. Second, under the Chinese conflict rules then, the designation of the governing law should be made *before* (but *not during*) the hearings. See also L. Spagnolo, '*Iura Novit Curia* and the CISG: Resolution of the Faux Procedural Black Hole', in this volume.

112 See, *e.g.*, CIETAC Arbitration proceeding, China, 5 February 1996, available at <http://cisgw3.law.pace.edu/cases/960205c2.html> (cited as: *Antimony ingot case*); *Caffeine case, supra* note 80; CIETAC Arbitration proceeding, China, 4 April 1996, available at <http://cisgw3.law.pace.edu/cases/960404c1.html>; CIETAC Arbitration proceeding, China, 15 November 1996, available at <http://cisgw3.law.pace.edu/cases/961115c1.html>; CIETAC Arbitration proceeding, China, 4 April 1997, available at <http://cisgw3.law.pace.edu/cases/970404c1.html> (cited as: *Black melon seeds case*); CIETAC Arbitration proceeding, China, 20 November 1997, available at <http://cisgw3.law.pace.edu/cases/971120c1.html>.

113 CIETAC Arbitration proceeding, China, 26 March 1993, available at <http://cisgw3.law.pace.edu/cases/930326c1.html> (noting that 'the applicable law is the Law of China referring to the International Convention').

114 CIETAC Arbitration proceeding, China, post-1992, available at <http://cisgw3.law.pace.edu/cases/930000c2.html> (referencing the CISG in the absence of provisions in Chinese law on a particular issue at stake).

115 See, *e.g.*, CIETAC Arbitration proceeding, China, 27 February 1993, available at <http://cisgw3.law.pace.edu/cases/930227c1.html>; *Lian Zhong (Hong Kong) Co. v. Xiamen Trade Co.*, Xiamen Intermediate People's Court, China, 31 December 1992, available at <http://cisgw3.law.pace.edu/cases/921231c1.html>; *Hong Kong International Industrial C Co. v. Hardware Machinery, Industrial Chemicals and Chinese Medicine Import-Export Co.*, People's Court (court's name unknown), China, 1993 (date unknown), available at <http://cisgw3.law.pace.edu/cases/930000c1.html>; *Zhanjiang Textiles v. Xian Da Fashion*, Guangdong High People's Court, China, 7 March 1994, available at <http://cisgw3.law.pace.edu/cases/940307c1.html>; CIETAC Arbitration Proceeding, China, 30 July 1998, available at <http://cisgw3.law.pace.edu/cases/980730c1.html> (cited as: *Cold rolled steel plates case*).

Kong (hereinafter 'Sino–British Joint Declaration'),[116] confusion arose in practice regarding the status of Hong Kong under the CISG. In effect, the practices in this regard are diverse.

The CISG has been applied to a number of cases involving parties from Hong Kong and a Contracting State, under Article 1(1)(a) CISG. In *CNA Int'l, Inc. v. Guangdon Kelon Electronical Holdings*,[117] the U.S. District Court for the Northern District of Illinois conducted a detailed analysis of the SAR's status in the light of Article 93 CISG. The Court concluded that since China had not made an Article 93 CISG declaration, the CISG was extended to Hong Kong, and hence the Convention should apply. The reasoning of that decision was followed by the U.S. District Court for the Western District of Arkansas in the more recent *Electrocraft Arkansas, Inc. v. Electric Motors, Ltd*[118] . Moreover, the status issue was discussed in passing in the Austrian *Tantalum powder case*,[119] where the Court of Appeal ruled that the CISG should apply to Hong Kong 'due to the restricted autonomy of [the region] in international and foreign affairs'. In a few other cases, however, the courts jumped to the conclusion that the CISG applied (under Art. 1(1)(a) CISG) without touching upon the Convention's applicability to Hong Kong.[120]

The CISG has also been applied in numerous Chinese interregional cases, involving parties from Hong Kong and the Mainland, on grounds other than Article 1(1)(a) CISG. In numerous cases, the Convention was applied based on parties' designation,[121] either by

116 Full text available at <http://www.hkbu.edu.hk/~pchksar/JD/jd-full2.htm>.

117 *CNA Int'l, Inc. v. Guangdong Kelon Electronical Holdings*, 2008 U.S. Dist. LEXIS 113433 (N.D. Ill.), 3 September 2008, available at <http://cisgw3.law.pace.edu/cases/080903u1.html>.

118 *Electrocraft Arkansas, Inc. v. Electric Motors, Ltd.*, 70 UCC Rep.Serv.2d 716, U.S. District Court (W.D. Ark.), 23 December 2009, available at <http://cisgw3.law.pace.edu/cases/091223u1.html>.

119 For a synopsis of the ruling of the Court, see Supreme Court, Austria, 17 December 2003 (7 Ob 275/03x), available at <http://cisgw3.law.pace.edu/cases/031217a3.html>.

120 See, *e.g.*, *Tantalum case*, *supra* note 65; *Index Syndicate Ltd. v. NV Carta Mundi, District Court Turnhout*, Belgium, 18 January 2001 (A/00/691), available at <http://cisgw3.law.pace.edu/cases/010118b1.html; *NV Carta Mundi v. Index Syndicate Ltd.*, Appellate Court Antwerpen, Belgium, 14 February 2002 (2001/AR/551), available at <http://cisgw3.law.pace.edu/cases/020214b1.html>.

121 Sometimes the CISG was also incorporated in the contract by reference. See, *e.g.*, CIETAC Arbitration proceeding, China, 14 February 2002, available at <http://cisgw3.law.pace.edu/cases/030626c1.html>. In that event, the CISG would be taken as contract terms. For further discussion in this respect, see Y. Xiao & W. Long, 'Contractual Party Autonomy in Chinese Private International Law' (cited as: *Contractual Party Autonomy*), in: A. Bonomi, *et al.* (Eds.), *Yearbook of Private International Law*, Vol. 11, 193, at 201 (2009).

choice within the underlying contracts,[122] or during the arbitral proceedings.[123] As demonstrated by the *Wool case*,[124] this approach could also be adopted in international cases involving Hong Kong parties. Equally interesting is the *Ink cartridge case*,[125] where a provision of the CISG was considered as 'a commonly observed international usage' applicable to the issue at stake. Yet in some other Chinese interregional cases where the CISG was applied, the reasons for its application were missing.[126]

By contrast, the applicability of the CISG to Hong Kong was determined in other cases in the negative. In the recent French *Telecommunications products case*,[127] the *Cour de Cassation* concluded that the CISG was not applicable to Hong Kong. In so doing, it ruled that China had made a declaration under Article 93 CISG, thereby precluding Hong Kong from the scope of the CISG. This line of reasoning was followed in the more recent Australian decision on *Hannaford v. Australian Farmlink Pty Ltd.*[128] The applicability issue was also treated in a less extensive manner in *Innotex Precision Limited v. Horei Image Products, Inc.*,[129] in which the U.S. District Court for Georgia also recognized the purported existence of China's Article 93 CISG declaration regarding Hong Kong. The same stance was taken by the Austrian Supreme Court in the *Tantalum powder case*.[130] Finally, in a number of Chinese cases, where the court did not apply the CISG to Hong Kong, the courts

122 See, *e.g.*, CIETAC Arbitration proceeding, China, 2 April 1999, available at <http://cisgw3.law.pace.edu/cases/990402c1.html> (cited as: *Gray cloths case*); CIETAC Arbitration proceeding, China, 10 August 1999, available at <http://cisgw3.law.pace.edu/cases/990810c1.html> (cited as: *Raincoat case*); CIETAC Arbitration proceeding, China, 2000, available at <http://cisgw3.law.pace.edu/cases/000000c1.html>; CIETAC Arbitration proceeding, China, 14 January 2004, available at <http://cisgw3.law.pace.edu/cases/040114c1.html> (the parties agreed that 'the CISG could be referenced').

123 The parties were deemed to designate the CISG usually because they cited the CISG in their pleadings and defenses. See, *e.g.*, CIETAC Arbitration proceeding, China, 29 September 2000, available at <http://cisgw3.law.pace.edu/cases/000929c1.html>; CIETAC Arbitration proceeding, China, 11 February 2000, available at <http://cisgw3.law.pace.edu/cases/000211c1.html>. Probably also CIETAC Arbitration proceeding, China, 5 April 1999, available at <http://cisgw3.law.pace.edu/cases/990405c1.html>.

124 CIETAC Arbitration proceeding, China, 28 February 2005, available at <http://cisgw3.law.pace.edu/cases/050228c1.html>.

125 CIETAC Arbitration proceeding, China, 30 January 2000, available at <http://cisgw3.law.pace.edu/cases/000130c1.html>.

126 See, *e.g.*, CIETAC Arbitration proceeding, China, 23 January 1998, available at <http://cisgw3.law.pace.edu/cases/980123c1.html>.

127 Supreme Court, France, 2 April 2008 (Pourvoi no. 04-17726), available at <http://cisgw3.law.pace.edu/cases/080402f1.html>.

128 See *supra* note 100. For comments on this case, see Spagnolo, *Last Outpost*, *supra* note 8, at 203-204.

129 See *Innotex Precision Limited v. Horei Image Products, Inc.*, 679 F.Supp.2d 1356, U.S. District Court (N.D. Ga.), 17 December 2009, available at <http://cisgw3.law.pace.edu/cases/091217u1.html>.

130 See *supra* note 119.

either mentioned in passing that Hong Kong was not a Contracting State to the CISG,[131] or simply ignored the status issue before reaching their decisions.[132]

Although the approaches employed by judges and arbitrators diverge as to the applicability of CISG to Hong Kong, many of the above-mentioned cases are unhelpful in determining the status of Hong Kong under the CISG.[133] As shown above, in cases where the court did not apply the CISG, the status of Hong Kong was often ignored or left open. Only a few cases have addressed the matter in detail. To further clarify the status of Hong Kong under the CISG, the following discussion will briefly examine two main issues in this respect.

Disqualification as a Contracting State

The first issue that requires clarification is whether Hong Kong can be regarded as a Contracting State. In this respect, the governing provision is Article 91(3) CISG,[134] which provides that a territorial entity may become a Contracting State by way of accession. Under Article 151 of the Basic Law of the Hong Kong Special Administrative Region of the People's Republic of China (hereinafter 'Hong Kong Basic Law'),[135] Hong Kong may on its own conclude agreements in appropriate fields notably including international trade. Apparently, the CISG falls within such fields. However, it should be noted that Article 91(3) CISG is open for accession by *states* only. Although Hong Kong enjoys a high degree of autonomy, it lacks sovereignty over its own territory, and does not have a government

131 See, *e.g.*, *Wuhan Yinfeng Data Network Co. Ltd. and Wuhan Cable Broadcast Television Network Co. Ltd. v. Xu Ming, et al.*, Hubei High People's Court, China, 19 March 2003, available at <http://cisgw3.law.pace.edu/cases/030319c1.html>; *Possehl (HK) Limited v. China Metals & Minerals Import & Export (Shenshen) Corp.*, Guangdong Higher People's Court, China, 2005, available at <http://cisgw3.law.pace.edu/cases/050000c2.html>. See also *Raincoat case*, *supra* note 122 (noting that the CISG could not apply under Article 1(1)(a) CISG, but applying the CISG based on the parties' choice).

132 *Sino-Add (Singapore) PTE. Ltd. v. Karawasha Resources Ltd.*, Guangxi Beihai Maritime Court, China, 5 March 2002, available at <http://cisgw3.law.pace.edu/cases/020305c1.html>.

133 Also noted in *Innotex Precision Limited v. Horei Image Products, Inc.*, *supra* note 129.

134 The CISG is applied as the putative applicable law here. This approach is similar to that employed in conflict of laws situations, such that one must interpret the law that might apply (in the form in which it would apply, presumably as modified by agreement) in order to determine whether and to what extent there is a conflict which needs to be resolved. The same scenario arises for arbitration clauses and determination of their validity. Schlechtriem makes this point in the workshop transcript published by H.M. Flechtner, 'Transcript of a Workshop on the Sales Convention: Leading CISG scholars discuss Contract Formation, Validity, Excuse for Hardship, Avoidance, Nachfrist, Contract Interpretation, Parol Evidence, Analogical Application, and much more', 18 *J. L. & Com.* 191, at 223 (1999). In other words, in order to work out whether the CISG applies, it can arguably be treated as the putative law and its own terms will determine whether it applies in a particular case. For a similar argument for this position, see L. Spagnolo, 'Opening Pandora's Box: Good Faith and Precontractual Liability in the CISG', 21 *Temp. Int'l & Comp. L.J.* 261, at 261-310 (2007).

135 Full text available at <http://www.basiclaw.gov.hk/en/basiclawtext/index.html>.

capable of independently entering into relations of all types with other States.[136] Therefore, Hong Kong cannot meet the criteria for statehood.

Indeed, within the framework of 'One Country, Two Systems', Hong Kong is an SAR of China. This position is not only stipulated by the Chinese Constitution,[137] the Sino-British Joint Declaration[138] and the Hong Kong Basic Law,[139] but is also in line with the practice of the Secretary-General of the United Nations,[140] the depositary for more than 500 multilateral treaties including the CISG. Accordingly, Hong Kong cannot accede to the CISG, and hence cannot become a Contracting State to the Convention in its own right.[141] For this reason, statements such as 'Hong Kong is a Contracting State under the CISG', as made in the *Electrocraft Arkansas, Inc. v. Electric Motors, Ltd*,[142] are to be regarded as inaccurate.

Qualification as Part of a Contracting State

Since Hong Kong cannot become a Contracting State in its own right, the Convention's territorial scope within the meaning of Article 1 may only extend to the region if Hong Kong is part of a 'Contracting State'. To answer the question as to whether Hong Kong meets this criterion, the rules applicable to the issue should be determined.

136 Hong Kong only possesses a limited treaty making power. The SAR may on its own enter into international treaties in limited fields. See Arts. 116, 133–34 and 155 of the Basic Law of the Hong Kong Special Administrative Region of the People's Republic of China, 4 April 1990, available at <http://www.basiclaw.gov.hk/en/basiclawtext/images/Basic_Law.pdf> (cited as: Basic Law). For elaboration on the capacity of Hong Kong to conclude treaties, see A. Aust, *Modern Treaty Law and Practice*, 67-71 (2007). Also A. Peters, 'Treaty Making Power', in: R. Wolfrum (Ed.), *The Max Planck Encyclopedia of Public International Law*, para. 30 (online ed., 2008), available at <www.mpepil.com>. In addition, Art. 152 Basic Law provides that Hong Kong 'may participate in international organizations and conferences *not limited to states*' (emphasis added).

137 See Art. 31 Constitution of the People's Republic of China (cited as: Chinese Constitution). Full text of the Constitution is available at <http://www.lawyee.net>.

138 See Section 2 Sino-British Joint Declaration.

139 See Preamble and Art. 1 Basic Law.

140 See Summary of Practice of the Secretary-General as Depositary of Multilateral Treaties, United Nations Treaty Collection, ST/LEG/7/Rev. 1 (1999), para. 97, available at <http://untreaty.un.org/English/Summary.asp>.

141 Also expressly making this point, J. Shen, 'Cross-Strait Trade and Investment and the Role of Hong Kong' (cited as: *Cross-Strait Trade*), 16 *Wis. Int'l L.J.* 661, at 668 (1998). Similarly M. Bridge, 'A Law for International Sales', 37 *Hong Kong Law Journal* 17, at 17-40 (2007) (observing that Hong Kong is not a Contracting State).

142 *Electrocraft Arkansas, Inc. v. Electric Motors, Ltd*, U.S. District Court (E.D. Ark.), 2010 WL 3307461, 19 August 2010. The contract at issue was between parties from Hong Kong and the U.S. During the proceedings, the parties submitted a joint statement stating that 'Hong Kong is a Contracting State under the CISG'. Based on the statement, the Court held that since 'Hong Kong is a Contracting State', the CISG applied to that action (under Art. 1(1)(a) CISG). For prior proceeding, see *supra* note 118.

In this regard, the Chinese domestic rules are not to be taken as a starting point. True, pursuant to the Sino-British Joint Declaration[143] and the Hong Kong Basic Law,[144] the application to the Hong Kong SAR of international agreements to which China is a party shall be decided by China's Central People's Government, in accordance with the circumstances and needs of the SAR, and after seeking the views of the SAR Government. However, unless permitted by the treaty or consented to by other treaty members, intranational arrangements regarding treaty applicability normally have no binding effect on third parties.[145] Indeed, for conventions which *per se* provide for automatic extension of application to a newly recovered territory, their extension does not depend solely on a decision to that effect by the state concerned.[146] In fact, this position is also endorsed by China. Before the handover of Hong Kong, China had made it clear that it would accept such automatic extension, if any, to Hong Kong of treaties to which China was a party.[147]

Having noted that the extension of the CISG to Hong Kong is to be determined multilaterally, it is then necessary to identify the applicable international rules. In this respect, the public international law rules on succession of states, especially the rule of 'moving treaty boundaries' embodied in Articles 15(b) and 31(1) Vienna Convention on Succession of States in Respect of Treaties (hereinafter the '1978 Succession Convention'),[148] need not be consulted at all. Indeed, neither China nor the U.K. is a party to the 1978 Succession Convention. Moreover, whether or not the 1978 Succession Convention represents established customary norms, and articulates law grounded in consistent State practice, judicial precedent or juristic opinion' is a matter of some controversy.[149] Even if such customary rules exist, one may well question their applicability to the succession of treaties regarding Hong Kong, given that Hong Kong's special case defies easy categorization.[150]

---

143 See Ann. I, Section XI Sino-British Joint Declaration.

144 See Art. 153 Basic Law.

145 Similarly R. Mushkat, 'Hong Kong and Succession of Treaties', 46 *Int'l & Comp. L.Q.* 181, at 194 (1997). Thus, in terms of the application of a multilateral treaty to Hong Kong, a decision made by the Chinese Central People's Government can only have legal effect on third parties if it conforms to the relevant provisions of the treaty, or, in the absence of such provisions, if the decision is not objected to by the parties to that treaty. For detailed discussions in this respect, see Aust, *supra* note 136, at 391.

146 Shen, *Cross-Strait Trade*, *supra* note 141, at 666-667.

147 See *infra* notes 173, 180 and accompanying text.

148 Vienna Convention on Succession of States in Respect of Treaties, Vienna, 23 August 1978, United Nations Treaty Series, Vol. 1946, p. 3. The Convention entered into force on 6 November 1996.

149 Mushkat, *supra* note 145, at 181 (strongly challenging this). But see Aust, *supra* note 136, at 369-371 ('[c]ertain general (customary law) principles can be deduced with reasonable confidence'); Schroeter, *Hong Kong and Macao*, *supra* note 22, at 319 (observing that for practical reasons, the 1978 Succession Convention may be considered as codification of customary public international law).

150 Mushkat, *supra* note 145, at 45-46. According to the author, the originality of the 'One Country, Two Systems' configuration and Hong Kong's highly autonomous status make it questionable to locate 'the instant discourse within the subject known as "state succession"'. The author also observed that the 'moving treaty frontiers'

Even if these rules are considered applicable to the case of Hong Kong, owing to their supplementary nature, they apply only in the absence of an applicable rule in the treaty concerned,[151] that is, in the present case, the CISG. Therefore, one should first look to the CISG to see if it contains any applicable rule.

Within the CISG, Article 93 CISG is relevant to the case of Hong Kong. This Article deals with the applicability of CISG to the territorial units of a Contracting State in which, 'according to its constitution, different systems of law are applicable in relation to the matters dealt with in this Convention'. The provision entitles a contracting state to declare that the CISG is to extend to all of its territorial units or only to some of them.[152] Absent such a declaration, the CISG extends to all of the state's territorial units.[153] Article 93 CISG only explicitly permits declarations by states which, 'at the time of signature, ratification, acceptance, approval or accession', already have a constitutional division of power among their constituent units.[154] Yet the Article is silent on the admissibility of a declaration filed by a contracting state when, as in the case of Hong Kong, its power becomes constitutionally divided upon acquisition of a territory after its approval of the CISG.[155] Nevertheless, as cogently argued by Schroeter, Article 93 CISG expresses a general principle of the CISG within the meaning of Article 7(2) CISG,[156] that is, Contracting States described in Article 93 CISG should be given the chance to decide the applicability of the Convention to their particular territorial units. The implementation of this general principle requires a declaration to be admissible only if made at the time when a state, by acquiring sovereignty over a territory after its approval of the CISG, becomes one with a constitutional division of

---

rule is inapplicable to the succession of treaties regarding Hong Kong. The originality of the 'One Country, Two Systems' regime is also noted by Shen, *Cross-Strait Trade*, *supra* note 141, at 663.

151 Arts. 15(b) and 31(1) 1978 Succession Convention make it clear that the 'moving treaty boundaries' rule does not apply unless the respective treaty does not contain an applicable rule. See Schroeter, *Hong Kong and Macao*, *supra* note 22, at 320 (also pointing out the supplementary nature of the public international law rules).

152 See Art. 93(1) CISG.

153 See Art. 93(4) CISG.

154 See Art. 93(1) CISG.

155 Arguably, this is a matter governed by the CISG but not expressly settled in it, and hence an internal gap of the Convention. See Schroeter, *Hong Kong and Macao*, *supra* note 22, at 323.

156 It is controversial whether Art. 7 CISG governs the interpretation of Art. 93 and other final provisions of the Convention. For authorities arguing for the application of Arts. 31-33 Vienna Treaty Convention, in lieu of Art. 7 CISG, as the governing rules of the final provisions of CISG, see, *e.g.*, Enderlein & Maskow, *supra* note 79, at 54. Other writers have more convincingly advocated the priority of Art. 7 CISG over Arts. 31-33 of the Vienna Treaty Convention. See, *e.g.*, U. Schroeter, *Backbone or Backyard*, *supra* note 10, at 428.

power.[157] This interpretation has been followed by the court in *CNA Int'l, Inc. v. Guangdon Kelon Electronical Holdings.*[158]

China did not have constitutionally autonomous units until Hong Kong was returned in 1997, years after China's approval of the CISG. Since then, China has become a Contracting State in which, according to its constitution,[159] different systems of law are applicable to international sales issues covered by the CISG,[160] thereby falling within the scope of the above-mentioned principle underlying Article 93 CISG. Here, it should be noted that some commentators consider Article 93 CISG of interest only in relation to states with federal systems.[161] True, Article 93 CISG is often labelled a 'federation clause'[162] or 'federal state clause'.[163] However, this label alone 'carries no significance for the interpretation of the clause'.[164] Nor should the fact that Article 93 CISG was requested and has since been utilised by federal states[165] prejudice the applicability of the provision to China, a non-federal state[166] with constitutional division of power. Accordingly, Article 93 CISG applies *mutatis mutandis* to the question whether the CISG extends to Hong Kong.[167]

157 Schroeter, *Hong Kong and Macao, supra* note 22, at 323-324. According to Schroeter, the same conclusion can be reached 'when relying on the general law on the succession of States, which accepts that a newly independent State may formulate a reservation when making a notification of succession establishing its status as a Contracting State to a multilateral treaty'. *Id.*, at 324. To the present author, Schroeter's interpretation of Art. 93 CISG is desirable in that it enables the CISG to adapt to future legal developments in the Contracting States.

158 See *supra* note 117 (expressly citing Schroeter, *ibid*).

159 Art. 31 Chinese Constitution.

160 For a general discussion on Chinese interregional conflict of laws arising from the 'One Country, Two System' under the Constitution, see J. Huang & A.X. Qian, 'One Country, Two Systems, Three Law Families, and Four Legal Regions', (Spring) 5 *Duke Journal Comparative and International Law* 289, at 303-307 (1995).

161 See Honnold & Flechtner (Eds.), *supra* note 32, at 700, para. 468; Bridge, *International Sale of Goods, supra* note 32, at 542, n. 207. Probably also P. Schlechtriem, I. Schwenzer & P. Hachem, in: *Commentary on the CISG* (3rd ed.), *supra* note 3, Art. 93 para. 1.

162 See Enderlein & Maskow, *supra* note 79, at 375, para. 2.

163 See P. Winship, 'The Scope of the Vienna Convention on International Sales Contracts', in: N. Galston & H. Smit (Eds)., *International Sales: The United Nations Convention on Contracts for the International Sale of Goods*, Matthew Bender (1984), Ch. 1, at 1-1 to 1-53; Flechtner, *Several Texts of the CISG, supra* note 9, at 194 *et seq.* But see Aust, *supra* note 136, at 210-211 (categorizing Art. 93 CISG as a 'territorial clause').

164 Schroeter, *Hong Kong and Macao, supra* note 22, at 320. See also M. Torsello, 'Reservations to International Uniform Commercial Law Conventions', *Uniform Law Review*, 85 at 94 (2000-1).

165 Art. 93 CISG was included at the request of Canada and Australia. See Enderlein & Maskow, *supra* note 79, Art. 93 para. 1. So far, Australia, Canada, Denmark, the Netherlands and New Zealand have made use of Art. 93 CISG. See Status of the CISG, *supra* note 26.

166 In China, it is generally believed that China has a unitary government. See Y. Zhou (Ed.), *Constitution*, 245-254 (2000). But see Schroeter, *Hong Kong and Macao, supra* note 22, at 324 (seemingly regarding China as 'a non-unitary state').

167 For an elaboration on the applicability of Art. 93 CISG to the case of Hong Kong, see Schroeter, *Hong Kong and Macao, supra* note 22, at 320-322.

So far, there is only one document that might serve as China's Article 93 CISG declaration regarding Hong Kong, *i.e.*, the Note Regarding Multilateral Treaties Applicable to Hong Kong SAR as of 1 July 1997 (hereinafter 'Note Regarding Hong Kong'), sent from the Permanent Representative of the P.R. China to the Secretary-General of the UN, on 20 June 1997.[168] In fact, most cases that have directly addressed the status of Hong Kong have focused on this Note. It is therefore important to examine whether the Note Regarding Hong Kong qualifies as a declaration under Article 93 CISG.

To be a valid Article 93 CISG declaration, the Note Regarding Hong Kong must satisfy three requirements. The first two were noted in *Innotex Precision Limited v. Horei Image Products, Inc.*[169] First, pursuant to Article 97(2) CISG, a declaration under the CISG should be in writing; second, under Article 93(2) CISG, the declaration must be notified to the Secretary-General of the UN, the depositary for the CISG. As mentioned, the Note Regarding Hong Kong, obviously made in writing, was deposited with the Secretary-General on 20 June 1997. It therefore satisfies both requirements. However, there is a third requirement. Article 93(2) CISG requires that a declaration expressly state the territorial units to which the CISG extends. In this regard, a list of treaties applicable to Hong Kong as of 1 July 1997 was annexed to the Note Regarding Hong Kong.[170] The CISG was not explicitly mentioned therein. For this reason, the *Cour de Cassation* held in the *Telecommunications products case*[171] that China had effectuated a declaration under Article 93 CISG. To the present author, however, the court's ruling is hardly convincing,[172] since the Note Regarding Hong Kong also stated:

> With respect to any other treaty not listed in the Annexes to this Note, to which the People's Republic of China is or will be a party, in the event that it is decided to apply such treaty to the Hong Kong Special Administrative Region, the Government of the People's Republic of China will carry out separately the formalities for such application. *For the avoidance of doubt, no separate formalities will need to be carried out by the Government of the People's Republic of China with respect to treaties which fall within the category of foreign affairs or*

168 The Note Regarding Hong Kong was sent to the Secretary General of the UN in Chinese and English. The English version of the Note Regarding Hong Kong was a translation from the Chinese original. For the Chinese original, see Gazette of the State Council (in Chinese), 1997, Issue 39, at 1688-1701. For the English translation, see 36 *International Law Materials* 1675 (1997).

169 See *supra* note 129. Also noted by Schroeter, *Hong Kong and Macao, supra* note 22, at 324.

170 See *supra* note 168, Ann. I & II, at 1676-1683.

171 See *supra* note 127.

172 See also Wolff, *supra* note 98, at 480.

defence or which, owing to their nature and provisions, must apply to the entire territory of a State.[173]

Accordingly, as correctly noted in *CNA Int'l, Inc. v. Guangdon Kelon Electronical Holdings*,[174] the list of treaties annexed to the Note Regarding Hong Kong is not exhaustive. In determining whether the CISG falls within the category of treaties which, 'owing to their nature and provisions, must apply to the entire territory of a State', one must look to Article 93 CISG which in turn points back to the clause cited above. This 'chicken and egg' situation demonstrates that the Note Regarding Hong Kong is far from an express statement as required by Article 93(2) CISG.[175] Therefore the Note Regarding Hong Kong does not constitute an Article 93 CISG declaration.

According to Article 93(4) CISG, in the absence of an Article 93 CISG declaration by a Contracting State, the CISG is to extend to all territorial units of that State. Since China has not filed an Article 93 CISG declaration regarding Hong Kong, the CISG extended *ipso iure* to the SAR on 1 July 1997. Driven by compelling policy considerations,[176] this interpretation is aimed at providing a better legal environment for international transactions involving Hong Kong.

It is worth mentioning that the Hong Kong Department of Justice publishes an online list of treaties that are currently in force and applicable to Hong Kong,[177] but the list does not include the CISG. In line with this position, there is a lack of implementing legislation for the CISG in Hong Kong. Since Hong Kong follows a dualist approach to effectuating treaties in domestic law,[178] the CISG has not taken effect in Hong Kong. Nevertheless, bearing in mind that Article 93 is the applicable provision for present purposes, it can be said with confidence that the position hitherto taken by the Hong Kong Department of Justice has no binding effect on third parties, and hence does not affect Hong Kong's status as part of a 'Contracting State' within the meaning of Article 1 CISG.[179] The automatic

173 *Supra* note 168 at IV (emphasis added).

174 See *supra* note 117.

175 Similarly Schroeter, *Hong Kong and Macao*, *supra* note 22, at 324 (observing that the Note Regarding Hong Kong 'is silent on the issue of UN Sales Convention').

176 For further discussion, see *infra* notes 222-226 and accompanying text. The policy considerations articulated there apply here as well.

177 See Hong Kong Department of Justice, International Law Division, List of Treaties in Force and Applicable to the Hong Kong Special Administrative Region, available at <http://www.legislation.gov.hk/interlaw.htm>.

178 See Aust, *supra* note 136, at 234.

179 This was also noted by the court in *CNA Int'l, Inc. v. Guangdon Kelon Electronical Holdings*, *supra* note 117, which made a fine point that the absence of CISG on the list of Hong Kong Department of Justice 'is not determinative' to the status of Hong Kong under the CISG. Similarly Schroeter, *Hong Kong and Macao*, *supra* note 22, at 325; Wolff, *supra* note 98, at 479-480.

extension of the CISG to Hong Kong, it is submitted, is also in line with the Chinese central government's express intention to recognize in general the automatic extension of treaties which, 'owing to their nature and provisions, must apply to the entire territory of a State'.[180]

4.2 *The Case of Macao*

4.2.1 Before the Handover

In the past four centuries until 20 December 1999, Macao was separated from China and connected with Portugal. Contrary to some commentators' view that Macao was once a colonized territory of Portugal,[181] China took the position that Macao was not a Portuguese colony.[182] This position was not only recognized by the UN General Assembly,[183] but was also accepted by Portugal when China and Portugal established diplomatic relations in 1979.[184] Nevertheless, until the handover of Macao, China did not possess the power to conclude international treaties for the region.[185] Thus, although China approved the CISG in 1986, this had no legal effect for Macao. On the other hand, since Portugal – which at the time was responsible for the international relations of Macao – was not a party to the CISG,[186] the Convention was not applicable to Macao.

---

180 See the emphasized clause in the Note Regarding Hong Kong, *supra* note 173.

181 For a brief account of the development of Macao's historical status from a colony with special capacities, later to a territory artificially lumped with other Portuguese possessions in Asia, then to a territory leased from China, and ultimately to a territory under (transitional) Portuguese administration until 20 December 1999, see P. Cardinal, 'Macao: The Internationalization of an Historical Autonomy', XLI (122) *Boletin Mexicano de Derecho Comparado* 637, at 638-644 (2008). See also D. Kugelmann, 'Macau', in: R. Wolfrum (Ed.), *The Max Planck Encyclopedia of Public International Law*, paras. 2-5 (online ed., 2008), available at <www.mpepil.com>.

182 For this reason, it is China's contention that no 'transfer' of sovereignty took place upon the handover on 20 December 1999, since China merely 'resumed the exercise of sovereignty over Macao'. The quoted wording was employed in section 1 of the Sino-Portuguese Joint Declaration, full text available at <http://bo.io.gov.mo/bo/i/88/23/dc/en/>. See also W. Deng, 'On the Basic Law of Macao', *SAR* 18-31 (in Chinese, 2007).

183 According to a memorandum dated 8 March 1972, China formally stated this position at the United Nations. At its 27th session held on 8 November 1972, the UN General Assembly adopted a resolution containing a list of colonized territories. Macao was not included on the list. See Cardinal, *supra* note 181, at 642, note 14.

184 On 8 February 1979, the Joint Communique of the People's Republic of China and the Republic of Portugal was issued, thereby establishing the diplomatic relations of the two countries. On that occasion, China and Portugal reached the consensus that Macao is a Chinese territory.

185 According to Section 3 Sino-Portuguese Joint Declaration, during the period from 15 January 1988, on which the Declaration entered into force, to 20 December 1999, Portugal was responsible for the administration of Macao.

186 To date, Portugal remains a non-contracting state to the CISG. See Status of the CISG, *supra* note 26.

Interestingly, the CISG was negligently applied to Macao in a number of CIETAC arbitrations. In the *Wool case,*[187] involving parties from Mainland China and Macao, the CISG was held applicable under Article 1(1)(a) CISG because Portugal, to which Macao 'belonged', was mistaken for a Contracting State to the CISG. The same problem existed in the *Natural rubber case*[188] and the *Steel channels case.*[189] Nonetheless, the inappropriate application of the CISG in these cases mainly derived from the courts' unfamiliarity with the contracting status of the Convention, and hence is insignificant in determining the status of Macao under the CISG.

4.2.2 After the Handover

Since China's resumption of sovereignty over Macao on 20 December 1999 in accordance with the Joint declaration of the Government of the People's Republic of China and The Government of the Republic of Portugal on the question of Macao (hereinafter 'Sino-Portuguese Joint Declaration'),[190] the status of Macao under the CISG has been engaging increasing attention. So far, no reported cases have applied the CISG to Macao after the handover. This fact alone is unimportant in exploring the status of Macao, as none of the cases that failed to apply the CISG to Macao has made even passing mention of the issue. In fact, at many points, the case of Macao is similar and sometimes even identical to that of Hong Kong. This means that in regard to Macao, the current situation is not at all unproblematic. The following discussion will seek to clarify the situation by addressing the same two main issues discussed above in relation to Hong Kong.

Disqualification for a Contracting State

The first issue is whether Macao can be considered a Contracting State to the CISG. Again, the governing provision is Article 91(3) CISG,[191] according to which a territorial entity may become a Contracting State by way of accession. Under Article 136 Basic Law of the Macao Special Administrative Region of the People's Republic of China (hereinafter 'Macao Basic Law'),[192] Macao may independently, using the name 'Macao, China,' conclude agreements on international trade. However, Article 91(3) CISG is open for accession by *states* only. Similar to Hong Kong, Macao enjoys a high degree of autonomy but lacks

187 CIETAC Arbitration proceeding, China, 27 February 1996, available at <http://cisgw3.law.pace.edu/cases/960227c1.html>.
188 CIETAC Arbitration proceeding, China, 4 September 1996, available at <http://cisgw3.law.pace.edu/cases/960904c1.html>.
189 CIETAC Arbitration proceeding, China, 18 November 1996, available at <http://cisgw3.law.pace.edu/cases/961118c1.html>.
190 Full text available at <http://bo.io.gov.mo/bo/i/88/23/dc/en/>.
191 See *supra* note 134.
192 Basic Law of the Macao Special Administrative Region of the People's Republic of China (cited as: Macao Basic Law), full text available at <http://www.mfa.gov.cn/eng/wjb/zzjg/tyfls/tyfl/2626/t15467.htm>.

sovereignty, and its government is incapable of independently entering into all types of relations with other States.[193] Therefore, Macao lacks the required statehood. Like Hong Kong, Macao is an SAR of China, a position not only stipulated by the Chinese Constitution,[194] the Sino-Portuguese Joint Declaration[195] and the Macao Basic Law,[196] but also in line with the practice of the Secretary-General of the UN, depositary for the CISG. Thus, Macao cannot accede to the CISG, and hence cannot become a Contracting State to the Convention in its own right.

Qualification as Part of a Contracting State

The second, and more important, question is whether Macao is part of a 'Contracting State' within the meaning of Article 1 CISG. Given the fact that Macao cannot become a Contracting State to the CISG in its own name, its qualification as part of a Contracting State is the only way by which the Convention's territorial scope may extend to the region. The governing rules of the issue should be first identified.

With respect to the application to Macao of international agreements to which China is a party, the mechanism is similar to that for Hong Kong. According to the Sino-Portuguese Joint Declaration[197] and the Macao Basic Law,[198] the matter is to be decided by China's Central People's Government, in accordance with the circumstances and needs of the SAR, and after seeking the views of the SAR Government. As has been articulated above,[199] since the CISG *per se* provides for automatic extension of application to a newly acquired territory, its extension does not depend solely on a decision to that effect by China. Therefore, China's domestic arrangement is not determinative for present purposes, but rather the applicable multilateral rules. The lines of reasoning given in the case of Hong Kong[200] make sense here as well. Thus, the public international law rules on succession of states need not be referenced in the first place, as they are supplementary to and supplanted by Article 93 CISG which contains applicable rules on the issue.

---

193 Macao only possesses a limited treaty making power. The SAR may on its own enter into international treaties in limited fields. See Arts. 112, 136 and 140 Basic Law of Macao. See *supra* note 192. For elaboration on its limited capacity to conclude treaties, see Aust, *supra* note 136. In addition, Art. 137 Macao Basic Law provides that Macao 'may participate in international organizations and conferences *not limited to states*' (emphasis added).

194 See Art. 31 Chinese Constitution.

195 See Section 2 Sino-Portuguese Joint Declaration.

196 See Preamble and Art. 1 Macao Basic Law.

197 See Ann. I, Section VIII Sino-Portuguese Joint Declaration.

198 See Art. 138 Macao Basic Law.

199 See *supra* note 145-147 and accompanying text.

200 See *supra* notes 148-167 and accompanying text.

Also similar to the case of Hong Kong, so far there is only one document that might serve as China's Article 93 CISG declaration regarding Macao, *i.e.*, the Note Regarding International Treaties Applicable to Macao SAR as of 20 December 1999 (hereinafter 'Note Regarding Macao')[201] sent from the Permanent Representative of the P.R. China to the UN Secretary-General on 13 December 1999. Obviously, the Note Regarding Macao was made in writing, and notified to the UN Secretary-General, the depositary for the CISG, thereby satisfying the first two requirements for a valid Article 93 CISG declaration.[202] With respect to the third requirement, that is, that a declaration should expressly state the territorial units to which the CISG extends, a list of treaties applicable to Macao as of 20 December 1999 was annexed to the Note Regarding Macao.[203] The CISG was not mentioned therein. Furthermore, the Note also stated:

> With respect to any other treaty not listed in the Annexes to this Note, to which the People's Republic of China is or will be a party, in the event that it is decided to apply such treaty to the Macao Special Administrative Region, the Government of the People's Republic of China will carry out separately the formalities for such application.[204]

The Note Regarding Macao was modelled on the Note Regarding Hong Kong in many respects but excepting one: unlike its Hong Kong counterpart, the clause cited above did *not* stipulate that

> *[f]or the avoidance of doubt, no separate formalities will need to be carried out by the Government of the People's Republic of China with respect to treaties which fall within the category of foreign affairs or defence or which, owing to their nature and provisions, must apply to the entire territory of a State.*[205]

One might infer from this omission that China intended to preclude the automatic extension to Macao of any treaties not mentioned in the annexed list. However, this omission may not be as significant as it first appears. Over the years, China has demonstrated to the international community its commitment to fulfil international treaty obligations. Thus, to the extent that the CISG – to which China is a Contracting State – extends

201 Full text available at <http://www.people.com.cn/GB/42272/42280/43266/43268/3134018.html>.
202 For the three requirements for a valid declaration under Art. 93 CISG, see *supra* notes 169-170 and accompanying text.
203 Ann. I & II Note Regarding Macao.
204 Clause IV Note Regarding Macao.
205 See *supra* note 173 (emphasis added).

to Macao according to its own provisions, it goes without saying that China would not object to such extension without justification.

Nonetheless, if we assume for the moment that the above-mentioned inference from the omission is correct, it would still be premature to conclude that by annexation of an apparently exhaustive list of treaties, China made a declaration under Article 93 CISG. In this regard, attention is drawn to Article 93(2) CISG, which requires that a declaration 'state *expressly* the territorial units to which the CISG extends'. This means that a declaration must (a) directly mention the territorial units to which the CISG extends; or (b) less desirably but nevertheless 'expressly', directly specify the territorial units to which the CISG does not apply; or (c) both positively and negatively identify the territorial units to which the CISG applies. The first formula was followed by Canada[206] and the Netherlands,[207] the second formula by Denmark[208] and New Zealand,[209] and the third by Australia.[210] If one compares the declarations by these states with the Note Regarding Macao, one may well reach the conclusion that the Note is far from an express statement regarding the CISG and Macao. Furthermore, even if the Note was intended as an Article 93 CISG declaration, the existence of such a declaration does not appear to have been noticed by the depositary for the CISG.[211] Arguably, therefore, the Note did not even make 'a *prima facie* case' for qualification as an Article 93 CISG declaration. Thus, for the sake of legal certainty,[212] the Note Regarding Macao should not be treated as an Article 93 CISG declaration.

Again, under Article 93(4) CISG, in the absence of an Article 93 CISG declaration by a Contracting State, the Convention is to extend to all territorial units of that state. Since China has not filed an Article 93 CISG declaration regarding Macao, the CISG extended

206 Canada filed an Art. 93 CISG declaration upon accession to the CISG, stating that the CISG would extend to Alberta, British Columbia, Manitoba, New Brunswick, Newfoundland, Nova Scotia, Ontario, Prince Edward Island and the Northwest Territories. With two subsequent declarations received on 9 April and 29 June 1992 respectively, Canada extended the application of the CISG first to Quebec and Saskatchewan, and then to Yukon. In a notification received on 18 June 2003, Canada extended the application of the Convention to Nunavut. See Status of the CISG, *supra* note 26.

207 The Netherlands declared that the CISG applied to the Kingdom in Europe and Aruba, *id.*

208 Upon signature, Denmark declared '...under paragraph 1 of article 93 that the Convention shall not apply to the Faroe Islands and Greenland...'. The declaration was subsequently confirmed upon ratification, *id.*

209 New Zealand expressly declared the non-application of the CISG to the Cook Islands, Niue and Tokelau. See Status of the CISG, *supra* note 26.

210 Upon accession to the CISG, Australia declared: 'The Convention shall apply to all Australian States and mainland territories and to all external territories except the territories of Christmas Island, the Cocos (Keeling) Islands and the Ashmore and Cartier Islands.' *Ibid.*

211 So far, no Art. 93 CISG declaration by China has been mentioned on the UN's webpage concerning the status of the CISG. See Status of the CISG, *supra* note 26.

212 P. Schlechtriem, *et al.*, in: *Commentary on the CISG* (3rd ed.), *supra* note 3, Art. 93 para. 4 (also emphasizing the need for legal certainty).

to Macao on the date of the handover. Yet like Hong Kong, the Macao government publishes an online list of treaties that are currently in force and applicable to Macao, but fails to include the CISG on that list.[213] Apart from the question as to whether implementing legislation is needed for the application of CISG in Macao,[214] this situation alone would affect its implementation in Macao. Nevertheless, for the same reasons given in relation to Hong Kong,[215] this does not undermine Macao's status as part of a 'Contracting State' within the meaning of Article 1 CISG.

4.2.3 Possible Improvements from the *Status Quo*

The foregoing discussion sheds some light on the underlying problems in practice regarding the status of SARs under the CISG. The contributing factors to the current uncertainty are multifold. In the increasing number of cases explicitly addressing the issue, the respective Notes regarding Hong Kong and Macao have led to divided decisions on the status of SARs. To some extent, this divergence is also attributable to the courts' and arbitrators' varying acquaintance with the CISG as well as their interpretations of the Notes. However, the divergence seems also to be due to differences in how well parties were represented.[216]

Moreover, in view of the cases where no reasons were given for holding that the CISG applied to Hong Kong,[217] one may well suspect that in practice, courts and arbitrators ignore the doubt surrounding the applicability of the CISG to SARs. Thus, if neither party challenges the applicability of the CISG, it is not inconceivable that courts and arbitrators may jump to the conclusion that the CISG applies to SARs. In particular, this may occur when the issue is litigated or arbitrated outside of China, in the absence of Hong Kong counsel and Hong Kong arbitrators. By contrast, if the matter is brought before the courts in Hong Kong, due to the lack of implementing legislation of the CISG in the SAR, the courts will simply hold the CISG inapplicable. Consequently, this situation not only undermines the uniformity of the application of CISG, but also encourages forum shopping. Indeed, the current uncertainty is highly undesirable to say the least.

---

213 The list is available at <http://en.io.gov.mo/Legis/International/1.aspx>.

214 For a synopsis of the pros and cons concerning the approaches to the implementation of treaties in Macao after the handover, see A.M. de Magalhães, 'The Validity of the International Agreements of the Human Rights in the Juridical Order of the Special Administrative Region of Macau', in: J.C. Oliveira & P. Cardinal (Eds.), *One Country, Two Systems, Three Legal Orders - Perspectives of Evolution*, 608, at 608-612 (2009).

215 See *supra* notes 177-180 and accompanying text.

216 See *supra* notes 119, 127, 142 and accompanying text.

217 See *supra* notes 113, 114, 115, 120, 126 and accompanying text.

Whatever the reason for not filing declarations for the two SARs,[218] something must be done in order to clarify the current situation. First and foremost, the matter must be brought to the attention of the Chinese central government and the SAR governments. It is noteworthy that the lists of treaties annexed to the Notes regarding SARs were arrangements jointly made by the parties to the respective Joint Declarations.[219] Since neither the U.K. nor Portugal was a Contracting State, they are unlikely to have taken the CISG into account. On the other hand, China may have overlooked the legal effect of Article 93 CISG. In either case, attention is drawn to China's statement that 'no separate formalities will need to be carried out with respect to treaties which [...] owing to their nature and provisions, must apply to the entire territory of a State'.[220] This statement stands in line with China's commitment to honour its international treaty obligations,[221] including the CISG to which China is a Contracting State.

Currently, there are compelling reasons to apply the CISG to SARs and to implement it in the regions. Extension of the CISG to SARs will not only further the goals of the CISG, *i.e.*, to promote worldwide uniformity and enhance legal certainty in international trade, but is also in the very interests of the SARs themselves. To date, Hong Kong is one of the world's largest trading entities.[222] Most of Hong Kong's major trading partners, including Australia, Germany, Japan, Korea, Singapore, The Netherlands, and the U.S.,[223] are Con-

218 For further discussion on the desirability of clarification, see F. Yang, 'Hong Kong's Adoption of the CISG: Why do we need it now?', in this volume.
Wolff observed that 'one may speculate if this is because a Hong Kong-related declaration may lead to the politically sensitive question as to whether a similar declaration is required in relation to Taiwan, which is currently not a CISG member [...]', see Wolff, *supra* note 98, at 480.

219 In the case of Hong Kong, a Sino-British Joint Liaison Group was set up to ensure a smooth transfer of government in 1997. The Group considered, *inter alia*, actions to be taken by the two Governments to ensure the continued application of international rights and obligations affecting Hong Kong. See Sino-British Joint Declaration, *supra* note 116, Ann. II, Section 5(b). In respect of Macao, a Sino-Portuguese Joint Group was set up to conduct consultations on actions to be taken by China and Portugal, to enable the Macao SAR to maintain and develop external economic, cultural and other relations. See Sino-Portuguese Joint Declaration, *supra* note 190, Ann. II, Part I, Section 2(c).

220 See *supra* note 173.

221 At the UN Security Council Summit dated 23 September 2010, Chinese Premier Wen Jiabao stated that China 'will earnestly fulfil [its] international obligations and shoulder [its] due responsibilities'. See Statement by Chinese Premier Wen Jiabao at the UN Security Council Summit, available at <http://www.china-un.org/eng/hyyfy/t757366.htm>.

222 In 2009, Hong Kong ranked 11th among leading world traders accounting for 2.7% of overall world trade. See Hong Kong SAR's Position in World Merchandise Trade in terms of Total Trade, available at <http://www.tid.gov.hk/english/aboutus/publications/tradestat/tradestat_maincontent.html>. In 2008, Hong Kong ranked 13th among the leading world merchandise traders. See World Trade Organization, Leading Exporters and Importers in World Merchandise Trade (2008), at 12, Table I.8, available at <http://www.wto.org/english/res_e/statis_e/statis_e.htm>.

223 For a list of Hong Kong's major trading partners, see Hong Kong's Domestic Exports in 2009 by Main Destination, available at <http://www.tid.gov.hk/english/abou tus/publications/tradestat/ex09des.html>;

tracting States to the CISG.[224] Thus, extending the CISG to Hong Kong would mean a substantial part of Hong Kong's merchandise trade would be covered by the CISG, thereby removing legal barriers in Hong Kong-related international trade to a considerable extent. It should be kept in mind that it is China's aspiration to maintain 'the prosperity and stability of Hong Kong'.[225] The accomplishment of this goal would not be possible without a transparent and stimulating legal environment for international transactions involving Hong Kong.[226] Many of these reasons hold good for Macao as well.

Given these reasons, it is advisable that the SAR governments petition the Chinese central government to take action to improve the *status quo*. Alternatively, the Chinese central government can take the initiative, and seek the views of the SAR governments before taking further steps. Actions to be taken may include, *inter alia*, communications to the depositary of the CISG, clarification of the wording of the two Notes, and, in the event that China reaches the fortunate decision to implement the CISG in SARs, enactment of implementing legislation of the Convention, if necessary.[227]

5 Application of the CISG to SARs in Typical Scenarios

Since at this stage no action has been taken to officially clarify the status of SARs, it is important that judges and arbitrators, when making their decisions on the applicability of the CISG to SARs, accord sufficient attention to the text of the CISG and to the policy considerations articulated above. To illustrate how this could be done, the following discussion will explore the application of the CISG to SARs in four typical scenarios.

Hong Kong's Re-exports in 2009 by Main Destination, available at <http://www.tid.gov.hk/english/aboutus/publications/tradestat/rx09des.html>; Hong Kong's Imports in 2009 by Suppliers, available at <http://www.tid.gov.hk/english/aboutus/publications/tradestat/im09sup.html>.

224 See Status of the CISG, *supra* note 26.

225 See the Sino-British Joint Declaration, first paragraph, *supra* note 116. Similar statement regarding Macao was made in the Sino-Portugese Joint Declaration, first paragraph.

226 Similarly C. Xu, 'On the Continued Application of Economic Treaties to Hong Kong After 1997', 1996 *Legal Science* 56, at 59.

227 As mentioned, implementing legislation is definitely needed in the case of Hong Kong. In the event that the implementing legislation is promulgated in Hong Kong, for the sake of legal certainty, the legislation should require that courts in the region apply the CISG only to contracts concluded after the legislation enters into force. Yet such legislation would only be binding in Hong Kong. Courts in foreign countries may nevertheless hold otherwise.

5.1 *Parties: SAR versus Contracting State (other than China), Forum: Contracting State*

As has been explained, the CISG has internationally extended to Hong Kong and Macao under Article 93 CISG. Thus, if the present suit is filed before a court in a Contracting State, *e.g.* the U.S., the court should apply the CISG through Article 1(1)(a) CISG, provided that the parties have not opted out of the Convention. If, however, a Hong Kong court is seized of such a case, it is unlikely to apply the CISG on the same ground. This is because of Hong Kong's dualist approach to the implementation of international law, and there is no implementing legislation for the CISG. Similarly, given the fact that the CISG is not included in the official list of treaties applicable to Macao, it is unlikely that a Macao court will apply the CISG should it be seized of the case.[228]

It is worth mentioning that since Hong Kong and Macao have become part of China, a Contracting State, China's declarations under Article 95 and Article 96 CISG respectively should also extend to the two SARs.[229] This conclusion conforms to the principle of continuity. In the present scenario, the Article 96 CISG declaration is relevant. When the present suit is brought to an SAR court, there is no doubt – putting aside for the moment the lack of implementing legislation– that the declaration is binding.[230]

On the other hand, if the case is before a U.S. court, doubts may arise as to whether the Chinese Article 96 CISG declaration has the same effect, for the U.S. has not made a declaration under Article 96 CISG. Indeed, opinions are divided on whether an Article 96 CISG declaration by one Contracting State should also be observed by other Contracting States which themselves have not filed a similar declaration.[231] In the present author's view, the effect of an Article 96 CISG declaration derives from the provisions of the CISG which are part of the law of a Contracting State, regardless of whether that state is a declaration state. Thus, in the present example, China's Article 96 CISG declaration is foreign to the U.S. court, but its effect is not,[232] because the effect derives from Articles 12 and 96 CISG which is part of the U.S. law. Accordingly, the court should observe the wording of Articles

228 Similarly Wu, *supra* note 21, at note 22.

229 See Schroeter, *Hong Kong and Macao*, *supra* note 22, at 328.

230 Here, it is irrelevant whether the legislation of the SAR requires contracts to be concluded in or evidenced by writing. See *supra* note 88 and accompanying text.

231 For opinions in the affirmative, see Flechtner, *ibid*, at 197; Schroeter, *Backbone or Backyard*, *supra* note 10, at 447. *Contra*: M. Bridge, 'Harmonized Sales Law: Choice of Law Issues', in: J.J. Fawcett, *et al.* (Eds.), *International Sale of Goods in the Conflict of Laws* (cited as: *Uniform and Harmonized Sales Law*), para. 16.140 (2005); Torsello, *supra* note 164, at 105-106. Probably also Basedow, *supra* note 72, at 740-741.

232 But see Torsello, *supra* note 164, at 105: '[T]he adoption of a reservation by a single State is to be regarded as the enactment of a purely domestic provision addressed by the national legislator to the national courts of the reserving State, and hence producing its effects only within the reserving State'.

12 and 96 CISG that 'any provision [...] does not apply'. Therefore, China's Article 96 CISG declaration indeed has an *erga omnes* effect.

5.2 *Parties: SAR versus Non-Contracting State, Applicable Law under Conflict Rules: Non-Article 95 CISG Declaration State, Forum: SAR*

Owing to China's Article 95 CISG declaration which also applies to SARs, a SAR court under this circumstance – again, leaving to one side the lack of implementing legislation – is free from applying the CISG. Nonetheless, as has been argued above, the Article 95 CISG declaration only discharges the obligation to apply CISG, but by no means prohibits application of the Convention where appropriate. There is a general consensus that once effected in a Contracting State, the CISG constitutes part of the law of that State. Therefore, if the court's own conflict rules lead to the law of a Contracting State, it may apply the CISG as part of that national law.[233] In that event, although the CISG has not been implemented in Hong Kong, the CISG can be applied as non-Hong Kong law.[234] The same holds true of Macao.

5.3 *Parties: SAR versus Non-Contracting State, Applicable Law under Conflict Rules: SAR, Forum: Non-Article 95 CISG Declaration State*

In such a case, since the forum State does not declare that it 'will not be bound by' 1(1)(b) CISG, the court should apply the CISG through Article 1(1)(b) CISG.[235] Here, China's Article 95 CISG declaration, which extends to SARs, is irrelevant.[236] In this respect, com-

233 See also Bell, *Singapore*, *supra* note 43, at 64. See M. Evans, *Bianca & Bonell Commentary*, *supra* note 73, Art. 95 para. 3.4 (indicating that in the present scenario, the CISG may apply only when the court's own conflict rules lead to the law of a Contracting State which has not made a declaration under Art. 95 CISG).

234 Note that the CISG is not 'foreign' to Hong Kong, as it is part of the law of Mainland China. For general discussion on commercial law conventions as part of Mainland law, see Y. Xiao, *Conflict of Laws from a Jurisprudence Perspective*, 227 (2008).

235 See Bridge, *Uniform and Harmonized Sales Law*, *supra* note 231, at 980–981 (for an excellent discussion on the issue); Schwenzer & Hachem, in: *Commentary on the CISG* (3rd ed.), *supra* note 3, Art. 1 para. 38; F. Ferrari, 'The CISG's Sphere of Application: Articles 1–3 and 10', in: F. Ferrari, H.M. Flechtner & R.A. Brand (Eds.), *The Draft UNCITRAL Digest and Beyond: Cases, Analysis and Unresolved Issues in the UN Sales Convention*, 1, at 21, 52 (2004); B. Zeller, *CISG and the Unification of International Trade Law*, 38-40 (2007); F. Ferrari, 'What Sources of Law for Contracts for the International Sale of Goods? Why One Has to Look Beyond the CISG, 25 *International Review of Law and Economics* 314, at 322, note 64, 328 (2005); Bell, *Singapore*, *supra* note 43, at 63-65.

236 But see Honnold & Flechtner (Eds.), *supra* note 32, at 42-46; Schlechtriem, in: *Commentary on the CISG* (2nd ed.), *supra* note 31, Art. 1 para. 43; Schlechtriem, in: *Commentary on the CISG* (2nd ed.), *supra* note 31, Art. 95 para. 4; J. Ziegel, 'The Scope of the Convention: Reaching Out to Article One and Beyond', 25 *J.L. & Com.* 59, at 66 (2005). The cited authors argue that forums in non-reserving Contracting States should still respect an Art. 95 CISG reservation by the Contracting State whose law is found to govern the contract.

parison can be made to Articles 92 and 93 CISG. Article 92(1) CISG allows a State to opt out of Part II or Part III of the CISG. Article 92(2) CISG then provides that a State that opts out of a Part is not considered to be a Contracting State in respect of matters governed by that Part. Similarly, suppose that by virtue of a declaration under Article 93 CISG, the CISG does not apply to a territorial unit of the declaration state. Under Article 93(3) CISG, that unit is not considered to be a Contracting State for the purposes of Article 1(1) CISG. In contrast to these two articles, no similar provision is made regarding Article 95 CISG, and the omission is striking. Therefore, an Article 95 CISG declaration state (*i.e.*, China in our example) remains a Contracting State within the meaning of Article 1(1)(b) CISG.[237]

Accordingly, if the case at hand is heard by a court of Australia, the court should apply the CISG. This is because its conflict rules lead to the law of a Contracting State, thereby triggering Article 1(1)(b) CISG, which is binding on Australia. This is so even if the court's conflict rules lead to Hong Kong law. In this regard, the lack of implementing legislation in Hong Kong is an incidental matter as far as this court is concerned. Article 1(1)(b) CISG is not a conflict rule *per se*.[238] It only provides categorically that the CISG applies when the rules of private international law lead to the law of a Contracting State. It does not say that the CISG applies as part of the State law.[239] Therefore, in the instant example, the CISG shall apply regardless of whether it constitutes part of Hong Kong law.

The situation will be different, however, if the matter is litigated in a German court. When acceding to the CISG, the then Federal Republic of Germany declared, contrary to the understanding above, that it would not consider an Article 95 CISG declaration state to be a Contracting State within the meaning of Article 1(1)(b) CISG, and that it therefore assumed no obligation to apply the CISG when conflict rules lead to the application of the law of a declaration state.[240] Accordingly, a German court would not be bound to apply the CISG in this case. Nevertheless, the German declaration, like any other interpretive

237 See Bridge, *International Sale of Goods*, *supra* note 32, at 544, para. 11.46; Schroeter, *Backbone or Backyard*, *supra* note 10, at 446-447.

238 Ferrari, *Homeward Trend*, *supra* note 7, at 16.

239 Bridge, *Uniform and Harmonized Sales Law*, *supra* note 231, at 905, 908, 922; Bridge, *International Sale of Goods*, *supra* note 32, at 544, para. 11.46.

240 The declaration reads: 'The Government of the Federal Republic of Germany holds the view that Parties to the Convention that have made a declaration under article 95 of the Convention are not considered Contracting States within the meaning of subparagraph (a) (b) of article 1 of the Convention. Accordingly, there is no obligation to apply – and the Federal Republic of Germany assumes no obligation to apply – this provision when the rules of private international law lead to the application of the law of a Party that has made a declaration to the effect that it will not be bound by subparagraph (1) (b) of article 1 of the Convention. Subject to this observation the Government of the Federal Republic of Germany makes no declaration under article 95 of the Convention.' See *supra* note 26.

declaration,[241] is incompatible with Article 7(1) CISG and hence prohibited by the Article.[242] Thus, although this declaration (by virtue of domestic legislation) is binding in Germany, it produces no international legal effect under the CISG.[243] Therefore, to courts in other Contracting States, not only the declaration itself, but also its effect, is foreign.[244]

5.4 *Parties: SAR versus Mainland, Forum/Seat of Arbitration: Mainland*

Since the respective handovers, Hong Kong and Macao have become parts of China, a Contracting State to the CISG. Thus, unlike in cases before the handovers,[245] the CISG cannot apply through Article 1 CISG to post-handover contracts between parties from SARs and Mainland. This is because Article 1 CISG requires the parties to have their places of business in *different* Contracting States. Nevertheless, the CISG may be applied by other means. Although the instant scenario is purely domestic, it is of interregional character. Under the law of Mainland China, international cases[246] and interregional cases, *i.e.*, cases involving Hong Kong or Macao elements, are in principle treated equally in terms of choice of law, unless otherwise provided by international conventions and interregional arrangements.[247] The requirement for equal treatment of international and interregional cases applies to both litigation and arbitration in the Mainland. Accordingly, approaches (other than Art. 1 CISG) by which the CISG are applied in international cases may also be adopted in the present scenario.

5.4.1 CISG Chosen by the Parties

The first, and most frequently employed, approach is to apply the CISG via the parties' agreement. As shown above,[248] in cases involving parties from SARs and Mainland China, the CISG is often chosen by the parties to govern their contracts. These cases are to be

241 For a discussion on the qualification of this declaration as an interpretive declaration, see Schroeter, *Backbone or Backyard, supra* note 10, at 454.

242 For further elaboration, see *id.*, at 455.

243 Similarly Torsello, *supra* note 164, a 117.

244 See *supra* note 232 and accompanying text.

245 See *supra* notes 106-109 and accompanying text.

246 In Chinese conflict of laws, the term 'disputes involving foreign elements' instead of 'international disputes' are employed. According to Supreme People's Court's Interpretation on the General Principles of Civil Law of P.R. China, Art. 178, a dispute involves foreign elements if (a) at least one of the parties is a foreign or stateless natural person, or a foreign corporation; or (b) the subject matter is located in a jurisdiction other than Mainland China; or (c) the event giving rise to, altering or terminating the legal relationship takes place in a jurisdiction other than Mainland China.

247 See Art. 2(5) Supreme People's Court's Interpretation on Trials of Disputes Involving Hong Kong or Macao Elements, (1987) Fa(Jing)fa No. 28. For a case expressly noting this point, see CIETAC Arbitration Proceeding, China, 30 July 1998, available at <http://cisgw3.law.pace.edu/cases/980730c1.html>.

248 See *supra* notes 121-124 and accompanying text.

distinguished from the situation where, when incorporated into contracts by reference, the CISG is treated as contract terms.[249] Indeed, the CISG may come into play as the applicable law when opted into by the parties at the level of conflict of laws.[250] The permissibility of such opting-in must be determined in light of the applicable conflict rules of the forum or the applicable arbitration rules, respectively.[251] The legal framework regarding such opting-in before Mainland courts and in arbitration calls for separate treatment.

Litigation

For Mainland courts, the validity of a choice of the CISG in cases beyond the territorial scope of the Convention is a question of conflict of laws. Under Mainland conflicts law, the reference to the parties' choice of the applicable law is generally limited to choice of national laws.[252] This stance reflects the civil law reasoning that 'in principle State courts cannot avoid the application of State law'.[253] However, this 'State law requirement' has not been strictly adhered to in practice.[254]

Currently, China is envisaging a new statute on the conflict of laws. The first draft of this statute broke new ground by providing that parties to international contracts may designate international conventions as the applicable law of their contracts.[255] Accordingly, choice of the CISG *in its own right, i.e.*, not as part of the law of a Contracting State, was permitted under this draft. Yet the second draft of this statute stands by the position under the

---

249 See, *e.g.*, CIETAC Arbitration proceeding, China, 26 June 2003, available at <http://cisgw3.law.pace.edu/cases/030626c1.html>. The parties incorporated by reference the provisions of Parts II and III of the CISG, except to the extent that these provisions were inconsistent with the express provisions of their contract or contrary to the law of Hong Kong as the applicable law. Thus, the provisions of the CISG were merely contract terms which were subject to the law of Hong Kong.

250 For general discussion on opting-in at the conflict-of-laws level *vis-à-vis* that at the substantive law level, see Schwenzer & Hachem, in: *Commentary on the CISG* (3rd ed.), *supra* note 3, Art. 6 paras. 29-36.

251 Schlechtriem, in: *Commentary on the CISG* (2nd ed.), *supra* note 31, Art. 6 para. 11.

252 Art. 145 1986 GPCL provides: 'Unless otherwise provided by law, parties to a contract involving foreign elements may choose the applicable law of their contractual disputes.' Art. 126 1999 Contract Law provides: 'Unless otherwise provided by law, parties to a contract involving foreign elements may choose the applicable law of their contractual disputes.' For detailed analyses on the requirements for a valid choice of law by the parties under Chinese law, see Xiao & Long, *Selected Topics*, *supra* note 21, at 78-80; Xiao & Long, *Contractual Party Autonomy*, *supra* note 121, at 194 *et seq.*

253 See F. Vischer, 'General Course on Private International Law', in: *Recueil des Cours* 1 at 136 (1996).

254 For instance, in *Fayau v. Wujin International Trade Co.*, the Uniform Rules for Collections, ICC Publication No. 322 (1978) were applied as the applicable law chosen by the parties. See Jiangsu High People's Court, China, 2002 ((2002) Su Minsan Zhongzi No. 019). Similarly *Shanghai Lansheng Corp. v. Shanghai Branch of OCBC Bank and Citibank China*, Shanghai High People's Court, China, 2000 ((2000) Hu Gao Jing Zhongzi No. 335). These decisions on choice of law may be challenged, not only because of the State law requirement, but also because according to Art. 142(3) 1986 GPCL, international usages can only act as gap-fillers in the absence of relevant provisions in Chinese law on the issues at stake.

255 See Art. 50(1) of the first draft. For further discussion on the provision, see Xiao & Long, *Contractual Party Autonomy*, *supra* note 121, at 200-203.

existing Mainland law, *i.e.*, the parties may only choose 'law' rather than 'rules of law'.[256] Since the second draft will probably be approved by the Chinese legislature without substantial amendment, one may speculate that under future Mainland conflicts law, direct choice of the CISG as the governing law will not be sanctioned. This being said, it remains to be seen whether this state law limitation will be adhered to in future practice. Moreover, in cases between parties from SARs and Mainland, direct choices of the CISG may not be considered by Mainland courts as choices of a-national rules of law at all, since the CISG is in force in Mainland as part of Mainland law. Even if a choice of the CISG is considered as choice of a-national rules in the present scenario, the court, bearing in mind the principle of *favor negotii*, may well interpret the parties' choice as incorporating the CISG into the contract. Thus, as far as the CISG is concerned, distinction between opting-in at the substantive law level and that at the conflict-of-laws level may not be so significant in practice.[257]

CIETAC Arbitration

Under the arbitration rules of CIETAC (hereinafter 'CIETAC Arbitration Rules'), an arbitral tribunal shall make its arbitral award 'in accordance with law and the terms of the contracts, with reference to international practices and in compliance with the principle of fairness and reasonableness'.[258] Similarly, the 1994 Arbitration Law of P.R. China (hereinafter '1994 Arbitration Law') requires arbitrators to render their awards 'in accordance with law'.[259] In light of the wording 'law', some commentators deem that when the seat of CIETAC arbitration is in the Mainland, arbitrators hardly have any discretion in applying rules of law.[260] According to this view, parties' choice of the CISG *in its own right* in the instant scenario is presumably not permissible.

Yet, in CIETAC arbitrations seated in the Mainland and applying Mainland conflict of laws, direct choices of the CISG may not be considered as choices of a-national rules of law at all, on the basis that Mainland courts may take the view that the CISG is in force in

---

256 See Arts. 4 & 43 of the second draft of the statute, available at <http://www.npc.gov.cn/huiyi/cwh/1116/2010-08/28/content_1593162.htm>.

257 See Schwenzer & Hachem, in: *Commentary on the CISG* (3rd ed.), *supra* note 3, Art. 6 para. 36.

258 Since their initial promulgation in 1988, the CIETAC Arbitration Rules have been revised six times, most recently in 2005. See China International Economic and Trade Arbitration Commission (CIETAC), <http://www.cietac.org/index.cms>. Except for the 1988 CIETAC Arbitration Rules, which had no stipulations on the law applicable to the merits of a case, the revised versions of the CIETAC Arbitration Rules all provide: 'The arbitral tribunal shall independently and impartially make its arbitral award on the basis of the facts, in accordance with law and the terms of the contracts, with reference to international practices and in compliance with the principle of fairness and reasonableness.' See, *e.g.*, Art. 43(1) CIETAC Arbitration Rules.

259 See Art. 7 1994 Arbitration Law, People's Republic of China.

260 See M. Chi, 'Application of the UNIDROIT Principles in China: Successes, Shortcomings and Implications', 2010 *Uniform Law Review* 5, at 30-33. In particular, the author pointed out that 'Chinese arbitration law does [...] require that arbitrators must base their decisions on laws.' *Id.*, note 102.

Mainland as part of Mainland law. In effect, the CISG has been applied as the governing law via parties' agreement in cases between parties from the Mainland and Hong Kong, regardless of whether the choice was explicitly stated in contracts, or subsequently indicated during the arbitration proceedings.[261] In the latter situation, the parties were deemed to have such consensus usually because they cited the CISG in their pleadings and defences.[262] To the present author's knowledge, of all the CIETAC arbitration awards applying the CISG via parties' agreement, none has been set aside or denied recognition by Mainland courts on the ground that the CISG was erroneously applied. Moreover, it does not seem implausible to adopt a more liberal interpretation of the wording 'law' under Article 43(1) CIETAC Arbitration Rules and Article 7 1994 Arbitration Law.[263] Thus, in CIETAC arbitrations involving parties from Mainland and SARs, the parties may have ample freedom to opt into the CISG.

Finally, it is not infrequent for the CISG to be chosen in conjunction with Chinese domestic law in CIETAC arbitrations.[264] For this concurrent designation, a problem may arise as to which set of rules should be given priority in the event of differences between the two.[265] The present author proposes that arbitrators should enquire whether the parties have a solution in mind. Failing the parties' agreement on such a solution, it is advisable to prefer the CISG since it is presumably more suited to international transactions.[266]

---

261 See, *e.g.*, *Antimony ingot case*, *supra* note 112; *Caffeine case, supra* note 112.

262 In effect, direct designation of the CISG has also been allowed in cases involving parties both doing business in Hong Kong. See, *e.g.*, CIETAC Arbitration proceeding, China, 28 April 1995, available at <http://cisgw3.law.pace.edu/cases/950428c1.html>, and also international cases involving parties from China and (the then) non-contracting states to the CISG. See, *e.g.*, CIETAC Arbitration proceeding, China, 23 July 1997, available at <http://cisgw3.law.pace.edu/cases/970723c1.html>; CIETAC Arbitration proceeding, China, 21 May 1999, available at <http://cisgw3.law.pace.edu/cases/990521c1.html>; CIETAC Arbitration proceeding, China, 8 September 1997, available at <http://cisgw3.law.pace.edu/cases/970908c1.html>.

263 For elaboration on a more liberal interpretation in this respect, see Xiao & Long, *Selected Topics*, *supra* note 21, at 80-82.

264 See, *e.g.*, *Black melon seeds case*, *supra* note 112; *Gray cloths case*, *supra* note 122; *Raincoat case*, *supra* note 122. Concurrent designation of CISG and Chinese domestic law also occurred in Mainland courts. See, *e.g.*, *Lianzhong Enterprise Resources (Hong Kong) Ltd. v. Xiamen International Trade & Trust Co.*, *supra* note 110.

265 The test for 'differences' between the two sets of rules is also a pending question. For discussions on the differences with regard to several specific matters, see Shen, *Declaring the Contract Avoided*, *supra* note 20, at 7 *et seq.*; Yang, *supra* note 20, at 23-27.

266 This approach was followed by the tribunal in the *Elevators case*, where it was ruled that according to the principle that international conventions should prevail over domestic laws, the CISG should apply if there was a conflict between the Convention and Chinese domestic law, see *Elevators case*, CIETAC Arbitration proceeding, China, 9 September 2002, available at <http://cisgw3.law.pace.edu/cases/020909c1.html>. See also CIETAC Arbitration proceeding, China, 23 October 1996, available at <http://cisgw3.law.pace.edu/cases/961023c1.html> (where it was held that in case of any contradiction between Chinese law and any international treaty adopted by China, the latter should prevail, and the CISG was subsequently applied).

5.4.2 CISG as Evidence of Usages

According to Article 142(3) GPCL, in the absence of relevant provisions in Chinese law and in treaties concluded or acceded to by China, international usages may apply. Again, this provision applies to both international and interregional cases. Thus, in cases involving parties from SARs and the Mainland, the CISG may be applied by Mainland courts if (a) Chinese law is designated by conflict rules as the *lex causae*; and (b) relevant rules on the issue at stake are absent in Chinese law; and (c) relevant rules of the CISG are qualified as evidence of international usages. Here, rules of the CISG act as the gap-fillers for Chinese law.

In CIETAC arbitration, to the extent that Chinese law is deemed applicable, the CISG may apply in the same justified manner under Article 142(3) GPCL as in Mainland courts. For instance, in the *Peppermint oil case*,[267] involving parties from the U.K. and China, the Tribunal seemingly considered the CISG as evidence of usages which should apply to matters not covered by Chinese law.[268] The reasoning in this international case may also apply to interregional cases concerning parties from SARs and China. Yet somewhat differently, in the *Ink cartridge case*[269] between parties from Hong Kong and Mainland, where Chinese law was held applicable, a provision of the CISG was treated as 'an international trade usage adopted commonly'. Thus, the CISG applied in parallel with Chinese law, rather than in the absence of relevant provisions in Chinese law. This concurrent application might be justified under Article 43(1) CIETAC Arbitration Rules, according to which a tribunal shall make its award 'in accordance with law [...] *with reference to international practices*'.[270]

6 Concluding Remarks

It is hoped that the foregoing discussion has shown that there are many good reasons to withdraw the two declarations by China under Article 95 and Article 96 CISG. During the past 20 years, great changes have taken place in regard to the Chinese legal system and its underpinning rationale. International trade is well received in China, with party autonomy

267 CIETAC Arbitration proceeding, China, 30 June 1999, available at <http://cisgw3.law.pace.edu/cases/990630c1.html>.

268 In so ruling, the Tribunal referred to Art. 5(2) 1985 FECL. The FECL has now been repealed by the 1999 Contract Law. Note that Art. 5(2) 1985 FECL is almost identical to Art. 142(3) GPCL. Therefore, the reasoning employed in this case may be followed in future cases under Art. 142(3) GPCL.

269 See *supra* note 125.

270 See *supra* note 258 (emphasis added). The emphasized wording is considered as mandating international practices as 'only secondary or auxiliary sources of law in CIETAC arbitration'. See Chi, *supra* note 260, at 32.

fully respected under contemporary Chinese law. Maintenance of the reservations will not only contradict China's attitude favoring a market economy and international transactions, but also create confusion in practice. Withdrawal of the reservations will eliminate all these inconsistencies and uncertainties, thereby bringing enforcement of the CISG into line with China's current policies, and promoting uniform application of the CISG with its full acceptance in China.

There are also compelling reasons to implement the CISG in Hong Kong and Macao. Implementation of the CISG in SARs accords with China's long-standing commitment to honour its international treaty obligations, including the CISG, to which China is a Contracting State. Implementing the CISG in Hong Kong and Macao will help to remove legal barriers in SARs-related international trade, thereby creating a suitable legal environment for international transactions involving the SARs. Therefore, implementation is also in the very interests of SARs themselves, and conforms to China's aspiration to maintain the prosperity and stability of Hong Kong and Macao. Finally, in the long run, implementation of the CISG in SARs will also further the goals of the CISG, that is, to promote worldwide uniformity and enhance legal certainty in international trade.

Teaching the CISG at U.K. Universities

An Empirical Study of Frequency and Method of Introducing the CISG to U.K. Students in the Light of the Desirability of the Adoption of the CISG by the U.K.

Anna Rogowska[*]

1 Introduction

The United Kingdom of Great Britain and Northern Ireland is among those European countries that have not yet acceded to the 1980 United Nations Convention on Contracts for the International Sale of Goods (CISG or Convention).[1] The U.K. Department of Trade and Industry, now called the U.K. Department of Innovation and Skill (BIS),[2] conducted two formal consultations in 1989[3] and 1997,[4] as well as a number of informal 'mini-consultations' between 1997 and 2007,[5] to inquire on whether the U.K. should accede to the

---

* Anna Rogowska, PhD Candidate (Essex), Magister (UAM Poznan), BA (EUV Viadrina), is a senior legal counsel at a leading investment bank in London City where her work includes negotiating commercial (energy) contracts and advising on corporate legal issues. She can be contacted at aarogowska@gmail.com.
The author would like to thank Prof. Ingeborg Schwenzer, Lisa Spagnolo and Alain F. Hosang for their kind assistance and support in reviewing this chapter as well as record her gratitude to Dr Camilla Baasch Andersen who commented on the Survey project in its initial stage.

1 United Nations Convention on Contracts for the International Sale of Goods (CISG), Vienna, 11 April 1980, available at <http://www.uncitral.org/uncitral/en/uncitral_texts/sale_goods/ 1980CISG.html>. Only four EU Member States have not yet acceded to the CISG: the U.K., Ireland, Portugal and Malta. A detailed list of the CISG Contracting States can be found at <http://www.uncitral.org/uncitral/en/uncitral_texts/sale_goods/1980CISG_status.html>.

2 For further information, see Department for Business, Innovation and Skills (BIS), <http://www.bis.gov.uk>, for further information.

3 Official Publication of Department of Trade and Industry, *United Nations Convention on Contracts for the International Sales of Goods, A Consultative Document* (London, June 1989).

4 Official Publication of Department of Trade and Industry, *United Nations Convention on Contracts for the International Sales of Goods (the Vienna Sales Convention), A Consultation Document* (London, October 1997).

5 As advised by the BIS in response to the author's official enquiry (personal email correspondence on 26 February 2010).

Convention. Those consultations, which were directed to the CISG-interested parties,[6] resulted in the ministers' approval for the U.K. to proceed with the accession.[7] However, the consultations also illustrated that business people and legal practitioners might have little desire for the U.K. to accede to the CISG.[8]

Although the U.K. actively participated in the CISG drafting process that started in the early 1970s, it has not ratified the Convention and no progress towards the accession has been made. There can be various explanations for this passive attitude of the U.K. government which, in fact, has never clearly declared its reasons for non-ratification. As pointed out by Sally Moss, a general lack of support or 'lobby' for implementation among industry groups and English legal professionals is one of the most important factors that hinders accession.[9] It can be claimed that the latter group often lacks interest in the CISG or underestimates the Convention as they are, for example, less familiar with it than their colleagues from other jurisdictions. It is suggested that this lack of knowledge may be in part due to ignorance or a lack of emphasis upon the CISG within U.K. universities.

It can be seen that some of the latest editions of the most popular English contract law textbooks and casebooks (particularly those recommended for first year contract law courses, *e.g.*: *McKendrick*,[10] *Beale, Bishop & Furmston*[11] or *Burrows*[12]) now include a separate chapter or section and/or comparative references throughout to the CISG,[13] with

6 These included, amongst others, trading companies, business associations, governmental institutions, practitioners and academics.

7 The initial approval was granted after the 1997 consultations, where the majority of the responses were in support of the CISG implementation, see S. Moss, 'Why the United Kingdom has Not Ratified the CISG', 25 *J.L. & Com.* 483, at 484 (2005).

8 For example, The Law Society of England and Wales and the Commercial Bar Association were against the implementation of the CISG during the 1997 consultations, see *id.*, at 484.

9 The arguments pro and contra accession have been widely discussed in a number of writings, see, *e.g.*, *id.*, at 484 *et seq.*; J. Linarelli, 'The Economics of Uniform Laws and Uniform Law Making', 48 *Wayne L. Rev.* 1387 (2003); A. Williams, 'Forecasting the Potential Impact of the Vienna Sales Convention on International Sales Law in the United Kingdom', in: *Pace Int'l L. Rev.* (Ed.), Pace Review of the Convention on Contracts for the International Sale of Goods, 9 (2000-2001); B. Nicholas, 'The United Kingdom and the Vienna Sales Convention: Another Case of Splendid Isolation?', in: Sacci, *Conferenze e Seminari* 9, Rome (1993), available at <http://www.cisg.law.pace.edu/cisg/biblio/nicholas3.html>.

10 E. McKendrick, *Contract Law* (2009); E. McKendrick, *Contract Law: Text, Cases and Materials* (2008) (taking into account the CISG, UNIDROIT Principles & PECL).

11 H. Beale, *et al.*, *Contract: Cases and Materials* (2008), referring only to the UNIDROIT Principles, *infra* note 17.

12 A. Burrows, *A Casebook on Contract* (2009). According to the *Preface*, at 5, references to the Principles of European Contract Law (PECL), *infra* note 18, only are provided 'so that students can compare PECL with English law […], given the ongoing talk of a European Contract Code […].'

13 However, no reference to international instruments of contract law was found in such recommended contract law textbooks and casebooks, as e.g. J. Poole, *Casebook on Contract Law* (2008); M. Furmstorm, *et al.*, Cheshire

Honnold[14] being probably the most frequently cited source on the CISG in the U.K. However, such material is usually not included in the syllabuses of the mandatory contract law course but rather offered as part of electives, such as international trade law, comparative contract law etc. Unfortunately, many academics further omit to embrace the CISG within mandatory courses they teach to undergraduates, as they do not consider it a necessary part of a student's general legal education.

Hence, it can be claimed that the U.K. students graduating with a degree in law have a deficiency in their knowledge of international sales contracts, in respect of a matter which could be necessary for their legal education as well as legal practice. Such deficiency could potentially cause either a reluctance to adhere to the CISG, or an explicit exclusion of the application of the CISG among present and future practitioners who are unfamiliar with this instrument.[15]

In order to get a better insight into the teaching of the CISG at the law schools across the U.K., the author conducted a survey on 'Implications of Teaching the CISG, UNIDROIT Principles and European Principles at U.K. Universities'.[16] The survey's main objective was to measure the attitude of the academics involved in the teaching of contract law, commercial law, international trade law etc., with regard to their knowledge and teaching of the CISG, UNIDROIT Principles of International Commercial Contracts (UNIDROIT Principles)[17] and Principles of European Contract Law (PECL)[18] to undergraduates.

Fifoot & Furmston's *Law of Contract* (2007); C. Elliott & F. Quinn, *Contract Law* (2009); E. Peel, *Treitel on the Law of Contract* (2007); J. O'Sullivan & J. Hilliard, *The Law of Contract* (2006).

14 J. Honnold & H. Flechtner (Eds.), *Uniform Law for International Sales under the 1980 United Nations Convention* (2009).

15 E. Brödermann, *The Practice of Excluding the CISG: Time for Change?, Comment on the Limited Use of the CISG in Private Practice (and on why This Will Increasingly Change)*, presentation at the Modern Law for Global Commerce: Congress to Celebrate the Fortieth Annual Season of UNCITRAL (9-12 July 2007), available at <http://www.uncitral.org/pdf/english/congress/Broedermann-rev.pdf>, who believes that 'ignorance, [...] fear, and [...] a reluctance to change existing patterns [...]' or '[a] lack of time and resources to concentrate on something new [...]' are often the reasons for explicit exclusion of the application of the CISG by many corporations, see *id.*, at 3.

16 The survey forms part of the author's doctoral research and was conducted in June 2009.

17 UNIDROIT International Institute for the Unification of Private Law, UNIDROIT Principles of International Commercial Contracts (2004), Rome, April 2004, available at <http://www.unidroit.org/english/principles/contracts/principles2004/integralversionprinciples2004-e.pdf>.

18 Commission on European Contract Law, Principles of European Contract Law (PECL), Part I and Part II (1999). The text of the PECL is available at <http://frontpage.cbs.dk/law/commission_on_european_contract_law/index.html>.

This chapter will present the empirical data from the survey related to the CISG only (with additional reference to the so-called Hague Conventions, ULFIS[19] and ULIS[20]), except for the last four survey questions that sought a joint opinion on the CISG, UNIDROIT Principles and PECL. Particularly, the following issues will be addressed:

1. What is the level of knowledge of the CISG among academics in the U.K.?
2. What courses taught at the schools of law in the U.K. incorporate the CISG?
3. Are the courses mandatory or optional?
4. Are the courses taught at undergraduate or postgraduate level?
5. What aspects of the CISG are taught?
6. Do any of the courses incorporate the ULFIS and ULIS?
7. Is CISG considered as a necessary part of the first year undergraduate student course on contract law?
8. Should the CISG be taught to postgraduate or to undergraduate students?
9. Do students have sufficient knowledge of the CISG?
10. What suggestions can be made for increasing awareness of the CISG in the U.K.?

It should be stressed that this paper can by no means form a complete analysis of how the CISG is being taught at U.K. universities. However, it is hoped that the conclusions presented below will encourage U.K. academics to take a fresh look at the importance of teaching the CISG, stimulate interest in placing the CISG into the mandatory courses of law and raise awareness of the CISG among the faculties members (and, thus, indirectly law students).

2 Related Work

To the best knowledge of the author, until now no such empirical research has been conducted in the U.K.; although some comparative studies related to the level of awareness and teaching of the CISG and UNIDROIT Principles were earlier undertaken in the United States in 1998 and 2006/2007.[21] Other major empirical projects on the CISG mainly

19 Convention Relating to a Uniform Law on the Formation of Contracts for the International Sale of Goods (ULFIS), The Hague, 1 July 1964, available at <http://www.unidroit.org/english/conventions/c-ulf.htm>.

20 Convention Relating to a Uniform Law on the International Sale of Goods (ULIS), The Hague, 1 July 1964, available at <http://www.unidroit.org/english/conventions/c-ulis.htm>.

21 One of the first attempts was performed by M.W. Gordon, 'Some Thoughts on the Receptiveness of Contracts Rules in the CISG and UNIDROIT Principles as Reflected in One State's (Florida) Experience of (1) Law School Faculty, (2) Members of the Bar with an International Practice, and (3) Judges', 46 *Am. J. Comp. L.* 361 (1998), with a follow-up survey by P. Fitzgerald, 'The International Contracting Practices Survey Project: An Empirical Study of the Value and Utility of the United Nation's Convention on the International Sale of Goods (CISG) and the Unidroit Principles of International Commercial Contracts to Practitioners, Jurists,

examined reasons for a limited use of the CISG in the practice and additionally measured familiarity with the Convention; those were conducted jointly in the United States and Germany in 2004/2005 and in China in 2007.[22]

In particular, a broad survey on 'the value and utility' of certain international instruments of contract law was undertaken by Professor Fitzgerald in the United States during 2006/2007.[23] This research measured, *inter alia*, levels of familiarity with the CISG and the UNIDROIT Principles and was addressed to U.S. practitioners, judiciary and academics. Interestingly, it concluded that the level of knowledge of the instruments was low among the practitioners;[24] most of the judiciary was 'not at all familiar' with the CISG and rather misperceived it as a 'foreign law' (although the United States are a Contracting State of the CISG).[25] It also showed that vast majority of both U.S. academics and practitioners and a number of judiciary representatives were in favour of increased education regarding the CISG and UNIDROIT Principles, mainly through inclusion in advanced law school courses.[26] Further, 67% of law professors, 69% of practitioners and 30% of judiciary also supported addressing the CISG in a 'basic Contract or Sales course'.[27] Furthermore, the survey examined to which extent the instruments were covered at law schools in the basic contract or sales courses. The study found that 78% of law professors surveyed addressed the CISG alone or in conjunction with the UNIDROIT Principles in basic contracts courses (however, with 83% of professors making only 'passing references' to the UNIDROIT Principles),[28] and all law professors studied covered them in basic sales courses (with two-thirds of professors making only 'passing references' to the UNIDROIT Principles).[29] As

and Legal Academics in the United States', 27 *J.L. & Com.* 1 (2008). For an analysis of other studies, see also in general L. Spagnolo, 'A Glimpse Through the Kaleidoscope: Choices of Law and the CISG (Kaleidoscope Part I)', 13 *Vindobona Journal of International Commercial Law and Arbitration*, 135 (2009), and L. Spagnolo, 'Rats in the Kaleidoscope: Rationality, Irrationality, and the Economics and Psychology of Opting In and Out of the CISG (Kaleidoscope Part II)', 13 *Vindobona Journal of International Commercial Law and Arbitration* 157 (2009).

22 A survey that targeted practising attorneys and investigated reasons for exclusion of the CISG and familiarity with the Convention was conducted by M. F. Koehler & G. Yujun, 'The Acceptance of the Unified Sales Law (CISG) in Different Legal Systems – An International Comparison of Three Surveys on the Exclusion of the CISG's Application Conducted in the United States, Germany, and China', 20 *Pace Int'l L. Rev.* 45 (2008).

23 Fitzgerald, *supra* note 21.

24 *Id.*, at 17.

25 *Id.*, at 8.

26 *Id.*, at 10.

27 The respondents expressed similar views as to the UNIDROIT Principles, however, to a lesser degree supported teaching them in the basic contract and sales courses, see *id.*, at 10-11.

28 *Id.*, at 20.

29 *Id.*, at 20-21.

Professor Fitzgerald summed up, 'it appears that we [academia] are substantially overrating both the bench's and bar's own familiarity and comfort with these instruments'.[30]

3 Survey Methodology and Participants

The survey 'Implications of Teaching the CISG, UNIDROIT Principles and European Principles at U.K. Universities' was conducted through an online questionnaire and was open from 9-30 June 2009.

The survey questionnaire was created using a professional online survey editor that enabled the design, collection and analysis of survey responses. Questions provided a series of choices to be ticked by participants. A number of the questions utilized an open comment format in order to allow participants to freely discuss issues of personal interest or concern. Some of these comments will be subsequently presented during the course of this paper. All survey responses were collected through the survey editor.

The survey questionnaire consisted of ten to 19 questions (depending on the respondent's answers). All questions were mandatory except those that might lead to the disclosure of the full identity of the participant.

The survey questions were as follows:

1. What is your level of knowledge of the CISG, UNIDROIT Principles and PECL?
2. Do any courses you teach incorporate the CISG, UNIDROIT Principles and PECL?
3. Are the courses mandatory or optional?
4. Are the courses taught at undergraduate or postgraduate level?
5. What aspects of the CISG, UNIDROIT Principles and PECL are taught?
6. Do any of the courses you teach incorporate ULFIS and ULIS?
7. Do you consider the CISG, UNIDROIT Principles and PECL as a necessary part of the first year undergraduate student course on Contract Law?
8. Do you think that the CISG, UNIDROIT Principles and PECL be taught to postgraduate or undergraduate students?
9. Do you think students in your department have sufficient knowledge of the CISG, UNIDROIT Principles and PECL?
10. What suggestions would you make for increasing awareness of the CISG, UNIDROIT Principles and PECL in the UK?

30 *Id.*, at 34.

The survey deliberately targeted U.K. academics involved in the teaching of contract law, commercial law, international trade law, or other courses related to international instruments of contract law, to both undergraduate and postgraduate students. Hence, the survey results do not concern all U.K. academics teaching law in general but only those who were likely to be involved in teaching of the CISG (as well as UNIDROIT Principles and PECL).

In order to reach a broad audience and encourage academics to participate in the project, an initial request for survey distribution was sent to an administrator of the U.K. Society of Legal Scholars (SLS).[31] Thanks to the kind response of the SLS, copies of the request were forwarded to SLS members registered in the SLS Contract, Commercial and International Law mailing lists. Additional information about the survey project was also included in a SLS newsletter which was sent to all SLS members via SLS representatives at their Law Schools. The newsletter was also available at the SLS website and some respondents might have accessed the questionnaire through this source.

Further requests for distribution among staff members involved in teaching contract law were sent by the author to law school administrators of the top 30 law schools in U.K. universities according to the *Times Good University Guide 2010.*[32]

The total number of participants who completed a full survey amounted to 42. The academics represented all of the U.K., *i.e.* England, Scotland, Wales and Northern Ireland. It is worth mentioning that among the respondents were some internationally renowned contract and comparative contract law authorities from the U.K. However, knowing that the survey questionnaire was sent to a very broad number of recipients and received only 42 responses could already indicate that, in principle, the CISG is not a popular research subject among U.K. academics.

The participants included ten professors, one reader, three senior lecturers, 18 lecturers and three teaching assistants; three respondents did not disclose academic position in their

---

31 SLS is a society registered in the U.K. with over 3100 members. It generally gathers those who teach law at U.K. universities or similar institutions, or who are practising law in the U.K. More information is available at <http://www.legalscholars.ac.uk>.

32 The universities included: University of Cambridge, University of Oxford, London School of Economics, University of Nottingham, University College London, King's College London, University of Birmingham, University of Aberdeen, Queen Mary University London, University of Durham, University of Edinburgh, University of Bristol, University of Southampton, University of Glasgow, University of Dundee, University of Strathclyde, University of Kent, University of Cardiff, University of Newcastle, University of Exeter, University of Leicester, University of Warwick, University of Reading, University of Liverpool, University of Sussex, Queen's Belfast University, University of Manchester, University of East Anglia, University of Hull and University of Sheffield. The Times Good University Guide 2010 is available at <http://www.thetimes.co.uk/tto/public/gug/?CMP=KNGvccp1-times%20good%20 university%20guide>.

departments and were thus categorized for survey purposes into a separate group 'other'. Consequently, the majority of survey respondents held either the position of a lecturer or a professor.

4 Limitations on the Scope and Nature of the Survey

A number of factors presented below limited the scope and nature of the survey. The first major issue arose at the design stage, which affected the scope of the evaluation, *i.e.* knowing that the CISG might be taught in a variety of undergraduate courses it was difficult to establish to which academics in particular the survey should be directed. Therefore, the survey request asked for response from all those who taught contract law, commercial law, international trade law, or other courses related to international instruments of contract law.

Secondly, due to the nature of the survey being deliberately directed to academics teaching in the U.K., only responses from that group of participants could be taken into consideration. Since four responses were received from participants teaching in another common law jurisdiction, only 38 responses as opposed to 42 were usable and analyzed from survey results. This, in turn, decreased the overall response rate.

Furthermore, the evaluation was not designed to assess actual knowledge of the CISG among the (undergraduate/postgraduate) students or of those students who are attending a Legal Practice Course to become a solicitor, or a Bar Professional Training Course to become a barrister in England and Wales. It would have been useful to measure this along with the level of knowledge of academics. However, practical considerations dictated that it was impossible at this stage to survey both academics and students; this would have required a different set of questions as well as a more complicated survey methodology. Indeed, for the purpose of this research it would be desirable to have an indication of the level of familiarity of the CISG among the above mentioned groups of students. Survey participants were provisionally asked to assess the level of knowledge of those instruments present among university students in their departments. However, a detailed study in this regard should be the subject of a separate research project.

To sum up, the above presented limitations can be overcome in a review or follow-up of the survey. Furthermore, despite these limitations, the participants of different departmental ranks constituted a representative group for the purposes of the survey and a detailed analysis of their responses will be provided in the following sections.

5 Survey Results

Before the survey results are analyzed below, the current section will briefly outline general assumptions of the research. This will help to clarify the hypothesis and main objectives of the study as well as assist in drawing general survey conclusions.

A general assumption of this research was that unification of the law of international commercial contracts is beneficial and practicable as it reduces legal barriers to cross border trade. Furthermore, unification is in line with the most recent attempts at the EU level to develop a European Civil Code (that primarily focuses on creating a unified law of contract).[33] Finally, the study assumed that the U.K. should no longer be isolated from the CISG.

Based on the broad assumptions above, this chapter argues that undergraduate students in the U.K. are not being sufficiently taught about the CISG, and in particular, not all U.K. academics potentially involved in teaching of contract law, commercial law, international trade law, or other courses related to international instruments of contract law, are aware of the Convention. The chapter also argues that a better integration of the instruments into undergraduate courses would raise awareness of the CISG. This could further aid the cause for the adoption of the CISG in the U.K. in the future.

Hence, the main objectives of the study were to assess and evaluate whether the above mentioned arguments are consistent with respect to the way the CISG is taught at U.K. universities. Subsequently, the author concludes that the CISG should be (to some extent) included in mandatory undergraduate courses on contract.

The following sections of this chapter provide a detailed summary of the survey results, including suggestions for increasing awareness of the CISG in the U.K. which are based on the comments of the survey participants. Since the last four survey questions were designed to gather joint data about all three instruments of international contracts law,

33 The European Parliament started calling for the codification of the European contract law and a creation of the European Civil Code, *inter alia*, in the following Communications: Communication From the Commission to the Council and the European Parliament on European Contract Law of 13 September 2001, COM(2001) 398 final, Official Journal C 255; Communication from the Commission of 12 February 2003 to the European Parliament and the Council – A more Coherent European Contract Law – An Action Plan, COM(2003) 68 final, Official Journal C 63 of 15 March 2003; Communication from the Commission of 11 October 2004 to the European Parliament and the Council – European Contract Law and the Revision of the Acquis: The Way Forward, COM(2004) 651. On further development on European Contract Law, *see* C. von Bar, E. Clive, *et al.*, *Principles, Definitions and Model Rules of European Private Law; Draft Common Frame of Reference (DCFR), Outline Edition* (2009).

i.e. the CISG, UNIDROIT Principles and PECL, without specific division, the results from those questions are relevant for all three international instruments of contract law. Meanwhile, a final section brings together all findings in order to draw general conclusions from the survey.

5.1 *What is the Level of Knowledge of the CISG among Academics?*

As Chart No. 1 at the end of this paper presents, most respondents were in general familiar with the CISG. The majority (42.1%) had either 'good' or 'very good' knowledge, whereas 15.8% declared 'excellent' familiarity, including publishing in this field. However, a quick literature review on the CISG shows that U.K. academics more often publish on the CISG in the foreign journals rather than in U.K. publications.

However, more than one third of respondents (36.8%) knew only the basics of the CISG. The remaining 5.3% (*i.e.* 2 lecturers and senior lecturers) declared no knowledge of the Convention. This confirms one of the general arguments presented above, *i.e.* that not all U.K. academics potentially involved in teaching contract law, commercial law, international trade law, or other courses related to the international instruments of contract law, are familiar with the CISG.

5.2 *What Courses Incorporate the CISG?*

Chart No. 2 at the end of this chapter illustrates that just more than half of respondents (57.9%) declared that they incorporate the CISG into their courses, whereas quite a substantial number of participants answered this question in the negative (42.1%).

Furthermore, as Chart No. 3 confirms, more than three-quarters of the courses that incorporated the CISG were optional (77.3%) whereas only 22.7% were mandatory. Then, as Chart No. 4 presents, the majority (68.2%) of the courses in which the CISG was taught were for postgraduates, with only 31.8% being for undergraduates.

As the comments from respondents explained, the CISG was mostly incorporated into such courses as: contract law, commercial law, European private law, international commercial law, international trade law, international sale of goods or international commercial contacts.

Finally, responses with regard to which aspects of the CISG taught varied; most of the respondents provided in their comments just a general overview of the CISG and comparison with domestic law (*i.e.* Sale of Goods Act 1979), or just the basic principles and CISG application; however, some taught all of it with a focus on obligations and remedies. It is anticipated by the author, that the latter is most likely taught in the more advanced and specialized courses for postgraduate students.

5.3 *Do any of the Courses Taught Incorporate the ULFIS and ULIS?*

The CISG is based on the so called 1964 Hague Conventions on Uniform Sales Laws (ULFIS and ULIS).[34] Back in the 1960s, the conventions were considered a first remarkable step towards unification of the law of sales. They were subsequently given effect in the U.K. by the Uniform Laws on International Sales Act 1967 (ULISA) and both remain applicable law.[35] Moreover, they are the only law in the U.K. that explicitly regulates international sales contracts. Such contracts are also generally subject to the Sale of Goods Act 1979[36] and the common law of contracts.

Considering the above, any course introduction to the CISG, or to international sales law, might have been expected to provide a brief overview of ULFIS and ULIS. However, the survey showed that the vast majority of respondents (81.6%) did not introduce ULFIS and ULIS to students in their courses, whereas only 18.4% of academics (seven individuals) did so: See Chart No. 5 below. This result is particularly worrying considering that more than half of respondents (57.1%) declared that they taught the CISG in their courses.

The survey question was not designed to identify courses that included ULFIS and ULIS (which are indeed beyond the scope of this chapter). However, it can be assumed that those courses that included ULFIS and ULIS were similar to those that include the CISG, *i.e.* generally not mandatory for all but available only for a limited group of postgraduate students who opted for specific courses on sale of goods or similar.

The reason for omission of those conventions might be that the academics were either unfamiliar with them or they simply did not consider them relevant for the students' education. Certainly, due to their limited mode of applicability, *i.e.* only by explicit inclusion

34 *Supra* note 20.

35 Further, the Department of Trade and Industry in its 1989 Consultative Document on the United Nations Convention on Contracts for the International Sale of Goods reported that it had found 'no reported case in the English, Scottish or Northern Ireland Courts involving the Hague Conventions and it would appear that the business community here have made little or no use of them in practice', *supra* note 3, at 8.

36 The U.K. Statute Law Database, Chapter 54, 1-34, available at <http://www.statutelaw.gov.uk/legResults.aspx?LegType=All Primary&PageNumber=1&BrowseLetter=S&NavFrom=1&activeTextDocId=1837068>.

by the parties, and thus their limited use in practice,[37] ULFIS and ULIS would not necessarily attract detailed analysis in undergraduate courses on contract law. However, given that the CISG is based on the ULFIS and ULIS, both of which technically remain applicable within the law in the U.K., some mention of their existence might be reasonably expected in an international commercial law or a comparative contract law course, whether optional or compulsory. In particular, any introduction to the CISG might be reasonably expected to acknowledge these two conventions and, consequently, any course that incorporates the CISG might be expected to include mention of the ULFIS and ULIS.

To conclude, ULFIS and ULIS are part of the domestic law of the U.K. and a lack of knowledge about them is, arguably, a gap in the learning of law students concerning international sale of goods. The lack of inclusion of these conventions into the curriculum of those surveyed can further undermine the potential for increased awareness of the role of the CISG, which is the successor of those conventions.

5.4 *Is the CISG Considered Necessary for First Year Undergraduate Student Courses on Contract Law?*

In the next question, participants were asked whether or not the CISG (as well as UNIDROIT Principles and PECL) were considered necessary for first year undergraduate contract law courses. The participants were further asked to provide a reason for their answer.

As illustrated by the responses, the majority of the participating U.K. academics (71.1%) did not consider the CISG (as well as UNIDROIT Principles and PECL) as required for the first year undergraduate courses on contract law. However, 28.9% of the academics are of the positive opinion on their inclusion into first year undergraduate courses on contract law: See Chart No. 6 below.

As seen from the participants' comments, there are essentially two main justifications for the prevailing negative opinion. Firstly, due to the complexity and length of English contract law material, any introduction of international contract law instruments would be difficult and would confuse rather than educate students. Secondly, since those instruments are not part of domestic law they should not be introduced into a first year undergraduate

37 According to the declaration under Art. 5 ULIS made by the U.K., and pursuant to Art. 1(3) Uniform Laws on International Sales Act 1967 (The U.K. Statute Law Database, Chapter 45, 1-26, available at <http://www.statutelaw.gov.uk/legResults.aspx?LegType=All Primary&PageNumber=1&BrowseLetter=U&NavFrom=1&activeTextDocId=1185417>, which implemented ULIS and ULFIS in the U.K., the parties to a contract would be bound by the ULIS only if they chose it themselves as the applicable law of contract.

course on contract law. Surprisingly, some respondents also reasoned that 'first year undergraduate students would not have the intellectual maturity to make meaningful use of these additional resources' or that 'it would hardly help to start adding stuff of dubious relevance (CISG, UNIDROIT) or speculative documents that may come to nothing'. However, it has to be pointed out that the majority of participants who were of the negative opinion noted that those instruments should nevertheless be taught to the students, although not in their first year contracts course.

Those who did consider the CISG (as well as UNIDROIT Principles and PECL) to be a necessary part of a first year undergraduate student course on contract law indicated they would rather refer to them only for comparative and supplementary purposes, *e.g.* 'to provoke enquiry into the rationale for rules which differ from those of the common law'. Such inclusion was further considered appropriate because, as explained by some participants, knowledge of the instruments is 'essential to ensure students are well equipped for the international environment', or to assist in the understanding of general development of contract law, particularly the recent initiatives of the European Civil Code. Finally, as noted by one respondent, 'in general, teaching of contract law is very egocentric in the U.K. and Northern Ireland and would benefit from a supranational element'.

5.5 *Should the CISG Be Taught to Students?*

The aim of the next question was to establish whether academics consider the CISG (as well as UNIDROIT Principles and PECL) suitable for an undergraduate course (not necessarily first year contracts), or rather for a postgraduate course only. The participants were allowed multiple responses and were further requested to state a reason for their answer.

As per Chart No. 7 below, 78.9% of the respondents believed that the CISG (as well as UNIDROIT Principles and PECL) should be taught to both undergraduate and postgraduate students, whereas 7.9 % of the participants considered that the instruments should be taught to postgraduate students only. Also, two individuals stated that the instruments should be neither taught to postgraduate nor to undergraduate students.

The comments from participants further show that many of the teachers surveyed would be happy to include those instruments in advanced undergraduate courses, such as *e.g.*: Commercial law or sale of goods law, or other undergraduate courses that concern comparative law.

Also, it has to be noted that, based on the comments, the academics studied differed in their opinion on what instrument should be most familiar to students graduating in law; for different reasons some thought that 'at least UNIDROIT Principles should be familiar', others thought that PECL should be taught 'at least in their outline' or that 'at least' or 'clearly' CISG should be taught as it is 'very important in certain industries in the EU and the world'; while very few opted for all instruments to be taught to undergraduates.

With regard to the two respondents who declared that the instruments should neither be taught to undergraduates nor to postgraduates, their comments explained that one wished to answer the question 'it all depends' whereas the other explained that, 'if by should is meant that some coverage should be required, then [the answer will be] no. But there is no reason why they should not be taught if that appeals to relevant academic staff'.

5.6 *Do Students Have Sufficient Knowledge of the CISG?*

The following survey question aimed to establish whether, from the point of view of the teaching staff, students have sufficient knowledge of the CISG (as well as UNIDROIT Principles and PECL). The participants were given the options, 'yes', 'no' or 'I don't know'.

The question did not divide between knowledge of a particular instrument as it is assumed that students should have an equal level of knowledge of all three instruments. Further, the question did not distinguish between undergraduate or postgraduate students and was aimed at gauging the level of knowledge of all students in general.

The results show that 57.1% of academics responded 'no', whilst 3.3% responded that they 'do not know' and only 9.5% responded 'yes': See Chart No. 8 below.

The results are alarming and clearly confirm that the majority of the participating U.K. academics consider students to have insufficient knowledge of the CISG (as well as UNIDROIT Principles and PECL) whereas only about 10 per cent of academics are confident that students are sufficiently familiar with the instruments.

This alarming perception by the majority of participants suggests there is a need to increase awareness among their students about the CISG (as well as UNIDROIT Principles and PECL) and to include those instruments to a greater extent in their syllabuses. Certainly, this would also require some of the teaching staff studied to become more familiar with the instruments given that, as shown above, not all of them were aware of the CISG.

Finally, the above question certainly assumes that students are required to have some knowledge of the instruments. It is insufficient for them to learn of the instruments belatedly in the course of professional practice. This is because, in many instances, it is unfamiliarity with the CISG in the first place that is the reason for the exclusion of the CISG from contracts by legal counsel, instead of difficulties with its application.[38]

5.7 *What Are Suggestions for Increasing Awareness of the CISG in the U.K.?*

The final question asked for participants' suggestions for increasing awareness of the CISG (as well as UNIDROIT Principles and PECL) in the U.K. This very general question ultimately aimed at generation of some discussion among U.K. academics on what further measures could be taken in order to increase awareness of the instruments. A further consideration was whether raising awareness was considered necessary.

The question did not specify among which groups of individuals concerned *e.g.* academics, students, legal professionals, industry people or policy makers, awareness of the CISG, UNIDROIT Principles and PECL should be increased. The question deliberately utilised an open format to enable participants to freely discuss the question posed.

In accordance with the comments received, it can be said that the vast majority of participants jointly agreed that in order to raise more awareness of these instruments at universities, they should be either better or indeed compulsorily integrated into existing subjects of the law degree; alternatively, a specialist (undergraduate or postgraduate) course devoted to those instruments should be established. The ratification of the CISG by the U.K. was another self-explanatory idea to increase awareness. Further proposals included teaching, extended research and publication on the topic, *e.g.* 'a conference or an SLS event – perhaps a special edition of the *Journal of Legal Studies*' as well as 'industry workshops and provisions of information' for business people or, interestingly, a '*Facebook*' fan club for students. All the initiatives would certainly raise awareness of the CISG and could ultimately help policy makers to take some steps towards the implementation of the CISG in the U.K. It would be, therefore, highly beneficial if any of those events were organised in the U.K. in the near future.

However, some participants thought that knowledge of the instruments ought not to be encouraged as 'there are plenty of other non-domestic legal forms with equal claim and

38 For this conclusion see also Spagnolo, *supra* note 21, at 141-142.

one cannot accommodate everything' or because 'they are of only peripheral significance, if any [...]; we do allocate a reasonable bit of time to *INCOTERMS*, which are international standard terms of sale and which are of real significance.' With regard to the latter statement, one should not forget that the CISG in its Articles 67-69 contains default rules relating to risk. However, *INCOTERMS* can be incorporated into a contract governed by the CISG to replace these default rules in accordance with Article 6.[39]

6 Conclusion

As can be seen from survey results, the majority, but not all, of the U.K. academics who responded to the survey, have extended knowledge of the CISG. However, only about half of the faculty members included it in courses they teach. The majority of courses that incorporate the CISG are optional and mostly offered to postgraduates. It should be hereby noted that the postgraduate degrees in law in the U.K. are generally completed by foreign, so-called 'overseas' students. Hence, if the current study is indicative of the broader situation throughout the U.K., one might conclude that British undergraduate students do not receive much exposure to the CISG during their studies. Moreover, the majority of the academics studied were of the opinion that students do not have sufficient knowledge of the Convention, UNIDROIT Principles and the PECL. This further means that participating teachers were aware of the fact that their students graduate with, arguably, inadequate knowledge of the CISG as well as the other international instruments. Furthermore, the vast majority of the surveyed U.K. academics did not teach ULFIS and ULIS in their courses although the conventions are part of the U.K. domestic law.

In view of the above, it might be difficult to ensure that English students obtain a full understanding of the general principles of contract law as a foundation for other courses in the law degree curriculum, knowing that certain aspects of general contract law, *i.e.* modern international instrument of contract law such as the CISG, might not be sufficiently taught in some of the U.K. universities.

The survey did not explicitly assess the reason for not including the CISG in courses taught by participating teaching staff. However, it can be seen from some comments of participants presented above, that a general reason for this practice is, at first, the complexity and length of material on domestic contract law that already needs to be covered with students; and,

39 Yet, there are various opinions on how the CISG and INCOTERMS interact, see, generally, J. Ramberg, 'CISG and INCOTERMS 2000', in: C. Baasch Andersen & U.G. Schroeter (Eds.), *Sharing International Commercial Law across National Borders: Festschrift for Albert H. Kritzer on the Occasion of his Eightieth Birthday*, 394-403 (2008).

secondly, the fact that the CISG has not been ratified in the U.K. and is not a part of U.K. contract law.

The CISG is inevitably connected to general contract and commercial law, and in particular, it is progressively becoming part of international legal education,[40] and, thus, should not simply be omitted in the syllabuses. Failing to teach it to students creates a potential risk of professionals not being aware of the CISG. Also professionals would be likely, for that reason, to exclude the CISG from application in their contracts.

In the author's opinion, all students need to have some, even if marginal, knowledge of the CISG. Further, incorporation (to some extent) into mandatory first year undergraduate contract courses will ensure that all students, not only postgraduate or those who choose to specialise in commercial or international trade law, are aware of the CISG. Students would also certainly gain better understanding of domestic law by some comparative references to the Convention, for example, by highlighting the differences related to the 'postal rule' or 'consideration' etc. Further, by indicating the influence of common law contractual principles in the wider context of international law of contracts, students would be even better informed about general contract law, which is now subject to wide harmonisation and/or Europeanization plans and cannot be simply overlooked as such in the law degree curriculum.

Hence, teachers should be required to include the CISG at least in the outlines of undergraduate contract law courses, if not in their lectures. Further, coursework questions that would require students to refer to the CISG could be set for a discussion in the tutorials. A general mention of its application as well as some comparative references would be sufficient for (first year) undergraduate students, whereas optional courses could discuss the CISG in detail. In addition, as mentioned earlier, several contract law textbooks and casebooks for first year students (as well as a variety of comparative contract law or commercial law textbooks and multiple online resources) now contain comparative references to the CISG, which should make it easier for teaching staff to introduce it to the students.

In addition, the CISG-critics who maintain that due to the fact that the Convention has not been applied in the U.K. and therefore, should not be taught to students, and particularly not as part of mandatory undergraduate courses, should be reminded that the CISG can nonetheless apply to the transactions of British businesses. For example, by virtue of rules

40 For example, through various annual international moots, such as *e.g.* the *Annual Willem C. Vis International Commercial Arbitration Moot* that takes place in Vienna or its sister moot, the *Willem C. Vis (East) International Commercial Arbitration Moot* that is conducted in Hong Kong. Further information is available at <http://www.cisg.law.pace.edu/vis.html>.

of private international law which may lead to the application of the law of a CISG Contracting State, or through the use of a foreign choice of law clause, as only an explicit exclusion of the CISG would preclude its application. It could also be applied by the courts or arbitral tribunals as an expression of the *lex mercatoria*.[41] Therefore, students should be taught about the CISG in order to be able to determine the applicable law of international sales contracts and its implications as well as to be able to advise their future clients on potential sources of applicable law.

To conclude, those who claim that due to complexity and length of material it is impossible to create a perfect compulsory curriculum for a contract law course that would provide for all domestic law principles supplemented by the CISG for both undergraduates and postgraduates, and those who argue that the Convention should be included only in optional courses related to commercial, European or comparative contract law, are therefore unconvincing. It is a reasonable expectation for all teaching staff active in the legal field of contract and international commercial law to increase awareness of the CISG among students, whilst also improving their general knowledge about the Convention and other international instruments relevant for the international sales transactions. The author recommends that U.K. academics do more to educate law students about the instruments. Indeed, due to time restraints, complexity and length of the material on English law of contracts it would be sufficient to provide at least a general introduction with some comparative references, even in basic contract law courses for undergraduate students. A wider discussion between academics and professionals could also certainly generate greater interest in the CISG and help inform discussion amongst policymakers who are working on the implementation of the Convention in the U.K. For that purpose, some of the initiatives promoting the Convention discussed in the earlier section could be undertaken by the U.K. academics.

Finally, if the U.K. wished to proceed with accession, the CISG would have to be incorporated into domestic law by a statute. Consequently, the U.K. parliament would need to pass an implementing act to that effect. However, at present, there appears to be no sign of any official parliamentary works on the CISG, and no further consultations by the BIS since 2007.[42] Therefore, it seems highly unlikely the CISG will be implemented in the U.K. in the near future. This is also apparent in the light of a following brief statement of the BIS representative issued in response to the author's enquiry on the U.K.'s current position regarding accession to the CISG:

41 See also A. Rogowska, 'CISG in UK: How does the CISG Govern the Contractual Relations of English Businessmen?', *International Company and Commercial Law Review* 226 (2007).

42 Statement from the U.K. Department for Business, Innovation and Skills (personal email correspondence on 2 March 2010).

'Further work on the CISG is not currently a priority for the Department for Business Innovation and Skills. We have carried out informal consultation and the prevailing view seems to be that there is little appetite amongst stakeholders to push this matter forward. Nonetheless we continue to welcome opinions and evidence to alter this position.'[43]

7 CHART OVERVIEW

Chart No. 1: What is the Level of Knowledge of the CISG among Academics?

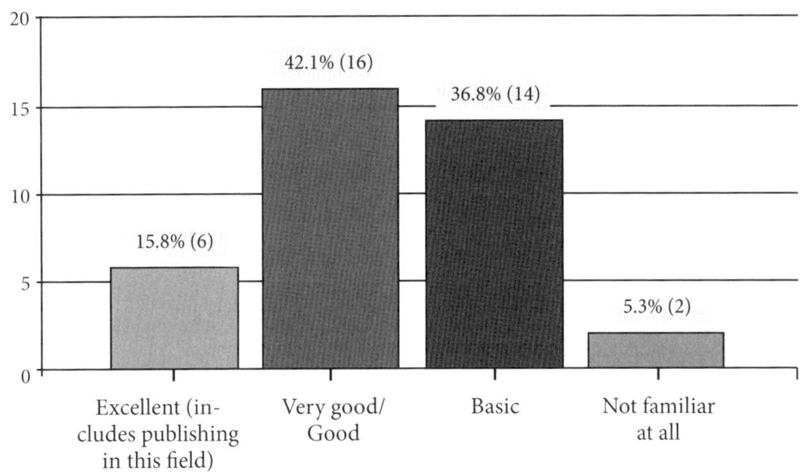

43 Statement from the U.K. Department for Business, Innovation and Skills (personal email correspondence on 29 January 2010).

Chart No. 2: What Courses Incorporate the CISG?

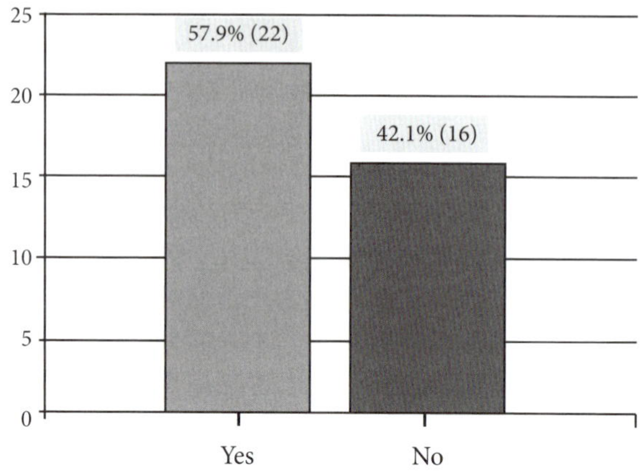

Chart No. 3: Is this Course Compulsory or Optional?

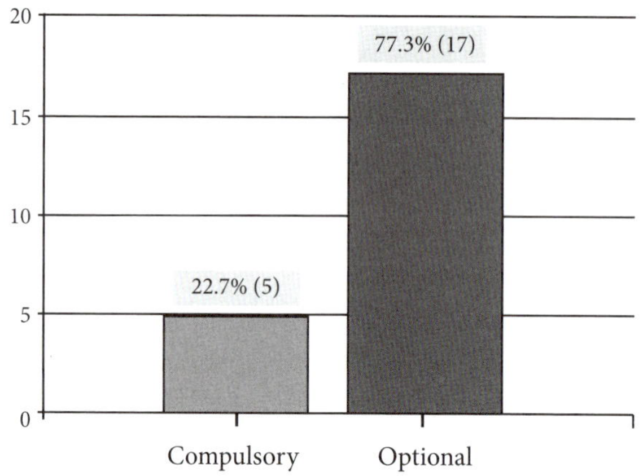

Chart No. 4: Is the Course at a Postgraduate or Undergraduate Level?

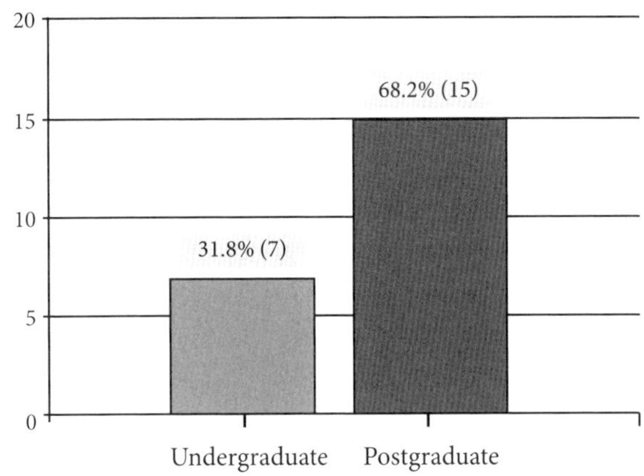

Chart No. 5: Do Any of the Courses Taught Incorporate the ULFIS and ULIS?

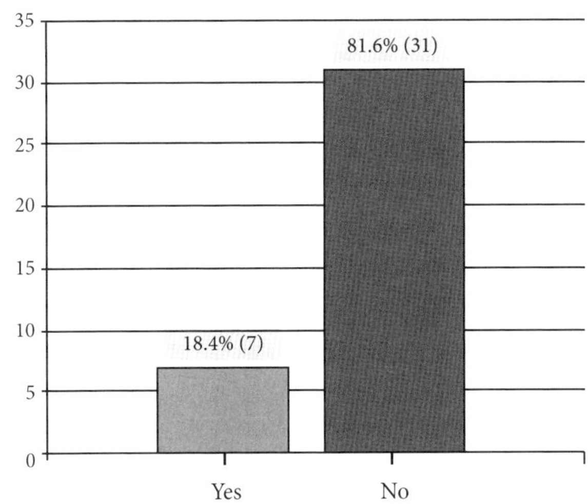

Chart No. 6: Are the CISG, UNIDROIT Principles & PECL Considered Necessary for First Year Undergraduate Student Courses on Contract Law?

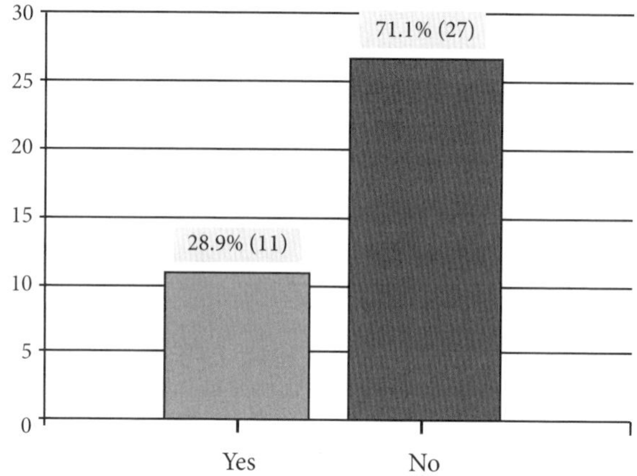

Chart No. 7: Should the CISG, UNIDROIT Principles & PECL Be Taught to Students?

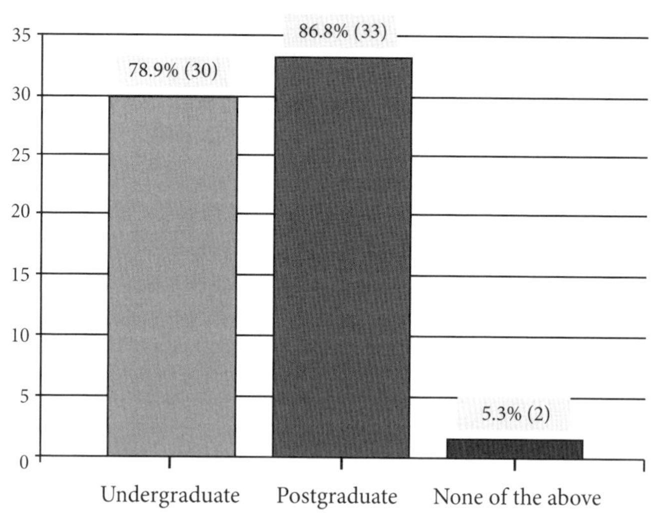

Chart No. 8: Do Students Have Sufficient Knowledge of the CISG, UNIDROIT Principles & PECL?

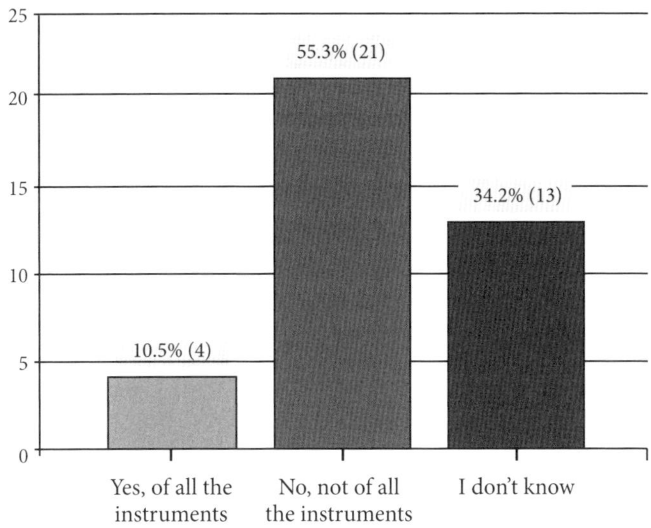

Global Sales Law – Theory and Practice

Ingeborg Schwenzer[*] *and Christopher Kee*[**]

1 Empirical Research

1.1 Previous Surveys

Despite the importance of global trade, until very recently little was known about how the law interacts with actual practice. There were many anecdotal stories being told. One of these stories, in particular, was that parties disliked the CISG and therefore were regularly contracting out of its application. In recent years there has been an increase in empirical research in this field, however these surveys have been limited as to the geographic area approached, as well as to the number of survey respondents. As far as geographic areas are concerned, these surveys focussed on Germanic legal systems (Germany,[1] Switzerland[2] and Austria[3]), the USA[4], and a rather small survey with under 50 respondents conducted in China.[5] There have been other surveys which did not directly address the CISG but

* Dr. iur. (Freiburg, Germany), LL.M. (Berkeley, USA), Professor for Private Law, University of Basel, Switzerland.

** Dr. iur. (Basel), LL.B., BA (Hons) (Deakin), Senior Researcher, Faculty of Law of the University of Basel, Adjunct Professor, City University of Hong Kong, and Honorary Fellow, Deakin Law School.

1 J. Meyer, 'UN-Kaufrecht in der deutschen Anwaltpraxis', 69 *RabelsZ* 457 (2005); M. Köhler & Y. Guo, 'The Acceptance of the Unified Sales Law (CISG) in Different Legal Systems – An International Comparison of three Surveys on the Exclusion of the CISG's Application Conducted in the United States, Germany and China', 20 *Pace Int'l L.J.* 45 (2008).

2 J. Meyer, 'UN-Kaufrecht in der schweizerischen Anwaltspraxis', 104 *Schweizerische Juristen-Zeitung* 421 (2008); C. Widmer & P. Hachem, 'Switzerland', in: F. Ferrari (Ed.), *The CISG and its Impact on National Legal Systems*, 281 (2008).

3 J. Meyer, 'UN-Kaufrecht in der österreichischen Anwaltspraxis', 20 *Österreichische Juristen-Zeitung* 792 (2008).

4 M. Gordon, 'Some Thoughts on the Receptiveness of Contract Rules in the CISG and UNIDROIT Principles as Reflected in One State's (Florida) Experience of (1) Law School Faculty, (2) Members of the Bar with an International Practice, and (3) Judges', 46 (Suppl.) *Am. J. Comp. L.* 361 (1998); Köhler & Guo, *supra* note 1; G. Philippopoulos, 'Awareness of the CISG Among American Attorneys', 40 *U.C.C. L.J.* 357 (2008); P. Fitzgerald, 'The International Contracting Practices Survey Project', 27 *J.L. & Com.* 1 (2008).

5 Köhler & Guo, *supra* note 518.

considered cross border transactions in Europe[6] and the worldwide use of transnational law.[7]

Against this research background our research group in Basel decided to conduct a global survey on the use and understandings of law in international sales transactions.

1.2 Global Sales Law Surveys

The Global Sales Law survey was conducted online in Fall 2009 and was supported by the United Nations Commission on International Trade Law (UNCITRAL). The survey was conducted in the six UN languages. Approximately 5000 individuals received personally addressed letters in United Nations envelopes. There were four target groups – practising lawyers, arbitrators, businesses engaging in trade and law schools. In addition various email lists were used to draw attention to the survey website. It is estimated that about 9,000 people across the globe would have received an invitation to participate. Approximately four weeks after the letters, follow up emails were sent. The survey was open for a period of six weeks ending in early November 2009.

The survey website run by our research team received more than 1,500 hits and 640 useable responses.[8] Responses were submitted from 85 countries,[9] of which 58% are CISG member states. Many of these countries have not been included in reported surveys before, especially countries from South America, the Middle East, Africa and Asia.

In addition to the online survey we continue to collect and review general terms and conditions of, thus far, more than 80 businesses[10] which were published and freely available in English, French or German on the internet.

6 S. Vogenauer & S. Weatherill, 'The European Community's Competence to Pursue the Harmonisation of Contract Law – an Empirical Contribution to the Debate, in: S. Vogenauer & S. Weatherill (Eds.), *The Harmonisation of European Contract Law*, 105 (2006).

7 K.P. Berger & H. Dubberstein, 'Anwendung Transnationalen Rechts in der internationalen Vertrags- und Schiedspraxis', 101 *Zeitschrift für Vergleichende Rechtswissenschaft* 12 *et seq.* (2002).

8 Initial analysis has identified useable responses per category to be: Arbitrators 98; Lawyers 347; Businesses 60; Law Schools 135.

9 Including lawyers from 66 different countries. The IP addresses of respondents were examined to determine this figure. There is a certain margin of error in this number as some respondents may have been using a proxy server which would have hidden their true location. The likelihood of this affecting the figures was considered minimal.

10 All companies searched are on the Forbes 500 list.

2 Results in Detail

2.1 Sales Cases in General

The increase in international trade is clearly reflected by a comparable increase in sales law litigation and arbitration. Practitioners in law firms were asked to report on the total number of sales law cases between 2004 and 2008. The results indicate a steady increase of approximately 5% per year which almost exactly equals the development of world trade during this period.[11] On average arbitrators indicated that 16% of their case load involved goods transactions over the last 10 years. If this percentage is applied to the total number of arbitrations reported by arbitral institutions during that period (not including ad hoc arbitrations) it can be hypothesised that nearly 5,000 arbitrations concerned the sale of goods over that period.[12]

2.2 CISG Cases

Having regard to the total number of sale of goods cases, the increase in the number dealing with the CISG is all the more impressive. Whereas throughout the 1990s CISG cases were scarce, at least in the majority of CISG member states, today it can confidentially be said that more than 2,000 cases are listed in the leading case databases on the CISG.[13] We estimate this is four times more than ten years ago. The significant majority of these cases have been decided by state courts. This is notable because it has been suggested – and is confirmed by our survey – that more than 60% of international commercial disputes are not litigated before courts but rather go to international commercial arbitration. Arbitral awards are typically not published as confidentiality is one of the main features of arbitration. Thus the real number of CISG cases must be a multiple of those published in the databases.

---

11 This figure can be found at <http://www.wto.org/english/res_e/statis_e/its2009_e/its09_world_trade_dev_e.pdf>, at 7.

12 This figure is based on the reported statistics published by the Hong Kong International Arbitration Centre (HKIAC), available at <http://www.hkiac.org/show_content.php?article_id=9>.

13 The precise number of cases is difficult to calculate and is in any event increased regularly. The Pace Website reports 2,500 cases, and the CISG-online website reports 2,094 – although some cases are reported on both sites, there are many that are only reported on one database. Consequently, the real figure may be closer to 3,000.

More than 100 decisions have been delivered by US courts alone,[14] however despite this in 2008 two decisions of the Southern District of New York claimed that there was 'virtually no American case law on the CISG'.[15] Presently there are more than 360 CIETAC arbitral awards that have been translated and reported on the Pace website. CIETAC is the China International Economic and Trade Arbitration Commission. As CIETAC only publishes a selection of its arbitral awards and even then only three years after they have been rendered, it can be expected that virtually thousands of arbitral awards concerning the CISG must exist in China.

The importance of the CISG in international litigation and arbitration is clearly mirrored in the results of our survey. Arbitrators in particular reported a significant increase in the numbers of CISG cases they were asked to determine. Over the last ten years respondent arbitrators indicated they had heard 1,306 cases in total involving the sale of goods; in 2008 alone 217 of these were CISG cases. Thus it can be extrapolated that a very high percentage of all sale of goods cases involve the CISG.

3 Familiarity with the CISG

Time and again it has been reported that unfortunately lawyers are still not very familiar with the CISG. In the surveys previous to ours, results regarding familiarity have varied greatly – from an almost 100% familiarity reported from Germany and Switzerland,[16] good familiarity reported from China and Denmark, to much less familiarity in mainly Common Law countries.[17]

---

14 As of 9 June 2010, there are 115 reported U.S. cases on the CISG-online website, available at <http://www.cisg-online.ch>, run by Prof. Ingeborg Schwenzer at the University of Basel, Switzerland, containing selected articles and numerous court decisions and arbitral awards, and 136 on the Pace website, available at <http://www.cisg.law.pace.edu>, run at Pace University, New York, U.S.A., containing numerous materials, scholarly writings, court decisions and arbitral awards. Other case law can be found on the Case Law on UNCITRAL Texts (CLOUT) database, available at <http://www.uncitral.org/uncitral/en/case_law.html>, which contains court decisions and arbitral awards to increase international awareness of UNCITRAL texts and to facilitate their uniform interpretation and application. See also UNILEX, available at <http://www.unilex.info>, run by Prof. Michael Joachim Bonell, containing materials, court decisions and arbitral awards on the CISG as well as the UNIDROIT Principles of International Commercial Contracts 2004.

15 *Hilaturas Miel, S.L. v. Republic of Iraq*, 573 F Supp 2d 781 (S. D. N. Y. 2008), 20 August 2008, CISG-online 1777, available at <http://cisgw3.law.pace.edu/cases/080820u1.html>; *Macromex Srl. v. Globex International Inc.*, 2008 WL 1752530 (S. D. N. Y. 2008), 16 April 2008, CISG-online 1653, available at <http://cisgw3.law.pace.edu/cases/080416u1.html>.

16 L. Spagnolo, 'A Glimpse Through the Kaleidoscope: Choices of Law and the CISG', 13(1) *Vindobona Journal of International Commercial Law and Arbitration* 135, at 138, note 14 (2009).

17 Spagnolo, *supra* note 16, at 138. For surveys on the U.S., see *supra* note 4 generally.

Our survey asked both law firm practitioners and businesses to state their relative familiarity with the CISG. As a percentage of the total number of respondents in each sub-survey, 78% of lawyers and 45% of businesses reported being familiar or somewhat familiar. However, to draw a meaningful comparison with other surveys it is necessary to examine the responses coming from CISG member states alone. The respective figures are 84% for lawyers and 63% for businesses. Although these figures are encouraging and higher than previous surveys,[18] the lack of familiarity on the part of businesses is alarming. This is particularly the case as only 13% of businesses reported using external lawyers.

Lawyers were also asked whether they discussed the CISG with their clients. Examining only the replies from those situated in CISG member states it can be seen that 45% always or sometimes raised the issue. Interestingly 5% indicated they never discussed the CISG. However, it is impossible to draw any significant conclusions from these statistics. A high percentage of respondents failed to provide any response (40% of those from CISG member states) and even fewer answered a subsequent question inquiring as to the circumstances in which the lawyers would raise the CISG.

Figure 1 Lawyer Familiarity in Contracting States as %

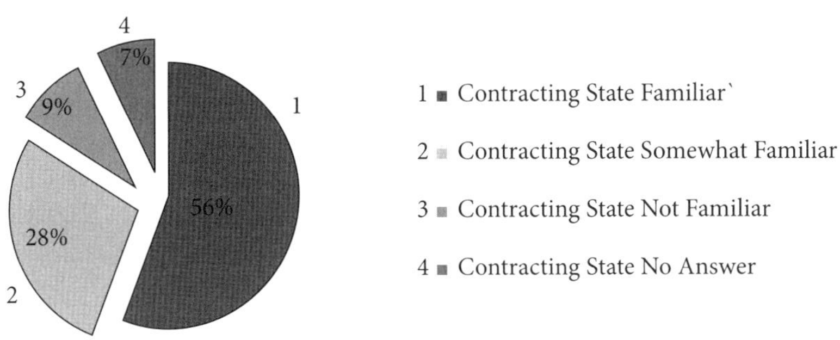

4 Exclusion of the CISG

The question of the extent to which parties are opting out, or excluding the operation of the CISG has become a perennial one. Hearsay suggests the number of opt-outs is considerable. The empirical evidence from other surveys is less emphatic, suggesting that between

18 Fitzgerald, *supra* note 4, at 41, citing 65% U.S. lawyers when all categories of familiarity are combined.

37% and 71% of lawyers promote opting out.[19] The 71% comes from a survey of U.S. lawyers, although the sample was very small.[20]

Our survey figures are considerably less dramatic. Of the lawyers from CISG member states who answered this question, only 13% reported always excluding the CISG, and a further 32% reported they did so sometimes. A considerable 55% answered that they never or rarely excluded the CISG. The respective figures for US lawyers who provided a response were: 12% always excluding, 42% sometimes excluding, and 46% never or rarely excluding. The responses from non-contracting states are similar to the US. Amongst that group 19% always excluded the CISG, 36% did so sometimes, while 45% rarely or never excluded it.

Figure 2 Lawyers Contracting Out in Contracting States as %

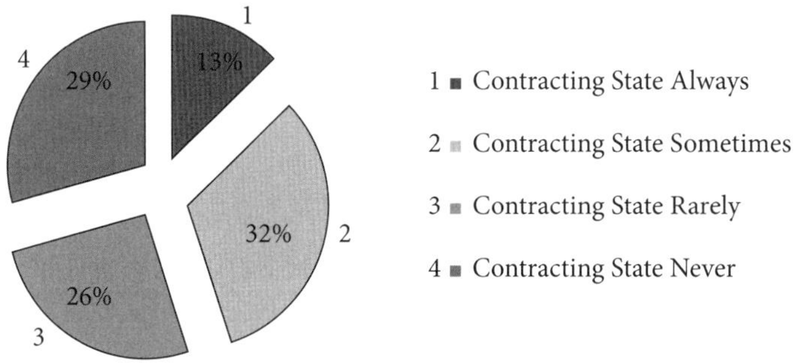

Unlike in other surveys, unfamiliarity with the CISG was seldom cited as a reason for excluding it by the lawyers who responded to the question, although many respondents who excluded the CISG indicated a certain preference for their own domestic law. Some respondents from South America expressed their concern about a lack of case law – the two jurisdictions in question were Brazil, a non-member state, and Chile, a CISG signatory. It is evident though that many of the respondents do carefully consider the most appropriate law to be applied to their client's situation and decide accordingly. This underscores the good degree of familiarity with the CISG already noted above.

19 Spagnolo, *supra* note 16, at 136.

20 M. Köhler, *Survey regarding the Relevance of the United Nations Convention for the International Sale of Goods (CISG) in Legal Practice and the Exclusion of its Application*, (2006), available at <http://www.cisg.law.pace.edu/cisg/biblio/ koehler.html>.

5 CHOICE OF LAW CLAUSES

Businesses were asked whether they included a choice of law clause in their standard terms and conditions. It is significant that 47% indeed did so; this coincides with the findings of other surveys that the possibility of choosing the applicable law is highly valued.[21] Such a choice cannot on its own be interpreted as a decision to opt out of the CISG, if for no other reason than that a choice of law clause is quite a sensible way to deal with those areas not covered by the CISG.

Businesses and arbitrators were also asked to identify which law parties were choosing in their contracts, and lawyers were asked to identify the law which they recommend. As might be expected, businesses and lawyers displayed a preference for their own national law.[22] Arbitrators reported a variety of generic laws such as the law of the seller, however consistently recurring references were made to English and Swiss law.[23] Especially among South American participants a reference to the law of the place of performance of the contracts was popular. This is not surprising as the conflict of law rules in this region usually designate this law as the proper law of the sales contract.[24] A further interesting response from a small number of arbitrators was the suggestion that the applicable law was that of the seat of arbitration, reminiscent of an old approach according to which the choice of the seat of arbitration also constitutes an implicit choice of law of that place.[25]

In this context it is also interesting that arbitrators indicated that between 20%[26] and 36%[27] of cases involving the sale of goods applied non-national laws such as PICC and *lex mercatoria*.

---

21 Vogenauer & Weatherill, *supra* note 6, at 120, 'Importance of Ability to Choose the Governing law'.

22 This finding concurs with Vogenauer & Weatherill, *supra* note 6, at 121.

23 This finding concurs with S. Vogenauer, *Oxford Civil Justice Survey - Civil Justice Systems in Europe: Implications for Choice of Forum and Choice of Contract Law A Business Survey Final Results*, available at <http://denning.law.ox.ac.uk/iecl/pdfs/Oxford%20Civil%20Justice%20Survey%20-%20Summary%20of%20Results,%20Final.pdf>, questions 17.1 & 17.2.

24 E. Muñoz Lopez, *Modern Sales Law in Ibero-America*, at 36 (2011).

25 For example, this was the position in the U.K. before it was rejected in *Compagnie d'Armement Maritime SA v. Compagnie Tunisienne de Navigation SA* [1971] AC 572, at 596.

26 Including non responses. See also Fitzgerald, *supra* note 4, at 43, reporting that 50% of all respondents were not familiar with PICC.

27 Valid percentage response.

6 Specific Contract Clauses

Our survey was also directed towards specific clauses contained in standard terms and conditions. Businesses were asked to report whether they included certain clauses. The results of these questions, as might be expected, reveal that limitation of liability clauses are very frequently included, with 55% of respondents indicating their use. Marginally in excess of one third of the respondents reported using both liquidated damages or penalty clauses, and INCOTERMS.[28] It is remarkable that at least 12% referred in their standard terms and conditions to the UN Global Compact or similar ethical guidelines.[29] All these results are supported by our study of general terms and conditions published on company websites.

7 Dispute Resolution Clauses

Our survey results clearly indicate that disputes in international trade are today primarily a matter for arbitral tribunals. 60% of business respondents reported including a dispute resolution clause in their general terms and conditions. While this on its own does not speak to the predominance of arbitration, it supports the other statistics which do. Arbitration was strongly preferred by lawyers, 60% of whom recommended it to their clients. To this figure can be added, probably to a significant degree, the 12% who recommend a multi-tiered dispute resolution clause. Only 21% recommended litigation in state courts, and 7% mediation alone. These results are supported by other surveys that also report that 60% to 65% prefer international arbitration over state court litigation.[30] Confidentiality and speed are still noted as the primary reasons.[31]

The preference for international arbitration is clearly reflected in the development of the reported case load across many arbitral institutions. The case load of some institutions, especially those in the Asian region, has doubled or even tripled in the last ten years.[32]

---

28 38% and 37% respectively.

29 For a discussion of the consequences, see I. Schwenzer & B. Leisinger, 'Ethical Values and International Sales Contracts', in: B. Leisinger & M. Probst (Eds.), *Human Security and Business*, 124 (2007).

30 Vogenauer, *supra* note 23, question 48, reporting that 63% of respondents preferred arbitration and 37% preferred litigation before a court when conducting a cross border transaction.

31 See, *e.g.*, Vogenauer, *supra* note 23, (questions 49.1 & 49.2).

32 HKIAC website, *supra* note 12; see also S. Greenberg, C. Kee, *et al.*, *International Commercial Arbitration - An Asia-Pacific Perspective*, para 1.127 *et seq.* (2011).

8 Conclusion

Laws tend not to be the engine room of an economy, rather they follow some steps behind. International trade, or perhaps more accurately, global trade, is no different. The globalisation of trade transforms law. Industrialisation at the beginning of the 19th century precipitated the codification and rationalisation of law worldwide at the level of nation states. Global trade in the 21st century is moving us towards the a-nationalisation and delocalisation of law.

Whether a truly global sales law that satisfies all the needs of global trade will ultimately emerge, and indeed whether it would be entirely desirable, is something we can debate. However, we can already recognise and acknowledge the important contribution the CISG has made and continues to make to international trade. One must also acknowledge the role of instruments like PICC and INCOTERMS, and last but not least, international arbitration. All of these enhance predictability, which in turn saves costs, and increases trade. More trade will mean more of the positive effects upon law referred to above, and the emergence of a positive spiral.

The Diversity of *Favor Contractus*: The Impact of the CISG on Japan's Civil Code and its Reform

Hiroo Sono[*]

1 Introduction

The goal of the United Nations Convention on Contracts for the International Sale of Goods (CISG) to unify and harmonize law of international sales is most directly achieved by application of the CISG to contracts for the international sale of goods.

However, that is not the only channel through which the CISG functions to unify or harmonize law. It also serves as a model for international, regional, and domestic law reforms.[1] In this article, I will refer to this process as uniformity or harmonization through 'assimilation'. Assimilation is most conspicuous in legislation influenced by the CISG: *e.g.*, China, Germany, Scandinavian countries (other than Denmark), former socialist states such as Russia and Estonia.[2] This process of 'legislative assimilation' is occurring also in Japan which has acceded to the CISG recently in 2008[3] (see *infra* Part 3.3).

On the other hand, there is a more discreet and indirect way in which assimilation is achieved. That is by interpretation of the existing domestic laws in light of the CISG, and thereby transforming understanding of existing laws. This process of 'interpretive assimilation' can also be observed in Japan even prior to its accession to the CISG (see *infra* Part 3.2).

---

* Professor of Law, Hokkaido University, Japan; member of the CISG Advisory Council (CISG-AC).

1 For examples of various impacts of the CISG beyond its original scope ('*Ausstrahlungswirkung*'), see F. Ferrari (Ed.), *The CISG and its Impact on National Legal Systems* (2008).

2 P. Schlechtriem, 'Basic Structures and General Concepts of the CISG as Models or a Harmonization of the Law of Obligations', 10 *Juridica International* 27 (2005); F. Ferrari, 'The CISG and its Impact on National Legal Systems – General Report', in: F. Ferrari (Ed.), *supra* note 1, 413 at 474-478.

3 For an account of the background, see H. Sono, 'Japan's Accession to and Implementation of the United Nations Convention on Contracts for the International Sale of Goods (CISG)', 53 *Japanese Yearbook of International Law* (2010 forthcoming). For an earlier account written while Japan was preparing for accession, see H. Sono, 'Japan's Accession to the CISG: The Asia Factor', 20 *Pace Int'l L. Rev.* 105 (2008).

One purpose of this paper is to provide illustrative examples of interpretive and legislative assimilations by taking Japan as an example.

Another purpose is to confirm or reconfirm the theoretical underpinnings of the CISG. Assimilation is not a process of carbon copying the CISG, but a process of selection.[4] An analysis of the selection will help to discern the distinctive characteristics of the contract law principles underlying the CISG (see Art. 7(2) CISG). Since it is impossible in this short paper to provide an overall examination of the assimilation process, the focus will be on one underlying principle of the CISG: the principle of *favor contractus*.[5] More particularly, the focus will be on the limitation of avoidance of contracts.

After exploring the meaning of *favor contractus* in the next section (Part 2), I will describe the assimilation of Japanese law with the CISG in respect of the principle of *favor contractus* (Part 3). I will then analyze the diverse versions of *favor contractus* and highlight the theoretical underpinning of the CISG (Part 4).

2 *FAVOR CONTRACTUS*

2.1 Favor contractus *in International Commercial Law*

In the field of international commercial law, the principle of *favor contractus* was perhaps first coined, or at the very least made familiar, by Michael Joachim Bonell in one of the early commentaries on the CISG,[6] and later in the context of the UNIDROIT Principles

4 Some countries have taken the ultimate form of legislative assimilation by enacting the provisions of the CISG as the law applicable to domestic transactions. Norway and the Tokelau Islands enacted the CISG as a sales law for both international and domestic sales law, see Schlechtriem, *supra* note 2, at 30; J. Lookofsky, 'The Scandinavian Experience', in: F. Ferrari (Ed.), *The 1980 Uniform Sales Law: Old Issues Revisited in the Light of Recent Experiences* 95, at 116-121 (2003). However, note that in the case of Norway, the order of the provisions has been reorganized, and discrepancies exist: *id.*

5 B. Keller, '*Favor* Contractus: Reading the CISG in Favor of the Contract', in: C.B. Andersen & U. Schroeter (Eds.), *Sharing International Commercial Law across National Boundaries: Festschrift Albert Kritzer*, 247 (2008) is an attempt to demonstrate through inductive inquiries that *favor contractus* is indeed a principle underlying the CISG.

6 M.J. Bonell, in: C.M. Bianca & M.J. Bonell (Eds.), *Commentary on International Sales Law: The 1980 Vienna Sales Convention*, Art. 7 para. 2.3.2.2 (1987). Bonell argues that the so-called *favor contractus* is a 'general principle' (Art. 7(2)) of the CISG which may be deduced from Arts. 19(2), 25-26, 34, 37, 48, 49, 51(1), 64 and 71-72 CISG. On the application of *favor contractus* to arbitration agreements in international commercial arbitration, see K.P. Berger, *The Creeping Codification of the Lex Mercatoria*, 199-201 (2010); S. Luttrell, *Bias Challenges in International Commercial Arbitration: the Need for a 'Real Danger' Test*, 272-273 (2009).

of International Commercial Contracts.[7] Bonell defines *favor contractus* as 'the aim of preserving the contract whenever possible, thus limiting the number of cases in which its existence or validity may be questioned or in which it may be terminated before time'.[8] Under the CISG, *favor contractus* appears in rules that facilitate contract formation, such as Article 19(2) and in rules that deny nullification of contracts due to initial impossibility (see Art. 68 sentence 2 CISG). It also appears in rules that limit avoidance of contracts: limitation of avoidance to cases of fundamental breach (Arts. 25, 49, & 64 CISG); seller's right to cure (Arts. 34, 37, 48 CISG); and permission of partial avoidance (Arts. 51(1), 71 & 72 CISG).[9]

Bonell justifies this principle by stating that 'it is normally in the interest of both parties to do [everything] possible to keep their original bargain alive than to renounce it and to look for alternative goods or services elsewhere on the market'.[10] In other words, favoring the contract is to favor and protect the purpose of the contractual arrangement.

Klaus Peter Berger also observes that '[in] both long term business relationships and arms' length bargains, the parties have a vital interest in upholding their contract. [...] From the perspective of legal theory, the principle of "*favor contractus*" correlates with the general significance of contractual consensus of the parties as the driving force behind the creation and evolution of transnational commercial law'.[11]

However, Berger's point in correlating *favor contractus* with the protection of contractual consensus poses the question of the relationship between *favor contractus* and the long standing contract law principle of *pacta sunt servanda* (agreements must be kept). We turn to this issue next.

2.2 Favor contractus *v. Pacta Sunt Servanda*

The principle of *pacta sunt servanda* calls for observation of the contract, which is one form of favoring the contract. Then why do we need a new principle of *favor contractus*? It is because they differ and there is even a tension between the two.

---

7 M.J. Bonell, *An International Restatement of Contract Law* (1st ed., 1994). The analysis is unchanged in its latest edition: M.J. Bonell, *An International Restatement of Contract Law* (2005). Citations from this book in this paper are taken from the latest edition.

8 *Id.*, at 102.

9 For a fuller account, see Keller, *supra* note 5, at 251-266.

10 Bonell, *supra* note 7, at 102.

11 Berger, *supra* note 6, at 199-201. See also *id.*, at 142.

One commentator recently explained that *pacta sunt servanda* focuses on 'compliance' with contractual commitments, and thereby allows avoidance of contracts even in cases of minor non-conformity, whereas *favor contractus* focuses on 'maintenance' of the contract.[12] However, this formulation is perhaps too narrow, because maintenance of the contract in itself is not the ultimate goal of *favor contractus*. *Favor contractus* does place a limit on contract avoidance but does not prohibit avoidance. When contract avoidance, and thus non-maintenance of the contract, is allowed, it is still in accordance with *favor contractus*. This function of sorting out which contracts are to be maintained and which are not, is inherent in *favor contractus*. This is in stark contrast with *pacta sunt servanda* which is only limited by external principles such as hardship[13] or *clausula rebus sic stantibus* (doctrine of changed circumstances).

Thus the focal point is under what conditions avoidance of contracts should be allowed. Under the CISG, this is when the breach of contract is fundamental (Arts. 49(1)(a) and 64(1)(a) CISG), *i.e.*, when a breach of contract substantially deprives the aggrieved party of what he was entitled to expect under the contract (Art. 25 CISG). Avoidance of the contract is also allowed pursuant to the so-called *Nachfrist* procedure when the breaching seller does not deliver the goods or when the breaching buyer does not pay the price or take delivery of the goods (Arts. 49(1)(b) and Art. 64(1)(b) CISG). All of these are, in essence, cases where the purpose of the contract has failed.

Thus, while *pacta sunt servanda* focuses on 'compliance' with the initial contractual commitment, *favor contractus* focuses on 'compliance' with the purpose of the contract.[14] In other words, *pacta sunt servanda* focuses on 'presentiation' whereas *favor contractus* focuses on the 'purpose' of the contract. The term 'presentiation' is attributed to the late Ian Macneil, the proponent of relational contract law theory,[15] in describing the core principle of classical contract law. To 'presentiate' means to bring the future into the present; or more plainly, to fix the future contractual relationship at the time of the conclusion of the contract, in order to maximize predictability.

12 Keller, *supra* note 5, at 248-249.

13 For rules on hardship, see *e.g.* 'UNIDROIT International Institute for the Unification of Private Law', *UNIDROIT Principles of International Commercial Contracts (2004)*, Rome, April 2004, available at <http://www.unidroit.org/english/principles/contracts/principles2004/integralversionprinciples2004-e.pdf>, Arts. 6.2.1-6.2.3.

14 O. Morita, *et al.*, 'Rikoseikyuken to Keiyakusekinin wo Kataru' [Talks on Right to Performance and Contractual Liability], 1244 *Hanrei Taimuzu* 22, at 29-32 (2007).

15 The major writings of Ian Macneil on relational contract law are collected in D. Campbell (Ed.), *The Relational Theory of Contract: Selected Works of Ian Macneil* (2001).

With this in mind, we proceed to the illustrative examples of how Japanese law has been assimilated with the idea of *favor contractus*, particularly the aspect of limiting avoidance of contract. Interestingly, the idea of *favor contractus* itself has been a source of inspiration in this assimilation process.[16]

3 The Process of Assimilation

3.1 *Pre-Assimilation Japanese Law*

3.1.1 The General Rule on Avoidance

By way of background, let me explain the rules of Japanese law prior to assimilation. The general rule of avoidance under Japanese law is the rule of *Nachfrist* avoidance (Art. 541 Japanese Civil Code).[17] In order to avoid a contract in case of breach, the aggrieved party must first set a reasonable period of time for performance, and only if the breaching party does not perform within that period of time may the aggrieved party avoid the contract by giving notice to that effect.

Another point that has profound implications is that traditionally, 'fault' on the part of the breaching party was considered to be a requirement for avoidance. This is because avoidance was regarded as a 'sanction' imposed upon the breaching party. Given this

16 S. Tsuburaya, '*Favor Contractus*' (Keiyaku no Soncho), in: S. Tsuburaya, *et al.* (Eds.), *Gendai Keiyakuho no Tenkai* [The Development of Modern Contract Law] 3 (2000); T. Uchida, *Keiyaku no Jidai* [The Era of Contracts] (2000); H. Sono, 'Minpo Kaisei no Doko (3): Amerika, Kokusaiteki Hotoitsu' [Trends in Civil Law Reform, (3): US & International Uniform Laws], in: T. Uchida & A. Omura (Eds.), *Minpo no Soten* [Issues in Civil Law] 36 (2007). *Favor contractus* is analyzed also in the context of the Civil Code reform debate most notably by Osamu Morita: O. Morita, '<Minpoten> to iu Mondai no Seikaku: Saikenho Kaisei no Bunmyakuka no tameni' [Characterization of the 'Civil Code' Question: For the Contextualization of the Obligations Law Reform], 1319 *Jurisuto* 36 (2006); O. Morita, 'Riko Seikyuken ka remedy approach ka: Saikenho Kaisei no Bunmyakuka no tameni' [Right for performance or remedy approach?: For the Contextualization of the Obligations Law Reform], 1329 *Jurisuto* 82 (2007); O. Morita, '"Keiyaku no Soncho (favor contractus)" ni tsuite' [On "Favor contractus"], in: Endo Mitsuo Moto Saikosaibansho Hanji Kiju Kinen Bunshu Henshu Iinkai (Ed.), *Endo Mitsuo Moto Saikosaibansho Hanji Kiju Kinen Bunshu [Festschrift Mitsuo Endo]* 199 (2007); Morita, *et al.*, *supra* note 14, 1244 Hanrei Taimuzu 22; K. Saigusa, 'UCC Dainihen Kaisei Sagyo ni okeru "Keiyaku no Soncho (favor contractus)"' ['Favor contractus' in the Revision of UCC Article 2], 84 *Waseda Hogaku* 191 (2009) analyzes *favor contractus* in the context of the Uniform Commercial Code.

17 English translation of the provisions of the Japanese Civil Code in this paper is taken from the Japanese Government's 'Japanese Law Translation' website available at <http://www.japaneselawtranslation.go.jp/?re=02>.
Article 541 (Right to Cancel for Delayed Performance) 'In cases where one of the parties does not perform his/her obligations, if the other party demands performance of the obligations, specifying a reasonable period and no performance is tendered during that period, the other party may cancel the contract.'

characterization, it was natural to bring avoidance in conformity with the fault principle for civil liability to which Japanese law adheres.[18]

3.1.2 Exceptions

However, this general rule is subject to two groups of exceptions. The first exception consists of a group of provisions which allow 'immediate avoidance' without resort to the *Nachfrist* procedure. The second exception is a case law development which has limited the availability of *Nachfrist* avoidance.

3.1.2.1 Immediate Avoidance

There are three categories of provisions which allow immediate avoidance. The first category relates to the case of subsequent impossibility.[19] In case of subsequent impossibility, the aggrieved party may avoid the contract provided that the impossibility is caused by the breaching party's fault (Art. 543 Japanese Civil Code).[20] It certainly would be futile to require adherence to the *Nachfrist* procedure where performance is impossible.

---

18 Art. 415 Civil Code, although a literal reading suggests otherwise, is unanimously considered to exemplify the fault principle.
Article 415 (Damages due to Default) 'If an obligor fails to perform consistent with the purpose of its obligation, the obligee shall be entitled to demand damages arising from such failure. The same shall apply in cases it has become impossible to perform due to reasons attributable to the obligor.

19 Japanese law adheres to the *impossibilium nulla obligatio est* principle although there is no explicit provision to that effect. Thus, a contract is void in case of initial impossibility. Accordingly, the consideration of avoidance for 'impossibility' in the text is limited to cases of subsequent impossibility.

20 **Article 543** (Right to Cancel for Impossibility of Performance) 'If performance has become impossible, in whole or in part, the obligee may cancel the contract; provided, however, that this shall not apply if the failure to perform the obligation is due to reasons not attributable to the obligor.'
If impossibility was not caused by the breaching party, avoidance is not allowed (nor is a damages claim allowed). The question of whether the aggrieved party must perform its counter-obligation in that case (*e.g.*, whether the buyer has to pay the price when the seller cannot deliver the goods due to impossibility), is decided by the rules of 'assumption of risk' (*Gefahrtragung, Theorie de risques*) under Arts. 534-536. The general rule is that the aggrieved party is discharged of its counter-obligation (Art. 536), which in function is tantamount to *ipso facto* avoidance.
Article 536 (Obligors' Assumption of Risk)
'(1) Except in the cases provided for in the preceding two Articles, if the performance of any obligation has become impossible due to reasons not attributable to either party, the obligor shall not have the right to receive performance in return.
(2) If the performance of any obligation has become impossible due to reasons attributable to the obligee, the obligor shall not lose his/her right to receive performance in return. In such cases, if the obligor gains any benefit as a result of being released from his/her own obligation, the obligor must reimburse the obligee for the benefit.'
However, a different rule applies to sales contracts. If the seller's obligation becomes impossible to perform, and if that impossibility is not due to the seller's fault, the buyer has to pay the price provided that the object of the sale has been already identified to the contract (Art. 534 para 1 and para 2).
Article 534 (Obligees to Assume Risk)

The second category is when time is of essence, and the purpose of the contract cannot be accomplished if performance is late (Art. 542 Japanese Civil Code).[21]

The third category appears in provisions of 'warranty' or 'guaranty liability' (*Guarantiehaftung, Garantie*) of sellers and contractors. Here, I will provide a rough sketch of the provisions in respect of the seller's guaranty liability. If the buyer is deprived of ownership because the subject matter of the sale belonged to a third party or because a third party has enforced a security right attached to the subject matter, the buyer may avoid the contract without use of the *Nachfrist* procedure (*e.g.*, Arts. 561 and 567 Japanese Civil Code).[22] The buyer may also avoid the contract if the purpose of the contract cannot be accomplished because the buyer is unable to use the subject matter due to a third party's proprietary

'(1) In cases where the purpose of a bilateral contract is the creation or transfer of real rights regarding specified things, if the things have been lost or damaged due to reasons not attributable to the obligor, such loss or damage shall fall on the obligee.
(2) The provisions of the preceding paragraph shall apply to any contract regarding unspecified things from the time when the things have been identified in accordance with the provisions of Paragraph 2 of Article 401.'

21 **Article 542** (Right to Cancel for Delayed Performance where Time is of the Essence) 'In cases where, due to the nature of the contract or a manifestation of intention by the parties, the purpose of the contract cannot be achieved unless the performance is carried out at a specific time and date or within a certain period of time, if one of the parties has failed to perform at the time that period lapses, the other party may immediately cancel the contract without making the demand referred to in the preceding Article.'

22 **Article 561** (Seller's Warranty when Selling Rights of Others) 'In the cases set forth in the preceding Article, if the seller cannot acquire and transfer to the buyer the rights the seller has sold, the buyer may cancel the contract. In such cases, if the buyer knew, at the time of the contract, that the rights did not belong to the seller, the buyer may not demand compensation for damages.'
Article 567 (Seller's Warranty in cases of Mortgage or Other Rights)
'(1) If the buyer loses his/her ownership of immovable property that is the object of a sale because of the exercise of an existing statutory lien or mortgage, the buyer may cancel the contract.
(2) If the buyer preserves his/her ownership by incurring expenditure for costs, he/she may claim reimbursement of those costs from the seller.
(3) In the cases set forth in the preceding two paragraphs, the buyer may claim compensation if he/she suffered loss.'

right of use (*e.g.*, easement) attached to the subject matter (Art. 566 Japanese Civil Code),[23] or because of latent defect of the subject matter (Art. 570 Japanese Civil Code).[24]

3.1.2.2 Limitation of Avoidance for Breach of Ancillary Obligations

A second exception, developed by case law, is a limitation on the availability of *Nachfrist* avoidance. The language of Article 541 Japanese Civil Code allows *Nachfrist* avoidance for *any* non-performance. However, in its judgment in 1961[25] the Supreme Court of Japan decided to impose a limitation on *Nachfrist* avoidance for non-performance of ancillary obligations.

It concerned a contract for the sale of land in which the transfer of property rights in the land as well as its possession and payment of price were performed in full. The parties agreed, however, to leave the registration of ownership of the land with the seller for the time being, pending resale of the land by the buyer.[26] The purpose of this arrangement was to save the registration fee by transferring the registration of ownership directly from the seller to a third party to whom the buyer was to later resell the land. However, since land taxes are levied on the person who appears as the owner in the land registry, the seller paid the taxes and claimed reimbursement from the buyer in accordance with the prevalent trade practice. The existence of the buyer's obligation to reimburse was not disputed. The buyer failed to reimburse the seller, and the seller declared the contract avoided under Article 541 Japanese Civil Code. The buyer in turn sued the seller and sought transfer of the ownership registration.

23 **Article 566** (Seller's Warranty in cases of Superficies or Other Rights)
'(1) In cases where the subject matter of the sale is encumbered with for the purpose of a superficies, an emphyteusis, an easement, a right of retention or a pledge, if the buyer does not know the same and cannot achieve the purpose of the contract on account thereof, the buyer may cancel the contract. In such cases, if the contract cannot be cancelled, the buyer may only demand compensation for damages.
(2) The provisions of the preceding paragraph shall apply mutatis mutandis in cases where an easement that was referred to as being in existence for the benefit of immovable property that is the subject matter of a sale, does not exist, and in cases where a leasehold is registered with respect to the immovable property.
(3) In the cases set forth in the preceding two paragraphs, the cancellation of the contract or claim for damages must be made within one year from the time when the buyer comes to know the facts.'

24 **Article 570** (Seller's Warranty against Defects) 'If there is any latent defect in the subject matter of a sale, the provisions of Article 566 shall apply mutatis mutandis; provided, however, that this shall not apply in cases of compulsory auction.' See *supra* note 23 for Art. 566.

25 Supreme Court Judgment, Japan, 21 November 1961, 15 Minshu 2507.

26 It should be noted that under Japanese law, the transfer of ownership is severed from the transfer of the ownership registration, see Art. 176 of the Japanese Civil Code:
Article 176 (Creation and Transfer of Real Rights) 'The creation and transfer of real rights shall take effect solely by the manifestations of intention of the relevant parties.'

The issue was whether the buyer's failure to perform its obligation to reimburse the seller for tax payments could be a cause for avoidance of the contract. The Supreme Court held that it was not a sufficient ground for avoidance.

> The reason why law allows avoidance of contract in case of non-performance of an obligation is to provide a remedy for cases where the purpose of the contract cannot be accomplished due to non-performance of a core obligation of the contract; unless there are special circumstances, an aggrieved party may not avoid its contract if the non-performance is only that of an ancillary obligation which is not indispensable for accomplishing the primary purpose for which the parties entered into the contract.[27]

Since both parties in this case had already performed their primary obligations, *i.e.*, transfer of ownership and payment of price, the court did not allow avoidance of the contract and held in favor of the buyer. Hence the court narrowed the availability of *Nachfrist* avoidance from any non-performance to non-performance of primary obligations, and ancillary obligations only if they are indispensable for the accomplishment of the purpose of the contract.

3.2 *Interpretative Assimilation*

Against that backdrop came the impact of the CISG. In addition to those who were committed to the promotion of the CISG and interested in the CISG as such, civil law scholars in Japan started to write about the CISG in the 1990s. This was soon after its entry into force in 1988, but long before Japan's accession to the CISG in 2008. Therefore, their interest was not in development of the CISG, but instead in the use of the CISG as a source of inspiration in developing domestic civil law. This interest was ignited by the legal scholarship in Germany where the CISG was ratified in 1989 and entered into force in 1990. German civil law scholarship traditionally has had a strong influence in Japan.[28] The flourishing of CISG scholarship in Germany as well as the many imprints of the CISG upon the debates surrounding reform of the BGB, has affected Japanese scholarship yet again.

---

27 Supreme Court Judgment, *supra* note 25, at 2508.

28 See, generally, Z. Kitagawa, *Rezeption und Fortbildung des europäischen Zivilrechts in Japan* (1970); Z. Kitagawa & K. Riesenhuber (Eds.), *The Identity of German and Japanese Civil Law in Comparative Perspectives* (2007).

What captured the interest of Japanese civil law scholars most was the limitation of the contract avoidance to cases of fundamental breach. Examination of the CISG rules on fundamental breach led to a reevaluation of the function of avoidance. First, it led to a shared understanding that the function of avoidance is not to sanction the breaching party, but rather to release the aggrieved party from the contract. This in turn led to the opinion that 'fault' should be abandoned as a requirement of avoidance.[29] Second, it became widely understood that release from the contract is only necessary when the purpose of the contract is frustrated.[30]

The time was ripe for a revised explanation of the Japanese rules of avoidance.[31] The revised explanation centers on the concept of failure of the purpose of the contract. First of all, among the rules that allowed immediate avoidance as exceptions to the general requirement of *Nachfrist* avoidance (see 3.1.2.1 above), there were rules that explicitly required failure of purpose for avoidance. These are the rules found in Articles 542 (time of essence) and 570 (guarantee against latent defects) Japanese Civil Code. Furthermore, among the exceptions to the general requirement of *Nachfrist* avoidance, there were rules which did not explicitly require failure of purpose, but which *by definition* required failure of purpose. These were the rules in Articles 543 (impossibility), 561 (eviction) and 567 (enforcement of security right) Japanese Civil Code. Also, the case law which limited avoidance due to non-performance of ancillary obligations discussed above at 3.1.2.2 could also be interpreted in the same way: denial of avoidance for non-performance of ancillary obligations when they are dispensable in relation to the accomplishment of the purpose of the contract, amounts to a limitation of contract avoidance to cases where the contractual purpose fails.

This revised interpretation of the Japanese law is an attempt to replace the traditional general rule with what used to be the exceptions to it: avoidance of contracts, including *Nachfrist* avoidance, is allowed only when the purpose of the contract cannot be accom-

29 B. Tatsumi, 'Keiyaku Kaijo to Kiseki Jiyu' [Avoidance of Contracts and Attributability], in: R. Hayashi & M. Kai (Eds.), *Taniguchi Tomohei Sensei Tsuito Ronbunshu* [In memoriam Tomohei Taniguchi], Vol. 2, at 331 (1993); Y. Shiomi, 'Saiken Soron' [Obligations in General], 430 (1994); M. Goto, 'Keiyakukaijo no Sonzaiigi ni kansuru Oboegaki' [A Memorandum of the raison d'etre of Avoidance of Contracts], 28 *Hikaku Hogaku* 1 (1994).

30 T. Watanabe, 'Wiin Baibai Joyaku' (CISG) ni okeru Keiyakumokuteki no Jitsugen to Keiyaku karano Ridatsu (1) & (2)' [Achievement of the Purpose of the Contract and Release from the Contract under the Vienna Sales Convention (CISG) (1) & (2)], 42 *Otaru Shoka Daigaku Shogaku Tokyu* 177 (1992) & 43 *Otaru Shoka Daigaku Shogaku Tokyu* 131 (1992); T. Yamada, 'Keiyaku Kaijo ni okeru "Judai na Keiyakuihan" to Kisekijiyu (1) & (2)' ['Fundamental Breach' in Avoidance of Contracts and Attributability (1) & (2)], 110 *Minshohozasshi* 273 (1994) & 110 *Minshohozasshi* 462 (1994); Shiomi, *supra* note 29, at 429 *et seq.*

31 See, *e.g.*, Y. Shiomi, *Saiken Soron* [Obligations in General], Vol. 1, at 431-432 (2003) for an expanded explanation of Shiomi, *supra* note 29, at 261; H. Sono, 'Keiyakukaijo no Yoken-Koka' [Avoidance of Contracts], in: K. Kamata, *et al.* (Eds.), *Minjiho* [Private Law], Vol. 3, at 76 (2005); S. Kagayama, *Keiyakuho Kogi* [Lectures on Contract Law], 279-287 (2007).

plished. The increasing support for this view[32] is a clear example of assimilation of Japanese law with the CISG.

3.3 *Legislative Assimilation*

3.3.1 The Civil Code Reform

The revised interpretation above has been carried over to reform of the Civil Code. The reform plan officially started in October 2009 and is expected to end in 2012. The reason for the Japanese reform plan is twofold. First, one obvious reason is that modernization of the Civil Code is needed. The Japanese Civil Code was enacted in 1896, and is already more than a century old. There are new socio-economic realities to which the law must adapt. Secondly, there is a need to enhance the visibility of law. In the past 100 years, the Civil Code of 1896, except for parts on family and succession laws, has undergone only sporadic and minor reforms. Instead, various special statutes were enacted and numerous case law developments provide many important private law rules which supplement the Civil Code. This obscures the current state of law, and it is felt that these scattered rules should be incorporated into the Civil Code itself.[33]

As a prelude to this official reform plan, there was a semi-official effort to produce a Draft Proposal (hereinafter referred to as the 'DP') for reform. This task was undertaken during the period of 2006 to 2009 by a privately formed group of leading academics known as the Japanese Civil Code (Law of Obligations) Reform Commission.[34] Their work resulted in the DP which was published in April 2009.[35] Although a mere proposal, it is generally considered that this DP will have strong influence on the outcome of the reform carried out by the government. Interestingly, the drafting of these proposals took place side by side with Japan's preparation in 2006-2008 toward accession to the CISG, although these were two independent projects.

32 See, in addition to the citations in *supra* note 31, H. Hirano, *Minpo Sogo* [Comprehensive Civil Law], Vol. 5, at 181 (2007).

33 Takashi Uchida, an eminent figure in the ongoing reform, often adds another reason: the need to adapt to the continuing global convergence of contract law. He makes the point that the creation of a new model of contract law will contribute to the worldwide harmonization process. T. Uchida, *Saikenho no Shinjidai* [The New Era of Obligations Law], 31-34 (2009).

34 The Japanese Civil Code (Law of Obligations) Reform Commission's website is available at <http://www.shojihomu.or.jp/saikenhou/English/index_e.html>.

35 Minpo (Saikenho) Kaisei Kento Iinkay [The Japanese Civil Code (Law of Obligations) Reform Commission] (Ed.), *Saikenho Kaisei no Kihon Hoshin* [Draft Proposals of Obligations Law Reform] (2009). An English translation of the DP (black letter proposal only) is available at <http://www.shojihomu.or.jp/saikenhou/English/index_e.html>.

3.3.2 *Favor contractus* in the Draft Proposal

The DP shows several significant departures from the current Civil Code, and convergence with the CISG in various aspects. To name a few, the current 'mirror image rule' in offer and acceptance[36] is relaxed to allow contract formation if there is no substantive modification within the acceptance.[37] This is in line with Article 19(2) CISG. Another example is the abandonment of the current rule that initial impossibility will nullify a contract (*impossibilium nulla obligatio est*).[38] This abandonment is also in line with the CISG (see Art. 68 sentence 2 CISG). The fault principle in contractual liability[39] is also abandoned, and non-performance without more is a ground for liability in damages.[40] This is one of the pillars of the CISG (see Arts. 45(1)(b) & 61(1)(b) CISG). An exemption similar to Article 79 CISG is also proposed in a much simpler form.[41]

The proposed rules on avoidance of contracts also show the obvious influence of the CISG. Under Proposal 3.1.1.77 of the DP, contracts may be avoided ('cancelled' according to the terminology of the DP) only when there is a fundamental non-performance ('serious non-performance' in the terminology of the DP).[42] This is clearly in line with Articles 49(1)(a)

---

36 **Article 528** (Acceptances which Modify Offer) 'If the offeree has accepted the offer by adding any condition or by making any other modification, it shall be deemed that the offeree has refused the offer and has made a new offer.'

37 Under the DP, the 'knock out rule' will apply as for the terms of the contract thus concluded.
Proposal 3.1.1.24 (Acceptance adding modifications to the offer)
'(1) If the offeree adds modifications to the offer and then accepts it, it is deemed that the original offer was rejected and a new offer was made; provided, however, that if in light of the intention of the parties and the nature of such contract, no substantive modifications have been made to the offer, the contract is formed through the contents excluding the parts which were modified.'

38 **Proposal 3.1.1.08** (Impossibility of performance/impossibility of expectation existing at the time of conclusion of the contract) 'Even if the performance of the contractual obligation was already impossible to perform at the time of conclusion of the contract or it was otherwise unreasonable to expect the obligor to perform as such in light of the intent of the contract, such contract is valid provided that the parties have not agreed otherwise.'

39 *Supra* note 18.

40 **Proposal 3.1.1.62** (Damages caused by non-performance of an obligation) 'The obligee may demand compensation from the obligor for damage incurred through non-performance of an obligation.'

41 **Proposal 3.1.1.63** (Grounds for exemption from damages)
'(1) If an obligation is not performed through causes which had not been accepted by the obligor with regard to the contract, the obligor shall not be liable for the damages of Proposal 3.1.1.62.
(2) If the obligor has the right of defense provided for in Proposals 3.1.1.54 or 3.1.1.55 the obligor shall not be liable for the damages of Proposal 3.1.1.62.'

42 **Proposal 3.1.1.77** (Requirements of accrual of the right to cancellation)
'(1) If there is a serious non-performance of the contract on the side of one of the parties to the contract, the other party may cancel the contract.
(a) A serious non-performance of the contract shall be when one of the parties to the contract does not perform an obligation and as a result the other party loses reasonable expectation with regard to the contract.
(b) In cases where, through the nature of the contract or manifestation of intention of the parties, the object of the contract cannot be achieved unless the obligation is performed by a specified date or within a certain

and 64(1)(a) CISG. Fundamental non-performance (or serious non-performance) is also defined in a similar fashion to Article 25 CISG: a non-performance is fundamental when one of the parties to the contract does not perform an obligation and as a result the other party loses what it is reasonably entitled to expect under the contract (DP 3.1.1.77(1)(a)), or when performance is delayed and time is of essence (DP 3.1.1.77(1)(b)). The first definition is very similar to the definition of fundamental breach in Article 25 CISG.[43] Thus the idea of *favor contractus* with regard to avoidance of contract is embedded in the DP.

However, a careful look into the definition of fundamental breach in the DP will reveal a significant divergence from that of the CISG: the 'unless' clause of Article 25 CISG which requires 'foreseeability' at the time of the conclusion of the contract[44] is missing in the DP's definition. This produces a significant difference to which we turn in the next section.

4 Diversity of *Favor contractus*

What does the lack of foreseeability requirement mean? It means that there can be varieties of *favor contractus*. The lack of foreseeability requirement in the DP means that the idea of fundamental breach in the DP focuses purely on 'failure of the purpose of the contract'. If the purpose fails, avoidance of contract is allowed, whether or not the failure of purpose by the breach in question was foreseeable at the time of the contract. In other words, *favor contractus* is given maximum weight in the DP by providing protection to the 'purpose of the contract', while the idea of 'presentiation' (or *pacta sunt servanda*) which provides protection to predictability, is given little weight. A similar rule exists in the DP in relation

---

period, when that time has passed without one of the parties performing the obligation, this shall fall under a serious non-performance of the contract.

(2) In cases where one of the parties to the contract does not perform an obligation, if the other party has demanded performance stipulating a reasonable period of time and non-compliance with the demand constitutes a serious non-performance of the contract, the other party may cancel the contract.

(3) With regard to a contract concluded between business operators, in cases where one of the parties to the contract does not perform an obligation, if the other party demands performance stipulating a reasonable period of time and no performance is made within this period, the other party may cancel the contract; provided, however, that this shall not apply if non-compliance with the demand does not constitute a serious non-performance of the contract.'

43 Interestingly, *Nachfrist* avoidance (see Arts. 49(1)(b) and 64(1)(b) CISG) is merged with avoidance for fundamental performance by requiring a showing that non-compliance with the *Nachfrist* demand for performance 'constitutes a serious non-performance of the contract.' (Proposal 3.1.1.77(2)).

44 Although the language of Art. 25 CISG is not explicit on the question of the relevant time of foreseeability, this is the understanding of the overwhelming majority. See, *e.g.*, U. Schroeter, in: I. Schwenzer (Ed.), Schlechtriem & Schwenzer, *Commentary on the UN Convention on the International Sale of Goods (CISG)*, Art. 25 para 32 *et seq.* (2010).

to the scope of damages as well. Proposal 3.1.1.67 is the relevant provision.[45] Paragraph 1 of that provision provides that the scope of damages is limited by 'foreseeability' which is determined with reference to the 'time of conclusion of the contract'. However, the second paragraph provides that foreseeability is decided with reference to the 'time of non-performance' if the obligor did not take reasonable measures to avoid the damage. Calculation of damages on the basis of this second paragraph will overturn the parties' presentiation or the prediction of the future contemplated by the parties at the time of the conclusion of the contract. According to one of the leading figures in the drafting of the DP, the rationale for this proposal is that since the obligor has undertaken to provide the obligee with a certain interest by way of performance, the obligor should not simply sit back and leave the obligee to incur loss which the obligor foresaw or should have foreseen at the time of non-performance, if the obligor could have prevented the loss.[46] Here again, protection of 'presentiation' is weak in the DP while *favor contractus* in the sense of protection of the purpose of the contract by way of monetary compensation is strong. Weak presentiation and strong *favor contractus* may be translated as recognition of the ongoing nature of contractual *relationship* which is not frozen at the time of contract. This stands out as a characteristic of Japan's DP.[47]

In comparison to Japan's DP, the CISG's version of *favor contractus* is milder, in that the CISG is diligently loyal to 'presentiation' (*pacta sunt servanda*) and thus predictability. Foreseeability at the time of the contract is a requirement both for fundamental breach[48] and for the scope of damages (Art. 74 CISG). The lack of rules on hardship in the CISG also points in the same direction. Thus, under the CISG, presentiation is given weight, and the pursuit of *favor contractus*, although a significant underlying principle, seems to give way to *pacta sunt servanda.*

45 **Proposal 3.1.1.67** (Scope of damages) '(1) With regard to a claim accruing based on the contract, the obligee may make a demand to the obligor for compensation of damage as the result of non-performance which, at the time of conclusion of the contract, both parties foresaw or should have foreseen.
(2) Even in cases where the obligor foresaw or should have foreseen the damage [only] after the conclusion of the contract up until the point of non-performance of the obligation, if the obligor did not take reasonable measures to avoid the damage, the obligee may make a demand to the obligor for such compensation.'

46 Uchida, *supra* note 33, at 92-93 (2009). Uchida also adds that this is a restatement of the consistent position of Japanese case law.

47 Another example is the proposal with regard to the rules on adaptation of contracts due to changed circumstances or hardships. See Proposals 3.1.1.91–3.1.1.93.

48 *Supra* note 44.

5 Conclusion

Where does this analysis lead us to? First of all, there can be diverse varieties and graduations in the idea of *favor contractus*. On one end of the scale, the CISG exemplifies a mild version of *favor contractus*; on the other end is Japan's DP which employs a radical version of *favor contractus*.[49] Which version suits the commercial reality better is a question beyond the scope of this paper. However, the recognition of this feature of the CISG should be kept in mind when engaging in analysis of the underlying principles of the CISG.

Another conclusion is that the CISG functions as an impetus toward uniformity through assimilation. This happens not only in Contracting States, but also in non-contracting states. The CISG is often referred to as the *lingua franca* of international trade. Whether it is really a *lingua franca* as applicable law is not necessarily clear, because there are many instances where the parties agree to opt out of the CISG (Art. 6 CISG). However, application is not the only function of the CISG. The CISG provides a common platform to a worldwide constituency in the process of assimilation, and in that sense, the CISG is a *lingua franca* shared not only by Contracting States but also by non-contracting states.

49 The UNIDROIT Principles of International Commercial Contracts, which this paper has not explored fully, perhaps stands in the middle. The UNIDROIT Principles are similar to the CISG in that 'foreseeability' in the definition of fundamental breach is determined with reference to the time of the contract (Art. 7.3.1(2)(a) UNIDROIT Principles). See P. Huber, in: S. Vogenauer & J. Kleinheisterkamp (Eds.), *Commentary on the UNIDROIT Principles of International Commercial Contracts (PICC)*, Art. 7.3.1 para. 37 (2009); Likewise, 'foreseeability' in calculating damages is also determined with reference to the time of the contract (Art. 7.4.4) which coincides with the CISG. On the other hand, UNIDROIT Principles contain rules which allow renegotiation and adaptation of contracts in case of hardship (Arts. 6.2.1 - 6.2.3), which is a limitation on *pacta sunt servanda*.

Iura Novit Curia and the CISG: Resolution of the Faux Procedural Black Hole

Lisa Spagnolo[*]

1 Introduction

A growing line of cases points to a potential black hole in the CISG. Through a combination of domestic procedural rules and waiver principles it seems many cases to which the CISG clearly applies are being determined on the basis of inapplicable law, simply because counsel failed to mention the CISG.

This result is at worst incorrect, and at best, unsatisfactory. In my view, judges (and to a lesser extent, arbitrators) who realize the CISG applies to the case before them rather than the local sales law presented by counsel, often should, and in many cases, must apply the CISG. In this article I will present the case for how and why this should occur, regardless of local procedural ground rules.

The chapter begins in Part 2 with a typical factual setting and examples of it in practice. Part 3 presents the traditional view, according to which the forum's procedural rules should provide the solution, outlines the nature of *iura novit curia*, and queries whether observed diversity in outcomes can be attributed to variance in procedural rules or interpretation of the CISG. The balance of the chapter attempts to provide a resolution to the problem that will improve certainty. Parts 4 and 5 respectively pose and analyse the questions so often obscured by the approach taken in the cases and by the traditional view: is there an obligation to apply the CISG if it is not pleaded? And if so, does failure to plead the CISG

* Faculty of Law, Monash University. The author can be contacted at lisa.spagnolo@monash.edu. While all errors remain mine, I wish to express my sincere gratitude to Prof. Ingeborg Schwenzer and Prof. Jeff Waincymer for their comments and suggestions on earlier drafts of this chapter. The author also thanks Juraj Kotrusz, Jorge Oviedo-Albán, Weidi Long, Sophie Nappert, Leandro Tripodi & Simon Greenberg. I am honoured to have had such wise and excellent assistance from around the world. A great global collaborator, Al Kritzer, sadly passed away while it was being completed. The last time I saw Al, he was, as always, amongst friends.

per se amount to an agreement to exclude it? Part 6 puts forward a range of practical solutions, and Part 7 draws some brief conclusions.

2 The Typical Situation

Let me describe the relevant situation. Two parties have entered a contract to which the CISG clearly applies, perhaps because the parties have their respective businesses in two different countries that have adopted the CISG,[1] and have failed to include a choice of law. Sometime later, a dispute arises. Counsel for each side present the case as if domestic sales law governed, and fail to mention the CISG.

This happens all too often. In a 2008 Chilean case[2] parties failed to plead or argue the applicable law of the CISG until appeal.[3] In an Austrian case,[4] both parties ignored the applicable CISG, and the court assumed domestic law applied. Only on appeal was the CISG considered.[5] In three Slovak cases, the court simply overlooked the CISG and incorrectly applied the Slovak Commercial Code.[6] In one Australian case the CISG was completely overlooked in argument and the judgment, an oversight not fully corrected upon appeal.[7] The failure to raise the CISG until too late in the trial hearing in the U.S. case of *GPL Treatment* precluded its application and almost cost the plaintiff the case.[8]

---

1 Thus the CISG would apply: Art. 1(1)(a).

2 *Industrias Magromer Cueros y Pieles SA v. Sociedad Agrícola Sacor Limitada*, Corte Suprema, Chile, 22 September 2008, available at <http://cisgw3.law.pace.edu/cases/080922ch.html> (*sub-nom Jorge Plaza Oviedo v. Sociedad Agricola Sacor Limitada*).

3 *Id.* The CISG was only argued in the Court of Appeal and Supreme Court: J. Oviedo-Albán, 'Exclusión tácita de la ley aplicable e indemnización de perjuicios por incumplimiento de un contrato de compraventa internacional (a propósito de reciente jurisprudencia chilena)', 14 *Int'l Law, Revista Colombiana de Derecho Internacional* 191, at 194 and 195 (2009) (stating the decision was incorrect).

4 *Boiler* case, Oberster Gerichtshof [Supreme Court](OGH), Austria, 2 April 2009, available at <http://cisgw3.law.pace.edu/cases/090402a3.html>.

5 Landesgericht [District Court](LG) Steyr, Austria, GZ 4 Cg 146/05m-45, 29 January 2008. At first instance, both parties and the court referred to domestic law including Art. 922 Allgemeines Bürgerliches Gesetzbuch 1811 [Austrian General Civil Code](ABGB): Oberlandesgericht [Appellate Court](OLG) Linz, Austria, 25 July 2008, GZ 3 R 46/08t-49.

6 Regional Court, Nitra, Slovak Republic, 15 October 2008, available at <http://www.cisg.sk/en/15cob-140-2008.html>; Supreme Court, Slovak Republic, 26 October 2006, available at <http://www.cisg.sk/en/3obo-247-2005.html>; Supreme Court, Slovak Republic, 28 February 2001, available at <http://www.cisg.sk/en/2cdo-114-2000.html>.

7 *Italian Imported Foods Pty Ltd v. Pucci Srl*, New South Wales Supreme Court, Australia, 13 October 2006, available at <http://cisgw3.law.pace.edu/cases/061013a2.html> (*Italian Imported Foods*). See L. Spagnolo, 'The Last Outpost: Automatic CISG Opt Outs, Misapplications and the Costs of Ignoring the Vienna Sales Convention for Australian Lawyers', 10 *Melbourne J. Int'l L.* 141, at 197-199 (2009).

8 *GPL Treatment v. Louisiana-Pacific Corp.*, 894 P. 2d 470 (Or. Ct App., 1995), 12 April 1995; aff'd 914 P. 2d 682 (Or, 1996), Oregon Court of Appeals, U.S.A., available at <http://cisgw3.law.pace.edu/

Even in China, which has a converse record of applying the CISG in situations when it is inapplicable,[9] there is at least one case where neither side argued the CISG and the court failed to mention it despite its applicability.[10]

On the other hand, there are cases in which the CISG was applied regardless of the fact that counsel did not present or inadequately argued the CISG.[11]

In many instances, the court or tribunal fails to appreciate that the CISG governs the matter. But what if the adjudicator *does* realize argument has been exclusively presented on the basis of the wrong law?

3 The Procedural Law of the Forum and Reasons for Diversity in Practice

3.1 The Traditional View

The resolution traditionally advanced by scholars is that procedural law determines the law to be applied where both sides have not presented argument on the law that is applicable, *ipso iure*. Pursuant to the traditional view, the course which a court must take is determined by the procedural law of the forum, and specifically, whether it follows *iura novit curia* (the court knows the law).[12] Naturally, since procedural rules vary, the traditional

cases/950412u1.html> (*GPL Treatment*) (the domestic 'in writing' requirement was displaced by the CISG, but counsel for plaintiff failed to raise this until too late, and the case was decided on the basis of the U.C.C.). See also, W.S. Dodge, 'Teaching the CISG in Contracts', 50 *Journal of Legal Education* 72, at 74 (2000); Flechtner, *infra* note 111, at 131; Ferrari, *International Legal Forum, infra* note 12, at 220, note 742.

9 Y. Xiao & W. Long, 'Selected Topics on the Application of the CISG in China', 20 *Pace Int'l L.Rev.* 61, at 70 (2008), available at <http://www.cisg.law.pace.edu/cisg/biblio/xiao-long.html> (describing this 'phenomenon' of application in Chinese cases).

10 *Gammatex International Srl v. Shanghai Eastern Crocodile Apparels Co. Ltd.*, Shanghai First Intermediate People's Court, China, 21 August 2002, available at <http://cisgw3.law.pace.edu/cases/020821c1.html>. It is unclear whether the court was unaware of the CISG's applicability, or was aware but did not apply it due to the parties' failure to raise it: W. Long, email to author, 2 March 2010; Xiao & Long, *id.*, at 71.

11 Tribunale di Vigevano, Italy, 12 July 2000, available at <http://cisgw3.law.pace.edu/cases/000712i3.html>; Appellate Court (OLG) Hamm, Germany, 9 June 1995, §§ I & II, available at <http://cisgw3.law.pace.edu/cases/950609g1.html>; Landesgericht [District Court](LG) Landshut, Germany, 5 April 1995, available at <http://cisgw3.pace.edu/cases/950405g1.html>. See also, M. Torsello, 'Italy', in: F. Ferrari (Ed.), *The CISG and Its Impact on National Legal Systems*, 187, at 191-195, notes 20, 22 and 209 (2008); Oviedo-Albán, *supra* note 3, at 204; F. Ferrari, 'CISG Rules on Exclusion and Derogation: Article 6', in: F. Ferrari *et al* (Eds.), *The Draft UNCITRAL Digest and Beyond: Cases, Analysis and Unresolved Issues in the UN Sales Convention*, 114 at 131 (2004) (Digest & Beyond).

12 *UNCITRAL Digest of Case Law on the United Nations Convention on the International Sale of Goods,* Art. 6 para. 10 (2008), available at <http://www.cisg.law.pace.edu/cisg/text/digest-art-06.html> (UNCITRAL

view has the potential to foster divergent outcomes. Depending on whether or not the forum follows the principle of *iura novit curia*, the court may either be obliged to apply the applicable law, irrespective of whether parties have invoked it, or conversely, may be prohibited from applying it at all.[13]

The traditional approach has influenced decisions in practice. Thus the procedural principle of *iura novit curia* has been explicitly relied upon to justify application of the CISG in cases where counsel did not plead it.[14] Criticism has also been levelled at a case where the CISG was not applied on the basis that the court failed to observe the procedural law of the forum which was subject to *iura novit curia*.[15]

In terms of the CISG, this traditional view effectively treats the issue as an external gap, that is, that the duty of the adjudicator is a matter not covered by the CISG itself. It therefore denotes the issue as one for determination under domestic procedural law. In this chapter, I seek to challenge that view.

On its face, it seems inevitable that leaving the matter to domestic procedural law would produce diverse outcomes. But should we be concerned about this in any event? After all,

---

Digest); F. Ferrari, 'Applicability and Applications of the Vienna Sales Convention (CISG)', 4 *Int'l Legal Forum* 138, at 220 (1998) (Ferrari, *International Legal Forum*); Oviedo-Albán, *supra* note 3, at 203, note 22 and 214 (denying applicability of the CISG unless the parties invoke it or *[i]ura novit curia* applies) (my translation); Oviedo-Albán, *id.*, (citing a similar statement by Illescas-Ortiz & Perales Viscasillas); M. Reimann, 'The CISG in the United States: Why It Has Been Neglected and Why Europeans Should Care', 71 *RabelsZ* 115, at note 48 and accompanying text (2007); M. Bridge, 'Uniform and Harmonized Sales Law: Choice of Law Issues', in: J. Fawcett *et al* (Eds.), *International Sale of Goods in the Conflict ofLaws*, 905 at 917 (2005); Torsello, *id.*, at 191–192 and note 20; F. Ferrari, 'Remarks on the UNICITRAL Digest's Comments on Article 6 CISG', 25 *J. L. & Com.* 13, at 30–31 (2005) (Ferrari, *Remarks*); P. Schlechtriem & P. Perales Viscasillas, *Case note on decision of Court of First Instance of Tudela (Spain)* 29 March 2005, at note 10 (2005), available at <http://www.cisg.law.pace.edu/cisg/biblio/perales4.html> ('Whether counsel pleading for the parties properly introduced the applicable provisions of the CISG is not known to these annotators, but would be irrelevant, since *jura novit curia*'); A. Pribetic, *An 'Unconventional Truth': Conflict of Laws Issues Arising under the CISG*, at 27, presented at the Continuing Legal Education Program, Toronto, 10 March 2009; F. Mazzotta, 'The International Character of the UN Convention on Contracts for the International Sale of Goods: An Italian Case Example', 15 *Pace Int'l L. Rev.* 437, at 443 (2003); F. Ferrari, 'Applying the CISG in a Truly Uniform Manner: Tribunale di Vigevano (Italy), 12 July 2000', 1 *Uniform L. Rev.* 203, at 211 (2001).

13 See also, S.L. Sass, 'Foreign Law in Civil Litigation – A Comparative Survey', 16 *Am. J. Comp. L.* 332, at 334-335 (1968) (breaking the potential scenarios into three categories).

14 Tribunale di Vigevano, 12 July 2000, *supra* note 11, para. 5; Tribunale Civile di Cuneo, Italy, 31 January 1996, available at <http://cisgw3.law.pace.edu/cases/960131i3.html>; *Georgia Pacific Resins, Inc. v. Grupo Bajaplay, S.A. de C.V*, Baja California, Fourth Panel of the Fifteenth Circuit Court [Federal Court of Appeals], Mexico, 9 August 2007, available at <http://cisgw3.law.pace.edu/cases/070809m1.html> (*Georgia Pacific Resins* case); Tribunale di Padova, Italy, 25 February 2004, available at <http://cisgw3.law.pace.edu/cases/040225i3.html>.

15 See, *e.g.*, criticism of the Chilean decision in the *Industrias Magromer* case, *supra* note 2, by Oviedo-Albán, *supra* note 3, at 203, note 22 and 214.

perhaps the court or tribunal should be content that both sides have presented their case on the basis of the same law, and proceed to apply the law argued.

In truth, the effect goes beyond the immediate parties concerned. First and foremost, obligations of international law are at stake. Generally, the administration of justice is hindered by 'incorrect' application of the substantive law, but when the governing law is a treaty, a court's failure to apply the applicable governing law can amount to a breach of international obligations.[16] At a practical level, it reduces the extent of influence on uniformity that would be otherwise achieved by the CISG. It deprives the expanding body of CISG case law from valuable additions, and robs the CISG of visibility in those jurisdictions where it is needed most; where the unwillingness of counsel to engage with it may arise from low levels of CISG litigation in their jurisdiction.[17] It signals to other counsel that they really need not bother to plead the CISG, even where it governs. The situation often leads to appeals and wastage of judicial resources and time.[18] Finally, as lawyers we should all be concerned about the effect on the rule of law when an inapplicable law is applied in not just one case, but many.

3.2 *The Principle of* Iura Novit Curia

As mentioned, the traditional view answers the question as to the law to be applied by the court in the above situation by referring to the procedural law of the forum, specifically, whether it follows *iura novit curia.*[19] At its core, the procedural principle of *iura novit curia* allocates the burden of establishing the identity of the applicable law and ascertaining its content.[20] It defines the very roles and respective responsibilities of the court and parties in relation to the substantive law.[21]

The suggestion in the traditional view that the outcome depends on whether a jurisdiction follows the principle of *iura novit curia* presupposes its absence in some of them. In truth, some version of *iura novit curia* exists in all jurisdictions. Judges are presumed to know

16 See Part 4.1 below.

17 L. Spagnolo, 'A Glimpse through the Kaleidoscope: Choices of Law & the CISG', 13 *Vindobona Journal of International Commercial Law & Arbitration* 137, at 148 (Table 3) (2009).

18 In some cases like those from the Slovak Republic mentioned earlier, the decision is remitted back to the lower court with a direction that the court apply the CISG: *supra* note 6.

19 *Supra* note12.

20 T. Isele, 'The Principle of Iura Novit Curia in International Commercial Arbitration', 13(1) *Int'l Arbitration L. Rev.* 14, at 14 (2010). This is sometimes referred to as the 'burden of education': M.S. Kurkela, "Jura Novit Curia' and the Burden of Education in International Arbitration – A Nordic Perspective', 21(3) *ASA Bulletin* 486, at 490 (2003).

21 Sass, *supra* note 13, at 332.

and empowered to apply the law, or at least the domestic law.[22] A 'strict' approach to *iura novit curia* obliges the court to *ex officio* identify and apply the substantive law it considers applicable to the case. A 'soft' approach to *iura novit curia* authorizes this, but does not demand it.

While civil law jurisdictions overtly acknowledge the principle, it has been claimed that it has no application in common law jurisdictions.[23] Yet it is probably more accurate to say that common law courts operate under a 'soft' form of *iura novit curia* in relation to domestic law, since common law judges also have an inherent power to apply points of law not invoked by counsel, subject to due process concerns.[24] The same due process concerns obviously also apply in courts which overtly follow the *iura novit curia* principle.

In the present context, the most important due process issue is the principle of *audi alteram partem*, the right to be heard, the contours of which are defined differently in different jurisdictions.[25] The breadth or narrowness with which the right to be heard is defined essentially determines the degree to which the court will feel constrained in a situation where counsel have not presented the case on the basis of the relevant law, as the ensuing decision may be overturned for failure to accord due process if counsel have not been invited to comment.[26]

---

22 See Isele, *supra* note 20, at 14-15; Kurkela, *supra* note 20, at 489. See also, International Law Association, *Final Report: Ascertaining the Contents of the Applicable Law in International Commercial Arbitration* 3 (2008), available at <http://www.ila-hq.org/en/committees/index.cfm/cid/19> (ILA Final Report).

23 F.A. Mann, 'Fusion of the Legal Profession', 93 *L.Q.R.* 367, at 375 (1977) (stating absence of *iura novit curia* distinguishes English legal procedure vis-à-vis civil law). This has led to assertions of the so-called principle of 'judicial unpreparedness': Mann, *id.*, at 369.

24 In fact 'courts are typically expected to know their law': ILA Final Report, *supra* note 22, at 8. Isele also concludes some form of the principle applies in England: *supra* note 20, at 23, since 'the [English] judge may suggest new legal reasoning and is free to decide in accordance with such reasoning, and that rejection of application of law not pleaded in Goldsmith *v.* Sperrings Ltd [1977] 1 WLR 478, 486 (U.K.) was not due to 'lack [of] authority [in the court] to do so, but due to the lack of the opportunity to be heard on the specific legal issue': *id.*, at 15; Mann, *id.*, at 369 (English courts may put new legal questions to counsel, but are under no obligation to do so).

25 The right to be heard is often found in specific provisions designed to prevent 'surprise' decisions. For example, in Austria: Art. 182 Zivilprozessordnung [Austrian Code of Civil Procedure 1895] (Austrian ZPO); see *Boiler* case, *supra* note 4 (Austrian Supreme Court holding the Court of Appeal had infringed the ZPO Art. 182 in applying the CISG where parties had overlooked it, but ultimately the error did not affect the outcome). See also, Art.139 Zivilprozessordnung, Germany (German ZPO), (5 December 2005 version), available at <http://www.gesetze-im-internet.de/bundesrecht/zpo/gesamt.pdf>. Regarding common law approaches, see T. Ingman, *The English Legal Process* 491 (2008); M. Cappelletti & B.G. Garth, 'Introduction – Policies, Trends and Ideas in Civil Procedure', in: M. Cappelletti (Ed.), *International Encyclopedia of Comparative Law*, Ch. 1, Vol. XVI, Civil Procedure, at 81, §1-81 (1987).

26 Isele, *supra* note 20, at 15 noting the strict right to be heard in relation to legal reasoning in common law; M. Rosenberg *et al.*, *Elements of Civil Procedure: Cases & Materials* 9 (1970) (parties may otherwise be denied

Therefore it is the breadth of the right to be heard and its effect in triggering potential appeals rather than whether a particular jurisdiction overtly follows *iura novit curia* that might, under the traditional view, impact on outcomes. These will be taken into account in the solutions proposed in Part 6 below.

3.3 *Causes of Diversity in Current Outcomes*

There is no doubt that reactions to the failure to plead the CISG have been highly variable. As might be expected, domestic procedural rules have had an impact. However, the real causes of the diversity deserve closer attention, since differences in domestic procedural rules do not entirely explain the range of outcomes in the cases.

As mentioned earlier, some courts have directly referred to the domestic procedural principle of *iura novit curia* to justify the application of the CISG despite failure of counsel to mention it, in keeping with the traditional view.[27] Others have implicitly done so by relying upon the interplay between domestic procedural practice and due process rules to view such failures as a waiver pursuant to domestic conceptions. For example, in the U.S. case of *GPL Treatment*, counsel's failure to argue the CISG was held to amount to a waiver, which permitted the court to apply the inapplicable domestic law that had been pleaded.[28] The Court of Appeal made no attempt to interpret whether there had been an exclusion pursuant to the CISG, but merely dismissed the CISG by way of footnote in the dissenting judgment which concluded that because the 'attempt to raise the CISG was untimely [...] that they had waived reliance on that theory'.[29] It must therefore be taken as having concluded waiver pursuant to a domestic framework. Similarly, in the Australian *Playcorp* case, although the court was awake to the CISG's relevance, it was still convinced its application was 'unnecessary' not due to any conclusion that it had been excluded by the parties, but due to its purported similarity to domestic law. The case had been primarily argued on the basis of domestic law, and the court relied upon the absence of any suggestion

the opportunity to test or address research conducted by the judge outside of court). Similarly, see also, *supra* note 25.

27 *Georgia Pacific Resins* case, *supra* note 14 (where the court found it was irrelevant whether or not the parties had mentioned the CISG because of the principle of law 'da mihi factur, dabo tibi ius' and principle of 'iura novit curia'); Tribunale Civile di Cuneo, 31 January 1996, *supra* note 14 ('[a]lthough the parties did not refer to the CISG, its rules must be followed by this Court from the principle *iura novit curia*'); Tribunale di Vigevano, 12 July 2000, *supra* note 11, para. 5 ('[t]hus according to the principle *iura novit curia*, it is up to the judge to determine which Italian rules should be applied'); Tribunale di Padova, 25 February 2004, *supra* note 14 ('by virtue of the principle of *iura novit curia*, it is for the judge to determine the applicable Italian rules'). See also, for commentary in support of the traditional view, *supra* note12.

28 The CISG was raised in argument only very late in the trial: *GPL Treatment, supra* note 8. See also *Italian Imported Foods, supra* note 7.

29 *GPL Treatment, id.*, Leeson J (dissenting, at note 8).

by counsel that the CISG was 'inconsistent' with local sales law. It therefore determined it was permissible to apply the domestic law. Again, this conclusion was reached by way of domestic principles.[30]

Then there are cases in which courts appear to interpret the CISG in determining whether the conduct amounts to an exclusion. Yet, vastly different approaches are apparent amongst such cases. Italian and German courts have expressly denied that mere failure to argue the CISG amounts to an implicit agreement to exclude it.[31] One Italian case stated the fact that 'the parties based their arguments exclusively on [...] domestic law [...] cannot be considered an implicit manifestation of an intent to exclude application of the [CISG]'.[32] Other decisions have held that failure to argue due to a misapprehension that domestic law was applicable or because parties were simply unaware of the CISG does not support an imputation of intent to exclude it.[33] One case held that argument on German domestic law amounted to an agreement to apply German law, but not to exclude the CISG.[34]

On the other hand, the very same conduct has been construed as demonstrating an intention to exclude pursuant to the CISG. An implicit exclusion of the CISG was upheld in a Chilean case,[35] where the failure of parties to plead the CISG until the appellate stages was characterized as involving a tacit exclusion or implied waiver of the CISG pursuant

30 The implementing legislation stated the CISG was to have the force of law, and was to prevail to the extent of any inconsistency: ss. 5 & 6 Sale of Goods (Vienna Convention) Act 1987 (Victoria). The court elevated the 'inconsistency' concept to effectively bypass the force of law given to the CISG, and ignores the inevitability that the unique interpretive methodology of the CISG will always render it different to domestic law despite any superficial resemblances. See *Playcorp Pty Ltd v. Taiyo Kogyo Ltd*, Victorian Supreme Court, Australia, 24 April 2003, at [235] and [245], available at <http://cisgw3.law.pace.edu/cases/030424a2.html>.

31 Tribunale di Cuneo, 31 January 1996, *supra* note 14; Tribunale di Vigevano, 12 July 2000, *supra* note 11, paras.. 5 and 6; C. Sant'Elia, *Editorial Remarks*, available at <http://cisgw3.law.pace.edu/cases/000712i3.html>; Tribunale di Forli, Italy, 16 February 2009, §4.3.3, available at <http://cisgw3.law.pace.edu/cases/090216i3.html>; Appellate Court (OLG) Stuttgart, Germany, 31 March 2008, available at <http://cisgw3.law.pace.edu/cases/080331g1.html>; Appellate Court (OLG) Hamm, 9 June 1995, *supra* note 11; District Court (LG) Landshut, 5 April 1995, *supra* note 11, §II.1.a (the fact that both parties based their case on the BGB 'does not change anything'). See also, International Chamber of Commerce (ICC) Award No. 7565 of 1994, available at <http://cisgw3.law.pace.edu/cases/947565i1.html>; UNCITRAL Digest, *supra* note 12, Art. 6, para. 10.

32 Tribunale di Vigevano, 12 July 2000, *supra* note 11, para. 5 ('The fact that [parties] based their arguments exclusively on Italian domestic law without any references to the [CISG] cannot be considered an implicit manifestation of an intent to exclude').

33 Tribunale di Vigevano, 12 July 2000, *supra* note 11 (stating it was to be assumed 'the parties wanted to exclude the application of the [CISG] only if it appears in an unequivocal way that they recognized its applicability and they nevertheless insisted on referring only to national, non-uniform law'); UNCITRAL Digest, *supra* note 12, Art. 6 at para. 10.

34 Appellate Court (OLG) Hamm, 9 June 1995, *supra* note 11. The OLG Hamm decision stated that litigation exclusively based on BGB provisions implied a choice of German law, and hence the CISG applied; *id.*, I.

35 *Industrias Magromer* case, *supra* note 2.

to Article 6.[36] A Slovak court interpreted such conduct as a choice of law.[37] Although decided on other grounds, a Spanish court also determined the CISG was tacitly excluded partly due to the failure of parties to raise it until the appeal stage.[38] The French Cour de Cassation has in two cases applied the domestic law on the basis that failure by the parties to invoke the CISG was tacit exclusion under Article 6.[39] Furthermore, it seems the same may have occurred in China.[40] In all these cases the domestic law was ultimately applied despite the CISG's *prima facie* applicability.

This demonstrates current outcomes are unpredictable and diverse. It would be wrong to blame the differing outcomes completely on the natural consequences of the traditional view. As discussed above, all jurisdictions employ some version of *iura novit curia*, tempered by due process concerns, and plainly, some jurisdictions which overtly follow *iura novit curia* have interpreted such conduct as waiver, and applied domestic law instead. Indeed, even within a single jurisdiction, conflicting decisions have been reached.[41] Clearly, the domestic procedural rules are only partly the cause of the diversity.

Those cases approaching the matter as one dependent on domestic procedural rules are incorrect at law, at least in Contracting States. Likewise, decisions which instead rely upon

36 *Id.*; Oviedo-Albán, *supra* note 3, at 194, 195, 198, 199 and note 7.

37 Regional Court, Bratislava, Slovak Republic, 10 October 2007, available at <http://www.cisg.sk/en/3cob-102-2007.html> (interpreting failure to plead or argue the CISG as an exclusion of CISG and tacit choice of Slovakian domestic law pursuant to §9(1) of act no. 97/1963 Coll., on International Private and Procedural Law as amended) (translation by J. Kotrusz).

38 *BSC Footwear Supplies Ltd v. Brumby St.*, Audiencia Provincial de Alicante, Spain, 16 November 2000, available at <http://cisgw3.law.pace.edu/cases/001116s4.html> (deciding the CISG was tacitly excluded for three reasons, including failure to raise the CISG in pleadings and failure to argue the CISG until appeal); see also, P. Perales Viscasillas, *Abstract,* available at <http://cisgw3.law.pace.edu/cases/001116s4.html>.

39 *Société Muller Ecole et Bureau v. Société Federal Trait*, Cour de Cassation, France, 26 June 2001, available at <http://www.cisg-france.org/decisions/2606012v.htm> and <http://cisgw3.law.pace.edu/cases/010626f1.html> (stating that while French judges must apply the CISG as the substantive law of French international sales, the parties had tacitly excluded under Art. 6 by 'failing to invoke the [CISG] before the French court') (my translation); Cour de Cassation, France, 25 October 2005, CISG-online 1098, available at <http://cisgw3.law.pace.edu/cases/051025f1.html> ('that by invoking and discussing, without any reservation, the [French Civil Code] all of the parties [...] voluntarily placed the resolution of their dispute under French domestic law' by exclusion under Art. 6).

40 In *Gammatex International* case, *supra* note 10; Xiao & Long, *supra* note 9, at 71 (the court ignored the CISG's applicability despite fulfilment of the requirements of Art. 1(1)(a) and no apparent intent to exclude). From the Chinese text of the decision 'it is unclear whether the court is unaware of the applicability of CISG, or it is indeed aware of the applicability, but nevertheless did not apply the CISG because the parties did not raise the applicability issue' (translation by W. Long). Chinese law has now altered to allow parties to make choices of law until the end of the first instance oral hearings: Y. Xiao & W. Long, 'Private International Law in China: Selected Topics; Contractual Party Autonomy in Chinese Private International Law', 11 *Yearbook of Private Int'l L.* 193, at 199 (2009).

41 For example, compare Regional Court, Bratislava, 10 October 2007, *supra* note 37; Regional Court, Nitra, 15 October 2008, *supra* note 6; Supreme Court, Slovak Republic, 26 October 2006, *supra* note 6.

conclusions of implicit waiver or agreement to exclude based purely on the conduct of the case are also incorrect unless derived from an application of the CISG itself. By contrast, cases which rely on interpretation of the CISG in determining exclusion indeed rely on the correct source of law, but unfortunately presently display a wide range of inconsistent interpretations. While some might be explicable on their facts, most appear too quick to conclude there has been a tacit exclusion without careful consideration of the issue.

3.4 *Critique of Traditional View*

The manner in which the traditional view leaves the issue to the myriad of local domestic procedural rules is arguably unsatisfactory and in many circumstances, incorrect.

It is unsatisfactory because, to the extent of diversity in domestic procedural rules, the traditional view contributes to uncertainty of outcomes in the application of a uniform law, as seen above. It is often incorrect because it ignores the duty in certain fora to apply the CISG. This will be discussed in Part 4. Further, the traditional view demonstrates a lack of faith in the capacity of the CISG to deal with inferences from the failure to plead. It is submitted the CISG is more than capable of this, as discussed in Part 5.

The balance of this chapter seeks to provide a more satisfactory approach with the aim of improving certainty and predictability in outcomes. It attempts to do so by concentrating on the two crucial questions which must be answered in the typical situation described: if the CISG is not pleaded, is there an obligation upon the adjudicator to apply it? And secondly, does failure to plead the CISG amount to an exclusion of it pursuant to Article 6?

4 Is there a Duty to Apply the CISG if it Is not Pleaded?

If the CISG is the governing law of the contract, then to begin with domestic procedural rules is to start on the wrong foot. The first question to be asked is whether the CISG is applicable despite the failure to plead it. Essentially, one must ascertain whether there is an obligation upon the adjudicator to apply the CISG flowing from international law. Depending on the answer, domestic procedural rules may have no relevance at all.

The primary enquiry turns on the location and nature of the forum making the determination; whether the forum is a court or arbitral tribunal, and if it is a court, whether it is located in a Contracting State to the CISG. A further permutation is whether the matter is a trial or appeal case.

4.1 Courts in Contracting States

This presents the simplest permutation. Where a court in a Contracting State hears a matter at the trial stage, it would be incorrect to consider domestic procedural laws such as *iura novit curia* relevant in the decision as to which law the court should apply.

4.1.1 Obligation to Apply the CISG

In Contracting State courts where argument is solely based on inapplicable domestic law in relation to a contract to which the CISG applies, the court is *obliged* to apply the CISG to resolve the effect of such conduct. In my view, this is true irrespective of whether the Contracting State operates as a monist or dualist system, provided the CISG has been effected.[42] I will deal with each in turn.

In summary, a court in a monist Contracting State is obliged to apply the CISG to the extent it covers a particular issue, as a matter of international law. Any domestic procedural rules relating to issues of *iura novit curia* are therefore irrelevant due to this obligation. Only the right to be heard is not.

The obligation arises as a matter of international law, because of course the CISG is an international treaty. The Vienna Convention on the Law of Treaties 1969[43] at Article 26 states:

> Every treaty in force is binding upon the parties to it and must be performed by them in good faith.

Provided its basic criteria are met,[44] the CISG is the applicable law. The applicability of the CISG to the typical situation described earlier arises under Article 1(1)(a) CISG, but the same would be true should the CISG apply via Article 1(1)(b). Absence of argument from counsel on the CISG cannot alter the court's fundamental obligation, as an organ of a Contracting State to the CISG, to apply it under these circumstances.[45] The imposition of

---

42 The CISG is not necessarily in effect in all regions of Contracting States: see W. Long, 'The Reach of the CISG in China: Declarations and Applicability to Hong Kong and Macao' and F. Yang, 'Hong Kong's Adoption of the CISG: Why do we need it now?', both in this volume.

43 Vienna Convention on the Law of Treaties, Vienna, 23 May 1969, Vol. 1155 U.N.T.S. 331.

44 The CISG applies when its geographical, temporal and material criteria are satisfied: Oviedo-Albán, *supra* note 3, at 199; H.M. Flechtner (Ed.), J.O. Honnold, *Uniform Law for International Sales,* Art. 1, at 29-48 (2009) (Honnold 4th edn); F. Ferrari, 'The CISG's Sphere of Application: Articles 1–3 and 10', in: Digest and Beyond, *supra* note 11, 21, *passim*.

45 Stating the applicability of the CISG is not dependent on a claim by the parties, but is to be examined *ex officio* by the court: I. Schwenzer & P. Hachem, in: I. Schwenzer (Ed), *Schlechtriem & Schwenzer: Commentary*

a treaty obligation to apply the CISG as the applicable law *ipso iure* means that the court's obligation is a strict duty to apply the correct law rather than a softer authority to do so.

Lest it be thought that domestic procedural rules could still play a part in relation to waiver by conduct of the CISG as a directory substantive law, the Vienna Convention on the Law of Treaties at Article 27 states:

> A party may not invoke the provisions of its internal law as justification for its failure to perform a treaty [...]

Thus to the extent that any rule of domestic procedure interferes with the application of the CISG, its observance by a court in a Contracting State would amount to a breach of that State's international obligation to apply the CISG. This is true of both dualist and monist systems.

The description of the obligation to apply the CISG as a matter of international law is relatively unproblematic in monist states, where a theory of unity of legal systems and primacy of international law ensures that international treaty obligations directly bind national courts without 'transformation',[46] although this can be sometimes less than straightforward in practice.[47] However, the proposition will not generally hold true in dualist states, where the accepted theoretical construct suggests two distinct legal orders of international law and municipal law, and in which, consequently, international law is not necessarily recognized as directly binding upon national courts, until 'transformed' in a manner determined internally.[48]

It is interesting to contemplate how courts have dealt with this. In some dualist systems, particularly those in the EU, courts have evolved a more 'internationalist' approach over

---

on the UN Convention on the International Sale of Goods (CISG), Arts 1-6, at 19-20 para. 3 (2010)(Schwenzer 3rd edn).

46 Thus in Europe, municipal courts are 'accustomed to the doctrine of "direct effect" under community law', such that the content of clear and unconditional international norms apply directly once integrated into the domestic legal order: A. Bianchi, 'International Law and US Courts: The Myth of Lohengrin Revisited', 15 *Eur. J. Int'l L.* 751, at 758 (2004); B. Conforti, *International Law and the Role of Domestic Legal Systems*, 25 (1993); A. Cassese, *International Law*, 213-216 (2005).

47 Conforti, *id.*, at 26 (noting that even in some monist states there is reluctance to implement treaties without internal directives to do so). Also, consider regions within some Contracting States, such as Macao: see Long, *supra* note 42; Yang, *supra* note 42.

48 See (writing extra-curially) Chief Justice Robert French, *International Law and Australian Domestic Law*, presented at the Annual Conference of the Supreme Court of New South Wales, Hunter Valley, 21 August 2009, at 23, available at <http://www.highcourt.gov.au/speeches/frenchcj/frenchcj21aug09.pdf>; Cassese, *supra* note 46, at 214.

time to increasingly recognize the direct effect of international law.[49] Many courts in dualist systems have developed a presumption to the effect that domestic laws should be interpreted to conform to international law whenever possible, on the basis that, having entered into a treaty, the state is presumed to have intended to give it effect unless the contrary is evident.[50] However, in certain dualist states, even though such presumptions are recognized, they are seldom utilized.[51] Indeed, there is a much-criticized persistent reluctance in the U.S. to accept the integration of international law, expressed in the doctrine of non-self-execution.[52] Perhaps anachronistically,[53] in the U.K. and Australia, national courts are not bound by international law *per se*, and will uphold domestic law, despite the fact that to do so where the domestic and international laws conflict involves a violation of international treaty obligations on the part of the State.[54]

Whatever may be the case generally, the CISG presents a special case. First, the CISG has been integrated into the internal legal systems of Contracting States, in the case of dualist states, either by being 'incorporated' or 'transformed' at the domestic level.[55] For example,

49 This has been the case in Italy, without constitutional or statutory change, in relation to EU Regulations: Conforti, *supra* note 46, at 39. Of course, the EU itself is a monist system.

50 See, *e.g.*, Italy, see Cassese, *supra* note 46, at 229-230; Sweden, C. Ehrenkrona, 'The Impact of International Law Instruments on National Legislation', Report to the European Commission for Democracy through Law (Venice Commission), 7 July 2010, at 6, available at <www.venice.coe.int>. See, *e.g.*, Australia, see *Mabo v. Queensland* (No 2)(1992) 175 CLR 1, at 41-43, High Court of Australia; *Minister for Foreign Affairs and Trade v. Magno* (1992) 112 ALR 529, at 534-535, High Court of Australia (*Magno* case). See also, Conforti, *supra* note 46, at 42.

51 In the U.S.A. this is known as the 'Charming Betsy' rule of statutory interpretation: *Murray v. The Schooner Charming Betsy*, 6 U.S. 64, at 81; 2 Cranch 64 (1804); *Talbot v. Seeman*, 5 U.S. 1, at 76; 1 Cranch 1 (1801). See also, American Law Institute, *Restatement (Third) of the Foreign Relations Law of the United States*, at §114 (1987); Bianchi, *supra* note 46, at 761 and 771-773. By contrast, in Australia, international obligations have impacted upon interpretation of domestic common law in some of the most prominent cases: see *Magno* case, *id.*

52 In the U.S., constitutional norms govern the internal binding effect of treaties. Despite the constitutional Supremacy Clause rendering treaties self-executing, this is said to depend on construction of intent: see, *e.g.*, *Medellin v. Texas*, 555 U.S. 491, at 504-505 (2008), U.S.A.; *Hamdi v. Rumsfeld*, 316 F.3d 450 (4th Cir., 2003), U.S.A.. This has allowed a doctrine of non-self-execution to flourish, based on constitutional doctrine, including the separation of powers and federalism: J. Yoo, 'Globalism and the Constitution: Treaties, Non-Self-Execution and the Original Understanding', 99 *Colum. L. Rev.* 1955, at 1959-1960 and 1982 (1999); Bianchi, *id.*, at 759 and 760. The U.S.A. has signed but not ratified the Vienna Convention on the Law of Treaties.

53 Conforti, *supra* note 46, at 20 and 83 (pointing out that dependency of the judiciary on the executive to implement international law is inconsistently upheld and hard to justify).

54 Cassese, *supra* note 46, at 236 (describing this as extreme 'statism'); Conforti, *supra* note 46, at 40. See also, French CJ, *supra* note 48646, at 23-29; *R v. Jones*, [2007] 1 AC 136, House of Lords, U.K.; *Magno* case, *supra* note 50, at 534-535; Ehrenkrona, *supra* note 50, at 6 (commenting generally).

55 Note Ghana and Venezuela have signed but not ratified the CISG: UNCITRAL website, available at <http://www.uncitral.org/uncitral/en/uncitral_texts/sale_goods/1980CISG_status.html>. In Ghana, ad hoc legislation is required: Cassese, *supra* note 46, at 229; E. Laryea, 'Why Ghana Should Enact Certain Interna-

in Australia, the CISG has been adopted in the form of a statute in each of the jurisdictions within its federation.[56] In the U.S.A., even following the decision in *Medellin v. Texas*,[57] it is likely the CISG would be considered a self-executing treaty.[58] From a dualist perspective, there is no conflict between the international obligations of the Contracting State and domestic law. The CISG forms part of the domestic law, and its provisions incontrovertibly bind national courts in dualist systems.

Secondly, in Contracting States, the CISG applies automatically and dictates both when and how it is to apply. Where the CISG is applicable pursuant to Article 1, the domestic law itself demands its application. Thus in a dualist system, the court is charged by the domestic law with the task of enforcement of the CISG where it is the applicable law according to its own terms.[59] It might be argued that courts can still observe procedural rules or principles which recognize the freedom of litigants to run their cases.[60] However, implementation of the CISG is not left to the court as a matter of domestic procedure. There is no discretion granted to the court in relation to whether or not it should be applied.[61] The CISG sets out the hierarchy of laws in relation to matters within its scope in Article 7(2) CISG, and imposes upon courts in Contracting States a duty to take into account the CISG's international nature in its interpretation,[62] and a duty to interpret it in a manner that promotes uniformity, in other words, in accordance with the CISG's own internal methodology: Art 7(1) CISG.[63] Essentially, the domestic law *directs* the court to

---

tional Legal Instruments relating to International Sale of Goods Transactions', 19(1) *African J. Int'l & Comp. L.* 1, at 9-17 (2011). See also, Long, *supra* note 42; Yang, *supra* note 42.

56 Spagnolo, *supra* note 7, at 143, note 4.

57 *Medellin* case, *supra* note 52, at 505 and 520-523 (majority conclusion that to be self-executing treaties must convey by their textual provisions an intention to be so, and resort may be had to secondary sources).

58 M. Cantora, 'The CISG after Medellin v. Texas: Do U.S. Businesses Have It? Do they Want It?', 8 *J. Int'l Bus. & L.* 111, at 113, 114 (2009) (concluding that sufficient indications of an intention by the President and the Senate for the CISG to apply as a self-executing treaty pursuant to the principles espoused by the majority in *Medellin* can be found in a clear statement by the U.S. President to the Senate demonstrating an understanding that the CISG was self-executing).

59 *Contra* Bridge, *supra* note 12, at 917 (arguing that Art. 1 does 'not with sufficient clarity abridge' the longstanding freedom of litigants to ignore foreign law).

60 *Id.*

61 Other than (irrelevantly for present purposes) regarding specific performance orders: Art. 28 CISG.

62 Art. 7(1) demands that, in interpreting the CISG, 'regard is to be had to its international character'.

63 Describing theses as international obligations: P. Schlechtriem, 'The Borderland of Tort and Contract – Opening a New Frontier?', 21 *Cornell Int'l L. J.* 467, at 468-469 (1988) (*Borderland*); J.O. Honnold, *Documentary History of the Uniform Law for International Sales* 89 (1989); Honnold 4th edn, *supra* note 44, at 128 para. 92; Bridge, *supra* note 12, at 922; J.S. Ziegel, 'The Future of the International Sales Convention from a Common Law Perspective', 6 *New Zealand Business L. Q.* 336, 342, note 30 (2000); C.B. Andersen, 'The Uniform International Sales Law and the Global Jurisconsultorium', 24 *J. L. & Com.* 159, at 166 (2005) (recourse to foreign CISG jurisprudence is a duty); Spagnolo, *supra* note 7, at 167; Schwenzer & Hachem, *supra* note 45, Art. 7, at 123 para. 7 ('regard is to be had' as a 'command' directed to courts and tribunals).

honour the international obligations of the Contracting State in relation to the CISG in relation to individual cases.

Similarly, in *Fothergill v. Monarch Airlines Ltd* in relation to Article 32 of the Vienna Convention on the Law of Treaties and consultation of *traveaux préparatoires* by English courts in interpretation of a treaty, Lord Diplock stated:

> By ratifying that Convention, [the] Government has undertaken an international obligation on behalf of the United Kingdom to interpret future treaties in this manner and since under our constitution the function of interpreting the written law is an exercise of judicial power and rests with the courts of justice, that obligation assumed by the United Kingdom falls to be performed by those courts.[64]

Hence the issues foreshadowed above regarding dualist states are not problematic for present purposes. While in monist states, courts are bound by the direct effect of the CISG as international law, courts in dualist states are bound by the terms of the CISG as municipal law to implement the international obligations of the Contracting State, in a manner which reflects the CISG's nature as international uniform law. It could be argued that the CISG effectively 'pierces the armour' of the dualist international-domestic law dichotomy[65] in a practical sense. However, in any event, the direction within the CISG to apply it where it is the governing law *ipso iure* will bind courts in dualist Contracting States to apply the CISG *ex officio* if necessary, even if the obligation technically arises as a matter of domestic law.

It should be noted that when the court is in a Contracting State, the CISG is not a foreign law. Despite the fact it is simultaneously a treaty, it forms part of the domestic law of the jurisdiction – a part of the law of the forum.[66] Therefore in Contracting States, how the forum treats foreign law is irrelevant.[67] Its applicability and content are a question of law, not fact. Any default rule regarding substitution of domestic for a foreign law has no place

64 *Fothergill v. Monarch Airlines Ltd* [1981] AC 251 (U.K.). The House of Lords was concerned with the Warsaw Convention for the Unification of Certain Rules relating to International Carriage by Air, as amended (1955), implemented in the Carriage by Air Act (1961) (U.K.).

65 The description used in a different context by Cassese regarding the inroads modern international law has made into various municipal systems: *supra* note 46, at 217.

66 Similarly, see Bridge, *supra* note 12, at 916; Schwenzer & Hachem, *supra* note 45, Introduction to Arts 1-6, at 19 para. 3; L. Sevón, 'Method of Unification of Law for the International Sale of Goods', in: K. Buure-Hägglund (Ed.), *The Finnish National Reports to the Twelfth Congress of the International Academy of Comparative Law*, 11 at 14 (1986); *Georgia Pacific Resins* case, *supra* note 14.

67 See discussion below in Part 4.2, at note 78 and accompanying text.

in the process.[68] This will be true regardless of how the CISG applies. In the case of Article 1(1)(a), where the CISG's requirements for application are satisfied, the CISG applies automatically.[69] If, on the other hand, the forum's private international law leads to the law of a Contracting State in accordance with Article 1(1)(b), then a Contracting State court is still bound to apply the CISG.[70] Normally, once conflict rules have identified the applicable foreign law, the manner in which its content would be ascertained would turn on whether the forum's procedural rules treat foreign law as law or fact, as discussed below.[71] However, where the forum is located in a Contracting State, the CISG is not foreign law at all. Thus the CISG should always be treated as a matter of law *where it forms part of the forum's own law*. To the extent it governs a particular issue, the forum of a Contracting State is bound to apply it.

Most importantly, the obligation to apply the CISG *ex officio* arises from the CISG itself, not from any domestic procedural principle. This is contrary to the traditional view discussed above, and also contradicts cases which have upheld the CISG on the express basis of the local procedure of *iura novit curia*.[72]

4.1.2 Displacement of Domestic Procedural Rules

The corollary of this obligation to apply the CISG *ex officio*, is that, where the CISG covers an issue, its provisions take precedence over any domestic procedural rules which would interfere with the fulfilment of that duty by the court. The legitimacy of such rules is essentially limited by the extent to which they can be reconciled with the Contracting State's obligation to apply the CISG. Even domestic procedural rules themselves often recognize the need to modify default rules in light of international obligations.[73]

---

68 See discussion below in Part 4.2, at note 81 and accompanying text.

69 Honnold 4th edn, *supra* note 44, Art. 1, at 29-48; Ferrari, *supra* note 44, *passim*.

70 The only complicating factor here is whether or not the forum Contracting State, or indeed the Contracting State whose laws are determined applicable under conflicts rules have made an Art. 95 declaration. It is beyond the scope of this chapter to deal with this issue. See instead, Bridge, *supra* note 12, at 919-921 and 980-981; Ferrari, *id.*, at 52; see also W. Long, 'The Reach of the CISG in China: Declarations and Applicability to Hong Kong and Macao', in this volume.

71 See discussion below in Part 4.2, at note 78 and accompanying text.

72 See discussion of traditional view in Part 3.1, and see also, *supra* note 27 (cases expressly relying upon *iura novit curia* to apply the CISG).

73 T.C. Hartley, 'Pleading and Proof of Foreign Law: The Major European Systems Compared', 45 *Int'l & Comp. L. Q.* 271, at 287-288 (1996)(U.K.) (describing how the default rule of application of English law in substitution of an unproven foreign law is displaced by international obligations). See also, Hartley, *id.*, at 277, note 25 (mentioning that the Swiss default rule substituting the *lex fori* for foreign law may not apply where application is pursuant to an international obligation); Art. 142(2) 1986 General Principles of the Civil Law, China, which provides that to the extent of any inconsistency, treaty obligations prevail over substantive civil laws, unless China has made a reservation. In this regard, China's Art. 95 declaration may be relevant: see W. Long, 'The Reach of the CISG in China: Declarations and Applicability to Hong Kong and Macao', in this volume.

The issues addressed by domestic *iura novit curia* and tacit waiver in domestic law have the potential to interfere with the obligation of courts in Contracting States to apply the CISG. To that extent, such rules have no place in determining the appropriate course for such a court when faced with counsel who fail to plead the CISG. The duty requires the CISG to be applied to the extent of issues governed by it. While some disagree with blanket pre-emption,[74] others hold that the CISG applies exclusively in relation to matters covered by it, on the basis that, were it otherwise, the CISG could not implement uniform outcomes.[75] The CISG deals on its own terms with its exclusion by choice of law, as discussed below in Part 5.

At this point, there is no longer room for any domestic rule which says another law is be applied by the court, either because of procedural rules relating to the court's role, local concepts of waiver, or due to rules of pleading.[76] The function of determining which law should be applied by the court has already been performed by the duty imposed upon the court. Consequently, it would be impermissible for any domestic procedural rules to confine the court to the inapplicable laws argued. It follows that these rules have been effectively displaced, leaving only the residual effect of the right to be heard.

Thus the obligation of courts to apply the CISG uniformly and internationally inexorably leads to the imperative that the CISG prevails over domestic procedural rules, at least to the extent such rules allow application of inapplicable law.[77] A domestic rule of procedure which would enable parties to oust the CISG from a contract to which it applies without actual agreement, would relegate the Contracting State's treaty obligations to the unfettered whims of counsel and threaten the harmonizing effect of the CISG.

Displacement of local procedural rules by a uniform approach under the CISG may in any event further the very aims to which domestic procedural rules aspire; proper administration of justice, development and clarity of the law, and judicial efficiency in the reduction of wasteful appeals. It encourages counsel to properly argue the case on the basis of relevant

---

74 See, *e.g.*, J. Lookofsky, 'In Dubio Pro Conventione? Some Thoughts about Opt-Outs, Computer Programs and Preëmption under the 1980 Vienna Sales Convention (CISG)', 13 *Duke J. Comp. & Int'l L.* 263 (2003).

75 See generally: Schlechtriem, *Borderland, supra* note 63, *passim*; P. Schlechtriem & I. Schwenzer, in: Schwenzer 3rd edn, *supra* note 45, Introduction 8-9.

76 Inferences from rules of pleading that preclude entitlement to argue the CISG cannot be relied upon to demonstrate inferences of an intent to exclude, although it must be conceded that loss of entitlements due to issues outside the CISG's scope, such as limitation periods, will obviously have such an effect and are not displaced. See also, the discussion regarding appeals, Part 4.4 below.

77 The author has previously asserted this point: *supra* note 7, at 215, note 522. See also, Pribetic, *supra* note 12, at 27 (arguing that if applicable the CISG must be applied despite differences between common and civil law on this point).

law, or to inform clients of their rights and obligations under relevant law and advise them to expressly agree to exclude it.

Displacement is important to resolving the erratic and unpredictable outcomes seen in practice, as outlined in Part 3.3. A straightforward solution under the CISG will result in improvements to uniformity and certainty. The suggested range of practical solutions in Part 6 also seeks to address non-displaced considerations of due process.

4.2 Courts in Non-Contracting States

Obviously a court in a non-contracting state is not bound by any obligation to apply the CISG of the type discussed above in Part 4.1, even if its conflict rules point to the law of a State which has adopted the CISG. Application of the CISG in such circumstances amounts to application of a foreign law.

Since in this permutation the CISG applies as foreign law, the extent to which a court considers itself either obliged, empowered or prohibited from applying the foreign law will be influenced by whether the forum's procedural rules treat foreign law as a question of fact or law.

The classification profoundly alters the burden of discovering the foreign law and applying it.[78] Proof of foreign law is frequently a matter for the parties, who might bear the onus of proof of the foreign law as a matter of fact, even in jurisdictions where *iura novit curia* overtly applies to domestic law.[79] Also, irrespective of where the primary burden lies, courts can normally require parties to assist in establishing foreign law, irrespective of character-

78 English courts cannot take judicial notice of foreign law: S. Geeroms, *Foreign Law in Civil Litigation: A Comparative and Functional Analysis* 114 (2004); Cappelletti & Garth, *supra* note 25, at 29, notes 176-177, §1-26. In the US, foreign law is now treated as a question of law, and federal courts and certain state courts are empowered (but not obliged) to take judicial notice of it: Rule 44.1 Federal Rules of Civil Procedure, U.S.A.. See *Frummer v. Hilton Hotels International, Inc.*, 60 Misc. 2d 840, 304 N.Y.S. 2d 335, Supreme Court, New York, U.S.A., 18 August 1969 (courts can take judicial notice of foreign law, but are not obliged to raise it *sua sponte*, unlike domestic law). By contrast, a duty to establish foreign law *ex officio* if necessary exists in some jurisdictions: see, *e.g.*, F. Galgano, 'The New Lex Mercatoria', 2 *Ann. Surv. Int'l & Comp. L.* 99, at 105 and note 11 (1995) (Italian judges must ascertain and apply foreign law *ex officio*); Sass, *supra* note 13, at 357 and note 85 (Italy); B. Bastuck & B. Gopfert, 'Admission & Presentation of Evidence in Germany', 16 *Loy. L.A. Int'l & Comp. L. J.* 609, at 622-623 (1994)(Germany); G. Dannemann, *Establishing Foreign Law in a German Court, Joint Workshops on Comparative Litigation Practice,* presented at British Institute of Int'l & Comparative Law & British-German Jurists Association, 30 June 1994, at text accompanying notes 4-7.

79 See, *e.g.*, in Scandinavian countries different aspects of foreign law are treated variously as law or fact: I. Zajtay, Ch. 14, 'The Application of Foreign Law', in: K. Lipstein (Ed.), *International Encyclopedia of Comparative Law,* Vol. III, Private International Law, at 8, §14-13 (1972).

ization.[80] Finally, when the content of foreign law cannot be ascertained, pursuant to domestic procedural rules, domestic law usually operates as a default.[81] A non-contracting state court's classification of foreign law as fact or law is therefore crucial, and will influence the manner in which the CISG's applicability and content are to be ascertained.[82] In these circumstances, the forum's procedural rules are determinative. Clearly, the traditional view that domestic procedural law determines the law to be applied holds true in non-contracting states.

4.3 *Arbitrations*

Except for tribunals such as ICSID which have been established pursuant to Conventions and are therefore of a public law nature,[83] arbitral tribunals are private institutions. They are not organs of the state, and have no duty to fulfil treaty obligations. Arguably, the tribunal owes duties only to the parties involved.

Yet arbitral tribunals do not operate in a complete vacuum. Their authority is derived from the arbitration agreement and the *lex arbitri*, however tribunals may need to consider a host of laws and rules to determine the respective roles of the tribunal and parties in relation to identification and application of the substantive law. These include the *lex arbitri*, and in particular, its mandatory rules including rules of due process,[84] any arbitration

80 The court may require parties to assist in ascertaining foreign law in many jurisdictions. See, *e.g.*: Rule No. 44.1 Federal Rules of Civil Procedure, U.S.A.; Art. 293 German ZPO; Isele, *supra* note 20, at 15-16 (Germany & France); Sass, *supra* note 13, at 356-358 (Germany); Art. 12(6) Código Civil [Spanish Civil Code]; Isele, *id.*, at 15 (Switzerland); Art. 14 Lei de Introdução ao Código Civil Brasileiro 1942 [Brazilian Law of Introduction to the Civil Code], Decreto-Lei N° 4.657; Art 13 Code de procédure civile [French Code of Civil Procedure]; Sass, *id.*, at 356 (Italy); Kurkela, *supra* note 20, at 493 (Finland); J. Dolinger, 'Application, Proof and Interpretation of Foreign Law: A Comparative Study in Private International Law', 12 *Ariz. J. Int'l & Comp. L.* 225, at 235-236 and 247-248, notes 55-59 and 110-111 (1995)(Greece).

81 L. Collins (Ed.), 'Dicey & Morris: The Conflict of Laws', 221 (2000)(Rule 18)(U.K.); Hartley, *supra* note 73, at 285 (U.K.); R. Fentiman, 'Foreign Law in English Courts', 108 *L. Q. R.* 142, at 147 (1992) (asserting a different basis for the English rule); Dannemann, *supra* note 78, at text accompanying note 23 (Germany); Bundesgerichtshof [Federal Supreme Court](BGH), Germany, 23 December 1981, NJW (1982), 1215; Kurkela, *supra* note 20, at 486 and note 5 (Finland); J. Rajski, 'The New Polish Private International Law, 1965', 15 *Int'l & Comp. L. Q.* 457, at 463 (1966)(Poland); Geeroms, *supra* note 78, at 113 (France).

82 Noting classification of the CISG as foreign law in such circumstances: Schwenzer & Hachem, *supra* note 45, Art. 1, at 40 para. 31.

83 I. Kalniņa, 'Iura Novit Curia: Scylla and Charybdis of International Arbitration?', 8 *Baltic Yearbook Int'l L.* 89, at 95 *et seq* (2005).

84 G. Born, *International Commercial Arbitration*, 426 (2009); J. Lew, L. Mistelis & S. Kröll, *Comparative International Commercial Arbitration* 524 para. 21-17 (2003). Generally, see G. Cordero Moss, 'Can an Arbitral Tribunal Disregard the Choice of Law made by the Parties?', 1 *Stockholm Int'l Arbitration Rev.* 1, at 4 (2005).

rules agreed by the parties, and conflict rules under the *lex arbitri* or arbitration rules.[85] Additionally, unlike courts, arbitral tribunals have no default substantive law of the forum upon which to fall back.[86]

Debate has recently arisen as to whether a principle of *iura novit arbiter* should be employed by arbitrators facing the type of situation posed in this chapter. Arbitral tribunals are bound by the procedure contained within the relevant arbitral law and arbitration rules. The arbitral law of the seat normally requires the tribunal to follow the choice of law made by the parties, and provides it with discretion where no choice has been made.[87] A choice of particular arbitral rules can clarify the role of the tribunal, as some rules contemplate the *iura novit arbiter* issue. For example, Rule 22(1) LCIA Rules gives the tribunal the power to ascertain and apply the law *sua sponte*, provided the parties have not agreed otherwise.[88] Similarly, the U.K. Arbitration Act s. 34(1) & (2)(g) is an arbitration law that specifically deals with this aspect of procedure.[89] These point to a soft version of *iura novit arbiter*; the tribunal is empowered to look beyond party legal submissions (unless parties have agreed to the contrary), but is not obliged to do so. In the case of the LCIA Rules, the power is subject to the due process proviso that parties must be given an opportunity to comment on independent research or novel legal points.[90]

---

85 R. Goode, 'Litigation or Arbitration? The Influence of the Dispute Resolution Procedure on Substantive Rights', 19 *Pace Int'l L. Rev.* 53, at 56 (2007) (noting that while arbitrators often follow the conflict rules of the seat of arbitration, they are normally not *obliged* to do so); Lew *et al*, *id.*, at 427, para. 17-51; Schwenzer & Hachem, *supra* note 45, Arts 1-6, at 23 para. 13; G. Kaufmann-Kohler, 'Globalization of Arbitral Procedure', 36 *Vand. J. Transnat'l L.* 1313, *passim* (2003).The tribunal might also consider rules relevant to enforceability, although normally these are essentially similar to the requirements of the *lex arbitri*. For example, Art. 36 UNCITRAL Model Law on International Commercial Arbitration 1985, as amended in 2006, Gen. Ass. Res. 40/72, U.N. Doc. A/40/17, annex I, 11 December 1985, Gen. Ass. Res. 61/33, 4 December 2006 (UNCITRAL Model Law); Art. V Convention on the Recognition and Enforcement of Foreign Arbitral Awards, New York, 10 June 1958, 330 UNTS 38 (New York Convention).

86 See also, Kaufmann-Kohler, *id.*, at 1332 (tribunals only have foreign law, and 'no *lex fori*'); Isele, *supra* note 20, at 16 (arbitral tribunals have 'no forum law to fall back on').

87 See, *e.g.*, Art. 28 UNCITRAL Model Law.

88 London Court of International Arbitration Rules 1998 (LCIA Rules) Rule 22(1): 'Unless the parties at any time agree otherwise in writing, the Arbitral Tribunal shall have the power, on the application of any party or of its own motion, but in either case only after giving the parties a reasonable opportunity to state their views: [...] (c) [...] to conduct such enquiries as may appear to the Arbitral Tribunal to be necessary or expedient, including whether and to what extent the Arbitral Tribunal should itself take the initiative in identifying the issues and ascertaining the relevant facts and the law(s) or rules of law applicable to the arbitration'. See also, Art. 17(1) International Chamber of Commerce, Rules of Arbitration 1998 (ICC Rules 1998).

89 U.K. Arbitration Act 1996 s. 34(1) & (2)(g) states that unless parties agree otherwise, the arbitral tribunal may decide 'whether and to what extent the tribunal should itself take the initiative in ascertaining the facts and the law'. See also, Kurkela, *supra* note 20, at 493.

90 *Supra* note 88. Indeed, some rules require tribunals to take account of contractual terms and usages 'in all cases', which by implication includes those where parties have not invoked them: Art. 17(2) ICC Rules 1998; Art. 35(3) UNCITRAL Arbitration Rules 2010.

It is submitted that, even where LCIA Rules are not applicable, they encapsulate the preferable approach to which tribunals should aspire. The soft form *iura novit arbiter* achieves the right balance between the respective roles of the parties and the tribunal, and provides flexibility to deal with inadequate submissions.[91]

Why is this flexibility inherently useful? Unless the tribunal is expressly appointed as *amiable compositeur*,[92] its mandate is to decide the dispute *according to law*.[93] A tribunal cannot decide a matter capriciously. If the tribunal can ignore the relevant law, the duty to decide according to law is rendered purely fictional.[94] Treatment of applicable law as a merely evidentiary matter is not compatible with this duty.[95] Faced with counsel who fail to address the relevant law, flexibility ensures the tribunal can draw on its own experience and research to direct counsel toward the correct law.[96]

Moreover, the soft version of *iura novit arbiter* combined with a broad right to be heard maintains standards that safeguard against challenges to the arbitration or award.[97] The need for due process is an overriding principle of arbitration,[98] and while awards by tribunals employing a narrow right to be heard have been upheld, there are also awards that have been set aside for failure of due process, even in courts renowned for upholding narrow definitions of the right to be heard in relation to arbitral awards.[99] Careful observance of a broadly defined 'right to be heard' is therefore prudent.

---

91 ILA Final Report, *supra* note 22, Recommendation No.7 (the tribunal is not confined to sources invoked by the parties, subject the opportunity to be heard in Recommendation No. 8). *Contra*, Recommendation No. 6 (arbitrators should not generally introduce new legal issues unless due to public policy rules or issues which may later lead to challenges to the award); A. Dimolitsa, 'The Equivocal Power of the Arbitrators to Introduce Ex Officio New Issues of Law', 27(3) *ASA Bulletin* 426, at 427 (2009) (describing the power (but not obligation) of a tribunal to ascertain the contents of applicable law as 'a facet of their jurisdictional mission').

92 That is, appointed to decide *ex aequo et bono*. Generally tribunals must be expressly authorized to decide in this manner: see, *e.g.*, Art. 28(3) UNCITRAL Model Law; Art. 17(3) ICC Rules 1998. Nappert also alludes to this: S. Nappert, 'Observations', 3 *Stockholm Int'l Arbitration Rev.* 283, at 286 (2008). See also: ILA Final Report, *supra* note 22, at 6.

93 ILA Final Report, *id.*, at 19.

94 Kurkela, *supra* note 20, at 495.

95 *Id.*

96 Swiss courts consider *iura novit curia* to apply to arbitrations: Dimolitsa, *supra* note 91, at 431; ILA Final Report, *supra* note 22, at 14 and note 42.

97 Art. V New York Convention; Art. 34(2) UNCITRAL Model Law.

98 Kaufmann-Kohler, *supra* note 85, at 1322-1323; ILA Final Report, *supra* note 22, at 20.

99 See, *e.g.*, Bundesgericht [Federal Supreme Court], Switzerland, 4A_108/2009, 9 June 2009. 28(3) *ASA Bulletin* 553 (2010) (inapplicable law not invoked but applied by tribunal); *Louis Dreyfus SAS v. Holding Tusculum BV*, Quebec Superior Court, Canada, 8 December 2008 (*Dreyfus v. Tusculum*) (annulling an award imposing a remedy neither side had pleaded for failure of the right to be heard and *ultra petita*); S. Nappert, *Arbitral Activism: The Manifold Guises of Jura Novit Arbiter* (2010), available at <http://demo.kluwerarbitration.com/arbitration/Newsletter.aspx?month=march2009> (commenting on the *Dreyfus* case); B. Grob & G. von Segesser, available at <http://kluwerarbitrationblog.com/blog/2009/08/27/iura-novit-curia-the-right-

Naturally, this would mean that tribunals cognizant that the CISG applies would need to suggest this to the parties before they would be empowered to apply it pursuant to this approach. Some have remarked upon the potential threat to the appearance of neutrality that such intervention might invite, since this could lead to the award being set aside for bias.[100] Nonetheless, if attention of counsel is focussed on clarification of the legal point involved, the success of such a challenge is difficult to envisage.

Awards or indeed arbitrations can also be challenged on an *ultra petita* basis.[101] This will be particularly so if the tribunal awards relief not claimed or greater relief than claimed. Alternatively, the tribunal in applying novel legal points might be considered to have gone beyond its arbitral mandate.[102] However, such attacks are rarely upheld,[103] so provided the arbitration agreement submits 'all disputes arising out of or in connection with the contract' to the tribunal, decisions based on the CISG are unlikely to be beyond the tribunal's mandate, even if impeachable for breach of due process.[104]

There are parallels to the issues that face courts.[105] It may be true that, unlike court decisions, arbitral awards are not generally reviewable on questions of law,[106] but both are vulnerable for failures to observe due process. The competing constraints under which a tribunal operates of ensuring discharge of its obligation to render a decision according to law while affording due process, ensure that ultimately, tribunals are faced with much the same dilemma. Essentially this boils down to a policy choice between:

to-be-heard-decision-of-the-swiss-federal-supreme-court-as-of-9-june-2009-4a_1082009/> (discussing the Swiss Federal Supreme Court decision of 9 June 2009).

100 Dimolitsa, *supra* note 91, at 429 & 438; Isele, *supra* note 20, at 24; Kalniņa, *supra* note 83, at 101; ILA Final Report, *supra* note 22, at 21.

101 Art. 34(2)(a)(iii) Model Law; Art. V(I)(c) New York Convention; Born, *supra* note 84, at 2606-2607; ILA Final Report, *supra* note 22, at 19; Cordero Moss, *supra* note 84, at 2; Kurkela, *supra* note 20, at 490; Kalniņa, *id.*, at 90 and 110.

102 Kurkela, *id.*, at 297-298.

103 See, *e.g.*, *Werfen Austria GmbH v. Polar Electro Europe BV*, Supreme Court, Finland, 2 July 2007, reported in translation at 3 *Stockholm Int'l Arbitration Rev.* 260 (2008)(*Werfen* case). See, *e.g.*, Federal Supreme Court, Switzerland, 4A_220/2007, 21 September 2007, 26(4) *ASA Bulletin* 742. Upholding this ground: *Systembolaget Aktiebolag v. V & S Vin & Sprit Aktiebolag*, Svea Court of Appeal, Stockholm, Sweden, T4548-08, 1 December 2009 (translation by K.B. Vinge); *Dreyfus v. Tusculum*, *supra* note 99. See also, A.J. van den Berg, *Yearbook of Commercial Arbitration*, Vol. 28 at 656 (2003); Born, *supra* note 84, at 2589 and 2607-2608; Lew *et al*, *supra* note 84, at 675 paras. 25-38 to 25-39; Nappert, *supra* note 92, at 286; Cordero Moss, *supra* note 84, at 3. For discussion of the *Werfen* case, see Nappert, *id.*, and P. Kiurunen, 'Finality of Arbitral Awards – Common Grounds?, 3 *Stockholm Int'l Arbitration Rev.* 273, at 277 and 280 (2008).

104 See generally regarding applicable law, Cordero Moss, *supra* note 84, at 3-4.

105 See Isele, *supra* note 20, at 20-24.

106 Some jurisdictions still allow merits review: see Born, *supra* note 84, at 2646-2647.

(i) a decision based on the wrong law thus incorrect on its merits but with little chance of challenge (application of inapplicable, but argued law);[107]

(ii) a decision correct on the merits but which risks being overturned for procedural error (*ex officio* application of applicable but unargued law);[108] or

(iii) a decision both correct on its merits and with little chance of challenge (application of relevant law after affording an opportunity to either address it in argument or to agree to restrict the tribunal's discretion to apply that law).

Of course the preferable course is for the tribunal to suggest the parties agree openly on the procedural rules as a preliminary matter. The tribunal might propose a soft form *iura novit arbiter* rule with a broadly defined right to be heard and leave it to the parties to agree upon a more restrictive approach if they can.[109]

Thus although tribunals are not subject to the same obligation to apply the CISG as courts in Contracting States, nonetheless, the suggested approach to interpretation regarding exclusions in Part 5.3 and practical solutions proposed in Part 6 will hold relevance for arbitral tribunals as they seek to balance their own competing obligations.

4.4 *Appeals*

A range of approaches is evident in appeals. The Slovak decisions mentioned earlier in which the lower court applied the wrong law were remitted by the appeal court back to the lower court for re-determination under the correct law.[110] Other systems might limit the scope of appeal to grounds already raised by parties, sometimes due to specific rules limiting the subject matter of the jurisdiction of the appeal court. Thus an appeal court might be constrained from applying a law overlooked at the trial stage. For example, in

---

107 Unlikely to provide grounds for refusal of enforceability, unless mandatory rules are overlooked: ILA Final Report, *supra* note 22, at 17 and 22.

108 A rare example of the Swiss courts upholding breach of the right to be heard for 'surprise' is Federal Supreme Court, 4A_400/2008, 9 February 2009, 27(3) *ASA Bulletin* 501 (2009) (quashing Court of Arbitration for Sport (CAS) award on the basis that the tribunal applied without warning a law which was not only inapplicable, but went beyond legal argument by the parties). Doubting this is likely in Sweden: M. Wallin & K. Mild, 'Observations', 1 *Stockholm Int'l Arbitration Rev.* 148, at 149 (2007).

109 G. Kaufmann-Kohler, 'The Arbitrator and the Law: Does He/She Know It? Apply It? How? And a Few More Questions', 21(4) *Arbitration Int'l* 631, at 636 (2005); Nappert, *supra* note 91, at 287. See also, Dimolitsa, *supra* note 91, at 433; Kalniņa, *supra* note 83, at 103; ILA Final Report, *supra* note 22, at 16; J. Waincymer, *International Arbitration and the Duty to Know the Law* (forthcoming, *J. Int'l Arb.* 2010).

110 *Supra* note 6.

the *GPL Treatment* case in the U.S., the appeal court refused to hear CISG arguments.[111] Similarly, in accordance with rules of appeal and pleading, counsel was refused permission to amend pleadings to incorporate CISG argument for the first time at the appeal stage in the Australian case of *Italian Imported Foods.*[112]

Sometimes the grounds of appeal are matters of judicial discretion,[113] which itself might turn on whether new arguments would be 'futile'. Where this is so, preliminary CISG argument should always be permitted so as to gauge the extent of potential futility.[114]

It could be argued that appeal rules fall within the more general proposition asserted earlier, and that they are procedural rules displaced by the CISG. This chapter does not make this assertion. Instead, it is submitted that, where rules of appeal allow for judicial discretion regarding new grounds, the matters raised above should be carefully taken into account in the exercise of that discretion to the fullest extent possible. A view inclined to allowing new argument will support the aims of the CISG and more closely align them with its application in practice. It will also encourage closer attention to it by counsel and therefore enhance familiarity with it in the jurisdiction concerned.

5 Can the CISG be Excluded by Failure to Plead It?

Once it has been determined that the CISG is to be applied, then the remaining question is how the adjudicator should view the failure to plead the CISG and presentation of the case on the basis of inapplicable local sales laws. What is a court or tribunal to make of such conduct? Can failure to plead the CISG amount to a waiver or tacit exclusion of it?

Since the contract is governed by the CISG, the adjudicator must look to its provisions alone to decide if such conduct amounts to an exclusion. It is the CISG which controls the 'choice of law rule' when a CISG contract exists, not domestic procedural rules or domestic waiver principles. If parties choose to exercise that option during proceedings, they will

111 *GPL Treatment, supra* note 8. Counsel was not allowed to alter the pleadings and was held to have waived the CISG argument since it was not raised until late in the trial: *GPL Treatment, id.*, Leeson J (dissenting, at note 8); H.M. Flechtner, 'Another CISG Case in the US Courts: Pitfalls for the Practitioner and Potential for Regionalized Interpretations', 15 *J. L. & Com.* 127, at 129 and note 11 (1995).

112 *Italian Imported Foods, supra* note 7; see Spagnolo, *supra* note 7, at 197-199.

113 *GPL Treatment, supra* note 8; *Italian Imported Foods, supra* note 7; *Summit Chemicals Pty Ltd v. Vetrotex Espana SA*, Court of Appeal, Western Australia, 27 May 2004, available at <http://cisgw3.law.pace.edu/cases/040527a2.html> (*Summit Chemicals*); see Spagnolo, *id.*, at 193-199 (discussing this aspect of the *Italian Imported Foods & Summit Chemicals cases*).

114 Unfortunately, this is not always appreciated in applications to amend pleadings: Spagnolo, *id.*

need to comply with the CISG's internal requirements before their autonomous choice is effective.

The ability of parties to choose to exclude its application is therefore controlled by Article 6 which deals with exclusion. This is so whether parties seek to exclude the CISG within the original contract or sometime thereafter.

Until Article 6 is enlivened, the CISG remains the governing law of the contract. Whilst there is minority opinion to the contrary, the effect of the majority view is that any agreement to exclude must be formed pursuant to the formation provisions of the CISG, and will need to satisfy Article 6.[115] The CISG's applicability from the outset is not 'subordinated to the will of the parties' unless that will amounts to an agreement to exclude in accordance with the CISG, since the CISG already applies pursuant to Article 1.[116]

115 See, *e.g.*, Appellate Court (OLG) Oldenburg, Germany, 20 December 2007, available at <http://cisgw3.law.pace.edu/cases/071220g1.html>; *Golden Valley Grape Juice and Wine, LLC v. Centrisys Corp.*, 2010 U.S. Dist. LEXIS 11884 (E.D. Cal.), 22 January 2010, available at <http://cisgw3.law.pace.edu/cases/100121u1.html> (*Golden Valley* case); *Easom Automation Systems, Inc. v. Thyssenkrupp Fabco, Corp.*, 2007 WL 2875256, U.S. District Court (E.D. Mich.), 28 September 2007, CISG-online 1601, available at <http://www.cisg-online.ch/cisg/urteile/1601.pdf> (*Easom Automation* case); Spagnolo, *supra* note 7, at 205 (CISG should determine the matter, at least until the point at which exclusion is established under its formation provisions); Schwenzer & Hachem, *supra* note 45, Art. 6, at 104 and 105 (formation and interpretation of exclusion clauses subject to CISG rules); M. Schmidt-Kessel, in: Schwenzer 3rd edn, *id.*, Art. 8, at 177 para. 61 (incorporation of choice of law clauses including exclusions of CISG within the sphere of CISG formation provisions). But see P. Schlechtriem, in: P. Schlechtriem & I. Schwenzer (Eds), *Commentary on the UN Convention on the International Sale of Goods (CISG)*, Art. 6, at 85-89 paras. 7-10 (2005)(Schlechtriem & Schwenzer 2nd edn) (stating that rules of private international law determine the issue).

116 *Sté Ceramique Culinaire de France v. Sté Musgrave Ltd*, Cour de Cassation, France, 17 December 1996, available at <http://cisg3.law.pace.edu/cases/950926f1.html> (the CISG 'applies at the outset; its applicability is not subordinated to the will of the parties, express or tacit'). See also, Tribunale di Padova, 25 February 2004, *supra* note 14 ('[f]urther, the silence in the pleadings on the matter of the applicability of the law at issue is immaterial because, in the presence of all requisites mentioned above [the CISG] is applicable by operation of law').

In other words, once in, the only way out is via the CISG's own rules.

5.1 *Exclusion within the Original Contract*

Much has been written about 'opting out' at the contractual stage, so it is useful to examine these requirements for present purposes as a point of comparison.

Generally, courts and commentators have taken a rather restrictive approach to exclusion of the CISG within contractual clauses. The predominant view amongst scholars cautions against swift conclusions of implicit exclusion within the contract.[117] At a minimum, a 'certain' or 'real' tangible intent is required for implicit exclusion to be effective, as opposed to a hypothetical or 'theoretical' intent.[118] While some cases have upheld implicit opt-outs,[119] most courts and tribunals have been slow to infer exclusion where the contractual clause is unclear.[120] Thus a reference to INCOTERMS has been held insufficient to demonstrate an intent to exclude the CISG.[121] A choice of national law excluding ULIS was held not to exclude the CISG.[122] A few cases have gone further still, by denying even

117 Against implicit exclusion: F. Enderlein & D. Maskow, *International SalesLaw: United Nations Convention on Contracts for the International Sale of Goods: Convention on the Limitation Period in the International Sale of Goods: Commentary*, Art. 6, at 48-49 paras. 1.2 and 1.3 (1992)(Enderlein & Maskow); Schlechtriem, in: Schlechtriem & Schwenzer 2nd edn, *supra* note 115, Art. 6, at 88-89 para. 12 (noting reluctance of legal writers to infer exclusion). See also, UNCITRAL Digest, *supra* note 12, Art. 6 paras. 6-9. In support of implicit exclusion: M. Bridge, 'Choice of Law and the CISG: Opting In and Opting Out', in: H.M. Flechtner *et al* (Eds), *Drafting Contracts Under the CISG*, 65 at 77 (2008), but see *id.*, at 78 (cautioning parties bear the burden of making their intent plain); Honnold 4th edn, *supra* note 44, Art. 6, at 108-110 and note 19 para. 77.1.

118 Cour de Cassation, 17 December 1996, *supra* note 116 (implied exclusion must be 'certain'); Honnold 4th edn, *id.*, Art. 6, at 107-108 para. 77 (requiring 'real' and not 'theoretical' intent, thus exclusions must be 'express' or 'clearly implied in fact'). See also, Enderlein & Maskow, *id.*, Art. 6, at 48; F. Ferrari, 'Specific Topics of the CISG in the Light of Judicial Application and Scholarly Writing', 15 *J. L. & Com.* 1, at 88, note 614 (1996); Ferrari, *International Legal Forum, supra* note 12, at 220.

119 See, *e.g.*, *Olivaylle Pty Ltd v. Flottweg GmbH & Co KGAA (No 4)* (2009) 255 ALR 632, Federal Court, Australia, 20 May 2009, available at <http://cisgw3.law.pace.edu/cases/090520a2.html>; District Court (LG) München, Germany, 29 May 1995, available at <http://cisgw3.law.pace.edu/cases/950529g1.html>; Bezirksgericht [Lower District Court](BG) Weinfelden, Switzerland, 23 November 1998, available at <http://cisgw3.law.pace.edu/cases/981123s1.html>; Cour d'appel de Colmar, France, 26 September 1995, available at <http://cisgw3.law.pace.edu/cases/950926f1.html> (in a decision criticized in this respect on appeal by the Cour de Cassation, 17 December 1996, *id.*)

120 Schlechtriem, in: Schlechtriem & Schwenzer 2nd edn, *supra* note 115, Art. 6, at 88-89 para. 12 (noting the reluctance of courts to infer exclusion).

121 *Gasoline and Gas Oil* case, Supreme Court, Austria, 22 October 2001, available at <http://cisgw3.law.pace.edu/cases/011022a3.html>.

122 District Court (LG) Düsseldorf, Germany, 11 October 1995, available at <http://cisgw3.law.pace.edu/cases/951011g1.html>.

the possibility of implicit exclusion within the contract.[123] By contrast, one case in which a clause provided for 'exclusion of UNCITRAL law' was upheld as manifesting an intent to exclude the CISG.[124]

Frequently the issue arises when a choice of law clause indicates the law of a Contracting State governs the contract. The widely accepted view upheld by most courts and tribunals is that this will not exclude the CISG, since the CISG forms part of the law of the Contracting State.[125] Of particular interest is a long line of cases in the U.S.A.. These have also held that the CISG will not be excluded implicitly merely by a clause providing for a choice of the law of a Contracting State.[126] In only one recent U.S. case has choice of the law of a province within a Contracting State been upheld as sufficient to exclude the CISG.[127] On the other

---

123 See District Court (LG) Landshut, 5 April 1995, *supra* note 11, §II.1.a (stating '[t]he parties can only exclude the application of the CISG by explicit agreement'); *Orbisphere Corp. v. United States,* 726 F. Supp. 1344, Federal Court of International Trade, U.S.A., 24 October 1989, note 7, available at <http://cisgw3.law.pace.edu/cases/891024u1.html>; Tribunal of International Commercial Arbitration at the Russian Federation Chamber of Commerce and Industry, Award 54/1999, 24 January 2000, para. 1, available at <http://cisgw3.law.pace.edu/cases/000124r1.html>.

124 *Olivaylle Pty Ltd v. Flottweg GmbH & Co KGAA (No 4)*, 20 May 2009, *supra* note 119.

125 Cour de Cassation, 17 December 1996, *supra* note 116 ('[r]eferring only to the law of a Contracting State in a clause [...] is not sufficient'); Supreme Court, Austria, 26 January 2005, available at <http://cisgw3.law.pace.edu/cases/050126a3.html>; ICC Award No. 7565/1994, *supra* note 31; Federal Supreme Court (BGH), Germany, 25 November 1998, available at <http://cisgw3.law.pace.edu/cases/981125g1.html>; Kantonsgericht [District Court] Zug, Switzerland, 11 December 2003, available at <http://cisgw3.law.pace.edu/cases/031211s1.html>; Cour d'appel Paris, 6 November 2001, available at <http://cisgw3.law.pace.edu/cases/011106f1.html>. See also, UNCITRAL Digest, *supra* note 12, Art. 6 para 8; Schlechtriem, in: Schlechtriem & Schwenzer 2nd edn, *supra* note 115, Art. 6, at 90 para. 14 ('prevailing opinion [...] holds that a reference to the law of a Contracting State *in itself* does not amount to an exclusion').

126 *Valero Marketing & Supply Co. v. Greeni Oy*, 373 F.Supp.2d 475, Federal District Court New Jersey, U.S.A., 15 June 2005, available at <http://cisgw3.law.pace.edu/cases/050615u1.html>; *Ajax Tool Works, Inc. v. Can-Eng Manufacturing Ltd.*, 2003 U.S. Dist. LEXIS 1306 (N.D. Ill.), 29 January 2003, available at <http://cisgw3.law.pace.edu/cases/030129u1.html>; *American Mint LLC v. GOSoftware, Inc.*, 2006 U.S. Dist. LEXIS 1569 (M.D. Pa), 6 January 2006, available at <http://cisgw3.law.pace.edu/cases/060106u1.html>; *Travelers Property* case, *infra* note 131 ('absent an express statement that the CISG does not apply, merely referring to a particular state's law does not opt out of the CISG'); *Easom Automation* case, *supra* note 115; *Asante Technologies, Inc. v. PMC-Sierra, Inc.*, 164 F. Supp. 2d 1142, U.S. District Court (N.D. Cal.), 27 July 2001, available at <http://cisgw3.law.pace.edu/cases/010727u1.html>; *St. Paul* case, *infra* note 131 ('Where parties [...] designate a choice of law clause in their contract - selecting the law of a Contracting State without expressly excluding application of the CISG' this results in application of the CISG 'as the law of the designated Contracting state'); *BP International, Ltd. v. Empressa Estatal Petroleos de Ecuador*, 332 F.3d 333, U.S. Court of Appeals (5th Cir.), 11 June 2003, available at <http://cisgw3.law.pace.edu/cases/030611u1.html> ('Where parties seek to apply a signatory's domestic law in lieu of the CISG, they must affirmatively opt-out of the CISG').

127 See *American Biophysics v. Dubois Marine Specialties*, Federal District Court Rhode Island, 411 F.Supp.2d 61, U.S.A., 30 January 2006, available at <http://cisgw3.law.pace.edu/cases/060130u1.html> (upholding exclusion by choice of law of the state of Rhode Island). The case cited five earlier decisions for the (inaccurate) proposition that the CISG applies when the 'contract does not contain a choice of law provision'. Yet the cases relied upon simply used 'imprecise descriptions, in dicta': W. Johnson, *Understanding Exclusion of the*

hand, mention of a specific domestic statute or code is seen as denoting a choice of domestic non-uniform law.[128]

The unmistakeable impression is that, while implicit exclusion remains possible, an intent to exclude is not readily inferred via Article 6 within the original contract. Courts and tribunals in this context are slow to jump to the conclusion that parties intended to exclude.

Of course, each case turns on its particular facts, and the task of adjudicators is to balance competing inferences. At a positive level, this can be seen as a three step exercise conducted within the framework of Articles 6 and 8 CISG, whereby the adjudicator first considers an intent to exclude as the purported meaning of words used; secondly, considers any competing hypothesis for their meaning; and thirdly, determines on balance, which meaning is the most likely to have been intended.

What the cases demonstrate in the context of contractual clauses is that this balance generally tips in favour of non-exclusion where the facts do not support an inference of clear intent to exclude that is more plausible than any competing alternatives. This is because the burden is on parties to make their choice of law plain enough that it would be reasonably understood as bearing the purpose of exclusion: Article 8(2) CISG.[129] Selection of INCOTERMS concerns a narrow range of issues, therefore cannot of itself objectively manifest a clear intent to exclude the entire CISG rather than mere derogation of provisions relating to risk etc. On the other hand, a reasonable person would understand a clause excluding UNCITRAL law to evince an intent to exclude something, and it is difficult to envisage an alternative hypothesis as to what was intended other than exclusion of the CISG.

At a normative level, there are good policy reasons for adjudicators to set the evidentiary bar at this level. It accords with the timbre of the Diplomatic Conference, where the concern was that uniform law would be rendered ineffective if courts were too quick to find

---

CISG: A New Paradigm of Determining Party Intent (2010), at 20-21, available at <http://works.bepress.com/william_johnson/2>. The same imprecise proposition has since been repeated as dicta in the *Golden Valley* case, *supra* note 115, and in the *Easom Automation* case, *id.*, yet, despite the rote repetition, the analysis in *Easom* under the CISG was 'largely ultimately sound': Johnson, *id.*, at 22, and parties in the *Golden Valley* case agreed the CISG applied. Thus *American Biophysics* stands alone in actually applying the incorrect proposition.

128 Appellate Court (OLG) Stuttgart, 31 March 2008, *supra* note 31 (commenting that were German law to apply, it should not be assumed the BGB or HGB rather than CISG applied, since 'the CISG is incorporated into German law'. Words such as 'the provisions of the BGB are applicable' would be required to denote domestic non-uniform law).

129 Bridge, *supra* note 117, at 78.

exclusion.[130] The policy concern of governments to maximize uniformity in practice has therefore been realized by what might be termed a 'strict approach' to the burden of proof regarding inferences of exclusion at the contractual stage. Some cases have even recognized these policy implications in their reasoning.[131] Thus the norm now feeds back into the decision making process by way of Article 7 in the form of the guidance provided by the predominant view in cases and scholarship.

The question is whether this same 'strict approach' is appropriate for exclusions that occur after the contractual stage.

5.2 *Post-Contractual Exclusion*

Inexplicably, this stringent stance on *ex ante* implicit exclusion stands in stark contrast to the cases on implicit waiver of the CISG during proceedings. As we have seen, some courts have allowed mere conduct of litigation to stand as a choice of law subsequent to conclusion of the contract.

The paradox is even more puzzling when one takes into account that in determining *ex ante* exclusion, whether or not a CISG contract even exists is still in question.[132] By contrast, *ex post* waivers or exclusions are already within the CISG's gravitational pull. Undoubtedly, determination of the efficacy of any purported post-contractual exclusion must be made pursuant to CISG rules. After all, a CISG contract already exists. Even the minority who advocate the use of conflict rules to test *ex ante* exclusion clauses reject this stance in regard to post-contractual exclusions.[133] One might think that, if contractual exclusions are construed strictly, then post-contractual exclusions should be construed just as stringently. Why then do courts consistently show great restraint regarding *ex ante* exclusion, yet fre-

130 The Diplomatic Conference declined special reference to the ability to impliedly exclude the CISG 'lest the special reference [...] might encourage courts to conclude, on insufficient grounds, that the [CISG] had been wholly excluded': *Official Records of the United Nations Conference on Contracts for the International Sale of Goods*, Vienna, 10 March-11 April 1980, UN Doc. A/CONF.97/19, at 17.

131 *Travelers Property Casualty Company of America v. Saint-Gobain Technical Fabrics Canada Ltd*, 2007 WL 313591, U.S. District Court, Minnesota, 31 January 2007, available at <http://cisgw3.law.pace.edu/cases/070131u1.html> (*Travelers Property* case) ('an affirmative opt-out requirement promotes uniformity and the observance of good faith in international trade, two principles that guide interpretation of the CISG'); *St. Paul Guardian Insurance Company and Travelers Insurance Company v. Neuromed Medical Systems & Support*, GmbH, 2002 U.S. Dist. LEXIS 5096 (S.D. N.Y.), 26 March 2002, available at <http://cisgw3.law.pace.edu/cases/020326u1.html> (*St Paul* case) (stating that choice of the law of a Contracting State did not exclude the CISG, and that '[t]o hold otherwise would undermine the objectives of the [CISG]').

132 Schlechtriem, in: Schlechtriem & Schwenzer 2nd edn, *supra* note 115, Art. 6, at 89 & 91 paras. 12 and 14.

133 Schlechtriem, *id.*, Art. 6, at 89 and 91 paras. 12 and 14.

quently are ready to quickly accept *implicit or tacit* waiver as sufficient where a CISG contract already exists?

The absurdity of this proposition provides the key to its resolution. To recognize tacit waiver or implied post-contractual exclusion is to recognize a change to the governing law of the contract. Essentially, courts are endorsing exclusion by modification of a pre-existing CISG contract. This must be done by application of Articles 6, 14-24 and 29.

Yet the cases demonstrate that this approach is not always employed. Even amongst cases which purportedly apply these provisions, we find vastly divergent approaches.[134] Moreover, it appears in many cases that the evidentiary bar is set far lower than it is at the contractual stage, and in some cases the court appears eager to conclude tacit waiver without careful consideration of the issue. A greater level of predictability can be fostered by integration of the correct approach with an appropriate assessment of inferences.

5.3 *Exclusion by Failure to Argue*

Failure to invoke the CISG in argument can only constitute an *ex post* implied agreement to exclude if it actually modifies the pre-existing CISG contract. Thus, in addition to Article 6, the conduct would need to satisfy Article 29 and Articles 14-24.[135]

More coherent and uniform outcomes require Article 29 to be consistently applied to all post-contractual modifications, and a realignment of the *ex ante* and *ex post* interpretations of Article 6. This would redress the anomaly of the lax standard presently applied to post-contractual exclusions in the current context by comparison with the 'strict approach' applied to exclusions within the original contract. Likewise, there is a need to reconcile the restraint evident in modifications pursuant to Article 29 in more general settings with the tendency to jump to conclusions of tacit exclusion during proceedings.

---

134 See cases discussed above in Part 3.3, at notes 31-40 and accompanying text.

135 Schlechtriem, in: Schlechtriem & Schwenzer 2nd edn, *supra* note 115, Art. 6, at 91 para. 14; Schwenzer & Hachem, *supra* note 45, Art. 6, at 114 and 116 paras. 24 and 28 (agreements to derogate by modification are 'only' subject to the CISG, not conflicts rules). Contracts modifying contracts falling within CISG are also subject to CISG formation provisions: U. Schroeter, in: Schwenzer 3rd edn, *supra* note 45, Art. 29, at 472 and 473 paras 2 and 4; P. Schlechtriem, *Uniform Sales Law* 63, §A5 (1986)(*Uniform Sales Law 1986*); Ferrari, *supra* note 44, at 61 ('contracts modifying an international sales contract fall under the CISG as well, since they directly affect the [parties'] rights and obligations').

Article 7(1) requires courts to interpret the CISG in a manner that promotes uniformity.[136] While a general principle of party autonomy underlies the CISG and Article 6 undoubtedly permits post-contractual exclusion, the divergence observed demonstrates the need to develop a balanced and consistent approach as to *how* party autonomy may be legitimately exercised in the current context.

Unlike exclusion within the original contract, it is incontrovertible that CISG formation provisions apply to post-contractual exclusions.[137] This means that although parties can agree to exclude the CISG during litigation,[138] there must be appropriate evidence of a clear intent to exclude. An analysis of the provisions of the CISG, as well as certain pragmatic considerations discussed below, support the argument that the evidentiary balance should be set at a higher level than it is at present in many cases.

It follows from Article 14 CISG that *ex post* offers to exclude should exhibit an 'intent to be bound'. It is improbable that absence of argument on applicable law in litigation could constitute such an offer. Failure to mention the law sought to be excluded must render most purported offers to modify hopelessly indefinite pursuant to Article 14 CISG. Additionally, mere failure to object could only rarely amount to assent under Article 18 in this context. A defence which answers only those arguments raised by the claimant is a long way from what is generally understood as acceptance of a unilateral attempt to modify. In fact, generally speaking, under Article 29 CISG, failure to object to modification offers will

136 The need to promote uniformity in the CISG's interpretation is described by Schlechtriem as a 'maxim': *Uniform Sales Law 1986, id.*, at 38, §IVA.

137 Unlike exclusions within the original contract, about which there is still some disagreement. *Compare, supra* notes 115 and 133 and accompanying text.

138 Bridge, *supra* note 12, at 917 and 922. Note that Bridge argues that where the forum would otherwise be obliged to apply the CISG, parties can post-contractually agree to apply non-CISG domestic law if, for example, Art. 3(2) of the 1980 Rome Convention applies (now Art. 3(2) Rome I Regulation, *infra* note 155); Ziegel, *supra* note 63, at 342, note 30. See generally, Zajtay, *supra* note 79, at 9, §14-13.

be acceptance only in 'very exceptional cases',[139] since there is already a contractual balance of rights and obligations on foot.[140]

Moreover, if the original contract contained a 'no oral modification' clause, the potential for tacit waiver by conduct of the case is further reduced, unless there has been reliance on the conduct: Article 29(2) CISG. The 'mere fact that a party has not pursued his remedies against the other party should [...] not constitute a sufficient reliance' for the purposes of Article 29(2).[141] It must be doubted that in formulation of its response to claims, a respondent has relied upon any absence of form. A purported offer to modify must be understood as such by a reasonable person to be effective.[142] The intention to be bound must be tested objectively under Article 8(2), not 'rashly' assumed.[143] This is certainly so in the context of attempts to modify during the contractual performance phase, where caution has been urged in interpreting conduct as acceptance of offers to modify.[144] Mere performance of the contract is normally not enough,[145] and clear assent is required. Since

---

139 Schroeter, *supra* note 135, Art. 29, at 476 para. 11; U. Magnus, 'Incorporation of Standard Contract Terms under the CISG', in: C.B. Andersen & U. Schroeter (Eds.), *Sharing International Commercial law across National Boundaries: Festschrift for Albert H. Kritzer on the Occasion of his Eightieth Birthday*, 303 at 324 (2008); P. Perales Viscasillas, 'Modification and Termination of the Contract (Art. 29 CISG)', 25 *J. L. & Com.* 167, at 172 (2005-6); Schmidt-Kessel, *supra* note 115, Art. 8, at 172 para. 53; *Macromex Srl v. Globex International Inc.*, American Arbitration Association Award, 23 October 2007, available at <http://cisgw3.law.pace.edu/cases/071023a5.html> (aff'd 2008 WL 1752530 (S.D.N.Y.); aff'd 330 Fed Appx. 241, U.S. Court of Appeal (2nd Cir.) 26 May 2009) ('failure to object to a unilateral attempt to modify a contract is not an agreement to modify a contract'); *Solae, LLC v. Hershey Canada, Inc.*, 557 F.Supp.2d 452, U.S. District Court Delaware, 9 May 2008, available at <http://cisgw3.law.pace.edu/cases/080509u1.html> (*Solae v. Hershey*) ('Nothing in the [CISG] suggests that the failure to object to a party's unilateral attempt to alter materially the terms of an otherwise valid agreement is an 'agreement' within the terms of Article 29').

140 Magnus, *id.*, at 324; Schroeter, *id.*, Art. 29, at 476 para. 11.

141 Schroeter, *supra* note 135, Art. 29, at 486 para. 37.

142 Art. 8(2). Thus courts have rejected supposed offers to modify consisting of standard terms on the reverse of invoices sent after conclusion of the contract: *Solae v. Hershey*, *supra* note 139; *Chateau des Charmes Wines Ltd v. Sabaté USA Inc.*, 328 F.3d 528, U.S. Court of Appeals (9th Cir.), 5 May 2003, available at <http://www.unilex.info/case.cfm?pid=1&do=case&id=899&step=FullText>. See also, Schroeter, *id.*, Art. 29, at 475 and 476 paras. 10 and 11; Schmidt-Kessel, *supra* note 115, Art. 8, at 173-174 para. 58.

143 Schwenzer & Hachem, *supra* note 45, Art. 6, at 113 and 115 paras. 21 and 26.

144 Schroeter, *supra* note 135, Art. 29, at 476 para. 11 (urging 'particularly careful assessment' as to whether acceptance of an offer to modify has occurred); Schroeter, *id.*, at 480 para. 19, (arguing in the context of agreements to terminate that 'courts and arbitrators are well advised to exercise appropriate restraint in finding an agreement between the parties').

145 Acts of performance are not acts of assent: CIETAC Arbitration Award, China, 23 May 2000, available at <http://cisgw3.law.pace.edu/cases/000523c1.html> ('Partial performance of the Contract should not be deemed as a modification of the quantity of the goods under the Contract'); *Chateau des Charmes Wines v. Sabaté*, *supra* note 142 (payment of invoice containing new choice of forum clause); *Solae v. Hershey*, *supra* note 139.

in the current litigation context parties are frequently unaware of the 'right'[146] they supposedly relinquish, there will often be an objective absence of agreement to modify where the CISG is not raised in argument. As stated by one court:

> in the presence of all requisites mentioned above [the CISG] is applicable by operation of law [...] Neither can it be [sustained] that the silence of the parties constitutes an implied manifestation of the intent to exclude the application of [the CISG].[147]

Several commentators agree that the 'mere fact that the parties argue on the sole basis of a domestic law'[148] is anything but a clear indication of intent. Parties cannot intend to exclude the relevant law unless they are aware of its applicability.[149] Only then can parties 'knowingly' depart from the CISG by agreement.[150] Prof. Schlechtriem perhaps stated this most clearly when he said:

> [i]f the parties mistakenly ignore the applicability of the CISG and refer to provisions of domestic law in their pleadings or in the oral hearing in court, this cannot constitute an agreement to modify their contract. *Statements based on ignorance are not agreements, because they lack the necessary 'intention to be bound'*; therefore they cannot alter the contents of a contract.[151]

Failure by counsel to mention the CISG speaks of the likelihood it was simply overlooked. A belief that domestic law applies is not *per se* evidence of an agreement to exclude the CISG,[152] as echoed in better decisions on point.[153] Under these circumstances it would be

146 Schroeter, *supra* note 135, Art. 29, at 485, note 119 para. 33; Schmidt-Kessel, *supra* note 115, Art. 8, at 164 para. 38.

147 Tribunale di Padova, 25 February 2004, *supra* note 14.

148 Ferrari, *International Legal Forum, supra* note 12, at 220 (arguing that this cannot 'per se lead to the exclusion of the CISG'); Schlechtriem, in: Schlechtriem & Schwenzer 2nd edn, *supra* note 115, Art. 6, at 91 para 14.

149 Ferrari, *id.*; Appellate Court (OLG) Rostock, Germany, 10 October 2001, available at <http://cisgw3.law.pace.edu/cases/011010g1.html>; Tribunale di Vigevano, 12 July 2000, *supra* note 11.

150 Schwenzer & Hachem, *supra* note 45, Art. 6, at 113 para. 21 (stating that 'conduct of the parties still needs to sufficiently indicate [...] whether the parties knowingly departed from the otherwise applicable CISG'); Schmidt-Kessel, *supra* note 115, Art. 8, at 164 para. 38.

151 Schlechtriem, in: Schlechtriem & Schwenzer 2nd edn, *supra* note 115, Art. 6, at 91 para. 14 (emphasis added).

152 Ferrari, *International Legal Forum, supra* note 12, at 220; Schwenzer & Hachem, *supra* note 45, Art. 6, at 113 para. 21 (arguing that 'basing arguments on provisions of domestic sales law is simply a mistake on the part of the attorneys' rather than evidence of an intent to exclude); Schlechtriem, *id.*, Art. 6, at 90-91 para. 14.

153 See Appellate Court (OLG) Stuttgart, 31 March 2008, *supra* note 31 (failure by parties to base allegations on the CISG does not imply post-contractual exclusion, since '[t]here is no mutual agreement of intent [...] as this requires an express declaration of intent [...]; the application of the wrong provisions due to a legal

erroneous for a court to infer an intent to exclude, without carefully considering the competing inference of ignorance or misapprehension.

With these points in mind, the disparate standards can be now realigned. General restraint is shown before *any* type of post-contractual modification is upheld under Article 29 CISG. Clear intent is required for inferences in relation to exclusion clauses in the original contract pursuant to Article 6 CISG. In view of the fact that exclusion by modification during litigation involves *both* Articles 6 and 29, it is proposed that the appropriate measure of intent should be no less stringent.

In setting the evidentiary standard for exclusion during proceedings, it is important to keep in mind the pragmatic consideration that, by contrast with the contractual stage, the evidentiary record is not static. At any time during proceedings, greater levels of proof are attainable upon enquiry by the adjudicator, simply by asking counsel.[154] This means that provided the adjudicator raises the matter, whether before, during or after the hearings, the balance of inferences need not be hypothetical at all. A court can be sure that parties clearly intend to modify their contract to exclude the CISG at the litigation stage if counsel present an express agreement by informed parties to that effect during proceedings. On the contrary, a court can only rarely be sure that 'tacit agreements to exclude' by mere reason of the way counsel conducts the case evince a clear inference that satisfies both Articles 6 and 29. Adjudicators, in balancing inferences, must consider the alternative hypotheses; that counsels' conduct is, rather than demonstrative of tacit agreement by the parties, a product of counsels' own ignorance, misapprehension or simply convenience. Ignorance is not to be equated with intent. Thus the misapprehension of counsel or even stubborn refusal to argue the applicable law should never be accepted as manifesting an informed intent by the parties to exclude the CISG by modification of the contract. Consistently with the predominant view on contractual exclusions, the adjudicator should be

misapprehension does not meet this requirement'); Tribunale di Padova, 25 February 2004, *supra* note 14 (pleadings referring only to non-uniform domestic law cannot of themselves amount to an exclusion of the CISG, as an intent to exclude the CISG, 'it must clearly show that [the parties] were aware of its applicability, and that they nonetheless insisted on referring only to the domestic rule'); Appellate Court (OLG) Rostock, 10 October 2001, *supra* note 149 ('Merely referring to [the domestic provisions] is insufficient, because such reference might also be made because the parties think that that law was applicable anyway'); Appellate Court (OLG) Linz, Austria, 23 January 2006, available at <http://cisgw3.law.pace.edu/cases/060123a3.html>; Appellate Court (OLG) Hamm, 9 June 1995, *supra* note 11; Tribunale di Forli, 16 February 2009, *supra* note 31, at §4.3.3; District Court (LG) Landshut, 5 April 1995, *supra* note 11, §II.1.a (argument solely on the BGB 'does not change anything'); District Court (LG) Bamberg, Germany, 23 October 2006, available at <http://cisgw3.law.pace.edu/cases/061023g1.html>. See also, ICC Award No. 7565/1994, *supra* note 31; Tribunale di Vigevano, 12 July 2000, *supra* note 11, paras. 5 and 6; Tribunale di Cuneo, 31 January 1996, *supra* note 14 (although the latter two were based on the domestic procedural rule).

154 See also Xiao & Long, *supra* note 9, at 77 and 81-82.

careful to exercise caution before jumping to the conclusion of exclusion by conduct in proceedings. In keeping with Article 29, adjudicators should be slow in accepting inferences that conduct of litigation amounts to an offer to modify and acceptance of that offer. Such inferences should of course be accepted when they are the *most* plausible explanation for counsels' conduct, but rejected when more plausible reasons, such as those suggested above, exist.

This approach results in a standard of proof of similar rigour to that shown in cases dealing with *ex ante* exclusions, and the restraint apparent in relation to general modifications. The balance suggested need not interfere with party autonomy. On the contrary, it mirrors the requirement for free choice to be 'clearly demonstrated' in other private international law contexts.[155] It does no harm to the general principle of party autonomy to require a clear intent to alter the existing law of the contract, particularly when it is open to the parties to manifest that intent during proceedings. The current prevailing approach to waiver is anything but clear, and instead seems to facilitate confusion and avoidance of the applicable CISG by judicial fiat.

The requirement of a clear intent does not rule out the possibility of implicit intent altogether, but acknowledges that it will rarely satisfy the relevant provisions of the CISG when applied in an integrated and coherent manner. Adjudicators, above all, must be confident that, amongst the range of competing inferences, not only must an agreement to exclude the CISG be clearly capable of inference from counsels' conduct, but also that, on balance, that such an inference is much more plausible than any other.

This standard has the advantage of encouraging adjudicators to seek clarification, which would not only promote evidentiary efficiency,[156] but also reduce the number of wasteful appeals on this point.

Importantly, the suggestion realigns the standards relating to inferences of intent to exclude at the contractual and post-contractual stages, so that the balance of proof is consistent at each stage. This brings improved coherence throughout the CISG and ensures it can be

155 Art. 7(1) Hague Convention on the Law Applicable to Contracts for the International Sale of Goods, 39 October 1986, 24 I.L.M. 1573, 1575 (1985) ('[t]he parties' agreement on this choice must be express or be clearly demonstrated') and Art. 3(1) Rome Convention on the Law Applicable to Contractual Obligations, 1980 O.J. (L 266), 19 June 1980, 19 I.L.M. 1492 (1980) ('[t]he choice must be expressed or demonstrated with reasonable certainty'); Art. 3(1) Rome I Regulation (EC) No 593/2008 on the Law Applicable to Contractual Obligations, 2008 O.J. (L. 177/6), 4 July 2008 ('[t]he choice shall be made expressly or clearly demonstrated by the terms of the contract or the circumstances of the case').

156 The author thanks Prof. John Gotanda for this suggestion after presentation of this paper at the 13 March 2010 conference in Hong Kong.

more easily understood and consistently applied, while still providing a clear avenue for true expression of party autonomy, if indeed parties really wish to exclude at the litigation stage.

6 PROPOSED SOLUTIONS

If the above propositions are accepted, how in a practical sense should courts proceed once they realize the CISG applies?

For a court in a Contracting State the CISG constitutes the entire picture. Essentially, the obligation to apply the CISG *ex officio* approximates the strict version of the *iura novit curia* principle. This means that, irrespective of its own domestic procedural inclination, the court must take a less than passive role. The only remaining question is how to implement it, given the availability of appeal for failure of due process. This calls for some flexibility in implementation, and leads us to three potential solutions for courts within Contracting States.

6.1 *Simpliciter Application* Ex Officio

Domestic systems that already follow the strict version of *iura novit curia* and have a narrowly defined right to be heard might simply apply the CISG. Where the right to be heard is limited to questions of fact in respect of domestic law, there is arguably no need for counsel to address the CISG before the court is entitled to apply it. Yet it is important to note that this result flows not from application of the domestic procedural rule, but from the CISG itself. Such courts would also need to ensure appropriate interpretation of Article 29 so that merely failing to plead is not instantly seen as tacit waiver. Rather than jump to such a conclusion, the court should carefully consider the competing inferences in the manner suggested in Part 5.3 to determine whether counsels' conduct is a sufficient clear basis for an inference of intent to exclude, and whether such an inference is the most likely on balance.

What of jurisdictions which do not employ strict *iura novit curia*? It is not impossible to imagine application of the CISG even so. There have been cases where common law courts have applied the CISG despite a near (but not complete) absence of it from pleadings and/or argument. In the Australian *Roder Zelt* case,[157] nothing appeared in pleadings, and

157 *Roder Zelt - und Hallenkonstruktionen GmbH v. Rosedown Park Pty Ltd*, (1995) 57 FCR 216, Federal Court, Australia, 28 April 1995, available at <http://cisgw3.law.pace.edu/cases/950428a2.html>.

despite only a 'passing mention' in argument, the court applied the CISG at length. *Sua sponte* decisions might also occur in the U.S.

While possible to argue that all Contracting State courts should employ this solution on the basis of their obligation to apply the CISG, some will be uncomfortable with 'dusty' judges.[158] There is also a need to reconcile the obligation to apply the CISG with broader definitions of the right to be heard, which may still underpin grounds of appeal. In these circumstances less radical approaches might be more effective in practice, to reach similar ends by means that take account of differing conceptions of due process.

6.2 *Dismissal of the Claim*

The first type of compromise achieves a correct, but harsh result. It remains similar to the first solution in that, having formed the view that the CISG is applicable, the court gives it some effect.

Where the CISG is not mentioned in argument, the case can be justifiably dismissed on the basis that any local procedural rules which might have constrained the court to the law argued by counsel are effectively displaced by the CISG. The judge does not go so far as to apply the substantive provisions of the CISG, but pursuant to the court's obligation to apply the CISG *ex officio*, takes judicial notice of its existence and effect in displacing the law argued by counsel. Counsel has simply not made its case.

Of course, the fact that a valid case might have existed under the law that *is* applicable makes this result rather harsh. It may also offend more broadly defined rights to be heard. However, this may alert counsel to the need to argue the applicable law.

6.3 *Intervention by Warning & Invitation*

The final suggested compromise is that, upon realizing the CISG applies, counsel are warned that the CISG is the applicable law, and an indication is given that the court intends to apply it because it displaces domestic sales law. Ideally, the court should also explain to counsel that any local procedural rules that might otherwise constrain the court to the law

158 The reader will forgive my reference to a case describing the common law's discomfort with interventionist judges: *Yuill v. Yuill* [1945] P. 15, at 20 (U.K.) (Lord Greene MR warning a judge who questions the witness 'so to speak, descends into the arena and is liable to have his vision clouded by the dust of conflict').

argued by counsel are also displaced by the court's obligation to apply the CISG *ex officio*.[159] The case might appropriately be adjourned to allow counsel time to prepare CISG based arguments.

After an appropriate warning, the following range of possibilities might eventuate:

1. Counsel might return and present argument on the CISG. The court can then apply it. This obviously presents no problems, since the court can both comply with its obligation and accord the right to be heard on the law.
2. Counsel return and inform the court that an agreement has been reached that the CISG is not to apply. This also presents no problem, provided counsel have the informed consent of their clients. Express exclusion by agreement will invoke the operation of the CISG's modification rules pursuant to Article 29. Thus the court should make a formal ruling regarding the satisfaction of Articles 6 and 29 CISG in the manner indicated above in Part 5.3, taking care to apply the appropriate standard of proof in weighing conflicting inferences.[160] The court is then relieved of its obligation, and accordingly justified in applying the law indicated by (now applicable) domestic procedural rules. The court should not propose that, unless counsel objects, conduct of the case alone will be treated as an implicit agreement to exclude.[161] This course would effectively subvert the correct methodology, including application of Articles 6 and 29, and the weighing of competing inferences in accordance with an appropriate standard of proof. In making the suggestion, the court would breach its obligation to apply the CISG *ex officio*. Instead, the court should give an appropriate warning to counsel, in order to encourage proper investigation of the rights and obligations arising from the applicable law, and if desired, formation of an *ex post* exclusion agreement with the informed consent of the clients.
3. Counsel return and assert they do not need to argue the CISG, on the basis of that local procedural rules preclude *ex officio* applications of law. It is at this point that the issue of displacement is critical. If the court has already explained its view that such domestic procedural rules have been displaced, then in performing its inherent obligation to properly apply and interpret the CISG, it would be justified in then dismissing the case. Moreover, unlike the dismissal discussed in Part 6.2 above, a broad right to be heard will have been accorded.

159 Obviously in the case of arbitration, this will not apply. Instead, the tribunal would refer to the procedural law and/or procedural rules applicable to the arbitration as the basis for its intent to apply the CISG. See discussion in Part 4.3 above.

160 The court should also consider the effect of any 'no oral modification' clauses.

161 Taking such an approach, see Appellate Court (OLG) Köln, Germany, 28 May 2001, available at <http://cisgw3.law.pace.edu/cases/010528g1.html>.

It seems unbelievable, but this actually occurred in an Australian case.[162] During its five hearings neither counsel nor the court recognized that the CISG applied. Only after the fifth hearing had finished did the court subsequently realize the CISG was relevant. Counsel for the plaintiff was properly invited to make further submissions on the applicable law. Incredibly, counsel declined, stating that it was unnecessary. Despite being an uncontested claim in which default judgment had already been ordered, counsel's stance ultimately cost the plaintiff dearly. The court denied damages, saying the failure to address the CISG was 'fatal'.[163] Interestingly, this occurred in Australia, a country that does not overtly employ the *iura novit curia* principle.[164]

4. Alternatively, if counsel assert they do not need to argue the CISG, then rather than dismiss the case, provided the court has provided adequate warning and opportunity, it could proceed to decide the case by application of the CISG *ex officio* rather than dismiss it.[165] This solution will be available in most jurisdictions. Parties have been accorded an opportunity to be heard, yet chosen not to present argument on the applicable law. Clearly, the outcome would not result in a surprise application of law in a manner that could not be foreseen by parties, given the court's earlier warning. In my view, this approach is feasible even in common law courts, because it accords the broadest of opportunities to be heard.

Overall, the interventionist third solution is a sound compromise. It is practical, acceptable, and has the advantage of complying with broad conceptions of due process; parties cannot complain on appeal that they were denied the opportunity to be heard, or surprised by application of the CISG. Importantly, it maintains that local procedural rules are displaced by the CISG, and in accordance with the interpretation of Articles 6 and 29 suggested above, rejects the application of domestic law despite the conduct of the case.

The third solution fulfils the obligation of a court in a Contracting State to apply the CISG. At a minimum, it ensures displacement to the extent necessary to preserve the CISG's

162 *Perry Engineering Pty Ltd v. Bernold AG*, South Australian Supreme Court, 11 February 2001, available at <http://cisgw3.law.pace.edu/cases/010201a2.html>. See B. Zeller, *CISG Cases* (2004), available at <http://www.business.vu.edu.au/cisg/Cases.htm>. Something similar has also occurred in Germany: see Appellate Court (OLG) Rostock, 10 October 2001, *supra* note 149 ('The parties have not made such a declaration even though they had been informed of its necessity by this Chamber. Merely referring to [the domestic provisions] is insufficient, because such reference might also be made because the parties think that that law was applicable anyway').

163 *Perry Engineering, id.*, at para. 16.

164 This stands in stark contrast to other Australian cases where the CISG's applicability has sometimes been incorrectly bypassed on the basis of purely domestic interpretive principles: see, *e.g., Playcorp Pty Ltd v. Taiyo Kogyo Ltd*, 24 April 2003, *supra* note 30.

165 See, *e.g.*, cases cited *supra* note 27. However, contrary to the purported source in those cases, the *ex officio* power derives not from domestic procedural law of the forum, but rather the CISG itself.

integrity. At its maximum, it amounts to a form of *iura novit curia* which fits well with the CISG obligations and the due process sensibilities of most jurisdictions.

It was noted earlier that the solution to the procedural dilemma was more complex in arbitration than in litigation. Nonetheless, in some ways the solution is simpler too, since far more discretion is usually accorded to arbitral tribunals under arbitral laws and rules, and appeal is generally not available on the merits. In the case of arbitration, unless the tribunal's mandate has been specifically restricted to exclude consideration of the CISG, or procedural rules which constrain the tribunal's discretion have been agreed by parties, the third approach is also suitable for arbitrators. While it cannot be said that an arbitral tribunal is under any *obligation* to apply the CISG in the same way as a court in a Contracting State, it will still be bound to decide according to law. In these cases the interventionist third approach represents a safe solution. Arbitral tribunals adopting it will normally render an award impervious to challenge on the basis of *ultra petita*, failure of due process, or on grounds of bias.

Likewise, courts in non-contracting states that nonetheless conclude the CISG is applicable bear no *obligation* to apply the CISG, but may nonetheless find the third solution attractive and, in many instances, compatible with their own (applicable) procedural rules.

7 Conclusion

This chapter seeks to highlight a flaw in the traditional view that generally, the procedural rule of the forum is determinative of the law to be applied when the parties fail to present argument on the applicable law of the CISG. Courts in Contracting States in fact have a duty to apply the CISG to resolve the issue. This means that in many instances domestic procedural rules of *iura novit curia* and any domestic conceptions of waiver are displaced.

In my view, the only way a court in a Contracting State can discharge its obligation to apply the CISG in the absence of argument from counsel is by the proper application of Articles 6 and 29. This is the sole route by which a pre-existing CISG contract can be transformed into something else. The matter of exclusion by modification lies clearly within the CISG. Thus the CISG itself provides the means by which modification during litigation must be tested. It is submitted that mere failure to argue the CISG will rarely satisfy this test under a proper application of those provisions due to plausible competing inferences. A standard of proof in keeping with widely accepted interpretations of analogous situations under the CISG not only improves its coherence, but is particularly apt given the pragmatic consideration that it remains open to the parties during proceedings to agree to exclude. Such a balance also ensures the purpose of the CISG in creating practical uniformity is not diminished, and improves the predictability of outcomes in practice.

Provided courts and tribunals alert counsel to the applicability of the CISG and afford them an opportunity to either address it in argument or expressly agree to exclude it, they will conform with the broadest notions of due process and can render enforceable outcomes which apply the CISG as the governing law. In the case of courts in Contracting States, they have an obligation to do so. The preferred solution demonstrates how courts and arbitrators can provide less erratic outcomes and, in the interests of certainty, ensure international sales law gravitates towards uniformity.

Japan After Acceding to the CISG – Should we Consider Ratifying the Limitation Convention Next?

Yasutomo Sugiura[*]

Preface

2009 became one of the most historical years for Japanese international business persons and scholars as Japan became the 72nd Contracting State of the CISG.[1] As most of Japan's trading partners are Contracting States of the CISG, a company having its office in Japan can now enjoy the merits of the uniform law, *i.e.* it can foresee whether or not the remedies of the CISG apply to its international sale of goods. A number of Japanese companies are assessing the impact of the CISG on their businesses seriously.[2] However, when such a company sues a debtor in a foreign court, its claim may be rejected as a result of the application of an unexpected domestic short limitation period.[3] Limitation of actions or prescription is an issue outside the scope of the CISG, and the remedies in the CISG which would otherwise be available may be useless in such circumstances. Yet is rare that busy business people are aware of such risk. There is a wide variety of limitation periods and rules throughout the world, and it is unpredictable when a party's claims will no longer be permissible due to time limitation. Unification of limitation periods is therefore desperately needed. Attention should now be drawn to the United Nations Convention on the Limitation Period in the International Sale of Goods (Limitation Convention),[4] which has

* BA, Professor at the Law School of Nihon University, Japan; Senior Advisor of Ashurst, Tokyo.

1 United Nations Convention on Contracts for the International Sale of Goods (CISG), Vienna, 11 April 1980, available at <http://www.uncitral.org/uncitral/en/uncitral_texts/sale_goods/1980CISG.html>.

2 For example, the legal departments of three major Japanese trading companies set up a CISG committee under my supervision and assessed the impact of CISG on their business practice and studied whether or not their standard contract terms should be modified as a result of Japan's accession to CISG.

3 The prescription of claims for account receivables in Japan is two years, see Art. 173(1) Civil Code of Japan, Act No. 89 of 27 April 1896, English translation available at <http://www.japaneselawtranslation.go.jp/law/detail/?id=1&vm=04&re=01&new=1> (cited as: Civil Code of Japan). This is applicable to the sale of goods, whether domestic or international, and foreign parties may consider it too short.

4 United Nations Convention on the Limitation Period in the International Sale of Goods, Vienna, 12 June 1974, as amended by the Protocol Amending the Convention on the Limitation Period in the International Sale of Goods, Vienna, 11 April 1980, available at <http://www.uncitral.org/uncitral/en/uncitral_texts/sale_goods/1974Convention_limitation_period.html> (cited as: Limitation Convention).

achieved a unified limitation period (four years) applicable in the area of international sale of goods. The definition of international sale contracts to which the Limitation Convention applies is identical to that used by the CISG. Thus both the Limitation Convention and the CISG are expected to support each other and move towards uniformity in the area of the international sale of goods.

Looking at world trends in the recent reform of limitation periods, some of the rules stipulated in the Limitation Convention now look outdated. Take the commencement of the limitation period for example. Recent national reforms prefer a combination of a short limitation period starting from the time a subjective test is satisfied and a long limitation period starting from the satisfaction of an objective test, while the Limitation Convention provides for four years,[5] starting from the satisfaction of an objective test only, except in case of fraud.[6] Here an objective test uses an objectively ascertainable event as a starting point, while a subjective test depends on someone's knowledge. However, since the business practice of international sales requires a clear and simple standard and quick disposal of deals, the Working Group of UNCITRAL sought to avoid the use of events subject to conflicting evidence from the very beginning.[7] I think this was the right approach, and for the Limitation Convention, exclusion of the subjective test from the commencement of the time period was most suitable in the international business setting.

In this chapter, we will examine the contents of the Limitation Convention in more detail and see that the Limitation Convention is still appropriate for the international sale of goods. Taking the opportunity at a time when discussion is in progress in Japan on reform of the Civil Code in the area of contract law, including prescription, I would like to propose that Japan, after having acceded to the CISG, should seriously consider, together with other CISG Contracting States, acceding next to the Limitation Convention.

1 Present Status

The Limitation Convention was concluded in New York on 14 June 1974. As a result of the conclusion of the CISG, almost six years later, a Protocol to the Limitation Convention was adopted in Vienna on 11 April 1980 to make minor textual adjustments in line with

5 Art. 8 Limitation Convention. Certain matters may result in an extension of time. However, in any event, the limitation period may not exceed ten years, see Art. 23 Limitation Convention.

6 Arts. 9 and 10 Limitation Convention.

7 The first report of the Drafting Group is referred to in para. 18 of the UNCITRAL Working Group I, Report of the Working on Time Limits and Limitations (Prescription), First Session, 18-22 August 1969, A/CN.9/30, available at <http://daccess-dds-ny.un.org/doc/UNDOC/GEN/NL6/900/22/PDF/NL690022.pdf?OpenElement> (cited as: Working Group Report 1969).

the wording of the CISG.[8] The Limitation Convention and the Protocol entered into force on 1 August 1988. As of August 2010, there are 28 Contracting States to the Limitation Convention (of which eight have not adopted the Protocol). Adherents to the Limitation Convention include the United States of America, Belgium, Czech Republic, Slovakia, Egypt, Hungary, Norway, Mexico, Poland, Romania, Serbia and Ukraine. In my opinion, the number of member states is too low compared to that of CISG.[9] The Working Group and the Commission recognized the sufficiently serious situation arising from the different approaches and divergent rules of limitation or prescription in the world, and had made great efforts to create the uniform rules on limitation or prescription more than 36 years ago.[10] But as long as the Contracting States of the Limitation Convention remain at such low numbers, the underlined serious situation remains unchanged today.

2 Official Commentary

Unlike the CISG, there is an Official Commentary available on the original 1974 Limitation Convention. When the preliminary Draft Convention was discussed by the Working Group in 1970, the Secretariat was requested to prepare a commentary on its provisions instead of reporting the progress of the discussion in detail during the session.[11] The first commentary was therefore drawn up after the meeting, taking into consideration the discussion at the session, and modified in response to suggestions received from members of the Working Group.[12] Thereafter, each time the draft was modified the commentary was also modified. The final Official Commentary was prepared by Professor Kazuaki Sono, then

8 Protocol Amending the United Nations Convention on the Limitation Period in the International Sale of Goods, Vienna, 11 April 1980, UN Doc. A/CONF.97/18, Annex II, available at <http://www.uncitral.org/pdf/english/yearbooks/yb-1980-e/vol11-p162-164- e.pdf>. As both conventions were being discussed at the same time in parallel, the draft Limitation Convention had already anticipated and incorporated the draft CISG at the respective time. Therefore, few adjustments of the Limitation Convention were required by the Protocol, see F. Enderlein, in: F. Enderlein & D. Maskow (Eds.), *International Sales Law, United Nations Convention on Contracts for the International Sale of Goods, Convention on the Limitation Period in the International Sale of Goods* 393 (1992) available at <http://www.cisg.law.pace.edu/cisg/biblio/enderlein.html#aut>.

9 At the moment, there are 76 states that are member to the CISG. A detailed list of the CISG Contracting States can be found at <http://www.uncitral.org/uncitral/en/uncitral_texts/sale_goods/1980CISG_status.html>.

10 Commentary on the Convention on the Limitation Period in the International Sale of Goods, New York, 14 June 1974, UN Doc. A/CONF.63/17, available at <http://www.uncitral.org/pdf/english/yearbooks/yb-1979-e/vol10-p145-173-e.pdf> (cited as: Official Commentary), Introduction: Objective of the Convention, paras. 4-6.

11 UNCITRAL Working Group I, Working Group on Time-limits and Limitations (Prescription), Report on the Work of the Second Session, 10-21 August 1970, held in Geneva, UN Doc. A/CN.9/50, available at <http://daccess-dds-ny.un.org/doc/UNDOC/GEN/NL7/001/09/PDF/NL700109.pdf?OpenElement> (cited as: Working Group Report 1970), para. 7.

12 *Id.*, Annex II.

of Hokkaido University in Japan, and is available on the UNCITRAL website.[13] It is not a legally binding document but it is always referred to when accession is considered and is a very useful tool for interpretation of the provisions of the Limitation Convention. As few scholarly articles have been written on the Limitation Convention, the Official Commentary is highly appreciated.[14]

3 Composition of the Limitation Convention

There are only 46 articles in total contained in the Limitation Convention, and it is not a difficult law. It is divided into four parts. Part I deals with substantive matters including sphere of application (Arts. 1-7 Limitation Convention); duration and commencement of the limitation period (Arts. 8-12); cessation and extension of the limitation period (Arts. 13-21); modification of the limitation period (Art. 22); general limit of the limitation period (Art. 23); consequences of expiration of the limitation period (Arts. 24-27); calculation of the period (Art. 28 and Art. 29); and international effect (Art. 30). Part II deals with the implementation of the Limitation Convention, Part III with declaration and reservation, and Part IV with final clauses.

4 Characteristics

Before going into the details of the Limitation Convention, we should briefly examine its characteristics.

4.1 Unification of Widely Different Limitation Periods and Rules

It is really a remarkable achievement on the part of UNCITRAL that various limitation periods in the world have been unified to four years and divergent limitation rules replaced by one set of clear and simple rules. Subsequent reforms of limitation laws in various parts of the world have been affected to a greater or lesser degree by the Limitation Convention. For example, since the introduction of a single short limitation period by the Limitation Convention, when the domestic prescription or limitation is reviewed, the period tends to be simplified and shortened. Germany shortened its standard prescriptive period from

13 Official Commentary, *supra* note 10.

14 American Bar Association (ABA), Section of International Law and Practice, 'Convention on the Limitation Period in the International Sale of Goods, Report to the House of Delegates', 24 *Int'l Lawyer* 583 (1990).

thirty years to three years in January 2002,[15] France also shortened its period from thirty years to five years in June 2008,[16] and now Japan is trying to shorten its standard prescriptive period from ten years to either three, four or five years.[17]

4.2 *Limited Sphere of Application*

The Limitation Convention is applicable only to claims arising out of contracts of international sale of goods between commercial parties, while domestic limitation laws are applicable to various kinds of legal claims and parties. Commercial parties are thought to be experienced and knowledgeable in international business and therefore, unlike consumers, are not necessarily in need of protection.[18]

4.3 *The CISG and the Limitation Convention Use the Same Definition of the Term 'International Sales Contract'*

The Limitation Convention and CISG are intended to govern the same international sales contracts,[19] Consequently, many CISG Contracting States are expected to accede to the Limitation Convention.

4.4 *Exclusion by the Parties*

The Limitation Convention is a hard law, but it contains a flexible clause by which the parties can, if they so wish, exclude the Limitation Convention and apply national laws.[20]

---

15 Art. 195 German Civil Code (*Bürgerliches Gesetzbuch (BGB)*), available at <http://www.gesetze-im-internet.de/bgb/BJNR001950>896.html>.

16 Art. 2224 French Civil Code, available at <http://www.legifrance.gouv.fr/affichCode.do?cidTexte=LEGITEXT000006070721&dateTexte=20080225#/>, as amended by the Loi nº 2008-561 du 17 Juin 2008, portant réforme de la prescription en matière civile, available at <http://www.legifrance.gouv.fr/affichTexteArticle.do;jsessionid=EA0980AD57B080109AFA6B26F2F4EFD4.tpdjo09v_3?cidTexte=JORFTEXT000019013696&idArticle=LEGIARTI000019014273&dateTexte=20080619>.

17 Art. 3.1.3.44(2) Proposed Japanese Civil Code (Law of Obligations) Reform Commission, English version available at <http://www.shojihomu.or.jp/saikenhou/English/index_e.html> (cited as: Japanese Reform Proposal).

18 Consumer contracts are excluded from the scope of the Limitation Convention, see Art. 4(a) Limitation Convention.

19 Working Group Report 1969, *supra* note 7, para. 11.

20 Art. 3(2) Limitation Convention.

4.5 International Effect

An act by one party affecting the limitation period in one Contracting State must be recognized by all other Contracting States.[21] Thus, the parties will have no need to take legal proceedings before expiry of the limitation period in each state. This should be one of the great incentives for joining the Limitation Convention.

4.6 Practical Solution

One of the main concerns of the Commission was practical convenience for users rather than theoretical perfection. A specific difficulty was the problem arising from differences between civil law and common law systems. The *travaux préparatoires* quite often show that when the discussion went into too much technicality delegates were reminded of how the relevant problems would be seen by business people.[22] The key to the successful conclusion of this commercially-oriented convention was to take the 'user's view.' In my view, the user's view was taken well into account in the course of drafting the Limitation Convention, and this practical approach eventually worked very well for reaching consensus on the more difficult problems.

5 Sphere of Application

Article 1(1) Limitation Convention provides as follows:

> This Convention shall determine when claims of a buyer and a seller against each other arising from a contract of international sale of goods or relating to its breach, termination or invalidity can no longer be exercised by reason of

21 Art. 30 Limitation Convention.

22 For example, take the discussion on whether or not invalidity of contract should be deleted from the scope of the Limitation Convention. The delegates from the civil law countries strongly insisted on its deletion from Art. 1(1) Limitation Convention while those from common law countries were happy to retain it. This was one of the typical arguments arising from the difference between the two legal systems. Then, the representative of Australia pointed out that the problem should be resolved by relating it to the position of the business person because it would be odd for a business person to be told that he must bring an action for breach of contract within a period of four years under the Limitation Convention, and then to be faced later with an action for rescission for invalidity brought outside the Convention's time limit, but within the applicable domestic time limit. This argument seemed persuasive, and finally civil law delegates compromised by reserving their position in present Art. 35 Limitation Convention, see discussion at the 94th meeting of the Commission, as referred in the *United Nations Commission on International Trade Law Yearbook*, Volume III: 1972 Supplement, available at <http://uncitral.org/pdf/english/travaux/sales/limit/yearbook- 3-supplement-e/94th-art1%281%29-e.pdf> (cited as: Commission Record of Discussion), at 9.

> the expiration of a period of time. Such a period of time is hereinafter referred to as 'the limitation period'.

It was agreed that only claims of buyers and sellers and not those of third parties would be covered by the Limitation Convention. The terms 'prescription' or 'statute of limitation' were carefully avoided and 'limitation period' was selected as a neutral term.[23] This neutral term had to cover the different conceptions existing in national laws.[24] The issue of invalidity of contract is outside the scope of CISG,[25] but within the scope of the Limitation Convention.[26]

Although not amounting to a complete harmonization of CISG and the Limitation Convention, the respective spheres of application and general provisions of the Limitation Convention and of the CISG are almost identical.[27]

6 The Length of the Limitation Period

The limitation period laid down in the Limitation Convention is four years (Art. 8 Limitation Convention), commencing from the date of which the claim accrues (Art. 9(1) Limitation Convention), subject to the rules relating to cessation, recommencement and extension which will be considered later. Even if extended, the period may not exceed ten years: Article 23 Limitation Convention. This is a simple and definite period.

How was this four year period decided? There are a wide variety of national limitation periods in the world ranging from six months to thirty years. The Working Group had a common understanding that the limitation period should be a single basic period governing all claims by both parties to an international sales contract – subject only to limited exceptions for special problems, and nearly all delegates favoured a period within the range of three to five years with opinion about equally divided between these two periods.[28] When the 1971 preliminary Draft Convention was drafted, two alternatives, either three years or

23 Official Commentary, *supra* note 10, Art. 1(1) Limitation Convention, para. 1.

24 Enderlein, in: Enderlein & Maskow (Eds.), *supra* note 8, Art. 1 Limitation Convention, para. 6.

25 Art. 4(a) CISG.

26 See *supra* note 22. There was an objection to the inclusion of invalidity claims mainly from civil law countries at the Working Group meeting. But there was strong counter-argument that it would be much more complicated for the traders if claims of invalidity were subject to the domestic limitation rules while other claims were subject to the Limitation Convention.

27 Enderlein, in: Enderlein & Maskow (Eds.), *supra* note 8, at 394.

28 Working Group Report 1969, *supra* note 7, para. 49 *et seq.*

five years, were proposed.[29] To investigate the national laws and to solicit opinions on the uniform rules, a Questionnaire was distributed to governments and international organizations[30] and 35 replies were received.[31] The responses were divided: five years was supported by fourteen states; four years by five states; three years by fourteen states; and two years by two states.[32] Against this background, four years was proposed in the 1972 Draft Convention,[33] which was later accepted by the majority of delegates. The *travaux préparatoires* reveal how four years was proposed and decided, but not on what grounds. It seems that the four year period in the Limitation Convention was simply an arithmetical compromise. A different question is whether the four year period is adequate for international sales contracts. I am of the opinion that four years should be an adequate period for various reasons. First, particularly for international traders who are handling a large number of sales contracts every day, even under modern advanced IT systems, it is still burdensome to have to keep business records for very long periods. Shorter periods are better for international traders. Secondly, four years is neither too short nor too long. A certain period is absolutely necessary because the creditor needs time for investigation, negotiation for settlement or arrangement for legal proceedings. In such circumstances, geographical distance, and difference in language and legal systems must be taken into account. Thirdly, usage of prompt action in international sales requires quick action. For example, Articles 38 and 39 CISG require the buyer to take prompt action, and under a charter party the cargo owner must usually act very quickly so as not to incur unnecessary demurrage, and contracts of carriage require the consignee to claim for damage against the carrier within three days. If a party to international trade does not act quickly, he knows he must pay for it. Fourthly, for busy international traders, simple and clear limitation rules are absolutely important. They must be able to easily decide their course of action accordingly.

Incidentally, the limitation period under the United States Uniform Commercial Code is four years according to U.C.C. § 2-725.[34] According to the official comment of that section, a four year period was selected as the most appropriate to modern business practice, and

29 Working Group Report 1970, *supra* note 11, Annex I, Art. 6.

30 *Id.*, Annex III.

31 Analysis of Replies to the Questionnaire, and Comments made at the Fourth Session of the Commission by Governments, on the Length of the Prescriptive Period and Related Matters: Report of the Secretary-General, UN Doc. A/CN.9/70/Add.2, Section 14, 24 February 1972 (cited as: Analysis of Replies to the Questionnaire), para. 6 *et seq.*

32 Incidentally, the Japanese Civil Code (Law of Obligations) Reform Commission proposed the amendment to the standard extinctive prescription period in the Civil Code of Japan from ten years to either three years, four years or five years, see Japanese Reform Proposal, *supra* note 17. It seems that five years is the more favoured period in Japan.

33 Working Group Report 1970, *supra* note 11, Annex I, Art. 8.

34 Art. 2 Uniform Commercial Code (U.C.C.) can be found at <http://www.westlaw.com>.

because this is within normal commercial record keeping practices. This may also be true for international sale of goods.

In conclusion, whatever the history concerning the length of the limitation period in the Limitation Convention might be, the consensus of the four year period is the most remarkable achievement of the Limitation Convention, thus making possible the elimination of the legal uncertainty arising out of the different limitation periods around the world. Further, a four year period is an adequate limit for international sale of goods. Why should international traders and lawyers not be given this benefit?

7 Commencement of the Limitation Period

The length of a limitation period cannot be judged without knowing when it starts running. So the commencement time is extremely important. When does the four year period start running? As there were so many options, this was one of the major topics on the agenda of the Working Group.[35] However, they kept in mind two elements: (a) the commencement event must be definite but flexible, when viewed from differing national perspectives regarding the parties' rights and the wide variety of individual contracts; and (b) it is important to avoid the use of events subject to conflicting evidence,[36] thus the subjective test was rejected by the Working Group which considered the objective test of time of breach of contract more suitable. The replies to the Questionnaire showed that there were many options under national laws.[37] For example, in the U.K. or United States, the period starts when the cause of action accrued, and in Japan when the right was exercisable.[38]

We can briefly examine the final structure of the Limitation Convention regarding the commencement. The basic rule is that the commencement date is the day on which the claim accrues (Art. 9(1) Limitation Convention). Claims for breach of contract accrue on the date of the breach (Art. 10(1) Limitation Convention), and in case of claims of non-conformity of goods, claims accrue on the date the goods are actually handed over to, or their tender is refused by the buyer (Art. 10(2)). For claims based on fraud, the period commences on the date at which the fraud was or reasonably could have been discovered (Art. 10(3) Limitation Convention). There are special rules in case of an express undertaking such as warranty (Art. 11), anticipatory breach (Art. 12(1)), and (c) instalment contracts (Art. 12(2) Limitation Convention).

35 Working Group Report 1969, *supra* note 7, para. 17.
36 *Id.*, para. 18.
37 Analysis of Replies to the Questionnaire, *supra* note 31, para. 10.
38 Article 166(1) Civil Code of Japan, *supra* note 3.

As we have just seen, the four year period commences from the moment an objective test is satisfied in the Limitation Convention (except for fraud claims). As mentioned earlier,[39] an objective test uses an objectively ascertainable event as a starting point, while a subjective test involves a test dependent on a persons' knowledge, and the Working Group considered a subjective test, but rejected it.[40] Yet, recent world trends show a preference for two-tier systems in which a short period commences from the subjective test and a long period commences from the objective test.[41] Is the rule in the Limitation Convention outdated? I do not think so. National limitation laws must cover various legal claims including torts or consumer claims, and the subjective test may be necessary to protect tort victims and consumers. By contrast, the Limitation Convention is expected to apply to international sale of goods between traders only. Tort claims and consumer contracts are outside the scope of the Limitation Convention. Further, a simple and clear commencement time should be the first priority under circumstances where traders have to deal with huge numbers of sales contracts effectively by means of standard contract forms. The objective test is simpler and clearer than the subjective test, because it does not require investigation of the person's knowledge, whereby relevant evidence is controlled by the person whose knowledge is in question. In my opinion, the objective standard is better suited to international sales.

8 Cessation of the Period

When the claimant commences legal proceedings (judicial, arbitral or administrative proceedings) against the debtor, or when it asserts its claim in existing proceedings, the limitation period under the Limitation Convention ceases to run. This means that the proceedings for the enforcement of claim must be brought before the period expires. This approach is universally accepted by almost all countries. A problem arises if legal proceedings terminate without a decision on the merits because of lack of jurisdiction, procedural defect or some other reason. What will be the effect on running of time? There are traditionally two kinds of approach to this issue: (a) When the legal proceedings commence the period will be suspended but if dismissed, the limitation period starts ticking again

39 See *supra*, Preface.

40 Working Group Report 1969, *supra* note 7, para 18.

41 Article 10.2 PICC, see UNIDROIT International Institute for the Unification of Private Law, UNIDROIT Principles of International Commercial Contracts (2004), Rome, April 2004, available at <http://www.unidroit.org/english/principles/contracts/principles2004/ integralversionprinciples2004-e.pdf>; Art. 3.1.3.44 Japanese Reform Proposal, *supra* note 17, in respect of the extinctive prescription in Japan. Also Germany and France have adopted the two-tier system, see Arts. 195 and 199(1), (3) and (4) German Civil Code, *supra* note 15, and Arts. 2224 and 2232 French Civil Code, *supra* note 16.

(*e.g.* in Germany),[42] or (b) when the legal proceedings start, the period will not be interrupted or suspended but keeps ticking, and the claimant may submit new litigation if initiated within a specific period (*e.g.* in U.S.A.).[43] The Convention did not opt for either approach, but instead elected for a third way.[44] The period is 'deemed to have continued to run' (Art. 17(1) Limitation Convention), but as this may put the creditor in a detrimental position, a one year period is guaranteed to allow the creditor enough time to initiate legal proceedings (Art. 17(2) Limitation Convention).[45]

9 Recommencement of the Period

When recommencement comes into operation, the full limitation period will start running afresh. What kind of acts shall then trigger the recommencement? In the Convention there are two acts which trigger recommencement, *i.e.* (a) service of a notice of demand or other performance by creditor (Art. 19 Limitation Convention), or (b) acknowledgement by the debtor (in writing or by payment of interest or partial performance which implies an acknowledgement of the debt): Arts. 20(1) and 20(2) Limitation Convention. In respect of the first trigger of notice of demand or other performance, there are two different approaches in the national systems, either: (i) such act has the effect of recommencing the limitation period without linking to the institution of legal proceedings; or (ii) such act will not recommence the limitation period and the creditor must institute legal proceedings.[46]

Article 19 Limitation Convention offers a good compromise between these two systems, *i.e.* if the creditor's act has the effect of recommencing the local limitation period in the debtor's country (not the creditor's country), then the limitation period will start again. In Japan, there is a system of the special demand which will interrupt the running of the prescription, but this is subject to initiating legal proceedings within six months.[47] Therefore, Japan falls into the category of countries adhering to approach (ii). In the meantime, the triggering act (b) described above is understandable and accepted in most countries.

42 Art. 207 German Civil Code, *supra* note 15.

43 UCC § 2-725(3), *supra* note 34.

44 H. Smit, 'The Convention on the Limitation Period in the International Sale of Goods: UNCITRAL's First Born', 23 *Am. J. Comp. L.* 337, at 341 (1975).

45 As long as the limitation period is deemed to have continued to run in the situation as provided in Art. 17(1) of the Limitation Convention, it should effectively be the same as under U.S. domestic law, but the difference would be, in case of the Limitation Convention: (i) termination is unqualified and absolute (unless it is deemed to have continued to run), see *id.*, at 342, and (ii) the limitation period is extended for a period not exceeding one year under the circumstances where Art. 17(2) of the Limitation Convention is applicable.

46 *Id.*, at 343.

47 Art. 153 Civil Code of Japan, *supra* note 3.

10 Extension of the Period

Where the institution of legal proceedings is prevented by a circumstance which is beyond the control of the creditor, and which the creditor could neither avoid nor overcome, the limitation period may be extended,[48] but in any event it may not exceed ten years.[49] These circumstances include war, interruption of communications and moratoria which are sometimes treated as events of force majeure or impossibility. Yet the Limitation Convention carefully avoids the use of the terms '*force majeure*' or 'impossibility' since they have different connotations in different legal systems.[50] Once such preventing circumstances cease to exist, if the remaining period exceeds one year, the limitation period will expire at the end of the normal limitation period. However, if less than one year remains at that time, the creditor is given a year to prepare legal proceedings.[51] By contrast, a two week period is given to creditors under the current Japanese Civil Code.[52] This period would be too short for the creditor to take legal proceedings in the case of an international sale of goods.

When negotiation for settlement commences between the parties, should the limitation period be extended for the negotiation period, or cease to run? There are negative and affirmative approaches to this question around the world. There was originally a clause dealing with this problem in the preliminary Draft Convention[53] but it was deleted in the final text of the Convention (Art. 22(1) Limitation Convention). A look at international rules and national statutes shows they are widely divided: in the case of the Principles of European Contract Law (PECL),[54] Germany,[55] France,[56] and the Japanese Reform Proposal,[57] either extension or cessation of the limitation period for negotiation is allowed; while in the case of PICC[58] and many other countries including the current Civil Code of Japan,[59]

48 Art. 21 Limitation Convention.
49 Art. 23 Limitation Convention.
50 Official Commentary, *supra* note 10, Art. 21 Limitation Convention, para. 1.
51 Art. 21 Limitation Convention.
52 Art. 161 Civil Code of Japan, *supra* note 3.
53 Working Group Report 1970, *supra* note 11, Art. 14.
54 Art. 14:304, PECL, see Principles of European Contract Law, 1999, available at <http://frontpage.cbs.dk/law/commission_on_european_contract_law/PECL%20engelsk/engelsk_partI_og_II.htm>.
55 Art. 203 German Civil Code, *supra* note 15.
56 Art. 2238 French Civil Code, *supra* note 16.
57 Art. 3.1.3.60 Japanese Reform Proposal, *supra* note 17.
58 According to Art. 10.7 PICC, *supra* note 41, the limitation period is suspended in case of ADR.
59 Art. 147 Civil Code of Japan, *supra* note 3, lists the causes of suspension of the prescription period but negotiation is not one of them.

there is no extension or cessation of time. The majority of respondents to the Questionnaire preferred the negative position.[60]

In my opinion it is not necessary to add negotiations to the events which cause extension or cessation because it is difficult to define precisely what amounts to negotiation, and to pinpoint when it starts and ends. Thus these problems themselves may be the cause of possible disputes between the parties. Further, it often happens that serious negotiations to settle a dispute only begin once legal proceedings have been instituted.

11 Modification of the Period by Agreement of the Parties

As mentioned earlier it should be noted that parties can agree not to have the Limitation Convention apply to their contract of international sale of goods under Article 3 (2) of the Limitation Convention, and further that parties can indirectly modify the limitation period by providing in the contract that a party must give notice to the other party within a period shorter than four years as a condition for the acquisition or exercise of its claim under Article 1(2) of the Limitation Convention.

However, in Article 22(1) Limitation Convention, no modification by any declaration or agreement is allowed in principle, except following two cases: (a) the limitation period can be extended by the debtor's written declaration after the limitation period has started running (Art. 22(2) Limitation Convention); and (b) it can be shortened by a valid arbitration clause in the contract whereby arbitration can commence earlier (Art. 22(3) Limitation Convention).[61] During the early stages of the Working Group deliberations the necessity of extension and shortening was discussed, but opposed by the majority of opinion.[62] It was thought that allowing the debtor to declare an extension of the time limit would prevent the hasty institution of legal proceedings in situations where the parties were still negotiating, but the limitation period was about to expire. Nonetheless, an agreement for extension at or before the time of contract was still rejected. Responses to the Questionnaire were

60 Analysis of Replies to the Questionnaire, *supra* note 31, para. 33 *et seq*. The following reasons were raised in the negative opinions:
(i). the parties in bad faith may prolong the negotiation to extend the limitation period;
(ii). if negative, the parties would have an incentive for serious negotiation in order to arrive at a settlement, but if affirmative, the situation would be reverse.

61 This kind of arbitration clause is frequently found in commodity transactions. It is sometimes provided that any dispute must be submitted to arbitration within a period of six months, see Official Commentary, *supra* note 10, Art. 22 Limitation Convention, para 5.

62 Working Group Report 1969, *supra* note 7, para. 93 *et seq*.

divided.[63] Recent trends seem to allow extension and shortening by agreement of the parties on the basis of freedom of contract.[64]

Is the approach of the Limitation Convention too rigid in light of recent world trends? In my opinion, Article 22 Limitation Convention is appropriate for the international sale of goods, because, first, even in countries where wide freedom of contract in respect of limitation periods is permitted, it is not an absolute freedom. In most of the countries, a maximum and minimum period is fixed within which any modification is valid, but beyond which it is not.[65] It should be noted that a certain public interest element in limitation periods cannot be denied even in those countries. Secondly, if a short and simple limitation period applies to claims of various kinds under national limitation laws, it may be necessary to allow parties to modify the limitation period to adjust their interests according to individual circumstances. Yet, the limitation period in the Convention applies only to international sale of goods, thus such adjustment of interests may not be necessary. Thirdly, as previously mentioned, international traders have to dispose of a large number of sales transactions effectively and quickly using standard contract forms, and my view is that they prefer a binding uniform limitation period which both parties must accept without negotiation at the time of the contract. I am therefore of the opinion that no further freedom of contract in respect of the limitation period is necessary beyond what the Limitation Convention now provides in Article 22.

12 CONSEQUENCE OF EXPIRATION OF THE PERIOD

Before examining the effect of expiration of the limitation period, it is noted that it should come into play only if invoked by the debtor (Art. 24 Limitation Convention). However, in some legal systems, the limitation is a matter of public policy and should not be subject to the discretion of private parties.[66] Therefore the state is allowed to reserve the application of this Article (Art. 36 Limitation Convention).

What effect will the expiration of the limitation period have? Article 25(1) of the Limitation Convention stipulates that 'no claim shall be recognized or enforced in any legal proceedings

63 Analysis of Replies to the Questionnaire, *supra* note 31, para 26 *et seq*.

64 For example, Art. 2254 French Civil Code, *supra* note 16 and Art. 10.3 PICC, *supra* note 41, allow the parties to agree to extend or shorten the prescription or limitation period within certain limits.

65 See, *e.g.*, Art. 2254 French Civil Code, *supra* note 16 which invalidates the shortening of the period to less than one year and the extension of the period to more than ten years, and Art. 10.3 PICC which neither allows the parties to shorten the short limitation period of three years to less than one year, nor permits the alteration of the long limitation period of ten years to either less than four years or more than fifteen years.

66 Official Commentary, *supra* note 10, Art. 24 Limitation Convention, para. 1 *et seq*.

[…]'. Emphasis should be placed on the phrase 'in any legal proceedings'. Matters other than those arising out of the legal proceedings will not be affected by the Limitation Convention. In Japan, the expiration of the prescription period extinguishes all the creditor's rights under substantive law.[67] The Limitation Convention has not adopted this principle, thus expiration of the limitation period will not extinguish the parties' other rights. A natural consequence therefore is that the defence of set-off against a claim from the other party is still possible (Art. 25(2) Limitation Convention), and any performance of an obligation after expiration of the limitation period is still valid (Art. 26 Limitation Convention).

13 International Effect

In my opinion, the international effect in the Limitation Convention is a great incentive to accede to the Limitation Convention. We have already considered the cessation, recommencement or extension of the limitation period. When the acts and circumstances halting or extending the limitation period have taken place in one Contracting State, the other Contracting States must ensure that those acts and circumstances are given the same effect, even if they have no such system under their own national laws. Without this effect, the creditor will need to institute legal proceedings in other states before expiry of the applicable limitation periods even as parties are negotiating an amicable settlement. This is too cumbersome for international traders.

As a result of the adoption of the Protocol, if the private international law of the forum situated in a Contracting State decides that laws of a Contracting State apply to a contract in which the debtor has its place of business in a Non-Contracting State, the Limitation Convention will apply to claims arising from that contract (Art. 3(1)(b) Limitation Convention). If the creditor institutes legal proceedings in a Contracting State, and the Convention applies, the effect of any act or circumstances taken in a Non-Contracting State will not be recognized by the Contracting State in determining cessation, recommencement or extension, according to Article 30 Limitation Convention. I believe that this article should have been amended when the Protocol was being prepared.[68] Nonetheless, this is not a fatal problem in the assessment of the significance of the international effect.

67 Art. 167(1) Civil Code of Japan, *supra* note 3.

68 Enderlein, in: Enderlein & Maskow (Eds.), *supra* note 8, Art. 30 Limitation Convention, para. 4.

14 Conclusion

As we can see from the *travaux préparatoires* of the Convention, the experts representing all regions and legal systems of the world at the Working Group and Commission discussed all the relevant problems of the uniform limitation laws in full and created one set of clear and simple rules. In addition to the CISG, I believe that the Limitation Convention is one of the most remarkable achievements by UNCITRAL. It unifies the wide variety of limitation periods and related rules. It provides clear solutions to the uncertainty of the limitation period applicable to international sales contracts. It offers great benefits to international traders and lawyers, but unfortunately, its existence is little known to them.

Therefore the Japanese government is urged to take a positive role to call on China and South Korea, both Contracting States of CISG in East Asia, and on other CISG Contracting States, to work together in acceding to the Limitation Convention in order to move towards even greater unity.

Hong Kong's Adoption of the CISG: Why do we need it now?

Fan Yang[*]

1 Introduction

As one of the most successful international uniform law instruments, the CISG has been adopted by 76 countries around the world.[1] As pointed out by Professor Ingeborg Schwenzer, it can be estimated that nowadays about 80% of world trade is potentially covered by the CISG.[2]

In 2008, Hong Kong Special Administrative Region (HKSAR) ranked 13th among leading world traders, accounting for 2.3% of total world trade.[3] Among the top thirteen world traders, only Hong Kong and the United Kingdom have not 'joined' the CISG. Hong Kong's major trading partners, including the Mainland of China, the United States of America, Singapore, Japan, the Netherlands, Germany and the Republic of Korea (South Korea) are all signatory states of the CISG. Hong Kong's trade with CISG jurisdictions accounts for 69.5% of Hong Kong's total domestic exports, 70.9% of Hong Kong's total outbound re-exports, 77.1% of Hong Kong's total inbound re-exports and 71.7% of Hong Kong's total imports.[4]

---

* LL.M., MCIArb., Barrister (England &Wales), Assistant Professor, School of Law, City University of Hong Kong. Email: fanyang.hk@gmail.com.

1 United Nations Convention on Contracts for the International Sale of Goods (CISG), Vienna, 11 April 1980, available at <http://www.uncitral.org/uncitral/en/uncitral_texts/sale_goods/1980CISG.html>. A detailed list of the CISG Contracting States can be found at <http://www.uncitral.org/uncitral/en/uncitral_texts/sale_goods/1980CISG_status.html>.

2 I. Schwenzer & P. Hachem, 'The CISG – Successes and Pitfalls', 57 *Am. J. Comp. L.* 457 (2009), available at <http://www.cisg.law.pace.edu/cisg/biblio/schwenzer-hachem.html>.

3 According to the World Trade Organization, total world trade is USD 32,492 billion in 2008. Also in 2008, Hong Kong Special Administrative Region (HKSAR) ranked 13th among leading world importers, accounting for 2.4% of world total imports, and 13th among leading world exporters, accounting for 2.3% of world total exports. See trade statistics published by the Trade and Industry Department of HKSAR, available at <http://www.tid.gov.hk/english/aboutus/publications/tradestat/wmt08tt.html>.

4 *Id.*

Hong Kong traders have long been exposed to the CISG,[5] but much to their detriment, HKSAR is not yet a 'party' to the CISG. Hong Kong as one of the major hubs of world trade is lagging behind other jurisdictions and running the risk of losing the opportunity to participate in the current 'Global Jurisconsortorium' which is one of the most important developments in the globalisation of law.

This chapter first examines the status of Hong Kong in the CISG after the reunification on 1 July 1997, then illustrates when the CISG applies to Hong Kong parties. It advocates why HKSAR should become a 'party' to the CISG and how Hong Kong would profit from making a clear stand in embracing the CISG.

2 Is HKSAR a 'Party' to the CISG: After the Reunification in 1997?

On 20 June 1997, shortly before Hong Kong's reunification with the Mainland of China, the People's Republic of China (PRC) deposited with the Secretary General of the United Nations a diplomatic note (PRC Diplomatic Note) announcing that treaties in Annex I to the note 'will be applied' to the HKSAR.[6] The CISG was not listed in Annex I among the 126 multilateral treaties to which China was a party at that date. Nor had the CISG been applied to Hong Kong before the reunification.[7] Hence, the Supreme Court of France (*Cour de cassation*) in the 2008 *Telecommunications products* case decided that the CISG is not applicable to the special administrative region of Hong Kong.[8] However, in the United States, there have been some conflicting court decisions on whether the CISG applies to HKSAR.[9]

5 F. Yang, 'CISG in China and Beyond', 40 *U.C.C. L.J.* 373, at 376 (2008).

6 See Letter of Notification of Treaties Applicable to Hong Kong After 1 July 1997, deposited by the Government of the People's Republic of China with the Secretary-General of the United Nations on 20 June 1997, Annex I, 36 International Legal Materials, vol. XXXVI, No. 6, November 1997, para. 1675 *et seq.*, available at <http://www.hku.hk/ccpl/database/annex1.html>.

7 See the List of Treaties in Force and Applicable to the Hong Kong Special Administrative Region, available at <http://www.legislation.gov.hk/interlaw.htm>.

8 French Supreme Court, 2 April 2008, CISG-online 1651, translation available at <http://cisgw3.law.pace.edu/cases/080402f1.html> (cited as: *Telecommunications products* case).

9 *Innotex Precision Limited v. Horei, Inc.*, 2009 U.S. Dist. LEXIS 117992 (N.D. Ga.), 17 December 2009, CISG-online 2044, available at <http://cisgw3.law.pace.edu/cases/091217u1.html> (cited as: *Innotex* case). For a contrary conclusion, see *Electrocraft Arkansas, Inc. v. Electric Motors, Ltd.*, 2009 U.S. Dist. LEXIS 120183 (E.D. Ark.), 23 December 2009, CISG-online 2045, available at <http://cisgw3.law.pace.edu/cases/091223u1.html>. See also *CNA International, Inc. v. Guangdon Kelon Electronical Holdings*, 05 C 5734 (N.D. Ill.), available at <http://cisgw3.law.pace.edu/cases/080903u1.html> (cited as: *CNA* case).

2.1 *The* Telecommunications Products *Case and the* Innotex *Case*

In the *Telecommunications products case*, the French Supreme Court held that 'the People's Republic of China has effectuated with the depositary of the Convention a formality equivalent to what is provided for in Article 93 CISG'.[10] The French Supreme Court emphasized the intention of the Chinese government as reflected on the 1997 PRC Diplomatic Note, in particular Annex I, which was considered to satisfy Article 93 CISG as the equivalent of a declaration that the CISG shall not apply to HKSAR after 1997.[11]

More recently, the United States District Court, Northern District of Georgia, Atlanta Division in the *Innotex* case also found that the CISG does not apply to HKSAR because Hong Kong is not a Contracting State. It pointed out that this conclusion is consistent with the position held by the Chinese government, the Hong Kong Department of Justice, the French Supreme Court, and numerous commentators.[12]

2.2 *Arguments against the Application of the CISG to HKSAR*

Arguments against the application of the CISG to HKSAR are mainly two-fold: (2.2.1) the 1997 PRC Diplomatic Note, in particular Annex I, constitutes an equivalent declaration that has satisfied Article 93 CISG; and (2.2.2) the intentions of the PRC Central Government and the HKSAR Government are not to apply the CISG in HKSAR.

2.2.1 Did the 1997 PRC Diplomatic Note Satisfy Article 93 CISG?

Concerning the interpretation of Article 93 CISG, it is a fact that the PRC did not 'at the time of signature, ratification, acceptance, approval or accession, declare that this Convention is to extend to all its territorial units or only to one or more of them' according to Article 93(1) CISG. The issue then is whether the 1997 PRC Diplomatic Note, and in particular Annex I, can be seen as a new declaration made by the PRC after its accession to the CISG in accordance with Article 93(2) CISG in that it 'state[s] expressly the territorial units to which the Convention extends'. Instead of adopting a textual interpretative approach, the French Supreme Court and the American District court in the *Innotex* case, stressed the intentions of the Chinese government and the HKSAR government not to apply the CISG in HKSAR.

10 *Telecommunications products* case, *supra* note 8, at para. B.

11 *Id.*

12 *Innotex* case, *supra* note 9.

By contrast, in the *CNA* case,[13] the United States District Court, Northern District of Illinois, interpreted Article 93 CISG by looking to its plain language and to 'the general principles' upon which the treaty is based,[14] and came to the opposite conclusion. The Court first decided that a plain reading of the provision permits China to make an Article 93(1) CISG declaration regarding the status of Hong Kong after gaining control of the territorial unit; therefore, the Court found that China had the legal opportunity to declare that the CISG should not extend to the Hong Kong SAR when it resumed sovereignty over Hong Kong.[15] Next, in deciding whether the Diplomatic Note satisfied the requirements set out in Article 93(2) CISG, the Court held that there are two requirements: first, the declaration must be notified to the Secretary-General of the United Nations who is the depositary of the CISG; and second, the declaration must expressly identify the territorial units to which the CISG extends. The Court held that the Diplomatic Note satisfied the first requirement but failed the second because Annex I says nothing with respect to the CISG, and clearly does not 'state expressly the territorial units to which the Convention extends'.

In interpreting Article 93 CISG, the American District Court in the *CNA* case stuck to the plain textual interpretative rule and concluded that the PRC has not yet filed an Article 93 CISG declaration, thus the CISG applies to HKSAR pursuant to Article 93(4) CISG.

2.2.2 What Were the Intentions of the PRC Central Government and the HKSAR Government?

As to the question whether the PRC Central Government and the HKSAR Government intend to apply or exclude the application of the CISG in HKSAR, it is submitted that the question is yet to be answered.

According to Section XI of Annex I to the Sino-British Joint Declaration (1984)[16] and its mirror Article 153 Basic Law of HKSAR,[17] the application to the HKSAR of international

13 *CNA* case, *supra* note 9.

14 The court cited *Chicago Prime Packers, Inc. v. Northam Food Trading Co.*, 408 F. 3d 894 (7th Cir. 2005), CISG-online 1026, available at <http://cisgw3.law.pace.edu/cases/050523u1.html>, citing Art. 7(2) CISG.

15 See generally U. Schroeter, 'The Status of Hong Kong and Macao Under the United Nations Convention on Contracts for the International Sale of Goods', 16 *Pace Int'l L. Rev.* 307, at 323 *et seq.*, available at: <http://www.schroeter.li/pdf/Schroeter_16_Pace_Intl_L_Rev_2004_307.pdf>.

16 Sino-British Joint Declaration, available at the website of the Constitutional and Mainland Affairs Bureau of the Government of the HKSAR: <http://www.cmab.gov.hk/en/issues/jd3b.htm#foreign>.

17 Art. 153 Basic Law of the Hong Kong Special Administrative Region of the People's Republic of China, 4 April 1990, available at <http://www.basiclaw.gov.hk/ en/basiclawtext/images/Basic_Law.pdf> states: 'The application to the Hong Kong Special Administrative Region of international agreements to which the People's Republic of China is or becomes a party shall be decided by the Central People's Government, in accordance with the circumstances and needs of the Region, and after seeking the views of the government of the Region. International agreements to which the People's Republic of China is not a party but which

agreements to which the PRC is or becomes a party shall be decided by the Central People's Government, in accordance with the circumstances and needs of the Region, and after seeking the views of the government of the Region.

Therefore, the fact that the CISG has not been listed in Annex I to the Diplomatic Note as one of the treaties to which China was a party at that date and which should also apply to Hong Kong, is not necessarily a conclusive indication that the Central People's Government has decided against the application of the CISG in HKSAR. We should bear in mind that Annex I was a result of series of strenuous negotiations between the British and Chinese government upon the transfer of the sovereignty of Hong Kong. The United Kingdom which is not a party to the CISG was unlikely to have added the CISG to their negotiation list, while the PRC might have overlooked the Convention.

Nonetheless, given Article 153 Basic Law,[18] whether the CISG applies to HKSAR shall be decided by the Central Government, in accordance with the circumstances and needs of the HKSAR, and after seeking the views of the government of the HKSAR. Therefore, two pertinent questions arise: (1) whether application of the CISG in HKSAR is in accord with the circumstances and needs of the HKSAR and (2) what should the current views of the government of the HKSAR be on the application of the CISG in HKSAR?

3 Whether the Application of the CISG in HKSAR is in Accord with the Circumstances and Needs of HKSAR?

As we know, the United Kingdom is not a party to the CISG.[19] Given the long standing tradition of following English law in Hong Kong, it may be argued that if the U.K. does not want the CISG, the HKSAR may well just do without. However, the circumstances and needs of HKSAR are dramatically different from those of the U.K.

Located in the centre of East Asia and with a rapidly growing Mainland China as its motherland, the HKSAR is an international business, trade and financial hub on its own right. Hong Kong external trade comprises merchandise trade and trade in services of

are implemented in Hong Kong may continue to be implemented in the Hong Kong Special Administrative Region. The Central People's Government shall, as necessary, authorize or assist the government of the Region to make appropriate arrangements for the application to the Region of other relevant international agreements.'

18 *Id.*

19 For a discussion about the reasons why the U.K. has not adopted the CISG, see M. Bridge, 'A Law for International Sales', 37 *Hong Kong L.J.* 17 (2007), available at <http://www.cisg.law.pace.edu/cisg/biblio/bridge3.html>.

Hong Kong with external parties.[20] Its external merchandise trade statistics are compiled based on information contained in import/export declarations. The HKSAR is a separate customs territory, as stated in the Basic Law of HKSAR.[21] An import/export declaration is also required of Hong Kong's merchandise trade with the mainland of China, and statistics relating to this are included in Hong Kong's external merchandise trade statistics.[22]

Have Hong Kong traders really felt the need for the CISG and are they particularly enthusiastic about it now? What about the costs of learning the CISG? Why cannot Hong Kong traders simply repeatedly opt out the CISG anyway? These concerns should be answered once the benefits of adopting the CISG in Hong Kong are fully understood.

3.1 *Benefits of Joining the CISG*

First, the phenomenal success of the CISG is evidenced in the number of its Contracting States and its wide acceptance in developed, developing, western, socialist, South-American, African and Asian countries. In particular, it is worth repeating here that Hong Kong's major competitors in the region, such as Singapore, Japan and South Korea are now all parties to this Convention. The CISG has now gained worldwide acceptance and is undoubtedly one of the most successful international conventions in the field of private law. It can be estimated that nowadays 80% of world trade is potentially covered by the CISG.[23] Over 2,500 – published – court decisions and arbitral awards, an abundant number of scholarly writings, numerous conferences and last but not least the Annual Willem C. Vis International Commercial Arbitration Moot[24] show the prominent contribution that the CISG has made and will continue to make in practice, legal science and legal education. The time has long been overdue for Hong Kong to make the CISG available to its own traders and show its trade partners and the world trade communities at large that it is committed to continue to build on its traditional free market economic policy and to further expand and facilitate trade both within the region and across the globe.

---

20 Hong Kong's external merchandise trade statistics cover movements of merchandise between Hong Kong and her trading partners, by land, air, water and by post. Movements of exempted articles, gold and specie are not included. See HKSAR Census and Statistics Department's website, available at <http://www.censtatd.gov.hk/hong_kong_statistics/statistics_by_subject/concept/external_trade/index.jsp>.

21 Art. 116 Basic Law of HKSAR, *supra* note 17: 'The Hong Kong Special Administrative Region shall be a separate customs territory.'

22 HKSAR Census and Statistics Department's website, *supra* note 20.

23 Schwenzer & Hachem, *supra* note 2.

24 For further information about the *Annual Willem C. Vis International Commercial Arbitration Moot* that takes place in Vienna or its sister moot, the *Willem C. Vis (East) International Commercial Arbitration Moot* that is conducted in Hong Kong, see <http://www.cisg.law.pace.edu/vis.html>.

Second, for the Hong Kong business and trade community, the benefit of using the CISG is readily apparent. Against the backdrop of globalization, international trade is a daily occurrence. Small and medium-size enterprises, in particular, are vulnerable in facing the legal technicalities involved in international trade. Small and medium-size enterprises would become the largest beneficiaries of the CISG, should it be applied to HKSAR. Once traders discover that the CISG is in effect in the majority part of the world, their attitudes change and their comfort level is enhanced when choosing the CISG as governing law. Adopting the CISG as the common international sales law can save the costs of dealing with diverse domestic laws, and transaction costs associated with negotiating choice-of-law clauses.

Third, the Mainland factor adds a strong reason for Hong Kong to join the CISG family. As pointed out by some experts, Hong Kong's longer-term economic prospects will be determined primarily by whether it can strengthen its competitive edge in Greater China, and by its role in China's market liberalisation.[25] Currently, many new opportunities are opening up for Hong Kong enterprises in the Chinese market, including closer economic integration with Guangdong/the Pearl River Delta (PRD), financial cooperation and capital market development, market deregulation under the Closer Economic Partnership Agreement (CEPA), and cross-border infrastructure links. The Pan-PRD Economic Zone enlarges the hinterland of Hong Kong. Given the strong linkage and resemblance between the CISG and the PRC domestic contract law, 'joining' the CISG would be a significant step for Hong Kong in enhancing the confidence of its trade partners in Mainland China and better serving and further collaborating with its Mainland Chinese trade partners, as well as traders from all other CISG jurisdictions.

Besides the Mainland of China, the same benefit applies to Hong Kong's trade with other East Asian countries. Hong Kong can serve as a bridge connecting the Pan-PRD with ASEAN countries. Given the diversity of legal systems among these countries, and the fact that many of these countries are either transition economies or economies in the process of developing their own legal infrastructures, the advantage of having one common sales law has become more attractive than ever. At present, China, Singapore, Japan and South Korea are the only East Asian States who are parties to the CISG. However, 'joining' the CISG would be a positive step for Hong Kong towards dealing with Asian diversity.

25 See Nomura Global Economics, The Ascent of Asia, February 2010 <http://www.nomura.com/research>.

3.2 *CISG Cases Involving Hong Kong Parties*

As will be shown in this section, in addition to the French Supreme Court, the American Courts, perhaps more importantly, the PRC People's Courts and in particular many CIETAC arbitral tribunals have already had to decide upon the application of the CISG to HKSAR despite HKSAR's own silence. A quick research of the Pace CISG database[26] revealed 56 cases in which the CISG has been applied to international sales involving a Hong Kong seller or buyer or both. Among them, 29 were decided in CIETAC arbitration, 12 in the People's Court in China, five in the United States, four in Austria, two in Belgium, and one each in France, Italy, Australia and Germany. Among these cases, the Hong Kong party was the plaintiff in 29 cases, the respondent in 25 cases, and in two cases both the respondent and the plaintiff were Hong Kong parties. In addition, there were about another 50 cases where Hong Kong was connected to international sales, either as the port of delivery, the place of payment or negotiation or conclusion of the sales contract to which the CISG applied. These identified and published cases probably represent only a small fraction of cases that involve Hong Kong parties in one way or another. The gravity of the CISG in Hong Kong can no longer be ignored.

There are at least the following four situations where the CISG has been applied to Hong Kong parties. First, the CISG can apply to Hong Kong parties pursuant to Article 1(1)(b) CISG, 'when the rules of private international law lead to the application of the law of a Contracting State'. The following case between a Hong Kong seller and a German buyer illustrates this point.[27]

In a 1996 German arbitration proceeding (*Chinese goods* case),[28] a dispute arose under a sales agreement. The German buyer terminated the contract, whereupon the Hong Kong seller commenced arbitration proceedings under the Arbitration Rules of the Hamburg Chamber of Commerce. Concerning the applicable law issue, the Tribunal decided that:

> [t]he applicable law must be determined according to German private international law. A choice of German law can be inferred, according to Art. 27 of the

26 PACE University CISG Database, available at <http://www.cisg.law.pace.edu/cisg/text/case-annotations.html>. See also the CISG-online Database, available at <http://www.cisg-online.ch>.

27 See similarly Austrian Supreme Court, 31 August 2005, CISG-online 1093, 2006 *Internationales Handelsrecht* 31, translation available at <http://cisgw3.law.pace.edu/cases/050831a3.html> (cited as: *Tantalum* case), in which the Austrian Supreme Court applied the CISG to a dispute between a Hong Kong seller and Austrian buyer.

28 See Court of Arbitration of the Hamburg Chamber of Commerce, 21 March 1996, CISG-online 187, 1996 *Neue Juristische Wochenschrift* 3329, translation available <http://cisgw3.law.pace.edu/cases/960321g1.html> (cited as: *Chinese goods* case).

> Introductory Law to the Civil Code (EGBGB),[29] from the agreement to refer disputes to a German arbitral tribunal.[30]

The Tribunal continued:

> [u]ndoubtedly, where the rules of private international law lead, as here, to German law, the [...] CISG [...], in force in Germany in 1990/1991, applies to sales contracts between parties in different States, by virtue of its Art. 1(1)(b) [CISG]. According to this provision, it suffices that the rules of private international law lead to the application of the law of one Contracting State – here: Germany. It is irrelevant whether the State where the other party has his seat is also a Contracting State to the CISG.[31]

As a result, the arbitral tribunal applied the CISG as the relevant German law under Article 1(1)(b) CISG to this dispute, to which the Hong Kong seller was a party.[32]

The second way in which the CISG can apply to Hong Kong parties is when it is applied to fill gaps in laws of the PRC. An example is the 2002 Guangxi Beihai Maritime Court case of *Sino-Add (Singapore) PTE. Ltd. v. Karawasha Resources Ltd*,[33] between a Hong Kong seller and a Singaporean buyer. The parties concluded a sales contract for 60,000 tons of Indian iron ore. The dispute concerned the underlying voyage charter for shipping

---

29 Introductory Law to the German Civil Code (*Einführungsgesetz zum Bürgerlichen Gesetzbuch (EGBGB)*), 18 August 1896, official German version available at <http://www.gesetze-im-internet.de/bgbeg/BJNR006049896.html>.

30 See *Chinese goods* case, *supra* note 28, (citing Palandt-Heldrich, BGB, 55th ed., no. 6 to Art. 27 Introductory Law to the Civil Code, *supra* note 29. In relation to German private international law, the tribunal cited German Federal Supreme Court, 21 September 1995, VII ZR 248/94, BB 1995, 2472. With regard to the Introductory Law to the Civil Code, the Tribunal cited Art. 27 Introductory Law to the Civil Code, *supra* note 29, which reads in its translation in the relevant part: 'The contract is subject to the law chosen by the parties. The choice of law must be explicit or must be determined with sufficient certainty from the provisions of the contract or the circumstances of the case.' See the English translation of the *Chinese goods* case, *supra* note 28, at note 3.

31 See *Chinese goods* case, *supra* note 28, (citing OLG Koblenz, Germany, 17 September 1993, 2 U 1230/91 RIW 1993, 934; Herber in von Caemmerer/Schlechtriem, CISG 2nd ed., Art. 1 nos. 37-40; Martiny in Münchener Kommentar BGB, 2nd ed., Art. 28 EGBGB App. II no. 27; references in Will, CISG International Bibliography, The First 150 or So Decisions, 1995).

32 Unlike Germany, the PRC made a reservation on Art. 1(1)(b) CISG pursuant to Art. 95 CISG. Therefore, the CISG shall not apply to PRC and Hong Kong parties according to Art. 1(1)(b) CISG. For a discussion about the PRC's two reservations, see F. Yang, 'PRC's Two Reservations and the Application of the CISG in CIETAC Arbitration Practice', 8 *International Law Review of Wuhan University* 307 (2008) [*in Chinese*], English version available at <http://www.cisg.law.pace.edu/cisg/biblio/yang2.html>.

33 *Sino-Add (Singapore) PTE. Ltd. v. Karawasha Resources Ltd.*, Guangxi Beihai Maritime Court, 5 March 2002, CISG-online 1383, translation available at <http://cisgw3.law.pace.edu/cases/020305c1.html> (cited as: *Sino-Add* case).

the goods. The parties did not choose the applicable law and the destination of the carriage of goods contract was located in Mainland China. The Guangxi Beihai Maritime Court accepted jurisdiction and in deciding the applicable law issue, the court held that

> [...] pursuant to Article 269 of the Maritime Law of the People's republic of China, which stipulates that where the parties do not choose the applicable law, the law of the nation holding the closest connection with the contract shall be applied", the Maritime Law of the People's Republic of China, the Contract Law of the People's Republic of China and the relevant international conventions shall be applied to this case.[34]

In deciding the buyer's claim for interest, the Court rejected the claimed interest calculated at the London Interbank Offered Rate, but held that to be fair, the interest shall be calculated at the contemporary lending rate of liquid capital promulgated by the People's Bank of China.[35] Although the court did not refer to any specific provision of the CISG, it is submitted that the court in fact applied the Article 78 CISG to fill a gap in the PRC Contract Law 1999, which did not provide any specific rules on parties' entitlement to interest until the Interpretation II of the Supreme People's Court which was promulgated and entered into force on 13 May 2009.[36] Similar to Article 74 CISG, Article 113 PRC Contract Law stipulates that the amount of damages shall be equal to the loss caused by the breach, including loss of profit, but shall not exceed the loss which the party in breach foresaw or ought to have foreseen, as a possible consequence of the breach of contract.[37] But, unlike Article 78 CISG which provides that interest is recoverable, the PRC Contract Law was silent on this issue. The Guangxi Beihai Maritime Court, sitting in May 2002, could not

34 *Sino-Add* case, *supra* note 33 (emphasis omitted). Art. 269 PRC Maritime Law 1993 states that '[t]he parties to a contract may choose the law applicable to their contract, unless the law provides otherwise. Where the parties to a contract have not made a choice, the law of the country having the closest connection with the contract shall apply'.

35 *Sino-Add* case, *supra* note 33. For a discussion on the interest rate under the CISG, see F. Mazzotta, 'Endless Disagreement Among Commentators, Much Less Among Courts', in: Pace Int'l L. Rev. (Ed.), *Pace Review of the Convention on Contracts for the International Sale of Goods* 123 (2003-2004), available at <http://cisgw3.law.pace.edu/cisg/biblio/mazzotta78.html>, citing this case and 275 other court and arbitral rulings,

36 Art. 21 of the PRC Supreme People's Court Judicial Interpretation on Several Issues regarding Application to PRC Law of Contract (2) states that '[t]he debtor shall pay interest and expenses in addition to the primary debt'. In its original Chinese language: 第二十一条 债务人除主债务之外还应当支付利息和费用 [...].

37 Although some may argue that Art. 113 PRC Contract Law 1999 provides for the recovery of interest, the Chinese word '利益' (profit) in Art. 113 was in fact misinterpreted in some English translations as 'interest' ('利息'). Art. 113 PRC Contract Law 1999 in its original Chinese language: '第一百一十三条 【损害赔偿的范围】当事人一方不履行合同义务或者履行合同义务不符合约定，给对方造成损失的，损失赔偿额应当相当于因违约所造成的损失，包括合同履行后可以获得的利益，但不得超过违反合同一方订立合同时预见到或者应当预见到的因违反合同可能造成的损失。"

at that time have applied the domestic PRC Contract Law to award interest, but must have relied upon the 'relevant international convention', *i.e.* the CISG, to grant interest.

The close connection and resemblances between the CISG and the PRC Contract Law 1999 cannot be overemphasised in this context. Many commentators have pointed out that the PRC Contract Law 1999 has followed closely the CISG and the UNIDROIT Principles of International Commercial Contracts 1994 (UPICC)[38] and, in some areas, the CISG and the UPICC have been reproduced in the PRC Contract Law 1999 article by article.[39] The CISG, a treaty to which the PRC is a party, is a formal source of Chinese domestic law.[40] It has often been applied to fill in the gaps of the PRC domestic laws, even when it does not apply according to its own provisions under Article 1 CISG. Sales with Hong Kong parties have long been treated as foreign-related transactions under current PRC law and practice,[41] therefore, the CISG will most likely be referred to. Even though it may not be the governing law, the CISG would still be highly relevant and persuasive.[42]

---

38 UNIDROIT International Institute for the Unification of Private Law, UNIDROIT Principles of International Commercial Contracts (2004), Rome, April 2004, available at <http://www.unidroit.org/english/principles/contracts/principles2004/integralversionprinciples2004-e.pdf>.

39 See L. Huixing, 'On the Third Draft of the Uniform Contract Law of China', 13 *Columbia Journal of Asian Law* 1 (1999), available at <http://www.cisg.law.pace.edu/cisg/biblio/liming-chuanxi.html>. See also J. Chen, *Chinese Law: Context and Transformation*, 450 (2008); Z. Yuejiao, 'Harmonization of Contract Law and its Impacts on China's Contract Law', presentation at the Modern Law for Global Commerce: Congress to Celebrate the Fortieth Annual Season of UNCITRAL (9-12 July 2007), available at <http://www.uncitral.org/pdf/english/congress/Zhang.pdf>; M. Zhang, *Chinese Contract Law, Theory and Practice* (2006); B. Ling, *Contract Law in China* (2002).

40 Art. 142 PRC General Principles of Civil Law 1986: 'If any international treaty concluded or acceded to by the People's Republic of China contains provisions differing from those in the laws of the People's Republic of China, the provisions of the international treaty shall apply, unless the provisions are ones on which the People's Republic of China has announced reservations. International practice may be applied on matters for which neither the law of the People's Republic of China nor any international treaty concluded or acceded to by the People's Republic of China has any provisions.'

41 According to the Official Reply of the Supreme People's Court on Several Questions in Dealing with Economic Dispute Cases Involving the Hong Kong-Macau-Taiwan Regions 19 October 1987, and more recently, in 2002, the Supreme People's Court issued the Provisions on Some Issues Concerning the Jurisdiction of Civil and Commercial Cases Involving Foreign Elements ("最高人民法院关于涉外民商事案件诉讼管辖若干问题的规定"), effective on 1 March 2002. Art. 5 of the Provisions stipulates: 'The jurisdiction of cases on civil and commercial disputes involving parties from Hong Kong or Macao Special Administrative Region or Taiwan Region shall be handled by the courts with reference to these Provisions [...]' ('第五条 涉及香港、澳门特别行政区和台湾地区当事人的民商事纠纷案件的管辖，参照本规定处理').

42 But see *Hong Kong Topway Trading Co. Ltd. v. Dongying Hongyu Import & Export Co. Ltd.*, Dongyang Intermediate People's Court of Shandong, 12 May 2008, CISG-online 2108, translation available at <http://cisgw3.law.pace.edu/cases/080512c1.html>, in which although the Hong Kong seller (plaintiff) pleaded on the basis of the CISG as a standard for performance of international sales contracts, the Court applied PRC Contract Law 1993, *supra* note 37 on the ground that the parties selected Mainland Chinese law as governing law. The Court did not discuss the applicability of the CISG in the case.

Third, the CISG can be applied to Hong Kong parties by the parties' explicit agreement on the choice of the PRC laws as applicable law.[43] In the 1999 CIETAC *Gray cloths* case between a Mainland seller and a Hong Kong buyer, the parties explicitly agreed in their sales contract that Chinese law and the CISG apply to their disputes.[44] Arbitration tribunals respect the parties' mutual agreement in such cases.[45]

Fourth, the CISG can be applied to Hong Kong parties by parties' implicit agreement. In the *Kidney beans* case,[46] the Mainland seller and Hong Kong buyer did not stipulate the applicable law in the contract. However, in the course of the arbitral proceedings, the parties referred to Chinese law and the CISG to support their arguments. Therefore, the tribunal deemed that the two parties had implicitly agreed that Chinese law and the CISG should apply.[47] In particular, the Tribunal decided that 'the [Seller] has fundamentally breached the Contract and caused the non-performance of the Contract [...]'. It is submitted that the concept of 'fundamental breach' is not contained in any provision of the PRC Contract Law 1999 and the Tribunal was in fact applying Article 25 CISG.[48] Alternatively, the Tribunal assimilated Article 94(4) PRC Contract Law 1999 to Article 25 CISG; the so-called 'applying the PRC Contract Law with reference to the CISG'.[49]

---

43 Note that some courts have taken a different view due to the declaration of the PRC according to Art. 95 CISG regarding application of Art. 1(1)(b) CISG.

44 China International Economic & Trade Arbitration Commission (CIETAC), 2 April 1999, CISG-online 1282, translation available at <http://cisgw3.law.pace.edu/cases/990402c1.html> (cited as: *Gray cloths* case).

45 See also CIETAC Arbitration proceeding, 4 April 1996, CISG-online 2106, translation available at <http://cisgw3.law.pace.edu/cases/960404c1.html> (cited as: *Three-ply board* case); CIETAC Arbitration proceeding, 28 January 1999, CISG-online 1206, translation available at <http://cisgw3.law.pace.edu/cases/990128c1.html> (cited as: *Refrigeration equipment* case).

46 CIETAC Arbitration proceeding, 27 June 1997, CISG-online 1069, translation available at <http://cisgw3.law.pace.edu/cases/970627c1.html> (cited as: *Kidney beans* case).

47 CIETAC Arbitration proceeding, 15 November 1996, CISG-online 1148, translation available at <http://cisgw3.law.pace.edu/cases/961115c1.html> (cited as: *Oxytetrecycline* case). See also CIETAC Arbitration proceeding, 4 April 1997, CISG-online 1660, translation available at <http://cisgw3.law.pace.edu/cases/970404c1.html> (cited as: *Black melon seeds* case).

48 Art. 94 PRC Contract Law 1999, *supra* note 37, stipulates in its translation that the parties to a contract may terminate the contract under any of the following circumstances: '(4) the other party delays performance of its obligations, or breaches the contract in such a manner that renders it impossible to achieve the purpose of the contract.' The author is of the view that Art. 94 PRC Contract Law 1999 is the provision which most closely resembles fundamental breach in Art. 25 CISG. See Art. 94(4) PRC Contract Law 1999, *supra* note 37, in its original Chinese language: '第九十四条【合同的法定解除】有下列情形之一的，当事人可以解除合同：（四）当事人一方迟延履行债务或者有其他违约行为致使不能实现合同目的。'

49 *Kidney beans* case, *supra* note 46; *Lianzhong Enterprise Resources (Hong Kong) Ltd. v. Xiamen International Trade & Trust Co.*, Xiamen Intermediate People's Court, 20 April 1993, CISG-online 1604, translation available at <http://cisgw3.law.pace.edu/cases/930420c1.html> (cited as: *Fish powder* case).

Nonetheless, in *Zheng Hong Li Ltd. Hong Kong v. Jill Bert Ltd. Swiss,*[50] the PRC Supreme Court decided that because the parties elected to apply the 'laws of the PRC' during the proceedings in the first instance, the Law on Foreign-related Economic Contracts[51] should apply, thus the Court of First Instance inappropriately applied the CISG. It is submitted that this is a case decided under the old 'three-pillar' contract law regime.[52] It is not clear whether the outcome would still be the same under the current PRC Contract Law 1999 regime.[53] Given the fact that the pre-1999 separate 'foreign-related' regime no longer exists, there would be problems in applying the PRC Contract Law 1999 without reference to the CISG in dealing with international/foreign-related sales contracts. This further reinforces the fact that the PRC Contract Law 1999 and the CISG are supplementary and complimentary to each other. Hence, it is predictable that the application of the CISG through PRC laws to Hong Kong parties cannot be underestimated and is likely to continue to increase.

4 What Current Views Should the HKSAR Government Have on the Application of the CISG in HKSAR?

Again, unlike in the United Kingdom, in Hong Kong there is no evidence to show that there is a real opposition to the CISG. Neither has there ever been any decision made to reject the CISG in Hong Kong. Is it a mere lack of awareness or manpower to attend to this important matter? Perhaps the legislative agenda has always been tight and full of other more pressing or controversial items. But the HKSAR Government can no longer afford to shut its eyes, ears or mouth to the CISG.

As some cases discussed above show, Hong Kong traders have already started to appreciate the merits of the CISG, either by opting into the CISG, or by arguing on the basis of the CISG, especially in the context of trading with Mainland China, and likely in the context of trading with the diverse legal systems of Asia.

50 *Zheng Hong Li Ltd. Hong Kong v. Jill Bert Ltd. Swiss*, Supreme Court of the People's Republic of China, 20 July 1999, CISG-online 1605, translation available at <http://cisgw3.law.pace.edu/cases/990720c1.html>.

51 This legislation was repealed and replaced by the current PRC Contract Law 1999, *supra* note 37.

52 See similarly *Hong Kong [...] Co. Ltd. v. Shanxi Yanquan Import & Export Corp*, Shanghai New Pudong District People's Court, 24 November 1997, CISG-online 2109, <http://cisgw3.law.pace.edu/cases/971124c1.html>; *Fish powder* case, *supra* note 49, in which the Xiamen Intermediate People's Court permitted the Law of the People's Republic of China on Contracts Involving Foreign Interest to apply, and therefore allowed the CISG and international customs to apply to this case, as the parties agreed during the court proceedings.

53 Shanghai Huangpu District People's Court, 30 August 2000, CISG-online 2107, available at <http://cisgw3.law.pace.edu/cases/000830c1.html>, in which the court applied the General Principles of Civil Law without deciding whether the CISG applies in this case between the Mainland seller and Hong Kong buyer.

If the HKSAR Government were to take the position that Hong Kong should remain outside the CISG, there would be costs to business not faced by competitors that have already implemented the CISG, including those in the Mainland China, Japan, Korea and Singapore. The absence of CISG actually imposes costs on Hong Kong business. First, not every Hong Kong trader can always convince their Mainland Chinese partner to agree on Hong Kong law or English law as the governing law. In fact, the rebalance of bargaining power and market change may well indicate that more sales contracts will be governed by the laws of the PRC. Uncertainty in the application of the CISG in HKSAR will prolong parties' negotiations on applicable law clauses which in turn delays the closure of commercial deals and this may mean parties even run the risk of failing to reach an eventual agreement, especially if a deadlock on the applicable law issue occurs.

On the other hand, if the HKSAR Government were to implement the CISG in Hong Kong, there would be costs of implementation, but the advantages would easily surpass the disadvantages, if any. Bearing in mind that Article 6 CISG permits parties to exclude the application of the Convention or, subject to Article 12 CISG, derogate from or vary the effect of any of its provisions, adoption of the CISG does not pose any threat to domestic law. Parties can always select national law to govern their contract. The CISG does not take away parties' freedom in this respect. It is not the intention of the CISG, nor does it have the ability to exterminate national laws or any particular legal system.[54] What the CISG does provide are some general principles and ground rules to facilitate international trade and commerce. The CISG provides an alternative body of rules outside of any national laws for merchants to select. The 'rootless' or 'less rooted' character of the CISG offers a unique 'neutrality' which is valuable and in some circumstances essential for international merchants to engage and thrive in cross-border trade.

Moreover, the CISG offers an opportunity for inspiration and further development of national laws. In Hong Kong, we have over the course of our history cited English jurists where their opinions are relevant. However, because the U.K. is not yet a party to the convention, the world CISG communities have not yet benefited from English jurisprudence in this important development of global sales law. If Hong Kong were to join the CISG, Hong Kong jurists would be able to contribute to the further development of this area of law by sharing Hong Kong jurisprudence with the global CISG community – with the jurisprudence of other countries – to help the world community benefit from the reasoning

54 As pointed out by Potter, the principles of the CISG drew heavily from the Uniform Commercial Code (U.C.C.) in the United States, which is based on a common law system. Hence, the adoption of the CISG does not exclude common law influence at all. See P. Potter, 'Law-making in the PRC: The Case of Contracts', in: J. Otto, *et al.* (Eds.), *Law-Making in the People's Republic of China*, 191 (2000).

of Hong Kong jurists on the evolution of international commercial law as participants in the global *jurisconsultorium* on the CISG.[55]

5 CONCLUSION

There can be no doubt that Hong Kong lawyers and businessmen are already well exposed to the CISG. When they leave their shores to do business it is not always as possible as it once was to take with them all the trappings of Hong Kong or even English Law. With the growth of new economies and trading blocks, bargaining power has changed, and Hong Kong parties cannot always guarantee that they will be able to contract for their own law, let alone their own jurisdiction. Hong Kong lawyers and businessmen are increasingly involved in cases to which the CISG applies. Inevitably much business is being done with the PRC to which CISG applies. The influence of the CISG on the laws of the PRC and the cases applying the CISG to Hong Kong parties unveiled in this paper,[56] when considered against Hong Kong's continuing growth in trade with China and Asia at large, should not deter Hong Kong from 'joining' the CISG, for it would not be likely to lead to the disappearance of Hong Kong or English law, or any national law. An international uniform sales law, as reflected in the CISG and the PICC, embraces influences from national laws at the same time as it nurtures the continued development of national laws. The question is not how long can Hong Kong wait to 'join' the CISG, but how long can it afford not to?

As Hong Kong courts will eventually be confronted with situations where application of the CISG appears likely, these courts will realize there is no clear Hong Kong or English authority on the topic, forcing them to consider decisions from other countries. By respecting and following, where possible, decisions in CISG cases, non-CISG jurisdictions will be assisting informally in the continuing process of harmonisation of international commercial law to which CISG has made such a significant contribution. This is especially

---

55 V. Rogers & A. Kritzer, 'A Uniform International Sales Law Terminology', in: I. Schwenzer & G. Hager (Eds.), *Festschrift für Peter Schlechtriem zum 70. Geburtstag*, 223 (2003), available at <http://cisgw3.law.pace.edu/cisg/biblio/rogers2.html>. See also C. Andersen, *Uniform Application of the International Sales Law: Understanding Uniformity, the Global Jurisconsultorium and Examination and Notification Provisions* (2007); F. Yang, 'CISG, CIETAC Arbitration and the Rule of Law in the P.R. of China: A Global Jurisconsultorium Perspective', in: C. Andersen & U. Schroeter (Eds.), *Sharing International Commercial Law Across National Boundaries: Festschrift for Albert H. Kritzer on the Occasion of his Eightieth Birthday*, 600 (2008).

56 See also Yang, *supra* note 5; F. Yang, 'The Application of the CISG in the Current PRC Law and CIETAC Arbitration Practice', 2006 *Nordic Journal of Commercial Law*, Issue 2, 1, available at <http://www.njcl.fi/2_2006/article4.pdf>.

so, given how increasingly easy it is to access CISG cases.[57] Were the HKSAR officially to join the family of the CISG, Hong Kong law may well assume greater influence over the development of national laws of other Contracting States such as the PRC. Perhaps one day, a Hong Kong case will be cited in the People's courts or Chinese arbitration tribunals and vice versa. International exchange should be a two-way street, not only in trade but also in law.

Last but not the least, it is hoped that the HKSAR government request the Central Government of the PRC to make the requisite communication to the United Nations for the CISG to apply to HKSAR. This paper has shown that there is no real reason why the CISG should not be made available to Hong Kong parties. If the HKSAR government wants the CISG to apply, there is no reason why the Central Government would not make the requisite communication to the United Nations to clarify the situation. Right now there is confusion as illustrated by this and other papers,[58] in particular the conflicting decisions among U.S. courts. The government of the HKSAR should not continue to be silent or do nothing on this important issue. Even if the government of the HKSAR decided not to make the CISG available to Hong Kong parties, again the HKSAR government should request the Central Government of the PRC to file a declaration according to Article 93 CISG to eliminate the confusion. Either way, it is time for the HKSAR government to act responsibly for the long term interest of Hong Kong without further undue delay.

57 Thanks to international comparative law and uniform law scholars and institutes, such as the PACE University CISG Database, *supra* note 27. See also the CISG-online Database, available at <http://www.cisg-online.ch> and the webpage of the Global Sales Law Project, available at <http://www.globalsaleslaw.com/index.cfm?pageID=2>.

58 Schroeter, *supra* note 16; see W. Long, 'The Reach of the CISG in China: Declarations and Applicability to Hong Kong and Macao', in this volume.

Facilitating Regional Economic Integration: ASEAN, ATIGA and the CISG

Bruno Zeller[*]

1 Introduction

As a general comment, looking at a political world map before World War I and comparing it with today's map it could be observed that there was a significant increase in the creation of new sovereign nations. Logically, therefore, an international trader would have to understand and potentially deal with more domestic laws which would add to the ever increasing complexity of engaging in world trade. However, this is not so. Legal scholars – specifically Ernst Rabel – have understood that there is a need to simplify and streamline the legal environment beyond mere transplantations of legal systems. Governments and world organisations like UNCITRAL have taken up the challenge. As a consequence an increase in the drafting of conventions, treaties and agreements has taken place which is now a feature of the legal landscape.

These developments have simplified the selection and understanding of a relevant governing substantive law but at the same time have also added a level of complication to the harmonisation efforts.

The result is that trade is conducted on several levels with interlocking legal regulations. Domestic law enriched by international conventions and transplantations must be understood against the backdrop of bilateral or multilateral trade agreements. The CISG[1] is one part of the complex legal framework regulating contractual relationships. The problem of today is not so much how to understand the diverse domestic legal systems but how to navigate through the maze of treaties. As an example, reservations of countries

* Dr. iur., Associate Professor at Victoria University, Melbourne, Australia, Adjunct Professor at the School of Law, Murdoch University, Perth, Australia; Associate at the Institute for Logistics and Supply Chain Management, Victoria University, Melbourne, Australia.

1 United Nations Convention on Contracts for the International Sale of Goods (CISG), Vienna, 11 April 1980, available at <http://www.uncitral.org/uncitral/en/uncitral_texts/ sale_goods/1980CISG.html>.

when adopting a convention need to be taken into consideration when dealing with a particular trading partner.

The outcome is that a multilayered legal regulation will govern the sale of goods which is the focus of this paper. This paper does not argue points of contention within the CISG nor will the discussion look at problems of private international law or, as common law lawyers understand it, conflict of laws issues. This paper will look primarily at the legal framework not within a country but a region, namely Asia, and will examine the economic integration and the consequences of such a legal landscape. The impetus to this inquiry is drawn from Ole Lando who noted that 'the contract laws of the world lag sadly behind the ongoing rapid growth of the world trade and communication'.[2]

2 The ASEAN Factor

It is useful at the onset to note that a clear distinction or separation between public and private international law in relation to commercial transactions is becoming difficult. The GATT/WTO treaty plays a part, as will bilateral investment treaties, free trade agreements (FTAs) whether bilateral or multilateral, and of course domestic laws. The reason a country enters into multilateral or bilateral agreements is to harmonise and facilitate the laws governing commerce. To that end, associations are formed such as the North American Free Trade Association (NAFTA) or in this case ASEAN.

ASEAN stands for the Association of Southeast Asian Nations. The following countries form part of ASEAN: Brunei Darussalam, the Kingdom of Cambodia, the Republic of Indonesia, Lao People's Democratic Republic, Malaysia, the Union of Myanmar, the Republic of the Philippines, the Republic of Singapore, the Kingdom of Thailand and the Socialist Republic of Viet Nam. However, the term ASEAN also includes the ASEAN Regional Forum, drawing together 27 countries. It is not primarily a trade agreement but rather a 'principal forum for security dialogue in Asia complementing the various bilateral alliances and dialogues'.[3] Amongst themselves, the ASEAN countries have concluded several multilateral agreements of which the ASEAN Trade in Goods Agreement (ATIGA) is of interest.[4] The complexity of aligning domestic contract law with international com-

2 O. Lando, 'CISG and Its Followers: The Proposal to Adopt Some International Principles of Contract Law', 53 *Am. J. Comp. L.* 379, at 384 (2005).

3 Chairman's Statement, of the First Meeting of the ASEAN Regional Forum, Bangkok, 25 July 1994, available at <http://www.aseanregionalforum.org/PublicLibrary/ARFChairmansStatementsandReports/ChairmansStatementofthe1stMeetingoftheASE/tabid/201/Default.aspx>.

4 ASEAN Trade in Goods Agreement (ATIGA), Cha-am, Thailand, 26 February 2009, available at <http://www.aseansec.org/22223.pdf>.

mitments has taken on a new dimension as Australia has just signed the first multinational free trade agreement, namely the ASEAN-Australia-New Zealand Free Trade Agreement (AANZFTA)[5] which was expected to come into force in January 2010.[6]

> AANZFTA contains regional rules of origin and substantial tariff reduction and elimination commitments, as well as World Trade Organization (WTO)-plus commitments in other areas such as services, which will provide commercially meaningful benefits to Australian business and further strengthen Australia's commercial ties with ASEAN.[7]

The achievements of ASEAN are on a government-to-government level which is clearly noted in the agreement.[8] However, the last step of integration at the level of domestic contract law has not yet been achieved. Much of the commercial law of Asia has been transplanted. In particular, contract law has 'been greatly influenced by Western law (either the common law or the civil law)'.[9] Of the ten ASEAN countries only Singapore has ratified the CISG. This begs the question; what is the significance of the CISG in relation to the ATIGA where all but one of the members are not signatories to the CISG?

The CISG is only relevant if a country becomes a signatory to the Convention. Article 1 of the CISG explains its sphere of application and describes two possible situations where it applies. First, when the contracting parties have places of business in different Contracting States[10] or 'when the rules of private international law lead to the application of the law of a Contracting State'.[11] At first glance, the CISG will be applicable only to contracts between

---

5 Agreement Establishing the ASEAN-Australia-New Zealand Free Trade Area (AANZFTA), Hua Hin, Thailand, 27 February 2009, available at <http://www.dfat.gov.au/trade/fta/asean/aanzfta/aanzfta.pdf>.

6 AANZFTA entered into force on 1 January 2010 for eight of the 12 countries that signed the Agreement. In addition to Australia and New Zealand, ASEAN countries that had notified other Parties of the completion of their internal requirements, and for whom the Agreement entered into force on 1 January 2010 are: Brunei, Burma, Malaysia, the Philippines, Singapore and Vietnam. Thailand notified on 11 January 2010 that it had completed its internal requirements. In accordance with AANZFTA, the Agreement entered into force for Thailand 60 days after this notification, on 12 March 2010. The remaining ASEAN countries (Cambodia, Indonesia and Laos) are working to complete their internal requirements at the earliest possible opportunity in 2010. The Agreement will enter into force for these Parties 60 days after the dates of their respective notifications. The dates of notification and the dates when AANZFTA will enter into force for those Parties will be published on <http://www.dfat.gov.au/trade/fta/asean/aanzfta/>.

7 Website of the Australian Dept. of Foreign Affairs & Trade, Overview of the Agreement Establishing the ASEAN-Australia-New Zealand Free Trade Area, available at <http://www.dfat.gov.au/trade/fta/asean/aanzfta/#Overview>.

8 Preamble, ATIGA, *supra* note 4.

9 G. Bell, 'Harmonisation of Contract Law in Asia – Harmonisation Regionally or Adopting Global Harmonisations – The Example of the CISG', 2005 *Singapore Journal of Legal Studies* 362.

10 Art. 1(1)(a) CISG.

11 Art. 1(1)(b) CISG.

ASEAN members and Singapore where the rules of private international law point to the substantive law of Singapore. However, this is not the case as Singapore has made a reservation according to Article 95 CISG which in effect makes the CISG only applicable if both countries are signatories to the Convention.[12] Another option would be to include an article in ATIGA to declare that the governing law in any sales contract should be the CISG. However, this is not possible for several reasons.

As already noted above, the CISG is implemented as part of domestic law and a country needs to first ratify the CISG. To otherwise include the CISG as a governing law would require contractual parties to specifically include ATIGA as the governing instrument in their contract. However, ATIGA is a public international law document. The preamble notes that the signatory states desire

> to move forward by developing a comprehensive ASEAN Trade in Goods Agreement which is built upon the commitments under the existing ASEAN economic agreements to provide a legal framework to realise free flow of goods in the region.[13]

Articles 3 and 4 ATIGA further define ATIGA coverage as inclusive of goods and products determined in accordance with the ASEAN Harmonised Tariff Nomenclature.[14] At this point, it becomes clear that there is no direct interaction between the CISG and ATIGA.

The difficulty of applying the CISG outside the ratification process can be illustrated by looking at the status of Hong Kong. At the handover of the colony, China and the United Kingdom established the Hong Kong Special Administration Region (HKSAR). Despite the fact that Hong Kong forms part of China, a Contracting State, there is no Hong Kong legislation implementing the CISG, thus the CISG is not applicable in Hong Kong.[15] Furthermore, Article 18(2) of the Hong Kong Basic Law expressly stipulates that '[n]ational laws shall not be applied in the Hong Kong Special Administrative Region except for those listed in Annex III to [the Basic] [L]aw'.[16] Considering that Article 93(4) CISG stipulates that if a country has territorial units where different laws apply (such as Hong Kong) and

---

12 China also made a reservation according to Art. 95 CISG.

13 Preamble, ATIGA, *supra* note 4.

14 Arts. 3 and 4 ATIGA, *supra* note 4.

15 U. Schroeter, 'The Status of Hong Kong and Macao under the Untied Nations Convention on Contracts for the International Sale of Goods', 16 *Pace Int'l L. Rev.* 307, at 326 (2004). See also, W. Long, 'The Reach of the CISG in China: Declarations and Applicability to Hong Kong and Macao', in this volume for a detailed discussion of this issue.

16 The Basic Law of the Hong Kong Special Administrative Region of the People's Republic of China, 4 April 1990, available at <http://www.basiclaw.gov.hk/ en/basiclawtext/images/Basic_Law.pdf>.

no declaration is made under Article 93(1) CISG, 'the Convention is to extend to all territorial units of that State'. As China did not file an Article 93 declaration the CISG should apply in Hong Kong. However, a French court noted in the *Telecommunications products* case:

> [T]he People's Republic of China deposited with the Secretary General of the United Nations a declaration announcing the conventions to which China was a party at that date which should apply to Hong Kong. The CISG did not figure on that list, nor had the CISG applied to Hong Kong before the retrocession of this territory to the People's Republic of China by the United Kingdom. Thereby, the People's Republic of China has effectuated with the depositary of the Convention a formality equivalent to what is provided for in Art. 93 CISG. Consequently, the CISG is not applicable to the special administrative region of Hong Kong.[17]

The difficulty of implementation through infra-State declarations is clearly illustrated by the Hong Kong example.

However, the purpose of this paper is to explore possibilities of further economic integration within ASEAN countries beyond the existing framework. Arguably, therefore, it would be of value to map the existing underlying ideas of cooperation and examine how these existing agreements can be widened to include private international legal frameworks, such as the CISG. It is evident that ASEAN has so far only generated protocols and agreements which regulate the public law aspects of trade.

3 ATIGA – The Thrust of the Agreement

The preamble notes that the goal of ATIGA is to 'establish ASEAN as a single market and production base characterised by free flow of goods'.[18] The ASEAN Economic Community Blueprint also clearly mandates that the community will create a single market and production base, a highly competitive economic region, a region of equitable economic developments and a region which is fully integrated into the global economy.[19] Such constant declarations arguably suggest that, once a single market is established, a common

17 French Supreme Court, 2 April 2008, CISG-online 1651, translation available at <http://cisgw3.law.pace.edu/cases/080402f1.html> (cited as: *Telecommunications products* case).

18 Preamble, ATIGA, *supra* note 4.

19 See ASEAN Economic Community Blueprint, Singapore, 20 November 2007, available at <http://www.aseansec.org/21083.pdf>, para. 4.

contract law would enhance and cement the relationships within ASEAN. However, this has not been the case. Article 21 ATIGA suggests that moves to create a single market with a sound legal framework is not merely a political ambition but has been given legal force. There are no indications that Article 21 extends to establishing a common sales law. Article 21 ATIGA merely makes it mandatory – with exact timelines – for each member state to issue a legal enactment in order to give effect to declarations.[20]

Furthermore, as there are now several agreements, a dispute settlement mechanism has also been introduced, namely the ASEAN Protocol on Enhanced Dispute Settlement Mechanism which caters for conciliation and mediation.[21] The Protocol also includes a review panel whose findings are binding pursuant to Article 15(1) of the Protocol. However, the dispute settlement mechanism only resolves disputes between states and is therefore not designed to extend to private contractual matters. There are also signs that the drafters of ATIGA did not specifically take international unified laws into consideration, as this agreement lacks the good faith proclamation which is now common in most uniform international laws such as Article 7 CISG. Furthermore, the definition of what constitutes 'goods' preceding the regulations in 'Chapter 3 – Rules of Origin' has no resemblance to Article 2 CISG.

Despite this, ATIGA may indirectly affect the influence of the CISG in the region. ATIGA can no longer be viewed from a confined regional perspective. The AANZFTA enlarged ATIGA beyond its borders. This, amongst other things, brings ASEAN countries into close economic contact with countries within the AANZFTA which have adopted the CISG. This is generally important, as the main trading partners of ATIGA nations such as Australia, China, the United States, the EU and Japan have all adopted the CISG.

4 ASEAN and the CISG

As a preliminary observation, currently, the United Kingdom is the only major trading partner of ASEAN which has not adopted the CISG. In addition, it should be noted that roughly 80% of international sales of goods are potentially subject to the CISG.[22] Despite the fact that the CISG is excluded in many sales contracts, the low volume of decided cases

20 Art. 21 ATIGA, *supra* note 4.

21 ASEAN Protocol on Enhanced Dispute Settlement Mechanism, Vientiane, Laos, 29 November 2004, available at <http://www.aseansec.org/16754.htm>.

22 Schroeter, *supra* note 15, at 309; I. Schwenzer & P. Hachem, 'The CISG – Successes and Pitfalls', 57 *Am. J. Comp. L.* 457 (2009), available at <http://www.cisg.law.pace.edu/cisg/biblio/schwenzer-hachem.html>.

on a global scale arguably suggests that the CISG is a successful instrument, understood by those applying it and hence, as a result, litigation or arbitrations are kept to a minimum.

As mentioned previously, within ASEAN unfortunately only Singapore is a party to the CISG. The question therefore is whether it would be possible for ASEAN countries to harmonise their commercial sales laws further and ratify the CISG. Arguably, there are no obstacles to doing so. It is interesting to note that the United Nations Conference for Contracts on the International Sale of Goods, Summary Records of the Plenary Meetings, 11th Plenary Meeting on 10 April 1980[23] where 'the Final Act of the Conference was adopted by acclamation',[24] none of the countries present voted against it, although nine countries including Burma and Thailand abstained. Furthermore, the United Nations Conference for Contracts on the International Sale of Goods, Summary Records of the Plenary Meetings, 12th Plenary Meeting, 12 April 1980[25] show that the Final Act was signed by representatives of Burma, the Philippines, Singapore and Thailand.[26]

It is instructive to note the attitude of the representatives of China and Pakistan, both non-ASEAN countries. The Chinese delegate noted:

> Mr. LI-Chih-min (China) expressed his satisfaction that five weeks of intensive work had culminated in the success of the Conference. The Convention, which was a step towards the harmonization of international trade law, would permit legal obstacles to international trade to be removed, facilitate trade and promote the establishment of an economic order *founded on equality and mutual interest.*[27]

The Pakistani representative speaking on behalf of developing countries was more cautious in his address.

---

23 United Nations Conference for Contracts on the International Sale of Goods, Summary Records of the Plenary Meetings, 11th Plenary Meeting on 10 April 1980, UN Doc. A/CONF.97/SR.11, available at <http://www.cisg.law.pace.edu/cisg/ plenarycommittee/summary11.html>.

24 United Nations Conference for Contracts on the International Sale of Goods, Summary Records of the Plenary Meetings, 11th Plenary Meeting on 10 April 1980, Doc. A/CONF.97/16, available at <http://www.cisg.law.pace.edu/cisg/ plenarycommittee/summary11.html>, para. 179.

25 United Nations Conference for Contracts on the International Sale of Goods, Summary Records of the Plenary Meetings, 12th Plenary Meeting on 11 April 1980, UN Doc. A/CONF.97/18, available at <http://www.cisg.law.pace.edu/cisg/ plenarycommittee/summary12.html>.

26 *Id.*, para. 2.

27 *Id.*, para. 8 (emphasis added).

> Mr. MEHDI (Pakistan) said that the Conference would bear the stamp of its President, who had succeeded in reconciling diverging views. The importance of the Convention which had been adopted could not be denied, but it should be noted that, although some of Pakistan's views had been taken into account, the views of the third world countries had not always been given sufficient consideration, although harmony between them and the other nations was a prerequisite for any progress. He [...] hoped that the Convention would enable more rational relationships between buyers and sellers to be established and would contribute to the creation of a more *just economic and social order.*[28]

The views of the creation of a 'just economic and social order'[29] founded on 'equality and mutual interests'[30] has been taken up by ASEAN but has not yet been taken to its logical conclusion. As seen above, harmonisation efforts within Asia have gone a long way in government-to-government relationships. It is interesting to note that AANZFTA has included a dispute resolution mechanism built – not on litigation – but on arbitration and conciliation. The only missing link in trade relations therefore is harmonisation of the contractual relationship between sellers and buyers.

Arguably, therefore, only irreconcilable differences between the Asian domestic sales laws would be a valid argument not to ratify the CISG which is arguably not the case. The CISG is a product of the 1980s and as the Pakistani representative argued, the 'view of the third world countries have not always been given sufficient consideration'.[31] What can be said is that the CISG predominantly is a mix of western legal traditions, civil law, common law and socialist law, considering that in the drafting stage of the CISG the three legal systems dominated the debates. The fact is that ASEAN contract law is historically based on civil and common law due to its colonial past.[32] In effect, sales laws in the ASEAN countries read

> very much like the original French or German civil codes, and in most instances, in common law jurisdictions, there is likely to be a Sale of Goods Act very similar to the version of the English Act of the same name.[33]

---

28 *Id.*, para. 12 (emphasis added).

29 *Id.*, para. 12.

30 *Id.*, para. 8.

31 *Id.*, para. 12.

32 The colonial powers, in particular England, France and the Netherlands, had an impact on the legal structure of their former colonies which is still clearly present in the modern legal structure of ASEAN nations.

33 Bell, *supra* note 9, at 364. For a more detailed discussion about the cultural issues surrounding the CISG and Islam within the Asian context, see G. Bell, 'New Challenges for the Uniformisation of Laws: How the CISG is Challenged by "Asian Values" and Islamic Law', in this volume.

The conclusion which can be drawn is that the content of the CISG is adaptable and hence is not difficult to include it in any domestic system. The advantage is obvious, especially within trading blocks such as the ASEAN countries, as it provides a uniform platform to regulate cross-border trade relations amongst businesses. Cultural differences are also not a stumbling block for the introduction of the CISG as the governing law within the ASEAN block countries. Such a view is reinforced by Bell who notes:

> cultural arguments are, by their very nature, not pan-Asian. Asia has many different cultural traditions and [for example] what might be true about Confucian attitudes in Singapore will not be true in Christian Philippines.[34]

Even a cursory examination of the CISG indicates that harmonisation of sales law in the ASEAN countries is not difficult. The preamble of the CISG notes that the broad objective was the establishment of a new international order and that international trade must be developed 'on the basis of equality and mutual benefit is an important element in promoting friendly relations among States'.[35]

The foreshadowed efforts of ASEAN countries to integrate not only with countries outside ASEAN but also to harmonise public commercial law amongst its member states leads to the argument that the overall objectives and intentions of the drafters of the CISG are already uppermost amongst ASEAN concerns. It is therefore a small step to harmonise contract law considering again that the preamble notes:

> that the adoption of uniform rules which govern contracts for the international sale of goods and take into account the different social, economic and legal systems would contribute to the removal of legal barriers in international trade and promote the development of international trade.[36]

The various treaties amongst ASEAN countries and their neighbours have already achieved a harmonised state-to-state legal regime. The only matter left now is achievement of a business-to-business harmonised legal environment. As noted in the drafting stage of the CISG, civil and common law views had to be reconciled, although this was not always possible. The CISG caters for differences by the inclusion of gaps. A good example is Article 4 CISG which states:

34 Bell, *supra* note 9, at 368.

35 Preamble, CISG.

36 Preamble, CISG.

> This Convention governs only the formation of the contract of sale and the rights and obligations of the seller and the buyer arising from such a contract. In particular, except as otherwise expressly provided in this Convention, it is not concerned with:
>
> (a) the validity of the contract or of any of its provisions or of any usage […].

Therefore, any cultural or mandatory requirements as to the validity of a contract are decided by the relevant domestic laws. An indication that the civil and common law traditions within ASEAN should not create any barriers for the implementation and application of the CISG is that both civil law countries, for example Germany – and common law countries, for example Australia – have both managed to adopt and work with the CISG.

China, an Asian neighbour and major trading partner of ASEAN countries is a useful case study which ought to be considered. China has adopted the CISG as one of the first countries to do so. It profited from reading and applying the CISG by incorporating general principles into the new Chinese contract law promulgated on 1 October 1999 such as good faith in Articles 6 and 60.[37] Furthermore, a study of Chinese decisions by CIETAC indicates that the interpretation and application of the CISG is in line with international developments.[38]

Such a finding is important as the Chinese Contract Law did retain unique Chinese legal principles such as those expressed in Article 59 which states:

> If the parties have maliciously concluded collusion to damage the interests of the State, a collective or a third party, the property thus acquired shall be turned over to the State or returned to the collective or the third party.[39]

Arguably, this is a regulation which is directed to the domestic audience, but as current events have shown can be used in international business relationships as well.[40]

Japan is another Asian country who has now acceded to the CISG. Parallels with China and ASEAN countries are obvious and should guide ASEAN countries in an endeavour to seriously investigate ratification. Japan has recognised that international trade is best

37 China Legal System Publishing House, *Contract Law of the People's Republic of China* (1999).

38 S. Singh, & B. Zeller, 'CIETAC's Calculation on Lost Profits under Article 74 of the CISG', 4 *Loy. U. Chi. Int'l L. Rev.* 211 (2007).

39 Contract Law of the People's Republic of China, 1 October 1999, available at <http://www.lawinfochina.com>.

40 See, *e.g.* the current investigation against executives of Rio Tinto in China.

served by choosing a governing law which values equitable solutions over certainty, unlike English common law which is characterized by strictness and emphasises certainty.[41] The diverse cultural and legal practices within ASEAN alone would suggest that a law favouring equitable solutions would be best suited to the success of a trading block, but this is especially so considering that most of the trading partners of ASEAN nations are countries which have acceded to the CISG. Japan has recognised that the success of the CISG cannot be ignored and the CISG 'is gradually becoming assimilated into Japanese law, and is starting to influence the interpretation of the Japanese Civil Code'.[42] It stands to reason that any ASEAN country dealing with Japan and China would come into contact with the CISG in cases where either Japanese or Chinese law governs the contract, therefore resulting in the CISG as governing law. A stumbling block for the introduction of the CISG into ASEAN countries is arguably the unfamiliarity of the current legal decision makers with international conventions. However, law schools in most parts of the world increasingly teach the global approach to law and competitions like the annual Vis moot have created a new generation of legal practitioners well versed in comparative studies and the CISG.[43] Perhaps a generational change in legal decision makers will see an introduction of harmonised sales laws in the ASEAN countries. No doubt the foundation stones have been laid.

A further consideration needs to be added, namely the requirements of a sophisticated legal system supported by quality legal services. The trend among major global legal firms towards establishing branch offices in ASEAN cities will no doubt facilitate and enhance the supply of sophisticated legal services. It is important to remember that once the CISG is applicable in ASEAN countries and familiarity with the CISG has been created, mutual benefits will flow immediately to the ASEAN community.

> Given the diversity of legal systems among [ASEAN] countries, and given that many of these countries are either transition economies or economies in the process of developing their legal infrastructures, the advantage of having one common contract law [in tandem with ATIGA] is becoming more attractive than ever.[44]

41 H. Sono, 'Japan's Accession to the CISG: The Asia Factor', 20 *Pace Int'l L. Rev.* 105, at 106 (2008).

42 *Id.*, at 108.

43 The Annual Willem C. Vis International Commercial Arbitration Moot is a student competition with over 250 university teams from over 60 countries in 2010. The Vis Moot has the goal to 'train law leaders of tomorrow in methods of alternative dispute resolution'. For further details, see the web page of the Vis Moot, available at <http://www.cisg.law.pace.edu/vis.html>.

44 Sono, *supra* note 41930, at 110.

This is specifically so as medium and small sized business will profit by being able to rely on the CISG, reducing the need to rely on lawyers to negotiate choice of law clauses, hence costs of contracting are kept to a minimum. A further point is that familiarity with the CISG enables ASEAN lawyers to represent their clients anywhere in the world if the CISG is the governing law, particularly if arbitration is the preferred dispute resolution mechanism. Without such familiarity with the CISG, local lawyers would need to be hired. The same applies if the private international law of an ASEAN country points to the application of a law of a state which has ratified the CISG. Conversely, unfamiliarity with the CISG will put ASEAN firms at a disadvantage even within their own jurisdiction if a contract where an ASEAN business is a party selects the law of a Contracting State such as Japan or China. It is well established that such a clause would trigger the application of the CISG.[45]

5 Conclusion

Why is it important to understand the state-to-state as well as the business-to-business legal frameworks? In order to advise clients, a modern lawyer needs to understand the interrelationships not only between countries but also the web of alliances between countries and the tangential points of FTAs and any other multilateral as well as bilateral agreements. As an example, Thailand, an ASEAN country, is not only a signatory to ATIGA but also to the AANZFTA. Furthermore, Thailand has also a bilateral trade agreement with Australia. The rules are not the same and specifically in relation to rules of origin, differences in compliances and costs can emerge. For example, customs officials will charge an Australian importer the general rate of import duty unless the importer clearly states under which agreement he wants to import the goods.

Furthermore, the relevant sales law needs to be specified as well. In order to create a level playing field, it is important that the international sales of a trading block such as ASEAN is wherever possible in line with that of their major trading partners. In this case, ASEAN has a significant volume of trade with Japan, China, the EU, Australia and New Zealand, all countries which are signatories of the CISG. Familiarity with the CISG will also assist inter-ASEAN trade relations, as not all of the members of the trade block belong to the same legal family. Currently, a level playing field is not present within the ASEAN block. Simply put, it can be strongly argued that an introduction of the CISG would create another

45 See, *e.g.* German Federal Supreme Court, 25 November 1998, CISG-online 353, translation available at <http://cisgw3.law.pace.edu/cases/981125g1.html>.

harmonised area on a different plane to enhance the public law aspects already achieved by ATIGA. This is especially important as the 'CISG opened the gates for a harmonisation of the law of contracts [...] and [...] has set a model for the future World Contract Law, which is now in sight [...]'.[46]

46 Lando, *supra* note 2, at 401.

International Commerce and Arbitration (Series editor: Ingeborg Schwenzer)

Volume 1: Mariel Dimsey, The Resolution of International Investment Disputes: Challenges and Practical Solutions, ISBN 978-90-77596-52-4
Volume 2: Sarah E. Hilmer, Mediation in the People's Republic of China and Hong Kong (SAR), ISBN 978-90-77596-74-6
Volume 3: Christina Knahr, Christian Koller, Walter Rechberger and August Reinisch (Eds.), Investment and Commercial Arbitration - Similarities and Divergences, ISBN 978-90-77596-81-4
Volume 4: Markus Jäger, Reimbursement for Attorney's Fees, ISBN 978-90-77596-98-2
Volume 5: Olivier Luc Mosimann, Anti-Suit Injunctions in International Commercial Arbitration, ISBN 978-90-77596-99-9
Volume 6: Edgardo Muñoz, Modern Law of Contracts and Sales in Latin America, Spain and Portugal, ISBN 978-94-90947-03-3
Volume 7: Pascal Hachem, Agreed Sums Payable upon Breach of an Obligation, ISBN 978-94-90947-04-0
Volume 8: Ingeborg Schwenzer and Lisa Spagnolo (eds.), Towards Uniformity, ISBN 978-94-90947-10-1